ONE
NATION
UNDER
DEBT

ONE NATION UNDER DEBT

HAMILTON, JEFFERSON, and the
HISTORY of WHAT WE OWE

Robert E. Wright, Ph.D.

New York   Chicago   San Francisco   Lisbon
London   Madrid   Mexico City   Milan   New Delhi
San Juan   Seoul   Singapore   Sydney   Toronto

1 2 3 4 5 6 7 8 9 0 DOC/DOC 0 9 8

ISBN: 978–0–07–1543934–0
MHID: 0–07–154393–7

CONTENTS

PREFACE

"It is a happy talent, to be able at once to please, and to instruct: but there are cases that will not admit of such gentle treatment. The public debt is of that nature." Or so claimed British scribbler Patrick Murray in 1753. I hope this book will prove Mr. Murray quite wrong. The story that follows will be found by many present-day bond traders and other financial services employees an interesting, even scintillating, exploration of the historical roots of their trade. Historians and economists will find in these pages new, and I daresay intriguing, interpretations of early America and economic growth. Neophyte investors will find the basics of investing, unchanged over two centuries, laid bare. Finally, policy makers should take heed because herein are lessons galore, lessons that need their urgent attention lest America's current national debt, swollen by decades of fiscal irresponsibility, become its *last*.[1]

Like any tool, a national debt can be used for good, ill, or anything in between. Many observers focus on its virtues, others on its vices. A few, like the "Shareholder" character in Joseph de la Vega's classic study of the Dutch securities market circa 1688, *Confusion de Confusiones*, saw both sides:

> I really must say that you are an ignorant person, friend Greybeard, if you know nothing of this enigmatic business which is at once the fairest and most deceitful in Europe, the noblest and the most infamous in the world, the finest and the most vulgar on earth. It is a quintessence of academic learning and a paragon of fraudulence; it is a touchstone for the intelligent and a tombstone for the audacious, a

treasury of usefulness and a source of disaster, and finally a counter-
part of Sisyphus who never rests as also of Ixion who is chained to a
wheel that turns perpetually.

My goal in this book is to play the part of "Shareholder," to give both sides of
the story, the good and the bad, the beautiful and the ugly, an equal hearing.
Ambivalence here is more than a virtue; it is a necessity. Proponents and critics of the national debt have both made telling points at times. Unfortunately,
neither side has been above stretching the truth until it tore asunder.[2]

"I am sorry to say," an observer lamented in 1768, "we have but very few
able guides in this task, the study of finances having been greatly neglected."
To this day, financial history has been a subject little studied, especially in
proportion to its importance. As the great business historian Bob Sobel
once noted, many important chapters in American history are "half-
forgotten due to a scarcity of historians' interest in such matters." In the
last 15 years or so, however, financial history has finally begun to come
of age. The long list of people I need to thank for their help, direct and
indirect, knowingly and unknowingly, on this book is good evidence of
financial history's emergence from the scholarly shadows: Timothy Alborn,
Will Baumol, Howard Bodenhorn, Peter Coclanis, David Cowen, Christa
Dierksheide, Tom Downey, Max Edling, Niall Ferguson, Jennifer Goloboy,
Farley Grubb, Songho Ha, John Herzog, Woody Holton, Mary Inkrot, John
James, James Karmel, Richard Kilbourne Jr., Naomi Lamoreaux, Carl Lane,
Nelson Lankford, James Macdonald, Cathy Matson, Ron Michener, Ed
Perkins, Frances Pollard, Paul Rhode, George David Smith, Richard Sylla,
Jan Traflet, Joachim Voth, David Weiman, Robert Whaples, and Katherine
Wilkins. In addition, Stephanie Vasta and Mary Inkrot provided invaluable
research assistance, and, as always, I must thank my family, Deb, Madison,
Alexander, and Trevor, for putting up with me while I brought this project
to fruition.[3]

Institutions have also aided this endeavor, with funds and friendship.
This book would not have been possible without a Harvard Business School
Alfred D. Chandler travel grant, an Economic History Association Alfred H.
Cole Research Grant, a grant from the Berkley Center for Entrepreneurial
Studies at New York University and the Ewing Marion Kauffman Founda-
tion, and a Mellon/Betty Sams Christian Fellowship in Business History

at the Virginia Historical Society. My employer, the Stern School of Business, also aided the project with significant research funds. Finally, New York University's Bobst Library deserves my thanks for making it easy to do research electronically from home. I alone, though, must own all errors of fact and interpretation that may be discovered herein by readers present and future. I, too, must own the editorial choices I made while writing, the most material of which is that I silently modernized spellings and did not concern myself with the difference between old and new calendar dating styles. Some of my old acquaintances, like Craig Horle, will be appalled by this indiscretion but they must remember that this is a work of narrative and interpretation, not a reference work. My conclusions rest on a mountain of data and in no way hinge on dates, spellings, or the like.

For scholars and scholarly types who want to follow up on my work, I have provided copious endnotes and a bibliography containing the most important printed sources that I consulted. The endnotes also include references to the tables and figures provided in the Appendix for more numerically inclined readers. Finally, I have made available to the world, on Eh.Net, the entire database of federal bondholders underpinning the study, with the hope that other researchers will use it to uncover additional stories of interest and importance.

Robert E. Wright, Ph.D.
Abington, Pennsylvania
November 2007

A Twinkle in the Eye

The Importance of Government Debt

O nce upon a time, in a land not so far away, a subjugated but enlightened people cast off a great tyrant. But their liberty, won with promises as well as with the blood of patriots, came at a high price. Burdened by debt, weak government, a pressing scarcity of money, and an uncertain future, the people wallowed in idleness and rebellion. Men of brilliance met, theorized, compromised, and, over some weighty objections, soon constituted a new type of government, one that was powerful yet benign, led by the ablest but dedicated to protect all. Taxes were collected, new loans procured, and old debts repaid. The details flummoxed some but most people understood, and applauded. Throughout the land, they bought the new government's IOUs at high prices and sold them at will, sometimes to people in distant lands eager for good investments. Through such trading, the interests of the governed and the government became one. The debt blessed the nation as bankruptcy turned to honor and despair to hope. The fruits of their labors now secure, the people worked hard and smart. Not all of their innovations succeeded, but, all told, their farms flourished, as did their factories and ports. The nation's debt dwindled according to plan, only to rise to new heights in a second war against tyranny. Hard work, intelligent taxation, and disciplined leadership again combined forces to tame the fiscal beast. The debt, rightly considered an imposition on the unborn, soon disappeared completely.

But the people, not as enlightened as they once were, did not live happily ever after. Their leaders, now mere politicians instead of statesmen, began to accumulate massive new debts to ensure their popularity rather than to fend off encroachments upon liberty. As foretold, the blessings of debt became a great curse, one that looms larger every second of every day, threatening the people's happiness and the productivity of their raucous economy. This is their story and it is an important one because within it dwells a great truth about happiness and sullenness, progress and regress, prosperity and poverty.

∝

Why do women in Japan live 84.41 years on average, while those in Mozambique average only 31.63 years? Why do 72.8 percent of the people in Mali live on less than $1 per day while almost nobody in OECD (Organization for Economic Cooperation and Development) countries has to get by on so little? Why is the average annual income of people in Luxembourg $66,463.78 while that of people in Burundi is $84.29? "The consequences for human welfare involved in questions like these," Nobel laureate Robert Lucas once wrote, "are simply staggering.... Once one starts to think about them," he added, "it is hard to think of anything else."[1]

Until recently, such questions have obsessed and perplexed observers, especially, ironically enough, professional economists. David Ricardo was largely correct when he complained that economics properly understood was not "an enquiry into the nature and causes of wealth" but rather a narrower, more scientific and technical endeavor. "Every day I am more satisfied," he wrote, that studying the causes of wealth "is vain and delusive."

Professional economists, it appears, had grown too enamored of fancy mathematical models and abstractions like financing gaps, sundry types of deficits, and adjustment loans. Worse, they had forgotten, or more likely had never learned, the Enlightenment-era insight that what really matters when it comes to economic prosperity is good governance, trade, and incentives.[2] Adam Smith succinctly stated the Enlightenment view in his 1755 *Lectures on Jurisprudence*:

> Little else is requisite to carry a state to the highest degree of opulence from the lowest barbarism, but *peace, easy taxes and a tolerable administration of justice*; all the rest being brought by the natural course of

things. All governments which thwart this natural course, which force things into another channel or which endeavour to arrest the progress of society at a particular point, are unnatural, and to support themselves are *obliged to be oppressive and tyrannical.* [Italics added]

Unfortunately, Smith's lessons have been largely forgotten. Most people today seem to think that wealth is a function of cash aid (the more the better), culture (the more Protestant or Western the better), democracy (the more the better), education (the more the better), genetics (the more Caucasian or Mongoloid the better), imperialism (the less the better), natural resource endowments (the more the better), and stability (the more the better). As it turns out, none of those variables does a rich country make. Aid almost always comes to naught, some wealthy countries are neither Western nor Protestant, most countries become rich before they become democratic, levels of education generally lag behind wealth, and many former colonies have grown wealthy. Not only are natural resource endowments and wealth not closely correlated; many economists speak of the *curse* of oil, diamonds, and other resources. Genetics may explain why some individuals have higher incomes than others, but all theories tying national poverty to race have been thoroughly debunked. Stability is another great bugaboo. *Order* is necessary for growth, but stasis is often a recipe for poverty. (Cuba and North Korea, for example, were remarkably stable for half a century but have remained economically stagnant and poor.) Finally, populist notions about rich countries stealing from the poor are also way off base. The rich countries are not taking increasingly bigger slices of an economic pie of a fixed size. Rather, they are making the pie bigger each year.

Thankfully, a growing chorus of scholars has rediscovered and begun to extend the key insights of Adam Smith and other Enlightenment thinkers. The answer to the wealth question is in sight, and it looks something like a diamond. No, not diamonds, or other natural resources, but rather a metaphorical diamond composed of four key facets.[3]

⨀

For most of its existence, humanity has enjoyed no period of sustained economic growth. Incomes may have increased a little in a few places for short periods, golden eras, but most of the time they've hovered not far above the subsistence level. Peace and good weather were more likely to summon forth more people rather than more prosperity. When war, pestilence, and drought returned—and they always did—people died in droves. To many observers, humanity appeared doomed to spend eternity wet, cold, hungry, and grief-stricken. Recent centuries have proven the gloomy prognosticators if not wrong, at least too pessimistic. In the seventeenth and eighteenth centuries in Holland and Britain, people began to produce a little more each year and the gains were not completely erased by a growing population. On average, economic output per person increased about 1 percent a year. That was not a rapid rate of growth by contemporary standards, but it was impressive by historical ones. More impressive yet, the gains were durable and over time added up. Modern economic growth had arrived but remained rare. In most places, aggregate output remained around $400 (in 2005 dollars) per head per year, just enough to subsist.

Aggregate output, the value of all final goods and services produced by an economy, can be measured in various ways, including gross national product (GNP), gross domestic product (GDP), net national product (NNP), and others. All such measures, indeed all economic statistics, are akin to sausage in that if you like to consume them, you do not want to see how they are made. That is especially true for historical statistics, but it also applies to current figures, which are constructed with the aid of some heroic assumptions. Scholars and government statisticians are aware of the shortcomings of the data; attempts are made, but not always successfully, to render the measurements consistent from year to year and country to country. Although figures like GDP are not as precise as scholars would like, most agree that aggregate output is the best way to track the performance of national economies. It is inherently more objective than other measures, including sundry "standard of living" indices, because it emphasizes the market value of finished economic goods, including physical merchandise and services. Adding up trillions of such transactions presents a technical problem—hence the sausagelike quality of the data—but not a conceptual one. When someone buys an automobile or a haircut, he or she must value that good *at least* as much as he or she paid for it. With each purchase, people reveal their preferences. Other measures of economic performance are less objective because they are subject to choices imposed arbitrarily by government statisticians or scholars. If the index gurus weight annual snowfall heavily, for instance, places like Canada will rank high in standard of living. Conversely, if the statisticians weight mean temperatures heavily, Canada and other northern countries will drop in the rankings. In either situation, the rankings tell us more about the indexers than about reality. Not so, though, with market price–based measures like GDP.

Economic growth is generally defined as increased aggregate income, holding population and prices constant. The normative effect of growth, whether it is "good" or "bad," depends on the observer's perspective and interests. The cultural, political, and socioeconomic changes wrought by economic growth injure some people, especially in the short term. The big picture, though, suggests that economic growth enhances overall human welfare. People are no happier in rich countries than in poor ones (apparently, happiness consorts with humanity only infrequently); however, people in rich countries, even the poorest among them, on average live longer, healthier, and more comfortable lives. They also enjoy more choices. In rich countries, people can live in a tower in an urban center, a house in the suburbs, or a shack in the countryside. They can dress in rags or the latest fashions. They can walk, ride, or drive to a job of their own choosing. In poor countries, people must walk, often in bare feet and ragged clothes, from their mud-brick homes to the only job available in town. Little wonder, then, that most people strive, and mightily at that, to better their economic lot in life. Most have failed, but some have succeeded. My scholarly task has been to comb the historical record in search of the fundamental causes, the deepest roots I can dig up, of the pattern of economic success and failure observed in the world today.

In the nineteenth century, sustained economic growth spread from Holland and Britain to new areas—the northern part of North America, central Europe, Scandinavia, and, late in the century, Japan. In the twentieth, it spread to other places in the Pacific Rim, including Australia, Singapore, Hong Kong, Taiwan, and South Korea, and to southern Europe. Israel, Ireland, Chile, and a few pockets elsewhere also experienced rapid growth. Many of the newly rich, often called "tigers" or "dragons," grew extremely quickly, at 6, 8, even 10 percent per year, largely catching up to the leading economies in just a few generations. As the second millennium gave way to the third, several important areas, including China, India, and parts of Eastern Europe, appeared poised to experience sustained economic growth as well. Whether they will hold on to their recent gains or not, only time will tell.

At the same time, vast areas, including most of Africa, Latin America, Central Asia, the Middle East, and Micronesia, remain mired in poverty. The gap between the richest countries and the stagnant poor ones grows every year and is already massive. Circa 1800, the world's richest countries were only four times wealthier than the world's poorest. Circa 2000, the world's richest countries were about 50 times wealthier than the poorest. While people in rich countries spend billions to lose weight and keep their elderly alive another few months, billions of people elsewhere have just enough food to keep them going and often do not have enough medicine to keep their babies alive.

Why, then, have some countries grown rich while most remained impoverished? Only two things, it turns out, create new wealth: trade and increases in efficiency. Exchanging one thing for another creates wealth by enabling people to obtain what they want more cheaply than they could by making it themselves. By definition, trade occurs when two parties consent to exchange. Both must become better off for making the exchange or they would not bother doing it. (Economists call that good feeling you get when you buy [sell] something, consumer [producer] surplus, that is, potential wealth turned into actual or kinetic wealth by the mere process of exchange.) Interestingly, our species, *Homo sapiens*, appears genetically predisposed to engage in exchange and also is the only species yet discovered that trades extensively with nonrelated members of its own species. In addition to making them feel good, trade also allows people to specialize in the production of one good or service, and to obtain most of what they need from others. That is important because specialists are usually much more efficient than generalists.

Efficiency increases whenever the same inputs (land, money, labor) lead to a greater quantity and/or quality of outputs (wheat, movies, steel). (Or, to put it another way, when the same quantity and quality of output can be created from less input.) Economists use the term *technology* as shorthand for anything that leads to increases in efficiency. That is somewhat unfortunate because the word *technology* often conjures up images of rocket ships and computers when in fact something as simple as a twig can be a technology if it is used to, say, extract termites from their subterranean lair faster than digging with bare hands. Even a new way of doing something that required no new tool—packing the hold of a ship with the most needed items last, for example—would be a technology in economists' lingo.

That is all well and good, but a major conundrum remains. Why do some countries enjoy much more trade and technology than others? The answer to that question is intensely historical. The story of each country, rich, middling, or poor, differs considerably in detail. Nevertheless, important common threads run through the stories of almost all of them. Those commonalities are presented here as a historical model of economic growth, a heuristic (teaching) device designed to help readers to see the forest for the trees. Like all models, the development diamond model presented here simplifies reality but tries not to distort it.

Imagine a baseball or softball diamond. At the bottom of the diamond is home plate, the most important base in the game, where the player both begins and, if successful, ends his or her journey. Looking out from home, first base is at the right corner, second base is at the top of the diamond, dead ahead, and third base is at the diamond's left corner. To score a run, a player must return to home plate after touching first, second, and third base, in that order. Countries are no different than ballplayers in this regard. For a country to get rich, it needs to progress from base to base in the proper order.

In the development diamond, home plate is represented by government, first base by the financial system, second by entrepreneurs, and third by management. To succeed economically, a country must first possess a solid home plate, a government that at a minimum protects the lives, liberty, and property of its citizens. It must next develop a modern financial sector—quality is as important as quantity here—capable of efficiently linking savers-investors to people with good business ideas, the entrepreneurs at second base. The managers at third take over after a product has emerged and matured. Managers, entrepreneurs, and financiers also try to influence government, sometimes but not always with salubrious results.[4]

The development diamond is a powerful model because it can be applied to almost every country on earth. The poorest countries never left home plate because their governments killed and robbed their citizens. Poor but not destitute countries never made it to first base, often

The development diamond is a powerful model because it can be applied to almost every country on earth.

because their governments, while not being outright predatory, restricted economic liberty to the point that financiers and entrepreneurs could not thrive. Countries with middling income rounded the bases once or twice but found that managers, entrepreneurs, and financiers co-opted the government and implemented policies that rendered it difficult to score runs frequently. Meanwhile the rich countries continue to rack up the runs, growing stronger as players circle the bases in a virtuous or self-reinforcing cycle.

Technological gadgets are not at the heart of the development diamond, and justly so. Many important inventions were conceived long ago. The ancients were amazingly adept at the language of science and technology, mathematics, as the dimensions and celestial orientations of numerous structures bear out. By 100 BC a functioning steam engine, called Hero's Engine, had already been developed. In addition to an extensive network of stone roads, many of which are still in use, the Romans had indoor plumbing, bridges, aqueducts, and nifty military gadgets like prefabricated fortifications and the autoloading manuballista, a machine gun–like handheld catapult. After the fall of the Roman Empire, the inventions kept coming. What Leonardo da Vinci did not concoct, someone in China did. The problem with those early inventions was that few people had the ability or incentive to build, sell, or use the devices. So most lay fallow for centuries. It's not that inventions are unimportant; it's that they cannot spur economic change unless the development diamond is in place.

Culture is often invoked by those looking for a quick answer to the wealth question, but it cannot explain wealth, or poverty either. Poor countries worldwide do seem to possess antigrowth traditions. In Russia, one joke has a peasant finding a genie in a bottle. Once released the genie offers the peasant the obligatory wish. The peasant explains that he is sad because he has 3 cows while his neighbor Igor has 10. The genie asks if the peasant would like 7 more cows. "No," the peasant responds with indignation, "I want you to kill 7 of Igor's cows." In India, one joke has frogs from different countries placed into jars by a scientist. All of the jars have stoppers except for the one containing the Indian frogs. When asked why all but the Indian jar have stoppers, the scientist explains that if one of the Indian frogs tried to escape the other frogs would pull it back down. In many places in Africa, the inhabitants often give successful neighbors a "phd"—not an academic degree, mind you, but a "pull him down" much like the vindictive Indian frogs and Russian peasant.[5]

Such behaviors stem not so much from culture as from jealousy, a universal human trait if there ever was one, and one of the realities of life in a zero-sum (poor or stagnant) economy. People naturally seek to live at the same level of material comfort as their neighbors. In a poor country, the easiest way to maintain that level, to alleviate the jealousy that arises when one person gets ahead, is to issue the phd. In positive-sum (wealthy or growing) economies, people reduce the jealousy by catching up to their neighbors. Instead of frogs, dead cows, and phds, rich countries are littered with people trying to "keep up with the Joneses." While culture may at times drive economics, when it comes to economic growth we find that causation usually runs in the other direction or is ambiguous.[6]

> While culture may at times drive economics, when it comes to economic growth we find that causation usually runs in the other direction or is ambiguous.

For those reasons, culture and inventions are not integral parts of the development diamond. They are important but changing them is difficult and will not alone induce a poor country to grow rich. The world learned this lesson the hard way, when state-of-the-art factories donated to various poor countries failed to produce anything but disappointment and corruption. Changing the nature of government, by contrast, has profound effects. The gloomy prognostications of early economists referred to above were not so much rooted in pessimistic personalities as in thousands of years of economic stagnation brought about by government failures, the lack of a home plate. In many places, governments were outright predatory, existing to enrich a few leaders at the expense of the many. Instead of building a canal that would have expanded trade by linking the Mediterranean and Red Seas, the pharaohs of ancient Egypt wasted untold hours and lives erecting elaborate pyramid tombs for themselves and a few loved ones. Some governments castrated young males who only after mutilation could be trusted to guard the leaders' harems. More governments than I could possibly mention conscripted young men to fight offensive foreign wars on their behalf. Many of those young men lost life and limb, not defending home and hearth but aggrandizing their kings, popes, barons, emirs, and high priests.

Even where governments did not outright steal their subjects' lives and property, they made it difficult for them to pursue their own economic goals. By one estimate, 96 percent of the world's population was unfree in 1775. The vast majority of people were slaves, serfs, or vassals whose everyday activities were severely constrained by their lords and masters. Little wonder economic progress remained limited. Few people had any incentive to do more than live through the day. Before they will work and think hard to improve their economic lot, people need to feel that their lives, liberty, and property are secure. That security, that order, is a public good, meaning that only governments, not markets, can efficiently provide it. Where government fails to provide protection, poverty is inevitable. A person whose life, freedom to act within the bounds of law, or possessions may be snatched away at any moment by foreign invaders, rapacious neighbors, or their own leaders will do naught but subsist, dream of better days, and perhaps plot revolution. Conversely, a person whose continued existence, though never assured, is not at the pleasure of a capricious tyrant, who knows that she can do what she lawfully lists, and who can reap the benefits of her efforts has incentive to engage in trade and to seek out ways of becoming more economically efficient. Security of life, liberty, and property are therefore the sine qua non of economic growth.[7]

Innovators and inventors can hardly be expected to prosper where the government or pirates can easily steal new ideas, inventions, gadgets, and gizmos or where risks cannot be pooled, ameliorated, and shared.

This book touches all four facets of the development diamond: nonpredatory government, finance, entrepreneurship, and management. It pays particularly close attention to the first three: the formation of nonpredatory government or "Constitutional liberty," as some early Americans termed it; the development of a modern financial sector; and the proliferation of entrepreneurship. It must range widely because the bases of the growth diamond are interrelated and intimately connected. Innovators and inventors can hardly be expected to prosper where the government or pirates can easily steal new ideas, inventions, gadgets, and gizmos or where risks cannot be pooled, ameliorated, and shared. And financiers will find little profit where government does not allow businesses to sprout and flourish. America did not thrive on government, finance, or business alone, but rather from the codevelopment of each.[8]

The "square of power" framework developed by famed historian Niall Ferguson lays bare the intimate connection between home plate and first base. According to Ferguson, four key institutions link government to the financial system—the legislature, the tax bureaucracy, the national debt, and the central bank. The first creates and monitors the second, which makes possible the third, which, in turn, calls for the creation of the fourth. Finally, the national debt and central bank combine to facilitate the creation of additional financial markets, for business debt and equities, and intermediaries, particularly privately owned banks and insurance companies.[9]

All four corners of Ferguson's square feature in the story line of this book (the evolution of the U.S. economy), but the development of a modern national debt will remain the main focus. The first national debt of the United States is of primary interest, but first, European and colonial precedents will be probed in Chapters 2 and 3. America's national debt was not the world's first. When it came to government borrowing by selling bonds and other securities backed by future tax receipts, the Netherlands and Great Britain led the way (Chapter 2). The latter empire's colonies in North America were also adept borrowers by the time that British tax, trade, and monetary policies made a breach unavoidable (Chapter 3). The colonies' debts, however, were overshadowed by the immense sums necessary to conduct the Revolutionary War. To win that conflict the patriots had to cobble resources together from a variety of sources, some ancient, some traditional, others novel (Chapter 3).

The war was won but the cost was high. The nation began "the world (as it were) in debt." Some states began to repay their obligations and even a portion of the national debt owed by Congress, but the nation was hurting economically and the government was essentially bankrupt. The

Constitution was bitterly contested but its eventual ratification gave the new federal government the opportunity to salvage the nation's credit (Chapter 4). Despite considerable political opposition to his plans, Alexander Hamilton took full advantage of that opportunity by finding ways to fund (pay the interest upon) not only Congress's debts but those of the states as well. In the process, he helped to create the nation's first modern capital market, replete with three types of government bonds with different payment and maturity characteristics (Chapter 5).[10]

In the early 1790s, America's capital market, which had come to include corporate equities and bonds in addition to government bonds and ground rents (perpetual interest-only mortgages), was already quite liquid and able to withstand shocks like the Panic of 1792. The number and diversity of holders of U.S. government bonds was impressive and included a variety professionals, merchants, master artisans, former soldiers, farmers, planters, and foreign potentates and investors. For a brief moment in 1797, the prices of U.S. bonds exceeded those of British bonds in the London market! Political squabbling over the debt's efficacy and a quasi-war with France (an undeclared naval war, 1798–1800) soon put U.S. bonds back in their place, at a discount to British bonds, but the spreads were not usually large. As the years turned to decades, the U.S. capital market matured, helping the federal government to deficit-finance several wars and the purchase of Louisiana (Chapter 6).

Many holders of federal bonds lived in the urban North but they could be found in each state, even Thomas Jefferson's Virginia. There, owners of government bonds included agriculturalists, artisans, and women as well as merchants and professionals, city dwellers and rural folk, and rich and middling types, from each major section of the Old Dominion. They owned bonds for a variety of reasons, including speculation; the assurance of a certain income for long periods; a safe harbor for when economic storms brewed; and as secondary reserves, income-producing assets that could be sold for cash at a moment's notice if necessary (Chapter 7).

Private gains do not always mean public benefits (vide slavery), but they often do. By the 1820s, the blessings of the U.S. national debt were clear. America's financial system rivaled, and in some ways bested, those of Britain, Holland, and the rest of the developed world. The financial system helped to fuel transportation improvements, industrial development, and federal government budget surpluses (Chapter 8). Those surpluses, combined with a good dose of anti-debt and antifinance ideology, conspired to end the national debt's existence during the administration of Andrew Jackson. But from its ashes soon arose a second national debt and a plethora of state debts. Americans have been born in debt, sometimes

By the 1820s, the blessings of the U.S. national debt were clear. America's financial system rivaled, and in some ways bested, those of Britain, Holland, and the rest of the developed world.

more, sometimes less, ever since. Today, the burden of America's national debt, both the explicit debt and the liabilities inherent in Social Security, Medicare, and other redistribution programs, is the heaviest in peacetime history (Chapter 9).

Two quotations from founding fathers encapsulate the life of America's first national debt. Alexander Hamilton argued that "a national debt, if it is not excessive, will be to us a national blessing. It will be a powerful cement to our union." Thomas Jefferson, by contrast, claimed that "the principle of spending money to be paid by posterity under the name of funding is but swindling futurity on a large scale." Ergo, he wished to pass a balanced budget amendment to the Constitution by "taking from the federal government the power of borrowing."[11]

Hamilton was correct. Under the right conditions, the national debt could be kept to a size moderate enough to render it a blessing rather than a curse. By allowing the new government to consolidate the nation's existing war debts and to incur new debts for major projects, including necessary new wars and territory acquisitions, the national debt spread the tax burden over several generations. That, in turn, helped to maintain political stability in a country infamous for tax rebellions. It also minimized the economic distortions caused by taxes, especially high taxes.[12]

But that was not all. The national debt mostly took the form of government bonds, tradable financial instruments that served as a sure source of steady income for innocent investors (widows and orphans) and intermediaries (savings banks and trustees), provided commercial banks and insurance companies with liquid secondary reserves, and gave businessmen an asset that could secure loans even in the most dire circumstances. Perhaps even

Perhaps even more important, the establishment of a secondary market for government bonds opened the door to a wide variety of other capital market instruments, including corporate equities (stocks) and bonds.

more important, the establishment of a secondary market for government bonds opened the door to a wide variety of other capital market instruments, including corporate equities (stocks) and bonds. To the disgust of many, the new capital market became the plaything of brokers, jobbers, and speculators. But even speculators, the vilest creatures upon the exchange, played an important economic role.

Hamilton was also correct when he argued that the widespread ownership of government bonds among the more important classes of people would help to politically stabilize the young federal government. The nation's creditors were numerous, especially in the North, and of course wanted to see the new country succeed, if only out of a selfish desire to be repaid in a timely fashion. As Hamilton foretold, the national debt helped to "cement" the new nation, to make it, and keep it, as one. (If Hamilton, an ardent abolitionist, had been allowed to phase chattel slavery out of existence, the nation would have always remained as one; it was not coincidental that the U.S. Civil War occurred at a time when the national debt was trifling and concentrated mostly in New York.) In short, it was possible, in the words of Hamiltonian Robert Goodloe Harper, to "gather all the roses of the funding system without its thorns."[13]

None of this is to say, however, that Jefferson was wrong. In the long run, he proved quite prescient. An impecunious insolvent debtor most of his adult life, Jefferson knew the downside of debt from hard-lived personal experience. He also knew that most people in public office were politicians, not statesmen. They would, he realized, often find it easier to borrow than to raise taxes or slash expenditures. The government would eventually bloat with bureaucrats more intent on keeping, or better yet increasing, their salaries and perquisites than in aiding the common weal.[14]

That is not to imply, of course, that Hamilton would approve of America's current fiscal situation any more than Jefferson would. No fan of big government, despite a persistent myth to the contrary, Hamilton sought to create an efficient, energetic federal administration. He succeeded where many twentieth-century policy makers failed. We can bring back neither Hamilton nor Jefferson to help us, so ultimately we will have to solve our current predicament, which many think a grave one, ourselves. We can, though, learn a little something from the past. In the late nineteenth century, a few historians, driven by contemporary debates about the swollen national debt, turned their attention to the nation's early financial system. John Watts Kearny, for example, argued that the financial history of the early United States was "well worth special study, because of the signal ability and sagacity by which the Government brought its difficult problem to a successful issue." Indeed, the history of the first U.S. national debt shows, for instance, that foreign ownership of government bonds can be a very good thing. It also shows that national debts can be used to bolster domestic political stability and jump-start economic growth. Finally, this study demonstrates that it is possible to pay down a national debt, and even pay it off completely. Early-third-millennium America might not be able to achieve the latter goal, but the former would require only a boost in political fortitude and taxpayer willpower.[15]

2

PARENTAGE

European Precedents

D ikes, windmills, tulips, wooden shoes, legal prostitution, and marijuana bars. 'Tis a shame, but that is what comes to the mind of many Americans when they think of Holland. The Dutch are rightly known for such trifles but they rarely get credit for arguably the greatest invention of the second millennium AD, capital markets, especially markets for negotiable evidences of national debt. Believe it or not, Holland was once a world superpower. The ability of the Dutch government to borrow large sums at low cost enabled it to rule the seas—for a time. Holland's invention spread, first to Britain, then to America, both of which, in time, would also create national debts that helped them to build navies and forge empires of their own.[1]

To appreciate the magnitude of Holland's contribution to world history, we must quickly tour what earlier governments did to finance war and, to a lesser extent, peace. Early governments, by which I mean governments from the dawn of recorded history to just a few hundred years ago, usually did little between wars but maintain a semblance of law and order and erect the occasional public work—temples, irrigation works, and defense fortifications. Government officials also redistributed wealth from the poor to themselves to fund their personal consumption, which could be lavish. Nevertheless, their budgets were generally small, funded by a variety of taxes on polls (individuals), real estate (land and buildings), trade (customs or tariffs), production (excises), and, in some places in a rudimentary way, incomes (from salaries, business profits, investments). Effective rates were quite low because taxpayers, who saw little of what they paid returned in the form of public services, had a nasty habit of rebelling if pushed too hard, too often.[2]

Wars required more exertion on the part of both taxpayers and governments. The former could be expected to suffer higher taxes, especially during defensive wars, through the payment of new taxes and the more vigorous collection of existing ones. Governments were expected to pitch in too, by selling state assets—sometimes land but more often their crown jewels and stockpiles of precious gems, bullion, and other high-value, low-volume items. "The ancient revenue of ... kings," one early chronicler explained, "was not only sufficient to enable them to support the splendour of royalty and defray the national expenses, which under the feudal system were comparatively small, but also to furnish the means ... of hoarding up what were then thought considerable sums." Taxes and assets combined, however, were rarely enough to field a serious army and navy for a significant length of time, so early governments scrimped by with the help of other expedients. Military contractors and officers, who were often one and the same, could frequently be imposed upon by immediately taking possession of their spears, swords, arrows, guns, and rations but not paying for them until some weeks, months, years, or even decades later, if ever. Armies more than navies could live off the land, soldiers taking the food they needed from Mother Nature or defenseless farmers in their path. Finally, early soldiers and sailors were often happy to take equity stakes in campaigns, fighting for their share of the spoils of war if victorious. If they lost, well then it didn't matter whether or not they had been paid a wage, because they were either dead or enslaved.[3]

As a final expedient, early rulers could borrow on their own credit and individual account. The loans they took out differed from modern national debts in two important ways. First, their notes, bonds, and mortgages were not traded in open markets but rather remained the property of the lender (or his heirs). Second, their obligations were personal ones, in no way binding the nation that they ruled. Early rulers were notoriously bad credit risks. After all, they were kings whose powers were largely unchecked by rule of law. According to an early chronicler, Edward III of England "was

> Early rulers were notoriously bad credit risks. After all, they were kings whose powers were largely unchecked by rule of law.

driven to the necessity of extorting (under the pretence of borrowing) great sums of money, which were never repaid." Philip II of Spain in 1557, 1575, and 1594 turned short-term debts into long-term ones without the consent of his creditors. Other kings, like Philips III and IV of Spain, taxed away much of the interest paid to debt holders. About the only way to successfully lend to such tyrants was to hold some serious collateral. On more than a few occasions, monarchs had to hock the family jewels, including their very crowns, to pawnshops in order to raise the necessary funds. When rulers had no credit and nothing suitable to hock, they often forced wealthy citizens to "lend" to them. In most cases, such forced loans were simply a thinly disguised capital tax.[4]

During the Renaissance, the northern Italian city-states moved toward the creation of a modern national debt by making two innovations in public finance. First, they began to issue interest-bearing "refundable taxes." The idea, though simple, was revolutionary: the government might turn its taxes into a loan if the project being funded, usually a war, went well. The second innovation, as stunning as the first, was to allow the evidences of the refundable taxes to trade in the open market. Most of the refundable taxes turned out, not surprisingly, to be miserable investments. Interest payments were spotty and repayment of principal almost unheard of. The markets probably helped people to trade risk—those most willing and able to shoulder the risk of nonrepayment bought the evidences from those least willing to hold them—but they were speculative securities that did not appreciably enhance the revenues of government.

Entrez Holland and her sister provinces, collectively known as the Netherlands, where the experiences of the Italian city-states mixed with the financial practices of medieval Europe. The main form of private and public finance in the north, the long-term mortgage of land called a ground rent, morphed into the mortgage of tax revenues. In France, the tax mortgages became a tool of corruption as most were sold to crown cronies at scandalous discounts. In some German states, by contrast, they became public debts after local legislatures assumed administrative control of them. By the sixteenth century, Low Country local governments in cities like Leiden, Haarlem, and Amsterdam, as well as the Dutch provincial government, were also able to borrow long-term by mortgaging taxes. A long series of wars fought on behalf of their overlord, the Habsburg

Empire, forced the Dutch to borrow, and tax, heavily. In response, over the first half of the fifteen hundreds the financial and fiscal systems of the Netherlands, particularly the county of Holland, slowly strengthened. By the latter part of the 1550s, Holland was able to sell significant quantities of tradable long-term debt obligations to voluntary investors at both at home and abroad.[5]

By the 1560s, however, the burden of war and taxation induced the Dutch to rebel, sporadically at first but ultimately culminating in the great revolt of 1572. The long, nasty war of independence that ensued solidified and extended the improvements made in Dutch public finance during the latter part of Habsburg rule. Though outgunned and outmanned, the Dutch enjoyed two advantages over their Spanish oppressors, home turf and money. The first was the result of their goal being independence, not domination. The second sprang from their crowning glory, the invention of a modern public debt. Instead of making vague promises about maybe someday repaying taxes, the Dutch outright *borrowed*, in the name of the independent Dutch nation, not some prince or potentate. In other words, they made solemn promises, backed by real tax revenues, to repay everything they borrowed, with interest punctually paid. The loans were entirely voluntary and transferable at will. Investors bought the government's obligations in droves. They did so because they effectively controlled the rebel government and hence, in a sense, lent to themselves. (In fact, state officials often invested heavily in the loans.) They did not fear repudiation so long as their government remained free. In a very real way, then, the public creditors were republican government's greatest allies.[6]

Low interest rates on public debt fueled not only Dutch independence, finally won in 1648 with the Peace of Westphalia, but also Dutch imperial and mercantile expansion. Interest rates on Dutch debt dropped from around 8 percent in 1600 to about 4 percent at mid-century to a mere 3 percent by 1700. By the late part of the seventeenth century, Dutch cities and towns could also borrow at 3 percent and commercial credits could be had at 3, $3^1/_2$, or at most 4 percent "without pawn or pledge." Rates dropped to 2 and even $1^3/_4$ percent early in the eighteenth century, making Holland the envy of the commercial world. Such low rates were then unprecedented. For all of humanity's existence hitherto, lenders charged borrowers, even *good* borrowers (those with sterling credit histories and collateral to pledge),

10, 20, 30, even 100 percent per year. In ancient Sumer, the customary rates for loans of barley (grain) and silver were $33^1/_3$ and 20 percent, respectively. In ancient Egypt, interest rates on loans of silver and grain could exceed 100 percent. The ancient Greek city of Oreos once borrowed a talent of silver (about 57 U.S. pounds) at 12 percent. Other Greek cities borrowed for as little as $8^1/_2$ percent but still others had to pay up to 48 percent and the quantities that they could borrow were severely limited. Other rates in ancient Greece, on safe or heavily collateralized loans, ranged from 6 percent well into the double digits. In ancient Rome, interest rates dipped for a time to 4 percent on safe loans but spent centuries at 12 percent and above. And this was in those states at the core of the ancient world. In others, on the periphery, like Egypt, interest rates on money were often twice as high and those on grain could hit 50 percent. In Europe in the twelfth century AD, pawnshops charged 43 percent and up. The best borrowers could get money at around 50 percent, the worst at 120, though short-term commercial loans could be had for 10 to 20 percent in some places. Over the next few centuries, little changed, though rates appear to have trended downward a little. Yet as late as the sixteenth century, good commercial paper was rarely sold at less than 8 percent yield and most governments had to promise double-digit rates.[7]

The market for government debt helped to spur development of other parts of the Dutch financial system, including a quasi-central bank, a network of private banks and insurance companies, and vibrant markets for a wide range of corporate securities. By the late seventeenth century, Dutch securities markets were amazingly modern. In addition to buying and selling corporate and government securities for cash on delivery, investors could buy or sell securities for future delivery and/or payment. Futures contracts, where price differentials led to cash payments between counterparties, rather than physical delivery, were also available, as were call and put options. An early sort of exchange-traded fund, or ETF, small-denomination phantom shares, could be traded by the less affluent and the risk adverse. Those institutions and markets greatly aided Dutch economic growth. Although it has long since lost its world superpower status, the Netherlands remains one of the world's richest countries.[8]

⚉

The English government paid the Dutch little heed at first and continued to fund its wars, including its long civil war, in traditional, and suboptimal, ways. James I died considerably in debt; Charles I borrowed large sums on the Continent by pawning jewels and mortgaging his lands but could never get out of debt. During the Protectorate, the government kept expenses in check and the taxes flowing, so it had no need to borrow. After the Restoration, Charles II proved considerably more profligate. "His own prodigality and that of his mistress," complained one early historian, "continually exhausted his revenue and obliged him to be constantly borrowing of the London bankers at 8, 10, and even higher rates of interest." In 1672, Charles II "suddenly shut" the Exchequer (treasury) and kept it closed a year and a half or so although only five years earlier he had "issued a declaration for preserving inviolably the course of payments … both with regard to principal and interest." "The credit of the Stuart Government never recovered from this monstrous robbery," one late-nineteenth-century chronicler chortled. Another major grievance was that taxpayers could not be certain that their sacrifices were purchasing the era's most important public good, national defense. "King Charles II," one writer later complained, "suffered the Fleet of England to moulder away to Nothing."[9]

James II, the last of the Stuarts, fared little better, leaving a debt in excess of £1 million upon his abdication during the Glorious Revolution of 1688, when Parliament replaced the Stuart line with a Dutch head of state in a largely bloodless coup. That revolution brought to the British Isles a good dose of Dutch republicanism, finance, and public administration. Although the new government initially had no more credit than its predecessor, its adoption of Dutch practices and the ascendancy of the prodebt Whig Party eventually won the confidence of investors. "Nothing has contributed so much to the establishment of public credit upon a firm basis," one early historian argued, "as parliament taking the management of the national finances into their [sic] own hands … for, previously to this, the security of the public creditors was very precarious." At the same time, London, a great city but financially unimportant before the Glorious Revolution, began its long career as a financial center, first for Europe, then for the world. Within a generation, London was home to a quasi-central bank called the Bank of England, numerous private banks and insurance companies, publicly traded joint-stock corporations, sound public administration, and a modern national debt.[10]

Two "great Wars," one under William, and the other under Queen Anne, forced the creation of that debt. Some believed the wars could not have been successfully financed by taxes alone because, in the words of one contemporary, they "involved this nation in an expence unknown till then." Others thought that the wars could have been won on taxes alone but that the political inexpediency of a new king, and a foreign one at that, levying heavy taxes induced William to borrow what was needed, and to do so on the nation's account and not his own. By common accord, "nothing but the inestimable Advantages of the Protestant Succession [i.e., the Glorious Revolution] ... could have render'd" such a debt "tolerable" to the nation. At first, the new government experimented with lotteries and tontines (investment pools the returns from which were awarded to those who lived the longest) and paid "great Premiums and exorbitant Interest." In 1696, "all public securities, of whatever kind, were ... at a considerable discount" from their par or face value because "public credit, then in its infancy, was generally considered as having already been extended too far." Pay to the armed forces was in arrears and at one point there was no money to pay the country's civil servants and pensioners. Another problem was that each type of debt instrument was linked to a specific tax or taxes, with no way to subsidize them from other taxes or the general budget. So if collections on a particular tax fell short, the government defaulted on interest payments on the obligations to which those taxes were assigned. In modern parlance, Britain early on issued revenue bonds rather than general obligation bonds. Corruption and "general mismanagement of the public revenue" by tax collectors and treasury officers compounded the other difficulties.[11]

Within a few years, though, new taxes, cuts in expenditures, and administrative reforms revived public credit to some extent and brought the national debt down to just over £10 million from a high of almost £13 million. Ominous noises emanating from a hostile France, however, could send bond prices plummeting to as low as 50 percent (10 shillings on the pound). Reforms, including an extensive audit by men of "sense, honour, and courage," were afoot as the new century dawned. But by 1702, William's death, the ascension of Queen Anne, and a new war had again put Britain in a bit of a financial tizzy. The following year, the government raised money with "one of the most destructive expedients that was ever resorted to," cheap annuities. Success on field and sea by 1705, though, again allowed the government to borrow on more reasonable terms. As the war dragged on, the Bank of England began to play an ever-larger role in government finance through outright loans, securities sales, and debt administration.[12]

The government's strict attention to debt service, enforced by the Bank of England, which was "under the direction of men more intimately conversant in money-transactions than public ministers usually are, and more strongly impressed with a sense of the necessity of maintaining an inviolable punctuality in such transactions," made it possible to borrow on increasingly better terms. Debt-for-equity swaps, including the one that created the South Sea Company, also helped to restore public credit by simplifying the structure of the national debt. Another major help was that Parliament, which was increasingly under the control of prodebt Whigs rather than antidebt Tories, began to pass perpetual tax laws instead of ones that had to be periodically renewed. Finally, by about 1710, deficiencies in any taxes were automatically "made good" the next year and interest payments met out of other available funds. The investigation and prosecution of delinquent tax collectors and unscrupulous military supply contractors also enhanced public credit. The successful conclusion of the war, provision for the payment of arrears, economic growth and development, the creation of a "sinking fund," and the consolidation of the debt into perpetual bonds allowed the government to lower the interest paid on some portions of the debt to 5 percent. By the 1720s, the British government paid only slightly more than the Dutch for long-term funds. That spelled higher prices for land, it was claimed, because land prices rose when interest rates fell. Thus was the landed aristocracy eventually won over to the new order.[13]

> By the 1720s, the British government paid only slightly more than the Dutch for long-term funds.

In 1717, George I spoke seriously of "reducing, by degrees, the debts of the nation." It was not to be. War, rebellion in Scotland, and the financial panic associated with the South Sea Bubble flummoxed the debt reduction plans. Not everyone was disappointed, though, as some had come to see in the debt virtue instead of vice. "Your public credit, or national debt," one proponent noted, "has preserved your independence as a state, and rendered you formidable to your enemies, by supplying you readily, without delay, with the means of paying your fleets and armies, and of supporting your maritime force, on which your whole system of foreign commerce depends."[14]

With success in war also came success in business, many debt proponents asserted. "The Character of the Nation abroad, and its flourishing State at home," one argued, "justify us in what we have done." The debt did not crowd out private investment because "there is so much Wealth accumulated in many parts of Europe, as well as among ourselves, more than can well be employed in Trade." Moreover, significant holdings of British bonds by foreigners, particularly Dutch investors, meant that the debt was a way of attracting capital for use of the hungry British economy. Someone had to serve as a safe depository for Europe's excess funds, and better Britain than her enemies. Were the national debt to be paid off, it was argued as early as the 1720s, "the difficulty of employing money would become so great, that half of it would be found useless and be boarded up!" Furthermore, government bonds were extremely liquid, serving as a convenient means of payment "in all Sorts of large Payments." A popular saying even claimed that investors "can sell Consols on a Sunday." Government bonds, in short, constituted a new and useful type of asset, as secure and remunerable as land but almost as easily transferable as cash.[15]

Moreover, as in the Netherlands, markets for trading the national debt facilitated the development of markets for private securities, including stocks and bonds of a wide variety of financial institutions and other types of businesses. With the aid of the debt, Britain's economy flourished. All candid observers admitted that Britain was far from perfect, but all her problems stemmed from other causes, like improper marriage and migration laws. The economy showed its strength in the wide variety of goods available to a wide portion of the populace, made possible by stable real wages;

the numerous infrastructure improvements, like canals and turnpikes under construction or already bulging with trade; and "chearfulness and plenty" on the faces of farmers. High taxes caused the price of British manufactured goods to rise, but they were of such quality that foreigners still readily consumed them. "The very name English," one writer claimed, "is sufficient to enhance the value of all hard ware; and woollen manufactures." The thriving nature of the public debt, proponents also claimed, helped to enhance the private commercial credit of British merchants, whose bills of exchange (essentially, international checks) were "universally received and discounted at the common course of exchange… . No recommendations abroad are more honoured or respected, than those given by British merchants."[16]

"We are very considerably in Debt," one prodebt pamphleteer noted, "but with that Debt, it is certain that we are better able to bear any Expence than any other Power now in Europe." The reason was simple: "In free Nations … every Individual is concerned in the publick Transactions; and thinks himself so… . Every man is satisfied, that what is expended, is expended for the Benefit of himself, and his Family." So self-interest and the public good were one. In despotic states, by contrast, "Taxations have caused more frequent Murmurings, and even Seditions… . Here it is, that the great Difference between what is *taken*, and what is *given* makes itself to be felt" (italics in original).[17]

Many believed that the national debt also played a key role in the political success of the Glorious Revolution of 1688, a largely bloodless coup in which Parliament seized power over the monarchy by replacing the Stuart line with a Dutch aristocrat, whom it decreed William III. Rich bondholders sided with Parliament and William III against various disaffected interests. The maxim became "Borrow what you can, the more you borrow the more Friends you make." The South Sea Bubble, an infamous episode of speculation that spawned a severe panic in September 1720, threatened the balance temporarily

The maxim became "Borrow what you can, the more you borrow the more Friends you make."

because it united the "sufferers" of the scheme with "Jacobites [those who sought to return the Stuarts to the throne] and malecontented Pretenders." Clearer heads prevailed, however; "publick Credit reviv'd and Money was soon borrow'd at very low Interest, to carry on the Current Service of the Government." Thereafter, many again saw the national debt as one of the forces holding the country together, because the public creditors, though relatively few, were highly influential. At least one pamphleteer went so far as to claim that extensive foreign ownership of the debt served a similar purpose, wedded many influential foreigners to Britain, and rendered the resources of all Europe open to her during emergencies.[18]

The national debt also allowed Britain to smooth consumption over time. Without it, one proponent pointed out, during major wars "the whole Wealth of the Nation … would have pump'd out … at a few Strokes … . By chusing rather to go into Debt," he explained, "our Taxation with a longer Continuance have been more moderate; Peace shares the Burthens of the War; and the whole is moderate by being extended." The debt may also have limited warfare by astonishing and overawing "the states of Europe," Britain's traditional foes.[19]

Although sometimes affected by the machinations of speculators, the price of the government's bonds for the most part served as a barometer for measuring the public's views of its policies. "Publick credit," as one contemporary observer put it, "is the Pulse of the Nation." And, according to an anonymous financier (probably broker Thomas Mortimer), that pulse was strong in 1768. "The existence of the renowned British Empire—as an independent free state, is in no manner of danger;—that she still preserves … her credit and influence with the states of Europe—that her public credit … is built on a permanent foundation … that her national debt, is not any national grievance." If the British national debt was a problem, that same financier pointed out, that fact would be reflected in the price and quantity of government bonds. If the country was not opulent and well able to make interest payments, "it would have been impossible to have found purchasers of our funds, considering their immense amount, even at any price."[20]

For proponents of the debt, the British constitution, the unwritten rules that separated government powers, protected civil liberties, and provided other checks against the return of "arbitrary, despotic tyranny," partook of "human frailty" and hence was imperfect. Nevertheless, it was for them "the most perfect form of government that the wisdom of man could devise, for the full exercise of civil and religious liberty." The debt played an important role in holding the constitutional edifice together by ensuring the allegiance of the rich to the government. The very success of the debt, however, raised the hackles of critics who saw the government buying the influence of the great moneyed men with the blood and sweat of taxpayers. "The public debt," one such critic asserted in no uncertain terms, "is a gangrene in the commonwealth, and will submit to nothing but amputation." Writing in the early 1750s, that same critic lamented that Britain would have been much richer and more powerful than she was "had it not been for the public debt."[21]

⊗

"Unfortunately," one proponent of the debt wrote, "this nation is as much over-run with scribblers as Ægypt was formerly with flies and locusts."

Despite helping to raise Britain to the status of superpower, the debt troubled many—some think most—Britons. "Unfortunately," one proponent of the debt wrote, "this nation is as much over-run with scribblers as Ægypt was formerly with flies and locusts." Some of those scribblers feared the debt's economic burden, others its power to corrupt politics. Many saw in it Britain's impending doom. "The enormous National Debt," one writer stated in 1768, "is now becoming the alarming Object of every British Subject."[22]

Economically, government borrowing increased interest rates and thereby crowded out private investment, the exact opposite of what was claimed by debt proponents. (Both sides were correct, but at different times. As Sidney Homer and Richard Sylla explain in their magisterial *A History of Interest Rates*: "When the funds were high in price, that is, yielding around 3%, new private enterprises could be financed with ease at 4 or 5%; canals and turnpikes were projected, mortgages were floated to finance agricultural enclosure, and company promotions were stimulated. When the funds were low, that is, yielding 5% or so, only the government could borrow heavily, and private credit expansion was sharply curtailed.") "At present," one commentator complained in 1731, "People lay by their Money, in hopes by some Means or other to lend it to the Publick." Such actions, of course, "cramped" merchants and manufacturers, who found it costlier and more difficult to borrow. "'Tis certainly," one commentator noted in 1750, advantageous to "the Merchant, the Manufacturer, and Traders of all denominations … to procure Money at a low, rather than at a high Interest."[23]

Many Britons clearly saw that the taxes necessary to pay the interest on the debt decreased demand for heavily taxed land and distorted commerce and manufacturing. "New Excises and High Customs," one complained, "hurt the Foreign Traffick, and interrupt the Domestick Trade of Great Britain." Another called taxes "so many Clogs upon Trade." "If there had been a formed Design to ruin both our Trade and Manufacturers," another claimed, "it could not have been more effectually executed than by thus loading the Materials of Manufacturers with Duties, and rendering the Business of a Merchant so difficult and expensive." Many blamed the high cost of living on taxes. Robert Bird, for one, believed that taxes had caused prices to double in just half a century because "Taxes accumulate upon Taxes, till the burden is become intolerable." High prices at home of course dampened British exports abroad.[24]

Several critics, including Richard Price and Robert Bird, argued that the debt caused the depopulation of the British Isles by inducing people to engage in a form of tax arbitrage, fleeing the home islands for the tax havens of North America and the West Indies. Depopulation hurt economic growth and left the home islands dangerously exposed to foreign attack. Others feared that if the debt grew too large, the country would not be able to borrow much in time of war, leaving it vulnerable. "When a Nation runs in Debt in Time of War, and pays no Part, or but a small Part, off in Time of Peace, such Nation must be undone," one exclaimed, "by having at last neither a Fund nor Credit for carrying on the most necessary War it can be engaged in." Others pointed to the supposed loss the country suffered when foreigners became debt holders. One called it a form of "tribute" that would eventually destroy the economy. Others believed that the debt encouraged "idleness," by allowing investors who *could* work to get by without doing so. "The public debt is like some leeches," another lamented, "which will suck the blood from the whole body." Some of the leeches were brokers and other financiers, others were tax collectors.[25]

"The public debt," a typical critic complained, "has opened the iniquitous tactic of stockjobbing, and introduced a spirit of gaming amongst all degrees of men." Claims of market manipulation were ubiquitous, though probably exaggerated. The practices doubtless emigrated from Holland along with its securities markets and traders. In 1688, the year of the Glorious Revolution, one of Amsterdam's brokers, Joseph de la Vega, left posterity with vivid descriptions of the Dutch securities market. The market, he claimed, was just a "game" of misinformation and spin management that pitted bulls (those who profited from an increase in prices) against bears (those who profited from a decrease in prices).[26]

> The bulls are like the giraffe which is scared by nothing, or like the magician of the Elector of Cologne, who in his mirror made the ladies appear much more beautiful than they were in reality. They love everything, they praise everything, they exaggerate everything. And as Bias deceived the ambassador of Alyattes during the siege of Prience by showing him hills of sand covered with wheat and intimating to him that such a wealthy town would never surrender because of famine, so the bulls make the public believe that their tricks signify wealth and that crops grow on graves. When attacked by serpents, they, like the Indians, regard them as both a delicate and a delicious meal ... They are not impressed by a fire nor perturbed by a debacle ... . The bears, on the contrary, are completely ruled by fear, trepidation, and nervousness. Rabbits become elephants, brawls in a tavern become rebellions, faint shadows appear to them as signs of chaos. But if there are sheep in Africa that are supposed to serve as donkeys and wethers to serve even as horses, what is there miraculous about the likelihood that every dwarf will become a giant in the eyes of the bears?[27]

De la Vega went on to detail a dozen different ways in which cabals of bears tried to reduce securities prices. The net effect of such machinations, though, was unclear. Sometimes the bulls won, sometimes the bears won, but oftentimes their activities just canceled out. "Numerous brokers are inexhaustible in inventing involved maneuvers," de la Vega explained, "but for just this reason do not achieve their purposes." Moreover, it was clear that expectations rather than actualities already moved markets. "The expectation of an event," he noted, "creates a much deeper impression upon the exchange than the event itself." Finally, as investors learned the tricks of trading, they came to expect hyperbole, false rumors, sham sales, and the like.[28]

But to most observers, then as today, it certainly looked as if insider operators were controlling the show, to the detriment of the public. "Many investors believe implicitly," Peter Bernstein once noted, "that if prices are falling for no obvious reason, it's because They are 'taking 'em down.'" Moreover, investors "find comfort in the belief that their losses are invariably the product of some dastardly plot," all evidence to the contrary notwithstanding. Early investors were no different. But even if they believed that supply and demand usually prevailed, observers saw in stock market shenanigans nothing but waste.[29]

The reputation of securities brokers, dealers, and traders suffered yet further due to the South Sea Bubble of 1720, a year one early historian considered "pregnant beyond all others with romantic schemes and visionary projects." For reasons perpetually debated (and hence ignored here), investors were willing to pay large premiums for the stock of the South Sea Company after it initiated several debt-for-equity swaps for the government. The prices of other securities followed suit, which attracted considerable interest from investors, including many neophytes. "It seemed at that time," famous nineteenth century bubble historian Charles Mackay noted, "as if the *whole nation* had turned stock-jobbers.... *Every body* came to purchase stock" (italics in original). Unsurprisingly, numerous entrepreneurs also emerged from the woodwork to try to sell stock in sundry business schemes. "Innumerable joint-stock companies," Mackay wrote, "started up *every where*." Mackay, readers may begin to sense, disliked securities markets and was prone to exaggerate just a tad, so he interpreted as real numerous companies or bubbles that were, in fact, satirical. The most infamous of those faux proposals, including "A company for carrying on an undertaking of great advantage, but nobody to know what it is," were not bona fide attempts to bilk investors of money but rather jokes. (Such companies, by the way, exist today.) Investors may have been a bit slow on the uptake, but most were not outright stupid.[30]

Clearly though, too many securities had been issued and securities prices had become rationally unjustifiable so the more prudent investors sold out or stayed away from new schemes. When other early purchasers began to cash out, the number of sellers in the market swelled. As prices dropped, others wished to exit in case the price fell farther still. That pressure, of course, became a self-fulfilling prophesy. Within three weeks, the price of South Sea stock had fallen some 800 percent. That, I'm sorry to say for those who purchased near the top of the market, is no typo, though it does run afoul of current convention.[31]

The political fallout from the panic was intense and long lasting. After the cashier of the South Sea Company absconded, its directors and top officers, including several members of Parliament, were arrested and their papers seized. A Parliamentary committee of investigation claimed to have "discovered a train of the deepest villainy and fraud that hell ever contrived to ruin a nation." Mr. J. Aislabie, chancellor of the Exchequer, was also implicated, and committed to the infamous Tower of London when it was discovered that he had purposely destroyed accounts to hide his tracks. (And they say history doesn't repeat itself!) The directors and officers had to pay hefty penalties to the stockholders, proportioned by the size of their estates and the depth of their culpability. Instead of alleviating some of the burden of the national debt as promised, the South Sea Company fiasco ended up costing Britons over £3 million.[32]

Bad as it was, the bubble had a positive effect—it kept British securities markets pretty sober. "Enterprise, like Icarus," Mackay explained, "had soared too high, and melted the wax of her wings ... She has never since attempted so high a flight." Not until 1825 did British investors again grow so drunk that they stumbled. According to one late-nineteenth-century historian of the debacle, the Bank of England was driven to "within an ace of stopping payment" and the panic remained "well remembered after nearly fifty years." The financial cataclysm also kept the government on its toes. Officials held the episode in "perpetual remembrance" because it afforded "innumerable beacons to guide" policy.[33]

> Not until 1825 did British investors again grow so drunk that they stumbled.

Constant trading in the funds served no economic purpose, many believed, but served only to enrich commissioned brokers. "The trade of the Alley," it was thought, "consists in conspiring to pick the pocket of every body not in the secret." Operators and sharpers, many thought, "can make stocks rise and fall at pleasure, and pocket the difference." They could move prices "one or two per cent. at pleasure … by raising rumours and spreading fictitious stories" and engaging in sham sales, "pretending to buy or sell large quantities of Stock on a sudden." Moneylenders and those in the know—yes, supposedly mostly Jews—received what the speculators had lost, "though they have found no treasure, discovered no philosophers stone, nor imported a single farthing from abroad."[34]

But the securities speculators were not the only bloodsuckers. "Are there not," one critic asked, "Placemen and Pensioners, crafty Courtiers, and craving Civil Lists, Foreigners and Footmen enough about the court yearly to devour" immense sums that could be used to pay down the debt? (Today these are called earmarks.) Some suspected substantial economic gains if tax men, thought by some to number over 30,000, could be diverted to more productive occupations. The "swarm of tax gatherers," another pointed out, "cannot fail to be looked upon as the instruments of oppressing the very country which had a right to the benefit of their honest industry."[35]

Excise taxes were particularly hated because the laws governing them allowed the tax man to enter business establishments, even at night, and otherwise invade personal privacy. To replace them, some sought a tax on houses and on trade with the French. All seemed to concede that tax yields were simply too low, that Adam Smith's fourth maxim of taxation was being broken: "Every tax ought to be so contrived as both to take out and keep out of the pockets of the people as little as possible, over and above what it brings into the public treasury."[36]

Little wonder, then, that many critics of the debt noted that political dangers lurked as well. Several commentators raised the specter of a tax rebellion. "The Throne of that Prince, in a Free Nation, must be most firmly established," one warned, "whose Affairs will permit him to ask, or who desires to collect, the fewest Taxes from his People." Another suggested that the "enormous Burthen" would eventually lead to "a Crisis" well before all the objects of taxation had been exhausted. That rebellion eventually came, though it struck in the American colonies instead of the homeland.[37]

The debt, one critic argued in 1731, turned the "very Members of the House of Commons, who should be the Bullwork of the Peoples Liberties, [into] Pensioners, and Servants to the Court." Another called the debt "the most effectual Means of rendering the People Slaves" because it allowed the monarch's minions to "corrupt the Parliament" with "Places and Pensions." (By slaves the author did not mean New World chattel slaves but rather forcing people "to act, or not to act, according to the arbitrary will and pleasure of another.") The complicated tax system was too valuable a source of patronage plums to be dismantled, many critics believed. Some went so far as to claim that the debt holders themselves, or at least the most important of the 30,000 or so of them, controlled the government, citing "that old Maxim, *the Borrower is a Slave to the Lender*" (italics in original). A few critics believed that debt holders were naturally warmongers. "It is the interest of the stockholders," one claimed point-blank, "to involve the nation in war, because they get by it." The debt holders also fomented war, some believed, to divert people's attention away from policy debates regarding the debt and taxes.[38]

> Some critics showed their concern by concocting schemes, some harebrained or in jest, to pay off the debt in short order.

Some critics showed their concern by concocting schemes, some harebrained or in jest, to pay off the debt in short order. Some wanted to monetize all or part of it; others to tax all manner of vices, including fornication and blasphemy; still others to tax high living and nudity; others to tax the church back to its "primitive" state; several to crack down on smuggling; others to refinance the redeemable part of the debt at a lower rate of interest as soon as market conditions permitted; one to pay it off through a sort of tontine scheme; and a few to run it up and then repudiate it, or part of it. The greatest dreamers of all thought it a simple matter to decrease expenditures and increase taxes. One author thought that two additional taxes, one on land and the other on people, would pay off the debt in just a dozen years, provided these taxes were fully paid into the sinking fund, an institution designed to apply budget surpluses to debt repayment.[39]

One writer suggested paying off the debt by *cutting* taxes. Eliminating the highest and most distortionary duties, like those on salt and candles, he argued, a century and a half before Ronald Reagan's birth, would allow trade and manufacturing to thrive, thereby increasing the yield on other, more sensible taxes. Matthew Decker agreed, arguing that Britain should abolish its tax system and put in its stead "one general Tax." George Box made a similar plea, suggesting land, house, burial, marriage, and birth taxes. Robert Bird also concurred, noting that a capital levy of 5 percent on the value of the real and personal estates of Britons, estimated at about 2 billion, would pay off most of the nation's debt. As Bird seemed to intuit, such a tax would be less distortionary, less "complex" as he put it, than Britain's usual raft of customs, duties, and excises.[40]

Bourchier Cleeve also looked to tax simplification and economic growth to reduce the burden of debt and taxes, but not through supply-side trickle-down voodoo economics. "The great Increase of our Commerce," he explained, "will render this Nation the Grand Mart of the World." Trade and manufacturing would pull the nation, if not out of debt, at least out of danger by reducing the ratio of debt to aggregate annual income. Along this same line, another pamphleteer proposed free trade and nationalization of the East India Company as the nation's savior. "Those trades which are monopolized by companies," he suggested, "shall become open and free to all his majesty's subjects." That would stimulate trade and manufacturing, allowing the country to pull itself out of debt by vastly increasing its wealth.[41]

Others made proposals fancier still, suggesting that the government offer to exchange irredeemable fixed-maturity bonds of 20, 40, and 60 years for perpetuities redeemable at the government's pleasure. Investors could thereby avoid interest rate risk, to wit, the risk that market interest rates would sink enough to induce the government to redeem its higher interest rate debt. By giving the debt a fixed maturity, the author hoped, the government would raise the taxes necessary to pay it off when due rather than bear the risk that interest rates would be high when tranches of bonds came due. Combined with 20 years of peace, the author asserted, his scheme would do the trick.[42]

How much of this debate the American colonists followed is difficult to say. The most politically important of them probably understood the gist of it and they certainly knew that the "enormity of the national debt" after the French and Indian War (Seven Years' War, 1756–63) was used to justify Britain's attempt to tax them. After the Revolution, American policy-makers undoubtedly familiarized themselves with the debate, at least as seen through the eyes of Scottish political economist Adam Smith.[43]

Born near Edinburgh soon after the death of his father in 1723, Smith as a baby was kidnapped by Gypsies but abandoned in the next town unharmed. A precocious youth, he started college at the University of Glasgow at the age of 14. At age 17, he enrolled at Oxford University, where he toughed it out for 6 long years. He later taught college, tutored European aristocrats, wrote several books, and discussed sundry economic topics, including national debts, with the Enlightenment's leading minds, like the brilliant Scottish scholar and philosopher David Hume. By January 1775, when Smith was putting the finishing touches on the first edition of his now-classic *An Inquiry Into the Nature and Causes of the Wealth of Nations*, the British national debt stood at over £129 million, down from the £146 million owed at the end of the Seven Years' War but still so large that Benjamin Franklin claimed it would take 314 ships or 31,452 carts to carry it all, and 148 years, 109 days, and 22 hours to count it out.[44]

No friend of big government, Smith, influenced here by Hume, concluded his magisterial opus with a bitter diatribe against that debt, or to be more precise the political system that had allowed the debt to grow decade after decade virtually unchecked. The "enormous debts" were already oppressive, he believed, and "in the long-run" they would "probably ruin, all the great nations of Europe," including Britain. Though its tax system was superior—more efficient and less distortionary—than those of most other countries, Britain would eventually be forced to turn to less efficacious taxes, Smith warned. "When the wisest government has exhausted all the proper subjects of taxation," Smith argued, "it must ... have recourse to improper ones."[45]

"The want of parsimony in time of peace" was the major problem. Instead of saving for the rainy day to come, most likely a war, governments wasted surplus income on frivolities—trinkets, pageants, "splendid buildings ... and other public ornaments." During an emergency, like a major war, taxes inevitably proved too low and too slow to meet the need. Borrowing became a dire necessity.

Wealthy merchants and other moneyed men happily fulfilled the need, Smith argued. Government bonds earned investors a market rate of return without tying up their capitals. Moreover, their liquidity (their ability to be cheaply and easily transferred to other investors for cash) and low risk of default made them ideal investments for a portion of every business's balance sheet.

> Instead of saving for the rainy day to come, most likely a war, governments wasted surplus income on frivolities—trinkets, pageants, "splendid buildings … and other public ornaments."

That was not to argue, however, that the debt was an unmitigated economic good. For the most part, the purchasing power transferred to the government was wasted on wars and colonies, from, in Smith's words, "maintaining productive labourers to maintaining unproductive ones, and to be spent and wasted, generally in the course of the year, without even the hope of any future reproduction." Moreover, the taxes needed to fund the debt could distort economic incentives, and the public debt to some degree crowded out private investment. "The private revenue of the inhabitants of Great Britain is at present as much encumbered in time of peace, their ability to accumulate is as much impaired," Smith lamented, "as it would have been in the time of the most expensive war, had the pernicious system of funding never been adopted."

Cognizant of its ability to borrow in time of need, the British government first stopped trying to run budget surpluses, then got into the habit of anticipating some of its annual taxes. "Like an improvident spendthrift," Smith complained, the British government was "in the constant practice of borrowing of its own factors and agents, and of paying interest for the use of its own money." Seemingly congenitally incapable of keeping expenditures equal to revenues, it then mortgaged many of its revenues in perpetuity, and finally found it could pay only interest on an ever-increasing principal sum. "This practice," Smith sighed, "necessarily puts off the liberation of the public revenue from a fixed period to one so indefinite that it is not very likely ever to arrive … . When national debts have once been accumulated to a certain degree," he further noted, "there is scarce … a single instance of their having been fairly and completely paid."

The heart of the debt problem was, in Smith's view, political rather than economic. "To relieve the present exigency," he noted, "is always the object which principally interests [no puns intended, I'm sure] those immediately concerned in the administration of public affairs. The future liberation of the public revenue," he continued, again with great sagacity, the politicians "leave to the care of posterity." Even the institutional mechanism those politicians employed to pay down the debt, the so-called sinking fund, was nothing more, in Smith's view, than a contrivance, a fund to be raided upon the slightest excuse, a fact that was not lost on other Britons. Moreover, the funds were usually quite small compared with the debt, because countries that could borrow, did borrow, usually to the hilt.[46]

Would that was all! The ability to borrow large sums on the cheap not only made governments improvident, Smith believed; it also made them substantially more militant. "Unwilling, for fear of offending the people," to pay for wars entirely through taxation, governments like that of Britain could, "with a very moderate increase of taxes," pay for their expeditions by borrowing. (Indeed, between 1688 and 1815, England paid for her wars with two-thirds taxes and one-third loans.) So rather than quickly becoming "disgusted with the war," citizens, especially those who invested in government bonds, found violent conflict as profitable as it was entertaining and patriotic. Instead of following Smith's advice and jettisoning colonies that would not "contribute towards the support of the whole empire," the British government and, at least at first, a good chunk of the British populace chose war over conciliation.[47]

In the eighteenth century, Britain's national debt soared with each new war and barely decreased during the short interludes between them and there was no end to the cycle in sight.

Smith's cynicism was certainly justified. In the eighteenth century, Britain's national debt soared with each new war and barely decreased during the short interludes between them and there was no end to the cycle in sight. In the nineteenth century, though, Smith's cynicism appeared unfounded because both Britain and the United States paid down their national debts, and even paid it off in America's case. But in the twentieth and twenty-first centuries, the justice of Smith's view was reestablished as formal national debts and other governmental liabilities, like Social Security, again waxed ever larger in both countries and many others besides.

Wealth of Nations was not *widely* read in America until the nineteenth century, but the new country's best and brightest became conversant with it during the war, if only indirectly, via American reprints of British commentary. For example, the third edition of *Four Letters to the Earl of Carlisle from William Eden ... On the Public Debts,* which explicitly described and praised Smith's views, appeared from the New York press of loyalist printer James Rivington in 1780. After the war, direct imports of *Wealth of Nations* became possible, excerpts appeared in American newspapers, an American reprint edition appeared in 1789 (and a second in 1796), and by the 1790s important libraries had the book, and in some cases commentary on it, on their shelves. By the time Smith died in 1790, the book was quite successful on both sides of the Atlantic, one writer remarking that *Wealth of Nations* "was not at first as popular as it afterwards became." By the early 1790s, enough copies were available to fuel numerous references to Smith's work in American political and policy discourse and even some textbooks. One writer said the book was "worth its weight in gold to an American legislator," no small praise indeed given the book's great girth. Rather than ask candidates for political office what they believe, the writer suggested one only need inquire, "Have you read Smith's Wealth of Nations?" (Why do Washington reporters not ask such questions today?) Americans combed over all aspects of the book, not just the finale on public debts, but clearly gave that critical section close scrutiny. Some accepted Smith's views of national debts lock, stock, and barrel. Others, including Alexander Hamilton, who studied Smith's work carefully, expressed serious misgivings. The rift between the Smithians and Hamiltonians would play a large role in the politics of the early republic as well as in America's handling of the debt it would incur winning its independence.[48]

3

CONCEPTION

Financing Revolution

By 1775, the British Empire was enormous, powerful, and rich. King, Parliament, and their corporate minions controlled mainland North America to the Mississippi, numerous sugar-rich islands in the Caribbean, Gibraltar and Minorca in the Mediterranean, and enjoyed footholds in Central America, Africa, and India. Though still far shy of its Victorian zenith, it was already impressive, extensive, and expensive. For support, it needed the world's largest navy, the larger ships of which displaced over 300,000 tons in total, a third more than the navies of France and Spain and three times more than those of Russia and the Netherlands. Britain's navy did not rule the waves to the extent it would at the end of the Napoleonic Wars but in 1775 it was a formidable force nonetheless.[1]

The British military was so awesome, in fact, it lost only one big war in the eighteenth century, the war for American independence. How did a handful of colonies, some just a few decades old and none among the empire's richest, defeat the world's greatest power? According to historian Edmund S. Morgan, the rebels' "greatest asset was, in fact, their desire to be free." Morgan makes a good point. American sailors and soldiers indeed fought the good fight. "I cannot too frequently repeat how much I was surprised at the American army," one French officer commented. "It is beyond understanding how troops who were almost naked, badly paid,

> "It is beyond understanding how troops who were almost naked, badly paid, composed of old men, negroes, and children, could move so well, both on the march and under fire."

composed of old men, negroes, and children, could move so well, both on the march and under fire." "We have no instance in history," another contemporary claimed, "of an army, who discovered, and practiced more spirit, firmness, patience, discipline, fortitude and zeal ... than were found in our troops." But there must be more to the story. Dogged determination is not always enough to win, as the Southern states learned to their chagrin in the first half of the 1860s. Moreover, most Americans did not want freedom enough to pay for it, at least not in the form of traditional taxes. They went to war, after all, at least partly because they wished to unburden themselves of British taxes and debt. If the British "abound in resources as largely as ... [they] boast they do," one supporter of independence complained, "let them cease complaining of their poverty, and contentedly discharge their own national debt, rather than go on augmenting; or by their efforts to saddle it, with an unlimited pension-list, on America."[2]

Perhaps another crucial rebel asset was their financial system and their willingness to use it even though many Americans, following British critics, believed that a national debt was a source of corruption and economic malaise. France, according to this view, joined the fray because the Americans had proved that they could impose a financial drain on the mother country. Private Dutch investors eventually came to America's aid as well, just as they abandoned the British. Ultimately, then, America outlasted Britain in finance as well as on the field of battle, though both were desperate affairs. Contemporaries, too, saw the war as a financial as well as a military conflict. In March 1780, for example, "A Friend in Time of Need" wrote the *Pennsylvania Packet*:

> Britain, foiled in her attempts to conquer America by force, is now carrying on a war of finance. The field of battle is changed for the field of the budget; and the longest purse aided by the best schemes for raising or creating a revenue will in a great measure determine the point.... The last resource then is finance.[3]

There is more than a little irony here. From Holland via Britain public finance came to America. The colonists of mainland British North America were not as skilled at borrowing as their financial parents were, but they learned just quickly enough to win their independence. The first U.S. national debt owed its existence to the Dutch and British and shared much in common with the debt of those countries, but it exhibited characteristics not found in either parent, no doubt due to the radically different environment in which it was nurtured.

The first U.S. national debt owed its existence to the Dutch and British and shared much in common with the debt of those countries, but it exhibited characteristics not found in either parent, no doubt due to the radically different environment in which it was nurtured.

❧

In fact, the colonies of mainland British North America were the first governments—at least the first Western governments in the modern era—to borrow significant sums at zero interest by issuing so-called bills of credit.[4] Massachusetts led the way in 1690, followed by South Carolina in 1703. (In the late 1690s, the British government reformed its coinage by calling in and reminting silver coins, which were much clipped and worn. To help alleviate the shortage of cash during the recoinage, the Exchequer issued zero-interest bearer tax anticipation scrip in denominations as low as £5. The colonies may have drawn on that experience but seem to have been influenced mainly by Massachusetts's example.) The bills, which were nothing more than specially printed pieces of paper signed by one or more colonial officials, were bearer instruments that served as a medium of exchange. In other words, they were cash money, much like today's Federal Reserve notes, except they were not always full legal tender. Colonists accepted them in payment because they were superior to the other media of exchange available to them. Various commodity monies, including wampum, beaver pelts, wheat, and tobacco, were inconvenient for a variety of reasons. Some were subject to adulteration or wastage, rendering transactions and storage nettlesome. Others were heavy and bulky in relation to their value so that making and receiving payments, especially large ones, was costly. Many were subject to the vagaries of the climate. Due to British imperial trade regulations, silver and gold coins, bars, and plate were often in short supply because colonial merchants needed them to make remittances to their commercial brethren in Liverpool and London. Here is how one observer described the trade of South Carolina with Britain in 1718:

> The trade between South Carolina and Great Britain, does, one Year with another, employ 22 Sail of Ships, laden hither with all Sorts of Woollen Cloaths … Linnens … Nails of all Sizes, Hoes, Hatchets, and all Kinds of Iron-ware, … fine Earthen-ware, Pipes, Paper, Rugs, Blankets, Quilts … Gloves, Pewter-Dishes and Plates, Brass and Copper-Ware, Guns, Powder, Bullets, Flints, … Looking and Drinking Glasses … Pins, Needles, &c. In return for which are remitted from hence about seventy Thousand Deer-Skins a Year, some Furs, Rosin, Pitch, Tar, Raw-Silk, Rice, and formerly Indigo. But since all these don't balance the continual Demand for European Goods, and Negroe Slaves, sent us by the English Merchants, there is likewise sent to England, some Cocoa-Nuts, Sugar, Tortoise-shell, Money, and other Things, which we have from the American Islands…. [and obtained in exchange for] Beef, Pork, Butter, Candles, Soap … Rice, Shingles … and Heads for Barrels.[5]

The difficult part for the colonists was the money part, which tended to flow through the colonies rather than linger. Bills of credit, by contrast, passed from hand to hand only in the colonies. (Some claim only in the colony where issued, but they are wrong. The bills often crossed colony lines, but they never circulated overseas.) Bills of credit were also easily transported and, if not overissued or counterfeited, they were of lasting and uniform quality. (The penalty for involvement in counterfeiting, which ranged from cropping of the ears to death without benefit of clergy—which meant the government took the crime extremely seriously—did not stop fakes and frauds but undoubtedly deterred casual producers of the fake stuff.) Until British imperial authorities intervened, bills also had the virtue of being of elastic supply. If a colonial legislature thought the economy needed some monetary stimulus, it could emit more bills.

But the legislatures were not central bankers; the decision to issue bills of credit was usually based on fiscal rather than monetary concerns because the bills were the colonies' major source of borrowing. The principle was simple: the government used the bills of credit to purchase goods and services, usually war material and soldiers. Some early emissions, including that of South Carolina, bore interest but that feature was soon abandoned as the colonies found supporting interest-bearing bills a "great Burthen" and "the Interest gave Encouragement to People to Hoard them." When they paid no interest, the bills were a medium of exchange, passing from hand to hand as cash until returned to the colonial treasury, usually via taxes or the sale of state assets like frontier lands. The treasurer could then destroy the bills or pay them out again. Some colonies, including Massachusetts and Pennsylvania, also established loan offices that lent bills of credit to farmers and other business firms against the security of land or other tangible assets. For the most part, though, the supply of bills in circulation was a function of the state's financial needs, not the needs of the economy. That proved to be their downfall in both the colonial and Revolutionary eras.[6]

Bills of credit were not officially convertible into specie (gold or silver coins) or other commodities at any fixed rate, not even at the treasury or loan office that issued them, so their value was wholly a function of their quantity and the government's ability to redeem them via taxation. In the middle colonies, wars were relatively few and small, so governments found it possible to limit their issuance of bills. In the extreme southern and northern colonies, by contrast, relatively frequent and fierce wars made such fiscal constraint impossible. Colonial Georgia, for example, issued bills of credit because it found it difficult to collect taxes sufficient to run the government and prosecute a war. In the middle colonies, by contrast, bills stayed at or close to their par or face values and remained informally convertible into specie. Where many bills were issued, by contrast, people found it profitable to export their gold and silver, ending easy retail convertibility. If yet more bills were issued before the economy expanded to accommodate them, they began to depreciate in value, which is to say that the prices of all other goods expressed in terms of bills increased. Interest rates, too, increased while the volume of credit extended decreased, straining relations between net debtors and creditors. In early South Carolina, North Carolina, and New England, inflation was rampant and in the latter chronic until reforms were implemented in 1749–50 by Massachusetts and by British imperial authorities in 1751.[7]

Those and subsequent reforms, which included British repayments for colonial war expenditures in coins and bills of exchange drawn on London, provided New England, particularly at first Massachusetts, a money supply composed largely of silver and later gold coins. Unable and unwilling to issue bills of credit, the government of Massachusetts began borrowing money the Dutch and British way, by selling interest-bearing bonds. It took time for investors to treasure Massachusetts's bonds, but, as the mastermind behind the colony's currency reform noted, once they "found that the promise made by government was punctually performed … the publick security was preferred to private." Some small-denomination treasurer certificates, or treasury notes as they were called, found limited circulation among soldiers but most were "in large Sums & kept up as Securities" and hence changed hands relatively infrequently. They were, in other words, financial assets but not money. And they were hardly trivial. At any given time, hundreds of thousands of pounds' worth were outstanding. The governments of Connecticut and Rhode Island too were eventually able to sell interest-bearing bonds in lieu of issuing bills of credit.[8]

Encouraged by what they saw in New England, other colonial governments also began selling bonds instead of issuing bills to meet small portions of their financing needs. For example, Pennsylvania in the late 1750s borrowed some £10,000 to capitalize its commissioners of Indian trade. Henry C. Adams, an early public debt theorist, argued that the existence of a "money" market, a market where short-term debts were bought and sold, was the sine qua non of a market for public debt. Indeed, wherever we observe a vigorous money market, as in Amsterdam and London, a market for government securities, some of distant maturity, later arises. Where a money market was lacking, as in Latin America, government debts, where they arose at all, had to be sold and traded in London or other international financial centers due to a dearth of domestic markets. The American colonies were no exception. Before colonial governments began selling long-term bonds, local markets for short-term debts, mostly in the form of international bills of exchange, were already well established. Both the money and government debt markets eventually would play important roles in financing the Revolution but the rebellious colonies initially found it expedient to rely heavily on their old standby, bills of credit.[9]

※

When the Revolution began, the colonists knew a surprising amount about finance but with the expectation of the loss of British aid, they knew they would not have the wherewithal to keep their war machine humming smoothly for long. Luckily, some American financiers adapted to the situation and managed to stave off defeat, but just barely. That the rebels had a rough go of it financially is not surprising. "A Government created by a revolution hardly ever is" creditworthy, banking theorist and editor of *The Economist* Walter Bagehot correctly noted in the late nineteenth century. What is surprising is that rebel financiers managed to muddle through the war despite numerous obstacles, some practical, others ideological. Tom Paine, the rabble-rouser who swayed many a fence-sitter to choose independence, persuaded numerous Americans that a national debt could be a blessing. In his widely read pamphlet *Common Sense*, Paine argued that Americans ought not to worry about creating a national debt during their struggle for independence. They had no debt to speak of, but they also had no navy. Britain had a large debt, but also a large navy. If Americans went into debt not to feed consumption but rather to build an effective war machine that would ensure its independence, it would be well worth the interest they would pay. Paine also argued that "a national debt is a national bond," a nice pun by which he presumably meant that in addition to winning independence on the battlefield a national debt would help to forge the disparate colonies into a more unified whole. Finally, Paine noted that "when [a debt] bears no interest [it] is in no case a grievance." He was gravely mistaken on that point as the colonial experiences of New England and the Deep South described above bear out. But here was a clarion call for the colonists to issue bills of credit to fund their glorious war of liberation.[10]

And issue bills of credit they did, though more perhaps from financial necessity than Paine's prodding. To raise funds, governments have three major options: tax, sell assets, and issue debt. The state, nee colonial governments and the Continental Congress, the sorry excuse for a national government the colonies inherited from the imperial crisis leading up to the Revolution, did all three in proportions that varied over place and time. Through 1779, issuance of debt, especially bills of credit, was the preferred source of funds for a variety of reasons. Taxes were impractical as well as inexpedient. In many places early in the rebellion, extralegal revolutionary bodies simply assumed the reins of state, including their tax revenues. In South Carolina and New York, for example, existing duties and fees were simply paid into the treasury of the new government rather than that of the old. Seizing the fiscal apparatus of the state did not ensure a steady stream of collections, however, especially under uncertain wartime conditions that proved very conducive to tax evasion, resistance, and even outright revolt. In June 1777, for example, Samuel Albright and dozens of other Lancaster County, Pennsylvania, men and women upset at overly rambunctious tax collection armed themselves with scythes, pitchforks, and other deadly farm implements. Three people perished in the ensuing melee. In New York, the British occupied lands that had produced about 60 percent of the government's revenues in the late colonial period, so the state treasury was essentially born emasculated.[11]

Moreover, the colonies had never been very efficient tax collectors because most had never managed to reconcile conflicts between and among merchants, landowners, and artisans, and the war did nothing to unite their disparate interests. The impost, a tax on imports, was an important source of colonial tax revenue, but it was severely disrupted by the war. Taxes on land were also disrupted, in part because the new state governments wanted to keep the direct tax burden low so as not to increase the ranks of pro-British Tories. That was a particularly important policy choice in colonies deeply divided over the war. In Georgia, for example, the population divided nearly equally between Tories and patriots because the British government had been supportive of the colony, which formed just a few decades before the Revolution, and imperial commercial restrictions burdened its largely agriculture economy but little. The new national government had no power to tax the people directly but could only plead for funds from the states, which found levying and collecting taxes, even for their own use, inexpedient and difficult. Congress's inability to induce the states to pay their requisitions is an important subject to which we will return.[12]

Taxes on prizes, or the proceeds of seizures of British ships at sea, were popular with everyone except the privateers, the men who risked life and limb to seize spoils in seas infested with sharks, storms, and enemy ships.

Moreover, prizes and the taxes they generated vacillated with the fortunes of war and could hardly be depended upon.[13]

To raise funds the rebel governments could also sell state assets, like vacant land. Sales were difficult to consummate during wartime, however, particularly when the land was located on the frontier, much of which was a deadly war zone. Only after the war did sales of government land produce a decent trickle of revenue. Perhaps the most popular source of revenue was the lease and later outright sale of confiscated loyalist estates. Seizing and selling Tory assets, particularly real estate, was relatively easy and may have dissuaded neutrals from joining the Crown against the rebels. On the other hand, confiscation brought unease to many steeped in Lockean notions of the sanctity of private property, so in many places, like South Carolina, it was resorted to in a major way only toward the end of the war, when the line between friend and foe was fairly clear.[14]

The easiest tax to levy was the so-called currency tax imposed on the holders of depreciating bills of credit. Here is how one congressman put it: "Do you think, gentleman, that I will consent to load my constituents with taxes, when we can send to our printer, and get a wagon-load of money, one quire of which will pay for the whole?" The currency tax had the virtue of being very light at first. In many places, an absolute dearth of currency existed as mobilization for war began, so bills of credit emissions stimulated the economy without causing inflation. "This Currency, as we manage it," Benjamin Franklin boasted, "is a wonderful Machine" because it "pays and clothes Troops, and provides Victuals and Ammunition." Franklin understood the end game too, noting that "when we are obliged to issue a Quantity excessive, it pays itself off by Depreciation."[15]

Franklin was as right about depreciation as he had been about electricity. As the war dragged on, the supply of new money began to outstrip demand. Some think that the rebel bills depreciated because people lost confidence in them or because they were not sufficiently backed by tangible assets. Not so. There were simply too many of

The inevitable result of more money chasing the same amount of goods and services was inflation, or depreciation of bills of credit in the parlance of the day.

them at prevailing prices, or, as Tom Paine would later put it, "the market ... was glutted." The inevitable result of more money chasing the same amount of goods and services was inflation, or depreciation of bills of credit in the parlance of the day. (But inflation it was because, as Paine noted, "the same fate would have happened to gold and silver, could gold and silver have been issued in the same abundant manner as paper had been, and confined within the country as paper money always is.") Meanwhile, coins were exported or went into hiding, awaiting the day that they would be able to fetch great gobs of goods.[16]

The rebels were unable to stop the slide in the value of their currency for three reasons. First, the continent's monetary policy was not coordinated. Each state issued its own bills, as did the national government, which did not exert as much control over the situation as it might have. In late July 1775, the Continental Congress appointed George Clymer and Michael Hillegas "joint treasurers of the United Colonies." After Clymer quit in August 1776, Hillegas became the sole Continental treasurer, a post he held until the new government formed in the late 1780s. In February 1776, Congress established a committee, the Board of Treasury, to oversee his activities and provide policy direction. That arrangement might have worked had the board been more financially astute and less limp-wristed. Although a standing committee with more authority and longer tenure than temporary or ad hoc legislative committees, the board was a weak entity nevertheless. Nominally composed of five members of Congress, the board was perennially hampered by low rates of attendance and extremely high rates of turnover. Worse, it did not exert much policy leadership in Congress until it was too late.[17]

Attempts to stop the depreciation of bills via government price controls and legal tender clauses were also poorly coordinated and doomed to failure. "The very law which *compels* us to receive bills of credit as cash," Nathaniel Hazard later explained, "first causes distrust, and injures their circulation" due to the tender nature of public credit (italics in original). "To attempt to fix the value of money," the great American geographer Jedidiah Morse explained, "was as ridiculous as an attempt to restrain the rising of water in rivers amidst showers of rain." "The laws of the country interposed," wailed early historian David Ramsay, "and compelled the widow to receive a shilling, where a pound was her due. The blooming virgin, who had grown up with an unquestionable title to a liberal patrimony, was legally stripped of everything. The hapless orphan was obliged to give a final discharge on the payment of six pence in the pound. The poor became rich, and the rich, became poor."[18]

Second, the British engaged in unabashed economic warfare. Its army pillaged and marauded and its navy blockaded the coast, severely disrupting America's foreign trade. Battlefield losses, including soldiers and other valuable resources, spelled economic disaster for the rebels. When the British retook Savannah and overran most of the rest of Georgia in late 1778 and early 1779, for example, rebel tax collection ceased and economic output plummeted as, in the words of one historian, "near anarchy prevailed." Perhaps worst of all, the British and loyalists did everything they could to destroy the value of state paper money and Continentals, Congress's bills of credit. At the end of 1776, Philadelphia financier Robert Morris noted that the patriots' "internal enemies" had "always been undermining" the value of rebel bills of credit "by various artifices," including taking out insidious advertisements offering the insultingly low value of "one guinea per thousand" for their use as wallpaper! Far worse, the British began to counterfeit state bills and Continentals and infuse them into circulation. In October 1777, a Boston newspaper reported that several men had been employed by the British "during the last fall and winter, in bringing counterfeit bills from Long Island, in order that they might be spread throughout the country, to destroy the credit of our money." Other apparently large-scale incidents also took place and rogues posing as patriots were more than happy to join the fray on the side of monetary chaos. The precise extent of counterfeiting, British or otherwise, will never be known for certain, but on one night alone in January 1780 a squad of Americans raided a house near the Sandy Hook lighthouse where they were rewarded with "seven enemy prisoners ... 45,000 counterfeit continental dollars [and] a quantity of hard money." Currency warfare has become a mainstay of international conflict but in the eighteenth century it was considered a form of ungentlemanly behavior, which the Americans in any case could not easily have countered, given the printing technology and paper available to them during the conflict, which was so primitive that it was joked that the "only means of distinguishing the difference" between true bills and counterfeit "was said to lie in the superior execution of the spurious bills."[19]

Third, patriots had only limited means of withdrawing bills of credit from circulation. As described above, the rebel governments found it difficult to exact high taxes or sell many assets. They also found it difficult to sell interest-bearing bonds. To soak up bills of credit and thereby stave off depreciation, state governments, like that of South Carolina, began in 1776 to sell bonds to the public. Holding rebel paper money was a brave act, especially early in the conflict, but it was not a large burden as the bills could quickly and easily be exchanged for goods and services. Owning rebel bonds was quite a different proposition. In many places, state bond issues failed to attract investors until the terms—the rate of interest, term to maturity, negotiability, and the like—were made more favorable. Even then, though, the sums borrowed paled compared with the sums of paper money emitted. In South Carolina, for example, loans to the state barely exceeded 11 percent of the currency that state issued. By the late 1770s, increasing numbers of investors were induced to part with their money for promises of future repayment, with interest. The successful completion of the British invasion of South Carolina in May 1780 understandably killed off that revenue stream, though, just as it also rendered it impossible to collect taxes or print more paper money. Massachusetts also borrowed on bond, a clear continuation of its colonial practice, though it too spewed forth quantities of bills of credit too prodigious to be allayed.[20]

By October 1776, the Continental Congress was also selling bonds called loan office certificates. It too experienced modest success, especially after it raised the nominal rate of interest from 4 to 6 percent and began to pay interest in specie or its equivalent in bills of exchange drawn on its European loans (making real interest more like 8 to 30 percent due to the depreciation of the Continentals). Ultimately, however, the sums it collected fell short of the amount necessary to retire its increasingly plentiful Continentals. Even its lottery scheme fell flat, a rarity in a country infamous for its voracious appetite for gambling. General Washington even forbade his officers to gamble, urging them to buy lottery tickets instead, apparently unaware of the chicanery lottery officials indulged in.[21]

The banner year for bond sales was 1779. The year 1780 ranked second but nevertheless was a major disappointment because the number of bonds sold and their total value were only half those of 1779. All the loan offices combined brought in less than $65 million of Continental bills of credit between 1776 and 1783. Over that same period, the several states issued some $210 to $246 million of their respective bills of credit and the Congress between $200 and $242 million of Continentals, depending on whose figures one chooses to believe.[22]

Unsurprisingly, Pennsylvania led the way in terms of both total investors and total dollars invested. Touched directly by the war for only brief periods, Philadelphia was both the national capital and the commercial and financial center of the rebellious colonies and would continue to be its financial heart until the 1830s. Precious little is known of most of the more than 13,000 individuals and firms who purchased Continental loan office certificates. The list of purchasers is of course littered with first- and second-tier founding fathers, men ranging from George Washington of Virginia to George Clinton of New York to Caesar Rodney of Delaware. But little is known of some major purchasers, including Isaac Vanbibber of Maryland, who bought $116,400 worth of Continental loan office certificates between September 1778 and March 1779, Nehemiah Dunham of New Jersey, who acquired $127,000 worth of bonds between February 1779 and April 1780, or Robert Johnson of New York, who bought $35,600 worth of bonds between December 1778 and July 1780. And nothing is known of the numerous small purchasers, like Mary Hutchins of New Hampshire, who purchased two bonds with a total face value of $500 on April 22, 1779, or Maryland's Thomas Buckingham, who purchased a single $200 bond on February 24, 1779. Worse, no monument records their names or recognizes their sacrifice. That's a travesty, plain and simple, because their bond purchases were just as important to the war effort as the men and muskets their funds provided for. As a contemporary commentator put it, with his italics: "The sums due them, are their *dear, their painful earnings*; these claimants are the *soldiers who fought*, and the *citizens who supplied* them, when the *salvation of our country*, was the great *prize contended for*; it is owing to their virtuous and strong exertions, that we have *any thing left*." If only a few historians would devote full time to the task, instead of working on the umpteen-thousandth study of oft-studied figure X or the cultural implications of this and that, justice (scholarly justice anyway) could finally be done for these financial patriots![23]

⬥

In 1778, the Continental Congress asked British mathematician and national debt expert Richard Price to emigrate to America and take over its finances. He declined and rightly so. Who but a fool would place such a large wager on a winded, haggard horse? Bills of credit continued to pour from American (and British and rogue) printing presses but everyone sensed that the end was nigh. Congress tried to dispel rumors that it would allow Continentals to vanish valueless into the abyss, but many realized it was simply a matter of when, and how, the end would come. Even as the nominal value of bills of credit in circulation spiraled upward, their real value, the value of goods they could purchase, slid. In the second half of 1776, Continentals could purchase, all told, approximately $11.5 million of specie. That sum had dropped to $6.7 million by the first half of 1778 before increasing to $8.5 million in the second half of that year. But by the second half of 1780, Continentals could draw forth a mere $1.5 million of specie and soon thereafter could command none at all.[24]

The purchasing system employed by the rebel armies exacerbated the government's fiscal plight. Paid on a percentage commission basis, quartermasters had incentives to drive prices up. Opportunities for fraud abounded, temptations that many apparently found too strong to resist. Purchasing departments became, in the words of John Laurens, "somewhat more than deranged. They are shattered and distracted." Numerous important merchants and government officials accused of wrongdoing faced congressional investigations and public censure but ultimately few were condemned in an era when personal and public accounts mixed as promiscuously as sailors and prostitutes in a seaport brothel.[25]

On January 2, 1779, Congress initiated reforms that it hoped would stem the tide of depreciation. First, it called upon the states to pay $15 million into the Continental treasury in 1779 and $6 million per year for the next 18 years thereafter. It also ordered from circulation the emissions of May 20, 1777, and April 11, 1778, which totaled $41.5 million, because they had been heavily counterfeited by the British. Neither prong of its attack worked—the states did not come close to meeting their requisitions, paying in only a shade more than $3 million, and most of the bills of 1777 and 1778 remained in circulation. The government had egg on its face once again. Theodorick Bland of Virginia tried to make some sense of the situation but ran into insurmountable obstacles at every turn. He realized that a sudden appreciation of the currency, even if it could be effected, "would undoubtedly be attended with every evil which the depreciation brought," though this time the pain would be felt by debtors instead of creditors. Various schemes and reforms set forth by private parties were all found wanting. As a stopgap measure, Congress on August 26, 1779, allowed commanders to feed troops "an over proportion of a plentifull [sic] article in lieu and in full Satisfaction of such as are scarce or not to be had."[26]

Desperate, Congress on September 1, 1779, announced that the printing presses would cease when the nominal value of Continentals hit $200 million. As we have seen, it may have slid well past that mark but nevertheless crisis ensued because most people believed, correctly as it turned out, that Congress would stop the presses before it found other adequate sources of income. They assumed, again correctly, that enforcement of legal tender laws, statutes that forced creditors to accept bills of credit in payment, would be stepped up. All private credit accordingly vanished, denuding the economy of an important lubricant. Combined with losses in the field in the South and Benedict Arnold's treachery, which apparently was an act of exasperation and desperation, the Revolutionary cause hit its nadir.[27]

In March 1780, Congress attempted to reform the currency again, valuing old Continentals at 40 to 1 with Spanish-milled silver dollars and emitting a new tenor of bills that were supposed to retain their value because they were pledged on the faith of both the national and state governments, bore 5 percent interest, were repayable in specie in 6 years, and were limited in supply. Recalcitrant and beleaguered states, currency bears, and skeptical market participants again doomed the reforms. According to Arnold: "Congress have lost all Confidence and Credit with the People, who have been too often deceived and duped by them to pay any regard to their promises in future, the different Provinces have very little more Credit with the People than Congress." The damnable traitor was right. As David Cobb wrote from Boston, quartermasters, commissaries, and recruitment officers were forced to "borrow money ... tho' that is damn'd hard." No money meant no bounties for recruits, who knew they were not likely to be well fed or clothed once they joined up. As a result, Cobb noted, "the recruiting business is totally at an end." The only volunteers were "damn'd Rascalls" who often soon went AWOL.[28]

By the end of 1780, old Continentals passed at $75 to $100 for $1 specie and new tenor bills, of which there were few, sank to 3 for 1. In April 1781, old tenor bills were officially rated at 140 to 1 and in May vanished into infamy after Congress and the states finally repealed their legal tender laws. New tenor and state bills met similarly melancholy fates. The death of fiat paper money was, however, a great relief to many because it forced gold and silver out of hiding and into general circulation.[29]

Precious little of the precious stuff found its way into the coffers of state, however, so the death of paper money meant the government had to endure yet another fiscal crisis and at an important point in the war at that. James Madison admitted that the situation was "more truly critical" than any the rebel cause had yet faced. The patriots managed to muddle through to the end of the war, though, thanks to a potent combination of grit, luck, foreign aid, and financial innovation. Eighteenth-century armies could live directly off the land to some extent. They needed gunpowder, metal, and a few other manufactured goods to allow them to fight, but they could be to some extent clothed, sheltered, and fed from the countryside, especially if they were on the move in enemy territory. The rebels proved this to some

At Bucktooth, near present-day Salamanca, for example, American forces found 500 acres of corn and vegetables, upon which they gorged themselves for three days.

extent during their rampages through New York's Indian country in 1777 and 1778, when they feasted on the fat fields of vanquished Iroquois tribes. At Bucktooth, near present-day Salamanca, for example, American forces found 500 acres of corn and vegetables, upon which they gorged themselves for three days. The war on the frontier was essentially one of economic attrition, so they burned the rest, along with some 130 nearby homes, but not before removing sundry objects of booty that later sold for $3,000. (In addition to deerskins, Indians often owned other valuable assets, including gold and silver coins, a little appreciated fact.)[30]

Subsisting on home turf or when wintering (and hence stationary) was a more difficult proposition because outright pillaging was out of the question politically and the surrounding farmland could not support the artificially inflated population level for long. That the army had little in the way of cash did not help to summon forth what the surrounding countryside did have to offer either, a fact learned the hard way at Valley Forge, Morristown, and Petersburg, where the threat of imminent British invasion made prodigious hoards of food and supplies appear, much to the surprise and chagrin of army quartermasters.[31]

As a final resort, rebel governments in the winter of 1778–79 began for the first time in the war to impress large amounts of goods from Americans in exchange for IOUs promising future payment, with interest, in cash. Again in December 1779, the severe monetary and fiscal disorders made it necessary for the northern army to impress goods to keep itself alive. In South Carolina, too, the army resorted to this expedient after the British invasion made any other mode of taxation impossible. Clearly, the army had might on its side. But it also had a good dose of right. Military personnel also received IOUs instead of cash pay, so while there were still grounds for complaint it was clear the army was not enriching itself at the expense of the public. Moreover, impressment, confiscation, or expropriation was simply a form of taxation. Since the government was unwilling and/or unable to raise taxes in the traditional way, the military had to innovate to collect what it needed. In addition, the top brass endeavored to minimize the practice as they realized that too much forced impressment would sour the tempers and alienate the affections of the populace. As Benedict Arnold put it, "this force acts against Itself by Creating internal Enemies." Although obnoxious and inefficient, impressment actually worked to some extent in places like South Carolina, where rebel counterattacks funded by expropriations of food, horses, clothes, weapons, and even indigo drove the British from rural districts to a Green Zone–like enclave around Charleston.[32]

In November 1780, quartermaster Nathaniel Irish lamented that "the Difficulty in procuring Materials, Money to pay for them, and pay the Men with" caused "delays & disappointments" prosecuting the war. Congress responded to such complaints by asking the states to pay their requisitions in "such supplies as may from time to time be wanted for carrying on the war," specifically beef, rum, salt, hay, flour, Indian corn, tobacco, and rice. Like impressment, the system of in-kind taxes or specific requisitions was grossly inefficient. As Quartermaster General Timothy Pickering complained, payments were often received far from where they were needed. Because he had no cash to pay for transport, he had to inform Congress of "the impossibility of forwarding Provisions without selling part of them to raise Money for the purpose." He feared that such a system would be "liable to abuses," like below-market sales to cronies. Nevertheless, in-kind payments eventually got some provisions from the field into soldiers' bellies. Also in 1780, the states took up the task of compensating their respective soldiers and officers for back pay and for depreciation of the government's money. Most did so by issuing IOUs called depreciation certificates, which would later form a major category of state debts assumed by the federal government. When it came to provisioning the Continental army, however, the states, which had never given Congress much more than nearly worthless bills of credit, again disappointed and so much so that by June 1781 Colonel J. Scammel "shudder[ed] at the prospect of the ensuing campaign, not from fear of the enemy, but from apprehensions of starvation." About the same time, Colonel Charles Dabney in Virginia complained that his troops were "almost naked" and without arms. According to John Mathews, "a want of money totally unhinges every thing." Madison argued that the dearth of good money

Colonel Charles Dabney in Virginia complained that his troops were "almost naked" and without arms. According to John Mathews, "a want of money totally unhinges every thing." Madison argued that the dearth of good money was all that kept the cause in doubt.

was all that kept the cause in doubt. Just a few million guineas, he claimed, "would expel the enemy from every part of the United States." He was right. The requisite monies came from abroad and from hoards at home. But first, major reforms were needed.[33]

The administrative structure of the Continental treasury changed during the war's early years, growing both larger and more complex but not more efficient, especially when it came to settling the many small claims of the government's creditors. Reforms made in September 1778 created three major executive offices, those of comptroller, auditor, and treasurer, which were filled by Jonathan Trumbull Jr., John Gibson, and Michael Hillegas, respectively. A slew of commissioners and staffers were also appointed but many of the former did not accept and Trumbull soon quit. Such problems suggest that the treasury was not corrupt and paid salaries that were too low to attract and retain enough efficient workers. "The Machine is so clogged," Gibson complained, "as to defeat in a great Measure the Intention of having the public Accounts speedily settled."[34]

In 1779, Congress tried again, creating a new Board of Treasury composed of two congressmen and three members from outside that body. It also eliminated the office of comptroller and provided the auditor general with an assistant or vice auditor. None of the shuffling did anything to make the treasury more efficient, to fill its coffers, or to reduce the supply of bills of credit in circulation, so the reforms were akin to slapping a Band-Aid on the hemorrhaging stump of a limb amputee. They did, however, bring some permanence to the Board of Treasury, which remained an important policy advisor to Congress as well as the head of the treasury department. The state of the treasury in 1779 and 1780—not literally empty but with claims exceeding cash on hand by a wide margin—nevertheless ensured utter public contempt for the new arrangement.[35]

A bitter, largely petty, and personal dispute between Francis Hopkinson, the treasurer of loans, and the Board of Treasury also injured public confidence in the treasury. Born in Philadelphia in 1737, Hopkinson took his baccalaureate from the College of Philadelphia (University of Pennsylvania) in 1757 and his master's degree in 1760. The following year, he was admitted to the bar but did not excel as a lawyer, perhaps because his head "was not bigger than a large apple." "I have not met with anything in natural history more amusing and entertaining than his personal appearance," future president John Adams wrote his wife. "Yet," he was quick to add, "he is genteel and well-bred, and is very social." Hopkinson and his small head bounced around between New Jersey, England, Delaware, and Philadelphia until the Revolution broke out. He signed the Declaration of Independence for New Jersey and served the rebel cause in a variety of roles. A creative soul, he invented several minor items and was also the author of pamphlets, poems, and songs and would have left posterity with more cultural treasures had he not died of a sudden epileptic seizure in May 1791. While treasurer of loans, Hopkinson, without contract or authorization, designed a number of items for the use of the United States, including a national flag, seals, bills of exchange, and bills of credit. He invoiced Congress for his endeavors, first asking for a quarter cask of wine, then $7,200 in bills of credit, and finally a sum of specie. After a long delay, Congress refused to pay for his "fancy work," arguing that many people were engaged in the design process and that "little assistances" could be expected from "Gentlemen who enjoy a very considerable Salary under Congress" without further recompense. Meanwhile, Hopkinson and the Board of Treasury squabbled, the former accusing the latter of general neglect and incompetence. An investigative committee concurred, arguing that the board members behaved in a way that was "very reprehensible, [and] extremely disgusting." A second committee also concluded that the "Demon of Discord pervaded the whole Department," rendering it inefficient. Congress dismissed both reports but found in the government's continued financial crisis cause for yet another reorganization, one that more or less worked.[36]

Robert Morris and Thomas Willing were among the two most highly respected financiers in all of British North America. The latter was the London-educated son of a wealthy Philadelphia merchant who perished young, leaving his eldest son in charge of a small mercantile empire and a huge gaggle of young siblings. Under such stress, Thomas matured quickly, perhaps too quickly, soon coming to be known as "Old Square Toes" for his conservative ways. But that reputation for caution and probity served him well as the nation's first banker. So did his association with Morris. First an apprentice in Willing's firm, Morris soon became a full partner thanks to

> First an apprentice in Willing's firm, Morris soon became a full partner thanks to his uncanny and well-known knack for buying low and selling high.

his uncanny and well-known knack for buying low and selling high. In the colonial period, the pair became heavily involved in marine insurance and even tried to establish a commercial bank, but British regulators and a wary public stamped it out. Independence and the nation's financial crisis removed both barriers. That crisis and the seemingly endless warfare also helped to put those who supported a weak national government on the defensive. In 1780, they gave way in Congress to a group of conservative nationalists hell-bent on furthering the "publick good" and compelling "party spirit" and petty personal grievances like the Hopkinson affair to "hide its head," even if it was only apple sized.[37]

Perhaps the most important step taken by the ascendant nationalist forces was the unanimous appointment of Morris as "Superintendent of Finance," the powerful policy head of a streamlined treasury department, in February 1781. Morris conditionally accepted the appointment in mid-March after much soul-searching. He wanted to help his country but at the same time knew that he was being asked to risk his considerable wealth and reputation, so he pushed Congress to acknowledge on the record that he was extensively engaged on his private account. He also asked for the power to terminate the employment of personnel in the Treasury Office and agents who handled government monies if he found their services unnecessary or their conduct untoward. Congress consented to his conditions in April, in May Morris signed on, and finally, in late June, officially assumed office. He had already jumped into the policy hot pot with both feet, however. Even before taking office, he induced Congress to charter a commercial bank with national reach, the nation's first. The bank plan met slight resistance in Congress from several delegates, including James Madison, who felt the national government did not have the power to create corporations. Expediency won the day, though, as did the fact that several states, the most important of which was Pennsylvania, also chartered the Philadelphia-based bank. Then, soon after taking office, he initiated a new system for supplying army units via contracts awarded to the lowest bidder.[38]

Those were important victories in the war on penury. The new provisioning contract system, as well as other administrative reforms, helped to keep a lid on government expenditures. Morris's bank, styled the Bank of North America, began operations in January 1782, soon after its subscription books filled, with the aid of $254,000 in French specie subscribed on behalf of the national government. Led by Willing, the new bank filled several crucially needed functions. First, it provided the government with short-term but large emergency loans, some $1.25 million worth all told. Second, it supplied the economy, especially the commercial centers in the mid-Atlantic region, with money in the form of checkable deposits and bank notes. Although composed of paper, those monetary liabilities were convertible into specie upon demand at the bank. Bank notes lost some value as they moved further from the bank's office in Philadelphia because it took time and resources to return them there if one wanted specie instead of notes. And, checks drawn on the bank were subject to credit risk (the maker of the check might not have sufficient funds, to wit, the check might bounce), but neither depreciated across the board as bills of credit did. Most people immediately perceived the stark improvement of convertible bank liabilities backed by specie and loans over bills of credit and so embraced them quickly. Third, the bank helped to stimulate desperately needed economic growth by efficiently matching savings to positive net present value business projects.[39]

Morris's tenure also witnessed another triumph, the financing of the critical Yorktown operation during the latter stages of the 1781 campaign. Those were critical months financially as well as militarily because the Bank of North America had not yet formed and bills of credit were discredited. As noted above, specie appeared—the British and French forces imported and spent many millions of it in North America and it now had a reason to stay in circulation on the rebel side of the line. Little solid coin found its way to the Continental treasury, however. So, Morris placed his own money and credit into the breach by issuing his own notes, payable by him personally, and on sight to boot. (Many army officers like Edward Carrington also raised supplies on their personal credit.) Morris also made explicit promises to important suppliers, like Philip Schuyler of Albany, to whom he pledged himself to repay "with hard money wholly if required" for 1,000 barrels of urgently needed flour. "For your reimbursement," Morris added, "you may either take me as a public or a private man." Morris's notes drew forth the carts, horses, forage, and other materials needed to move the northern army into position to trap Cornwallis. An emergency loan of $20,000 in hard money from French general Jean Baptiste Comte de Rochambeau also greatly aided the cause though it fell short of the total need. Apparently interest-free loans of publicly and privately owned horses, oxen, yokes, chains, saddles, wagons, carts, and even field pieces, to be paid for only if destroyed, made up the difference. With that aid, Washington decamped from his base in New York on August 21, arrived in Yorktown on September 28, and laid siege to the trapped British forces until their formal surrender on October 19.[40]

Yorktown spelled the end of major land campaigns but was by no means the end of America's financial problems. Although the army shrank from about 29,000 soldiers in 1781 to 18,000 in 1782 to 13,000 in 1783, it had to be kept in fighting order lest the British be tempted to sally forth again. Warfare on the sea continued unabated, and the Americans were losing badly. The British blockade squeezed out much trade and made what did sneak through very expensive. Ports like Charleston were relatively open the first years of the war but the British became adept at intercepting reshipments by coastal packets, and overland carriage was extremely expensive. Smaller ships were faster and more likely to escape British patrols but they also had higher fixed costs. Without extensive foreign trade, crucial materials remained in short supply, coins remained scarce, interest rates high, and tariff receipts pitiful. Congress's inability to pass a national tariff or impost was thus mitigated by the cruel fact that Britain's blockade of American trade was so tight that little was making its way in or out of the country anyway. More fancy financial footwork by Morris and foreign loans filled the gap.[41]

> Yorktown spelled the end of major land campaigns but was by no means the end of America's financial problems.

Congress had managed to borrow relatively little abroad in the early years of the war. Most subsidies arrived in the form of war materials, not money. Cash receipts picked up in 1780, however, and loomed large in 1781 through 1784. (They would become important again in the early 1790s too, a topic to which we shall return.) Some of those funds were lent by allies, especially France, but much of the money after 1781 came from private investors, mostly Dutch. America's introduction to Amsterdam's capital market came in 1778 but its bond issue sank rather than floated, attracting only $32,000 in subscriptions. In 1781, though, France successfully floated a loan there earmarked for the American cause. In 1782, the United States, with the help of a syndicate of investment banks, made its first successful independent issue. Subscriptions were slow although the interest offered was high by Dutch standards and the commission to the investment banks was quite sizable. Dutch investors were right to hesitate as the American government planned to service its debt the way profligate college students do, by borrowing yet more money. Ultimately, though, America, home of the free, the brave, and an enormous natural resource endowment, looked like a better investment than Britain.[42]

Adam Smith and other astute students of the British economy, like John Earl, had surmised at the outset that a prolonged war with America could exhaust the mother country financially. (That is not to say that such a war would impoverish the British and indeed it didn't. A Russian visitor to Britain in 1780 observed that "everything presented an aspect of ... plenty" and that "no one object from Dover to London reminded me of poverty.") Said Earl: "This unnatural Civil War with America" was "a War of enormous and unknown Expence." The House of Commons rightly worried that its constituents already labored "under burthens almost too heavy to be borne ... . The great expenses of the war, the shameful abuses by which they were augmented, the rapid increase of the debt, and the terms on which" loans were made, especially late in the war, conspired to ensure the Revolution's success. "The Americans would not have dared to rebel," Robert Bird proclaimed, "unless they had known that this Nation was overloaded with Debt and Taxes." Bird was only half right—during the struggle, the British national debt nearly doubled before the pressure became too intense to endure. A soft economy in some sectors, high taxes, a ballooning debt, and higher yields (lower prices) for bonds spelled big trouble for British politicians. The jig was up when Dutch investors, long a great prop to the British capital markets, slowed their purchases of British bonds, making a "pretty general refusal ... to subscribe" to British loans, and began to buy American ones. Dutch complicity in the American victory was no coincidence. The Dutch saw in America themselves, republicans struggling mightily against a massive, distant imperial overlord.[43]

After Yorktown, Morris oversaw the importation of specie on public and private account from Havana, which hungered for American flour and was relatively easy to reach using quick and elusive ships designed to evade blockading British men-of-war. He also continued to support public credit with his own by issuing 60-day notes, or "Long Bobs" (in contrast to Short Bobs, which were payable at sight or a short time after being presented for payment). Unlike the Yorktown notes, which were completely personal obligations, later Morris notes were, technically, public obligations, but because they bore Morris's signature and his personal pledge to redeem them their value was greater. Treasurer Michael Hillegas, Paymaster General John Pierce, and other treasury officials also issued notes under Morris's authority. Some of the notes, like the subsistence notes issued by Hillegas to army officers, were of small enough denominations that they circulated in New Jersey and perhaps elsewhere hand to hand like money. Others, for larger sums in irregular amounts, changed hands only by endorsement between merchants, like bills of exchange. Like the bank's liabilities, the notes issued by treasury officials generally held their value well and certainly did not lose value daily as bills of credit had, partly because Morris enjoined his subordinates not to part with them "on any other Terms than as of the full value of Gold or Silver dollar for dollar." As "zeroes," or discount bonds, they actually appreciated as they approached their redemption date and place. To generate cash flow to meet his notes when due, Morris also engaged in sundry commercial operations and speculations on public account. He juggled all those trades, obligations, bills of exchange drawn on the expectation of foreign loans, and his other meager resources so adroitly that one late-nineteenth-century historian claimed that Morris possessed the "art or abuse of dazzling the public eye by the same piece of coin multiplied by a thousand reflections."[44]

The notes and smoke and mirrors were of course only temporary expedients. If too many notes were issued, or they were not paid in specie when promised, they would sink in value just as bills of credit had. Morris therefore pushed to collect taxes, including a Continental impost, and requisitioned specie (or its equivalent, including bank notes and Morris notes), not commodities, from the states. His notes could also be tendered, at par, for the purchase of government assets, including bills of exchange drawn on foreign loans, but also public buildings, army horses, and the like. In October 1783, for instance, the Quartermaster General Department offered for sale some of its buildings in Newburgh, New York for "cash, bank notes, Mr. Morris's notes, subsistence notes, or debts contracted in the quarter Master Generals department since the first of January 1782." The only way to redeem most of the notes, however, was taxation, which remained difficult, in the words of Morris's assistant Gouverneur Morris (no relation), "in a country like this, where the people are their own rulers." Nevertheless, the Financier, as Robert Morris came to be known, managed to cajole, coerce, and otherwise extract more cash from state coffers than any of his predecessors had.[45]

By 1782, Americans were weary of war, both psychologically and economically. To be sure, the war had stimulated the economy in some places in big ways and in all places in at least small ways. Nonetheless, since 1775 the war had drained between 15 and 20 percent of the nation's economic output, a strain far less than Americans would bear in World War II but on a par with the burdens endured during the Civil War and World War I. By December 1782, the situation had grown tense. Soldiers and their officers had not been paid in months and other public creditors began to wonder if they would ever be repaid. "The patience of the army has been equal to their bravery," Madison noted, "but that patience must have its limits." The same could also be said of others holding government IOUs.[46]

In January 1783, Morris resorted to kiting by paying off some of the soldiers' back pay with the proceeds of sales of bad bills of exchange drawn on exhausted foreign loans, a desperate tactic that induced one late-nineteenth-century historian to accuse Morris of having engaged in "the most vulgar kind of bill-kiting." (To "kite" was commercial slang for obtaining temporary credit by knowingly issuing an IOU against insufficient funds.) Morris realized he was treading on thin ice by thus risking his reputation, so he threatened to resign at the end of May if no progress was made on the tax front. He refused, he said, to serve as the "minister of injustice." Madison and others in Congress supported Morris. "Justice, gratitude, our reputation abroad, and our tranquility at home," Madison wrote, "require provision for a debt of not less than fifty millions." But several states, including Madison's own Virginia, again refused to give the national government the power to tax though they had given it the power to borrow. The threat that the U.S. government would become as corrupt and moneygrubbing as the British was just too palpable.[47]

But other grave and imminent threats also threatened the young nation's existence. By February 1783, the army encamped near Newburgh was on the brink of mutiny. Independence had been won—news of a preliminary peace agreement reached Congress on February 13, and by March 24 it was known that the war was effectively over. Nothing prevented outbreak of a new war, however, so all could be lost if the army rebelled or if the British smelled sufficient weakness. Moreover, some nationalists, including Morris and Alexander Hamilton, hoped to bring matters to a head, forming nebulous plans with some leading generals to put pressure on the government to make financial reforms or suffer vague but ominous consequences. Their plans spiraled out of control, though, when generals eager to take George Washington's place atop the military hierarchy joined the so-called conspiracy. Thankfully, at a crucial hour Washington staved off rebellion by giving a speech that brought tears to the eyes of battle-hardened men. "Gentlemen," he said, pulling reading glasses from his coat, "you will permit me to put on my spectacles, for I have not only grown gray but almost blind in the service of my country." The Newburgh conspiracy collapsed.[48]

Morris made certain Washington would not have to give an encore performance by paying off the army with $11 million worth of his notes. It dutifully disbanded in April 1783 without fomenting rebellion, though a few rabble-rousers caused a fuss in Philadelphia. The exertion strained Morris to the max according to Quartermaster General Timothy Pickering. As he told an assistant in May, Morris was "so embarrassed by the measures for giving pay to the army, that as far as possible he desires all other payments to be postponed." Unsurprisingly, financial and economic matters continued to deteriorate and little aid was forthcoming. Disgusted, Morris left office in November 1784, again leaving control of the national government's purse, holey bag that it was, to a bored board of incompetents. Another Dutch loan allowed him to honor his debts and leave a small sum in the treasury before he left. But the national and state governments were far from solvent. The best that could be done was to redeem some debt certificates via taxes and land sales and pay the interest on the rest by issuing yet more IOUs called indents. Domestic creditors received some payments from the states but all in all America was bankrupt. In August 1785, the Board of Treasury that replaced Morris in office wailed that "the present State of the Treasury requires immediate and vigorous aid from all the States." In 1786, Congress could not sell *any* of the $500,000 worth of domestic bonds it needed to bolster the federal army in the aftermath of Shays' Rebellion, and the state governments could have borrowed in Europe only on terms so ruinous no republican government would countenance them in peacetime. Congress found it difficult to muster a quorum much less a decent revenue. Morbid fear of tyrannical leaders had produced impotent government.[49]

※

Nobody knows, or can know, what the world would look like today had the U.S. federal Constitution failed to be ratified. Nevertheless, a scenario in which the world would be better off is difficult to imagine. Whether one considers recent U.S. policy as too imperial or not imperial enough, as stately or disgraceful, as indicative of an omnipotent hegemon or an impotent hedgehog, it is impossible to deny the positive economic, military, and political roles America played in the twentieth century, especially in World War II and its immediate aftermath. The U.S. government under the Articles of Confederation could not have fought off the Germans and the Japanese simultaneously. In fact, it is doubtful that Americans would have stretched across the continent had the Articles, which described itself as nothing more than "a firm league of friendship" among the states, remained in force. The area from Texas to California would still be part of Mexico, Canada would extend much further south, and Napoleon would never have exchanged the vast midsection of the continent for U.S. government bonds. The reason for all this is simple—the Articles created a loose military alliance rather than a unified country because it did not give the national government the "power of the purse." As one contemporary put it, "the authority to lay and collect taxes is the most important of any power that can be granted" and the national government simply did not have it.[50]

A wartime expedient, the Articles of Confederation did not inspire confidence among merchants, manufacturers, or urban artisans. Under this document, the national government could not directly tax, and therefore could not do much of anything. Two attempts to give it the power to collect revenues by taxing imports, the so-called impost, failed due to the intransigence of a single state, Rhode Island in 1781 and New York in 1783. Requisitions from the states trickled in, always well short of the need. Out of the $13.7 million Congress requested between October 1781 and August 1786, the states turned over about $5 million, only about $3.2 million of which was paid in gold or silver (specie) coin, the only type of money that Congress could use internationally and in all the different states. (Bills of credit circulated over political boundaries, but usually only in adjacent states or states engaged in significant commercial intercourse with each other.) That dismal record is explained by two simple realities: one, state governments *did not want to pay*, and two, they *could not pay*, owing to economic weakness and a dearth of political fortitude.[51]

The states maintained militia forces of unequal, and usually low, quality. If the United States were to be attacked, neither the national nor the state governments would be able to resist effectively, nor would they be able to borrow to fend off their foes. As Edmund Pendleton wrote in 1787: "Every man must be convinced of [the government's] imbecility on the subject of finan[ces]." Another Edmund, this one Randolph, was even more pessimistic: "the nerves of government seem unstrung, both in energy and moneys." The "associated republics" suffered from "increasing languor" due to the "stagnation in the receipt of Taxes at present throughout every State in the Union."[52]

State tax *rates* were generally higher than they were before independence but collections were lower because specie was in extremely short supply. Much of the coin the country had attracted after the death of bills of credit left again after the war to pay for imports of manufactured goods, "foreign fripperies" as one critic called them. Several new banks began operations but the Bank of North America had to pull in its horns—and its notes—when an

State tax *rates* were generally higher than they were before independence but collections were lower because specie was in extremely short supply.

aggressive state legislature revoked its Pennsylvania charter. It stayed in business until its charter was restored but in the interim had to play it safe. Little money meant high interest rates, which in turned spelled economic stagnation and, eventually, political unrest. Interest rates spiraled upward, as high as 40 or 50 percent according to Massachusetts yeoman-cum-political-economist William Manning, making it impossible to borrow, and the prices of land, labor, and produce plummeted. Depressed levels of exports meant that gold and silver were difficult to attract, even though prices were dirt cheap.[53]

The monetary situation was truly dire but little could be done. "Paper money died," wrote Manning using a metaphor common in the period. (People also likened inflationary periods to a game called Robin's Alive, an early version of "hot potato" in which children passed a lighted stick from hand to hand, punishing the poor sap holding it when the fire went out.) After the close of the war, seven states issued bills of credit in relatively small amounts, eagerly seeking a pulse. The bills all depreciated in various degrees; their failure demonstrated the futility of relying on colonial traditions. Rather than provide relief, the bills dried up private credit and made what little specie there was flee into overseas trade or local hoards. "I will not say," Maryland observer Alexander Hanson noted in 1787, "that no man possesses a faith in bills of credit; but I remark, that a very great part of the people do not." There were simply too many people like William Gamble of Bordentown, New Jersey, around. "During our revolutionary struggle of Independence," a contemporary explained, "this Gentleman was a Majr. in the State of Jersey militia." Gamble allowed his mansion to serve as "an asylum for the sick & weary soldiers of his country." Due to his hospitality, the "depredations of the Enemy & the ruinous depreciation of our paper currency, he & his amiable family became greatly straitned [sic] in his circumstances" and remained so for decades.[54]

Especially in more rural areas, the dearth of cash rendered tax collection economically difficult and politically costly. When people did not pay their tax bills, even when the ultimate cause was an absolute scarcity of money, collectors seized the delinquent's real

> When people did not pay their tax bills, even when the ultimate cause was an absolute scarcity of money, collectors seized the delinquent's real and personal property and sold it at auction to satisfy the tax.

and personal property and sold it at auction to satisfy the tax. Pressed to the limit and facing loss of their property, taxpayers rebelled, some by taking over state legislatures and voting relief, some by refusing to purchase tax-distressed property at auction, some by intimidating tax collectors, and more than a few by taking up the sword. "The dog of war was let loose upon them," Manning later reflected, and "this shook the government to its foundation." In every instance, state governments backed down.[55]

The net effect of the fiscal crisis, the monetary derangement, and the political upheavals they caused was a profound economic stagnation that stretched from the far north to the deep south and, perhaps worse, a profound sense of malaise among many who felt the Revolution was being undone. Like most places in America, New Hampshire wallowed in economic depression throughout the 1780s, and that despite the war having left the state's physical infrastructure relatively unscathed. "Trade in A great measure is cut off," wrote Portsmouth merchant Thomas Sheafe in September 1785. Decline in international trade hurt not only New Hampshire's merchants but also her shipbuilders, fishermen, lumber concerns, and, most important, her farmers. Demand for country goods dropped as domestic manufacturing and extractive economic activity, like mining and logging, decreased and foreign trade, long interrupted by the war, failed to regain its colonial footing. The death of paper money and the dearth of exports meant that there literally was not enough money, paper or coin, or credit, money's close cousin, to uphold the price level or consummate any cash transactions. Apparently, what little money there was served mainly to settle the occasional long-overdue account.[56]

Little money meant high interest rates which, in turn, spelled lower property values and higher debt burdens. Farmers stung by uncommonly bad weather struggled, many in vain, to scrape together enough cash to pay their taxes and private debts. Lawsuits during the decade numbered over 29,000, an amazingly high number given the state's population (142,108, all told, in 1790) and that this figure reflects just the surviving records. By one estimate, over the decade some 40 percent of the total population found itself sued in civil court at least once.[57]

The state government could not make payments for much of 1781 and 1782 and emerged from the war deeply in debt. The main problem was that it found it impossible to collect the taxes owed it. For example, by

January 1787 not a single New Hampshire town had paid a state tax passed in February 1786 (payable in May). On a later tax, only 67 out of 190 towns made even a partial payment. Delinquency rates by county ranged from 60 to over 93 percent! The *New Hampshire Gazette* groaned under the load of notices of farms being auctioned to pay back taxes even though many towns allowed local taxes to be paid in kind, with goods or labor. Receipts were so anemic that the state government struggled to provide even basic public goods, like a lighthouse and small garrison for Portsmouth.[58]

The result of all those shocks was an economy hamstrung. "Americans!" exclaimed the *New Hampshire Gazette*, "our vessels rotting by the wharves! our seamen starving! tradesmen out of employ! money there is none! and business of all sorts stagnated!" Many clamored for an emission of paper money, but the lessons learned during the Revolution were still so vivid that many others doubted its efficacy. "A new Emission of Paper Money," many predicted, would "either greatly depreciate or like Sampson at his Death pull down the Pillars of our Paper Fabrick and bury itself in the Ruins of the whole." In the end, the state passed some debtor relief legislation but did not emit bills. Its economy languished until after the passage of the Constitution and Alexander Hamilton's financial reform package.[59]

At the other end of the new country, the economies of Georgia and South Carolina also wallowed in the Revolution's aftermath. During their occupation of the Deep South, the British had freed slaves, killed off livestock, and otherwise devastated farms, plantations, roads, and bridges. After peace finally came, the British government did everything it could to impede the region's trade with the West Indies and even developed an alternative source of supply for indigo, an export important to South Carolina's economy. Trade restrictions were moot in some years, however, because poor weather meant short crops. Little wonder, then, that economic conditions in South Carolina deteriorated as they did in New Hampshire. High interest rates, low real estate and other asset prices, numerous lawsuits, and high rates of tax delinquency led to rioting in 1783, 1784, and 1785. According to Aedanus Burke, an Irish émigré to colonial South Carolina, patriot soldier, and judge, "trade and commerce" had come to "an end" in the South Carolina backcountry. Thieves stole the horses drawing wagons to market, rendering it difficult to earn money to pay taxes, not that there was much money to be had anyway.[60]

The state government could not service its debts in specie, so it issued IOUs to "pay" the interest on its IOUs. The IOUs were negotiable but were not bearer instruments and they traded well below par, so they were not an effective medium of exchange. A paper money emission in 1785 brought some relief to the people of the Deep South, but it was not enough. The government feared that if it issued too many bills, even though they were lent on good security and were to be recalled in just five years, inflation would ensue.[61]

Between those two geographical extremes the economy was good and bad, but mostly the latter. Some think the economy was pulling out of recession by 1786–87. Others think not. Writing in 1786, Rawleigh Colston complained to George Washington of the "great scarcity of money" in northern Virginia. About the same time, a "Farmer" in Maryland beseeched his friends to "consider well the ruinous State of your once flourishing country." He likely referred to the "tumultuary [sic] assemblage" that forced a nearby country court to "adjourn all *civil* causes" because the people thought it unfair to lose their farms, the value of which had plummeted to "a tenth part" of their real value due to low money supplies and high interest rates (italics in original). About the same time, "A Citizen of New York" lamented that "our prisons [were] crowded with debtors," that "the estates of many [were] selling by execution under their feet, to satisfy very trifling debts," and "the cries of all ranks of people among us for money."[62]

Daniel Shays and other tax rebels, including large numbers of rural Pennsylvanians, were also in the latter camp, arguing that the weak economy and dearth of money made it impossible to pay their taxes. When pressed for payment at the risk of their farms and freedom, their backs were to the wall and they had to rebel. Their desperate actions spurred the nationalists to strengthen the nation's government once and for all. Despite the obvious deficiencies of the Articles of Confederation, however, it almost carried the day. Such was the ignorance of many early Americans, and such was their fear.[63]

4

GESTATION

The Constitution and the National Debt

The Constitution crackled as it burned, 50 of its avowed enemies looking on with gleeful eyes, the sweet stench of freshly fired muskets filling their nostrils. People love to burn that which they hate. Flames regularly consume effigies, flags, draft cards, braziers, and despised decrees. As a corollary, people hate to see that which they love go up in flames. Americans alive in the tumultuous 1780s were no exception. So there would be hell to pay for those who dared to set a copy of America's proposed frame of government aflame.

Independence Day in 1788 fell on a Friday and under normal circumstances would have been a festive affair. On this Fourth of July, however, the atmosphere in Albany, New York, thickened with tension. For the first time since their revolution against Mother England and her wayward son King George III had effectively ended at the Battle of Yorktown in the early autumn of 1781, Americans were deeply divided. On one side stood the federalists, supporters of the new U.S. Constitution signed in Philadelphia in September 1787. On the other, stood the antifederalists, a large group opposed to the formation of a new government based on the Constitution. Each state held a convention, a sort of legislative session with specially elected representatives, to decide whether it would ratify the document and join the proposed union or not.

This fine Fourth, the antifederalist cause teetered on the brink of extinction. On June 21, 1788, New Hampshire became the ninth state to ratify the Constitution; nine was the minimum number required by the Constitution to launch the new national government. But two large and powerful states,

Virginia and New York, remained undecided and if they demurred the whole project could still fall apart, the antifederalists reassured themselves. On June 25, though, Virginia's convention also decided to ratify. The Old Dominion's decision was galloped north by horse, arriving in Poughkeepsie on July 2 and in Albany the following day. News of Virginia's ratification of the Constitution rankled New York's antifederalists, who now had to admit that formation of a new government was inevitable. New York's federalists were of course ecstatic to learn of Virginia's decision, because it put their antifederalist foes in a difficult position. Now if New York did not ratify, it would be surrounded by a powerful new country to the east and south, a colony of its enemy Great Britain to the north, and unknown numbers of testy Native Americans to the west. Federalists throughout the state wished to press home their advantage by using the impending holiday, already the holiest of profane days, to celebrate their victory and advertise their cause.

Accordingly, federalists in Albany proposed to hold a "procession," a sort of quasi-military parade. Albany antifederalists in effect told the federalists that they did not wish to have their noses rubbed in their defeat. As was customary, all the bells in the city had been rung until sunset the day the news arrived and that, they hinted, was quite enough. The federalists graciously gave up the idea of parading through Albany's streets but still celebrated the Fourth in high style, replete with speeches, huzzahs, music, flags, cannonades, alcohol-laden beverages, and all with the obligatory pomp and circumstance. About 50 antifederalists countered by marching through the city (an ancient one by New World standards and, with about 550 houses and 3,000 inhabitants, America's sixth largest). Upon reaching their destination, a vacant lot on the city's outskirts, they fired 13 muskets in honor of the 13 colonies that had rebelled against Britain. No harm in that. Shorn of most of its loyalists, America would show little affection for its former mother country until the late nineteenth century. But then, to the astonishment of onlookers, the antis pasted a copy of the Constitution and the notification of Virginia's ratification to a liberty post, a symbol of struggle against oppression since the late colonial period, and torched the entire ensemble.[1]

Outraged, the federalists decided to stage a procession after all. They marched peacefully along Albany's broadest and most populous thoroughfares—Pearl, Market, State, and Water Streets—undoubtedly admiring the city's many fine homes built in the old Dutch Gothic style, with the brick gable facing the street to facilitate drainage of their infamous water spouts. (Denizens of Albany, an old fur trading outpost, knew to walk in the middle of the street when it rained due to the spouts and the mostly dirt roads, which quickly turned to mud.) The houses were not large but in addition to their unique architecture they were kept spic-and-span by their owners, who mopped them almost daily and scoured them weekly, a notable characteristic in a still relatively poor and filthy country. Albany in this period, perhaps because of its hoary Dutch roots, was, in the words of one contemporary, "unique ... picturesque ... naïve ... beautiful ... antique, clean, and quiet." Albany this day though was hardly quiet. The federalist procession, a copy of the Constitution on a liberty pole leading the way, stopped periodically to fire 10-gun salutes to the states that had ratified.[2]

Then all hell broke loose. Emboldened with alcohol—more likely hard liquors than the small (light) beer that typically quenched their thirsty throats—the antifederalists decided to take a stand by blocking the procession as it funneled past their watering hole on Green Street, a narrow side road connecting State and Hudson Streets several blocks up from the river on the city's south side. After exchanging a few choice words, the two sides battled for control of the narrow alleyway with swords, bayonets, clubs, and stones. As the battle raged, a group of light cavalry led by Dirck Ten Broeck flanked the antifederalist position. The antis broke ranks, some retreating to the countryside, others to Hilton's tavern, where they had been imbibing most of the day. Not content with having breached the barricade, the federalists mobbed the tavern, inflicting considerable damage to the building

As the battle raged, a group of light cavalry led by Dirck Ten Broeck flanked the antifederalist position. The antis broke ranks, some retreating to the countryside, others to Hilton's tavern, where they had been imbibing most of the day.

and its occupants but ultimately giving quarter to their vanquished, drunken foes. Thankfully, no one on either side resorted to the use of firearms or the cannon, though according to one account some of the antis prepared to fire gravel out of their field pieces. (Less lethal than lead, but something to avoid nonetheless!) Several leading antifederalists were jailed, ostensibly for their own protection as the city was at this point in great disorder. Contradictory reports render it impossible to ascertain casualty figures, but by all accounts over a dozen men were wounded during the fracas, several seriously.[3]

Despite the altercation, the procession continued, though some surely wondered if the battle for Green Street had been the opening salvo in a civil war. The federalists were winning the struggle over ratification of the Constitution, but they knew that many Americans remained highly suspicious of the document and the type of national government it would create. Having lost their cause on the floors of the state ratifying conventions, might the antis try to win on the battlefield? The economy, not to mention the collective psyche, had yet to recover from the Revolution, but that did not mean that another bout of war and rebellion was not possible. The French were about to prove that. The Americans might have been no different.

Contrary to common conception, the Constitution's creation was no cakewalk. As best we can tell, most Americans in 1787 and 1788 were antifederalists, more fearful of a strong domestic national government than of a foreign invasion or rampant domestic strife. "I had rather be a free citizen of the small republic of Massachusetts," one blatantly claimed, "than an oppressed subject of the great American empire." "Infinitely preferable," announced another, would be "occasional wars" between states than "the fangs of despotism … . As passing clouds obscure for a time the splendor of the sun," he explained, "so do wars interrupt the welfare of mankind; but despotism is a settled gloom that totally extinguishes happiness."[4]

No one doubted that America could be invaded, but as the Revolution had shown, her coastal cities were far more vulnerable to foreign attack than her hinterland. Not surprisingly, sentiment for the Constitution was much stronger in coastal areas than in the interior. But other factors were at play, as the strong federalist contingents in Albany and other large inland towns suggested. Antifederalists tended to be rural folk, mostly farmers, who believed that they could get by without armies, navies, national debts, taxes, and the other trappings of a strong national government. They particularly feared debt and taxes, which they thought made the "people groan" under the weight of "enormous taxes" on everything from christenings to burials. The benefits of the Constitution to them seemed small and its risks great. Little wonder the antis thought the proposed frame of government a raw deal.[5]

People in the cities and towns and more commercially oriented farmers, by contrast, knew that they would remain relatively poor if they did not have ample access to world markets. To them, a strong government meant a fair chance to sell their goods and services at home and abroad. Both sides agreed that some type of government was necessary. "If men were angels," James Madison once noted, "no government would be necessary." Everyone, especially those who turned Albany's Green Street red with blood, knew that men were, if not demonic, at least not angelic. City folk and those engaged in relatively large-scale business, however, had learned something from their everyday experience that most small farmers had not. They realized that men could be made to behave *as if* they were angels, that they could be induced to behave themselves. So for big commercial farmers and urban dwellers, the Constitution offered much in the way of benefit and little in the way of risk. No wonder that Albany and Manhattan were ardently federalist while their agricultural hinterlands remained cool toward the new government.[6]

The nation was polarized and frighteningly well armed. (Just how well armed is a matter of some dispute. We know, though, that many merchants owned *cannon* and most adult males wielded a musket so they could pass militia muster without incurring fines.) Perhaps at the next encounter partisans on both sides would hurl sober musket balls and grapeshot rather than drunken stones and barbs at each other. If they did, all might be lost forever.[7]

Thankfully, the altercation at Albany was anomalous. Before the Civil War (1861–65), Americans preferred to fight each other with pens rather than swords, with broadsheets rather than broadsides, and with a flurry of invective rather than a volley of hot lead. Within four days of the Albany fracas, an observer reported that the two sides had in effect kissed and made up. Soon after the fight, some rural antifederalists descended upon the city looking for some payback. To their eternal credit they dispersed after some of the antis involved in the fray admitted that they had initiated the violence and that both sides had been all juiced up on rum and other arduous spirits. Early American politicians liked to duel and beat each other with canes but widespread political violence was rare. Even America's rebellions—Shays', the Carlisle Riot, Whiskey, Fries'—were relatively bloodless affairs. Violence played little part in the ratification of the Constitution. In fact, at the very moment that foes and proponents of the controversial document were bloodying each other in Albany, members from each side were dining together peacefully at New York's ratification convention in Poughkeepsie. They drank the following toasts under the discharge of 13 cannon:

1. The United States.
2. Congress.
3. The Allies of America.
4. The Governor of the state of New York.
5. General Washington.
6. The Convention, wisdom, and unanimity in their councils.
7. The memory of the departed patriots of America.
8. Science, agriculture, commerce, and manufactures.
9. Public faith and private credit.
10. A Federal Government, uniting energy with liberty.
11. Happiness at home and respectability abroad.
12. The American Fair.
13. The Day.[8]

The toasts reveal that both antifederalists and federalists shared the same goals, continued American independence and economic prosperity. What the toasts obscured, though, was that the two sides were bitterly divided over the means of achieving those goals. Political debate therefore revolved around the issue of what was the best form of government. The states had already worked out their own constitutions. Some, like that of Massachusetts, would stand the test of time. Although heavily amended, it remains in force to this day. Others, like that of Pennsylvania, would soon be completely revamped. The question in 1788, though, was about the nature of

> The question in 1788, though, was about the nature of the national government. Should it be weak or strong?

the national government. Should it be weak or strong? If the former, what would prevent civil wars, foreign depredations, national bankruptcy, and an anemic economy? If the latter, what would keep the national government from degenerating into tyranny? The Revolution would have been for naught if all it managed to do in the end was to replace King George with an American or foreign autocrat. No wonder tensions ran so high. All the sacrifices made to win the Revolution were at stake. "The state of our affairs at present," an anonymous essayist wrote in December 1787, "is of such moment, as even to arouse the dead."[9]

Much of the discussion at the Constitutional Convention and during ratification was highly technical in nature. Most participants understood that they were trying to solve a difficult problem, how to form a government that was energetic but not tyrannical. While not quite the demigods Jefferson thought they were, the delegates were well qualified to frame a new government. As Madison wrote Jefferson: "The names of the members will satisfy you that the States have been serious in this business." Their views of the solutions to the technical problems of governance differed based on numerous personal factors, including their unique life experience, type and level of education, social class, occupation, geographical location, and the nature of their assets. The Constitution as a whole was a "Pareto improvement"—a fancy way of saying that it improved the lives of many while making no one worse off so it is difficult to get upset over ratification, even if each delegate had made a fortune from it, as some have claimed. To develop this technocratic view of the Constitution fully here would require a substantial digression from the main story, so what follows is a discussion of the convention in terms of only those parts of the final document that bore most directly on the national debt, most of which appear in Article I, Sections 8, 9, and 10.[10]

Roger Sherman, the aged sage from Connecticut, noted that the "national debt & the want of power somewhere to draw forth the National resources, are the great matters that press." Small wonder that taxes and the debt excited such little controversy. The delegates agreed without debate or vote that the national government would have the power to tax. That power of the purse, however, was not unlimited. "All Duties, Imposts and Excises" had to be "uniform throughout the United States." Moreover, the national government could not enact a capitation or other direct tax except in proportion to population. The Constitution also forbade the taxation of exports and interstate trade. All in all, though, the tax clause breathed life into the new national government by allowing it to lay and collect the taxes it needed to implement its other clauses.[11]

The Constitution also stipulated that the national government could "borrow Money on the credit of the United States." This, too, gave the government control of its own destiny and met little resistance. The clause for borrowing money was agreed to "nem. Con."—*nemine contradicente*, which is to say without dissent.[12]

The form that such borrowing should take was slightly more controversial, but not much. So long as it was done on a specie basis, the Constitution did not prohibit or even limit state governments from borrowing, which would have, rightly, raised the hackles of the antifederalists. The Constitution, however, did seize control of monetary policy from the states by forbidding them to "coin Money, emit Bills of Credit; make any Thing but gold and silver Coin a Tender in Payment of Debts; pass any Bill of Attainder, ex post facto Law, or Law impairing the Obligation of Contracts" while simultaneously granting the national government the power "To coin Money, regulate the Value thereof, and of foreign Coin, and fix the Standard of Weights and Measures; To provide for the Punishment of counterfeiting the Securities and current Coin of the United States." Prohibition of state bills of credit was put to a vote on August 28 and carried overwhelmingly, 33 to 6. The delegates undoubtedly understood that states could still make loans to citizens if they saw fit, as New York and other states later did; they would just have to do it with real money. The vote would have been closer had Rhode Island bothered to send delegates to the convention, because that state was then controlled by a party that supported state-issued legal tender paper money. Its little experiment "convulsed the State nearly to a civil War" and disgusted people everywhere as the value of its bills plummeted, Continental-style, to 15 to 1. The six delegates opposed to the outright ban may have believed, like the plain, forcefully speaking Nathaniel Gorham of Massachusetts did, that allowing the states to issue bills of credit if they obtained federal consent would be a more flexible and politically astute alternative. Most, though, apparently agreed with Sherman that state emissions had to be completely barred lest the partisans of paper money "make every exertion to get into the Legislature in order to license it." That was a remarkable position for Sherman to take because he is perhaps best known as the convention's great compromiser, a critic of national power, and its leading advocate for maintaining states' rights. Of course he was also known to be as "cunning as the Devil" and as slippery as an "Eel."[13]

In any event, the power of the federal government to emit bills of credit was neither explicitly confirmed nor denied in the Constitution. Gorham argued that the Constitution need not give the federal government the explicit right to issue bills of credit because "the power as far as it will be necessary or safe, is involved in that of borrowing." Future Supreme Court Chief Justice Oliver Ellsworth of Connecticut thought the question moot: "Paper money can in no case be necessary. Give the Government credit, and other resources will offer."[14]

Some discussion of federal assumption of state debts took place at the convention. South Carolina bigwig John Rutledge moved "that a Grand Committee be appointed to consider the necessity and expediency of the U. States assuming all the State debts." Such a move would be both necessary and just because the "State debts were contracted in the common defence" and because "taxes on imports … the only sure source of revenue" would likely rest with the federal government. He also thought that "by disburdening the people of the State debts it would conciliate them to the plan." Rufus King, the handsome delegate with a "sweet high-toned voice" from Massachusetts also said that he "would have no objection to throwing all the State debts into the federal debt, making one aggregate debt of about 70,000,000 of dollars, and leaving it to be discharged by the Genl. Govt." King noted "that the State Creditors" would form "an active and formidable party" that would "be opposed to a plan which transferred to the Union the best resources of the States without transferring the State debts at the same time." (King would later move to New York where he would become a U.S. senator, a staunch supporter of Alexander Hamilton's funding and assumption plans, and a director of the Bank of the United States.)[15]

The matter was referred to a committee, which reported out a clause that explicitly gave Congress the power to pay off the Revolutionary War debt of both the national government and "the debts incurred by the several States during the late war, for the common defence and general welfare." It did not, however, force Congress to do so. The clause was shot down without a vote because it was thought that such a halfway provision might excite "great opposition" against the Constitution. Ultimately, the Constitution said nothing specific about assuming state debts, but the matter was far from dead.[16]

There was also some talk of further strengthening the federal government's commitment to repaying its debts. For instance, Rutledge moved "that funds appropriated to public creditors should not be diverted to other purposes." Virginia firebrand George Mason objected because he feared that "such a fetter might be dangerous in time of war." He also wished to prevent "the danger of perpetual revenue which must of necessity subvert the liberty of any Country," whereupon the convention unanimously agreed to consider a clause for "restraining perpetual revenue." Nothing came of it, though, unfortunately.[17]

Meanwhile, Gouverneur Morris's suggestion that Congress be constitutionally mandated to discharge the national government's debts carried, but Pierce Butler of South Carolina urged a reconsideration because he feared the clause would "compel payment as well to the Blood-suckers who had speculated on the distresses of others, as to those who had fought & bled for their country." Mason chimed in that "use of the term 'shall' will beget speculations and increase the pestilent practice of stock-jobbing." He also pressed for making a distinction between "original creditors & those who purchased fraudulently of the ignorant and distressed." He admitted, though, that he "did not mean to include those who have bought Stock in [the] open market" and that "drawing the line" between fraudulent and fair trades would be difficult. He also feared that the term "'shall' might extend to all the old continental paper," a form of debt no one wanted to resurrect.[18]

Elbridge Gerry of Massachusetts fired back at Mason, arguing that the "Stock-jobbers" performed the valuable service of keeping up "the value of the paper. Without them," he noted, "there would be no market." Creditors, especially soldiers, who had been defrauded should be compensated, though, he conceded. Virginia's Edmund Randolph broke the impasse by offering a clause that stated merely that all debts of the Confederation would be debts of the new government. It passed 10 states

> The national and state governments owed a wide variety of debts, some of which were concentrated into a relatively few hands and some of which were widely held.

to 1, with only Pennsylvania opposed. The debate and vote showed that the issue did not pit the wealthy classes against the masses. The national and state governments owed a wide variety of debts, some of which were concentrated into a relatively few hands and some of which were widely held. One out of four New York farmers, for example, owned a particular type of federal debt certificate.[19]

When it came to the debt and related matters, that was about it. The framers found it expedient to leave the details about federal bills of credit, state assumption, and discrimination between original and subsequent holders to the new government. The debates begun during the convention on those subjects would therefore rage again in a few years. The delegates agreed on the basic components of the fisc, specifically that the money of the United States should be based on specie, that the federal government should support its value by maintaining the sanctity of contracts and standards of weights and measures and valuing foreign coins, and that it should pay off its debts and would have the ability to tax (and borrow) to do so. Slavery, control of western territories, the basis of representation in the House and Senate, the balance between the states and the proposed national government, the roles of the three branches of the national government, and related questions took more time and were far more contentious issues. Eventually, the delegates worked out those thorny problems, although not before six delegates (Elbridge Gerry, John Lansing, Luther Martin, George Mason, Edmund Randolph, and Robert Yates) quit or refused to sign their names to the document, which they feared would create a leviathan, a monster that would swallow up their liberties in one mighty gulp.[20]

On September 17, 1787, the remaining members of the Constitutional Convention finally signed the document they had hashed out over the long, hot and humid summer, the worst since 1750 according to the old-timers. The convention then rose and adjourned into history. But the framers' efforts, labored and sweaty as they were, would have become a mere footnote had not the new sovereign, the people of the United States, accepted the validity of the document they created. In September 1787, Alexander Hamilton, James Madison, and their federalist friends had won a battle, and a major one at that, but the struggle for a new government was just beginning. Once the contents of the document, which the delegates had managed to keep mostly under wraps during the convention, became known, opposition was sure to arise. As Francis Hopkinson, of the apple-sized head, told Thomas Jefferson: "No sooner will the chicken be hatch'd but every one will be for plucking a feather." And there were many feathers to pluck. No one believed that the frame of government signed in Philadelphia was a perfect one, but all those who affixed their names to the document thought it was at least worth a try. Perhaps they were swayed by Hamilton's admonition that "if mankind were to resolve to agree in no institution of government until every part of it had been adjusted to the most exact standard of perfection, society would soon become a general scene of anarchy and the world a desert."[21]

A large number of Americans, however, thought the new government unacceptable and many more found it highly objectionable. So yes, an important battle had been won, but the war was far from over. In fact, in many ways the worst was yet to come. The Constitution still needed the approval of at least nine states before it would take effect. Even with that number, if several key states failed to ratify, the new union might go down in flames quite quickly. To win the war and gain ratification in all the states, the federalists needed to persuade their fellow citizens that a government could be both powerful and nonthreatening, that it could be entrusted to tax and incur debt and to maintain armed forces. Many efforts were made, but none as authoritative as that of Alexander Hamilton, John Jay, and James Madison under the title *The Federalist* and the nom de plume "Publius."

> To win the war and gain ratification in all the states, the federalists needed to persuade their fellow citizens that a government could be both powerful and nonthreatening, that it could be entrusted to tax and incur debt and to maintain armed forces.

Born a bastard and orphaned at an early age, merchant-lawyer-theorist Alexander Hamilton learned firsthand how to govern a multinational mercantile enterprise while still in his teens. After emigrating to America, he devoured numerous tracts on economic, legal, and political theory. His military experience further cemented his theories of proper governance. A towering intellect overflowing with ambition, Hamilton inspired awe in some but fear in others. One of the most controversial men of his or any age, he was clearly the moving force behind *The Federalist*, although its youngest contributor. Hamilton's career was short but spectacular. He was the only founding father who played leading roles in the painful, but ultimately victorious, campaigns of the Continental Army, in the creation and ratification of the Constitution, in the formation of the new government, and in the emergence of the country's modern financial and economic systems. More than any other individual, he was responsible for the crystallization of America's development diamond.

John Jay, attorney and state builder was, at just 42 years of age, the triumvirate's elder statesman. While still in his thirties, Jay had authored New York State's first constitution, served as chief justice of his native state's supreme court, and played an important role in a diplomatic mission to Europe, where he observed the machinations of Old World governments firsthand. Often sickly in appearance and constitution, Jay authored only five of *The Federalist* essays before taking ill. His contributions, though, were arguably the most important of the 85 essays.[22]

Like Hamilton and Jay, planter-scholar James Madison enjoyed a deep understanding of matters of governance, which sprang from extensive reading and reflection as well as life experience. At least one observer, politician Fisher Ames of Massachusetts, considered the erudite Madison "a little too much of a book politician," but the Virginia planter and slaveholder was well accustomed to solving real-world governance problems. The combination of thought and action proved a powerful one that allowed Madison, like Hamilton and Jay, to penetrate to the heart of the matter. "His language," Ames admitted privately, "is very pure, perspicuous, and to the point." It had to be, because his physical presence was less than daunting. One contemporary claimed that the slight Madison was "no bigger than half a piece of soap" and his voice was so low listeners often had to beseech him to speak up.[23]

The outline for *The Federalist* sprang almost fully formed from Hamilton's brain on the deck of a Hudson River sloop as he and wife Betsey traveled to Albany to attend the fall session of the state supreme court in early October 1787. In many ways, it was fitting that Hamilton would devise his brilliant defense of the Constitution on a sloop, an important instrument of commerce. Sloops, which by definition carried a single mast farther forward than cutters or other types of small sailing ships, were capable of transoceanic voyages. In fact, the second vessel to sail from New York to China, the aptly named *Experiment*, was a sloop. She sailed from Manhattan in 1785 laden with ginseng, furs, cash, and a heavy arsenal to fend off pirates. *Experiment* returned to New York unscathed and laden with tea, silks, and nankeens, but Chinese taxes and bribes ate up her profits. At a mere 85 tons, she was simply too small to turn a profit on such a long, dangerous voyage. But sloops like *Experiment* could be highly profitable when engaged in shorter coastal or inland routes where tariffs and armaments did not chew up margins. Before the ascendancy of the railroad in the mid-nineteenth century, sloops domi-nated the Hudson Valley. Usually of about 60 tons burthen and handled by a crew of four—captain, pilot, sailor, and cook—sloops carried beef, bricks, flour, lumber, pork, firewood, hay, cider, and sundry grains and vegetables from the north and foreign wares like tea and manufactured goods from the south. Passengers, like the Hamiltons, were also taken on, though as revenue gravy rather than the mainstay of the trade. (In the early nineteenth century, steamboats stole away much of the passenger trade but barely dented the sloops' control of the freight trade.)[24]

Ocean travelers had to endure days, weeks, even months of vast emptiness, league after league of nothing to see but more sea. Hudson River sloop pas-sengers, by contrast, were treated to the grandeur of the river valley's breath-taking views. Hamilton's heart may have beat with pride as he soaked in the stunning physical majesty of his adopted homeland. This is how Washing-ton Irving, one of early America's literati, made famous by short stories like "Rip Van Winkle" and the "The Legend of Sleepy Hollow," described his first excursion aboard a Hudson sloop, in an age when steamboats, railroads, and suburban sprawl did not spoil the valley's pristine beauty:

> What a time of intense delight was that first sail through the Highlands! I sat on the deck as we slowly tided along at the foot of those stern moun-tains, and gazed with wonder and admiration at cliffs impending far above me, crowded with forests, with eagles sailing and screaming around them . . . . And then how solemn and thrilling the scene as we anchored at night at the foot of these mountains, clothed with overhanging forests; and everything grew dark and mysterious; and I heard the plaintive notes of the whippoorwill from the mountain-side, or was startled now and then by the sudden leap and heavy splash of the sturgeon.[25]

Other travelers were less effusive but equally awed. The voyage between Albany and New York took from several days to well over a week, depending on the winds. Given the beauty of the trip, few seemed to mind, although some complained bitterly about launches delayed as captains sought to stuff the ship with merchandise and passengers before proceeding. Some also disliked living in close quarters with strangers of the opposite sex, but others were undoubtedly thrilled to sleep so close to mysterious fair maidens and handsome beaus.[26]

By the time he arrived in Albany, Hamilton's brain was probably stuffed with new and exotic ideas and that was why his remarks at a dinner party appeared to James Kent to be uncharacteristically "careless" and "desultory." Kent was one to know. Born in 1763 to Hannah Rogers and Moss Kent, an upstate farmer-lawyer (it was not uncommon to have two, three, even four, occupations in early America), Kent graduated from Yale in 1781. Although the British razed his grandparents' house in a wartime raid, Kent appreciated many things British, including the law. At age 15, he greedily consumed Lord Blackstone's famous but formidable treatise, *Commentaries on the Laws of England*, and determined to become a lawyer (and unlike his father, only a lawyer). After graduation, he prepared for the bar under state attorney general Egbert Benson and married Elizabeth Bailey. The couple lived happily together for 63 years, with three of their four children living to adulthood. The home front secure, Kent devoted his life to the study of the law, quickly becoming one of New York's most important early jurists. He was said to have memorized *The Federalist* and marveled at Hamilton's oratorical skills on public display at the New York ratification convention in Poughkeepsie, where Kent then lived. But already by autumn 1787, Kent deeply admired Hamilton and was perplexed to find his idol so out of sorts. After the first number of *The Federalist* appeared, it dawned on him that Hamilton's conversation was off because he had been composing in his mind while he made small talk at dinner.[27]

Other pressing matters distracted Hamilton as well. In addition to sketching the plan of the essays, Hamilton had to think about recruiting top talent for his authorial team. The task ahead was too much for even Hamilton, especially given that he could not devote his full time to the cause, which after all he took on pro bono. Candidates for the team, he concluded, should be well off, good to great writers, and intimately familiar with the proceedings of the Constitutional Convention.

Two of Hamilton's top choices, Jay and Madison, signed on to the project. Two others, William Duer and Gouverneur Morris, did not work out. The former essentially flunked out. The latter, though hounded by Hamilton, begged off due to the press of private business. Hamilton's failure to lure Morris was a major setback, because Morris would have been an outstanding addition to the team, especially if he had played an editorial role, sprucing up the language of the deep-thinking triumvirate.

In many ways, Morris was an odd fish. Although his mother remained loyal to the Crown during the Revolution, Morris was an ardent patriot. When still in his twenties, he served in the Continental Congress. Despite his high breeding, he was no stuffy intellectual or aristocrat. Women found his humor, charm, and peg leg irresistible. How many he bedded will never be known with certainty, but he probably bested Benjamin Franklin and Bill Clinton combined, which is quite an achievement. Morris made love to the written word the way he made love to the ladies in his prime, with sweet verbal caresses interspersed at appropriate intervals with deeply probing prose. His most famous work is the Constitution itself. He spoke more often than any other delegate and the power of his pen is evident in the final version of the document. A better choice for final draftsman, Madison concluded, could not have been made. The Constitution's famous Preamble portrays Morris's elegant control of language at just age 35:

> We the People of the United States, in Order to form a more perfect Union, establish Justice, insure domestic Tranquility, provide for the common defence, promote the general Welfare, and secure the Blessings of Liberty to ourselves and our Posterity, do ordain and establish this Constitution.

The Federalist was competently composed but if it had had the benefit of such consummate wordsmanship, its impact would have been even greater.[28]

Duer, on the other hand, was no wordsmith. He penned a few pieces thought to be "intelligent and sprightly" but ultimately found wanting. Duer's dismissal from the project was for the best. Although a staunch federalist, Duer ultimately cared more about himself than the cause. He showed his true colors a few years later when serving as Hamilton's undersecretary at treasury. Hamilton had to force him out of the administration because he treated the public purse as his own. The devilish Duer could not be induced to behave as if he were an angel, so he had to be cast out. In 1792, his highly leveraged securities speculations helped to cause a financial panic that could have destroyed the nation's fledgling financial system and economy. Hamilton intervened to prevent that catastrophe but could not keep his erstwhile friend out of debtor's prison, where he spent most of the rest of his short, impish existence.[29]

Another headache for Hamilton was finding publishers for his project. Then as now, finding the right outlet for a policy wonk was no piece of cake, and Hamilton did not have the luxury of an agent. Several newspapers printed the essays in serial form, as they rolled off the pens of the authors, because they were a good read and increased demand for subscriptions. And because early American newspaper editors shamelessly copied each other and rarely paid even for original content, they were a cheap source of words. Finding a publisher willing to put out the essays in book form, on the other hand, was a much more difficult proposition. Most early American publishers were mere printers unaccustomed to assuming the risk inherent in the manufacture and sale of books. They were happy to arrange for the creation of a book, so long as the author fronted the money. They were, in effect, more like "vanity" presses than modern publishers. Nevertheless, Hamilton was able to find a publishing team, John and Archibald McLean of Hanover Square, willing to take on the job and the financial risk. The McLeans were a good fit for *The Federalist* because they were federalists, and, although they specialized in religious works, they also had experience publishing policy pieces. John's first book, published in 1784, was Baron von Steuben's *A Letter on the Subject of an Established Militia*. Later that same year, John also helped to publish *Thoughts on Taxation* by Timothy Davis, a wonk if there ever was one. In 1787, the pair published the text of the Constitution and broadsheets announcing its ratification by New Hampshire and Virginia. (Perhaps their handiwork was burned by the Albany antis on July 4.)[30]

The McLeans likely calculated that they could turn a tidy profit on a timely political treatise of 200 or so pages. They might have, had the triumvirate held its ink, but it did not. When the trio finished seven months later, the essays numbered 85 instead of the originally planned 25 and contained an astounding 175,000 words, which filled two volumes and 620 pages. The poor McLeans barely broke even, several hundred copies of the tome wallowing unsold in a warehouse. *The Federalist* was the last policy book they ever published. John died in 1789 and Archibald in 1798. The following year, Archibald's estate bound and reissued the remaining unsold copies. Although initially a commercial flop, *The Federalist* was what people in the book trade call an "evergreen." Never a blockbuster, the treatise has nevertheless persisted in print for over two centuries. No fewer than four editions appeared in 1961 alone and there have been over 300 in total since 1800, including translations into Bulgarian, Chinese, Croatian, French, German, Hebrew, Italian, Japanese, Korean, Russian, Spanish, and other foreign tongues. Scores of publishers have profited from reprinting *The Federalist*, but the men who first made it widely available in book form had to rest content with only the knowledge that they had done well.[31]

Assigning responsibility for the essays was Hamilton's next task and was relatively easily accomplished. Each member of the trio would work, alone, on his area of expertise. Unlike, say, the translation of the King James Bible, the report of the Warren Commission, or the Constitution itself, *The Federalist* would not be written by committee. Rather, it was a compilation of essays composed by three very different minds under a single pseudonym and vision.[32]

Jay, the diplomat, took up foreign affairs. Madison, the scholar, discussed history and took up the trickier theoretical treatments. He also sketched the general outline of the new government as he had, after all, authored the victorious Virginia Plan. Hamilton handled the executive and judicial branches and some of the discussion of the Senate. The former and future military man and treasury secretary also discussed taxation and defense.

The easiest task of all was selecting a nom de plume. Hamilton at first settled on "Citizen of New York" but abandoned it after Madison, a Virginian, joined the team. He searched history, his own and that of the world, for a substitute, finally hitting upon Publius, a pen name he first used in 1778. Publius was short for Publius Valerius Publicola, one of the founders of the Roman Republic in 509 BC. In addition to helping to expel Lucius Tarquinius Superbus, the last Roman king, Publius helped to lay the foundation for the republic by enacting two laws, one that enjoined citizens to slay any man who dared call himself king, and one that allowed defendants to appeal to the people any condemnation delivered by a magistrate. From their formal education in school or their informal education during the imperial crisis leading up to the Revolution, many Americans would have recognized the symbolic connection between the historical Publius and the authors of *The Federalist*. Anyone who paid even the slightest attention would also have realized that the modern Publius set forth a much more complex plan for preventing the rise of tyranny than Publius Valerius Publicola had. The Roman Republic lasted almost 500 years before devolving into an empire ruled by an autocrat. Could the American republic last as long?

⚜

The first installment of the Federalist Papers appeared in the *Independent Journal* on October 27, 1787. It was hardly a thing of beauty. Early American newspapers were composed of just a few pages and generally contained more advertisements than news. Printed on heavy paper with a high rag or cotton content, they have survived the ages well but were, and are, difficult to read due to their small type. Illustrations were few and of course were in black and white. The perspicacity of the piece, however, made up for its lack of graphic attractiveness. In fact, more people probably heard the Federalist Papers read aloud, in taverns, post offices, and parlors, than read it silently to themselves, as is the norm today. By the end of the Revolution, most Americans could read and write but found more difficult pieces a tough slog. Moreover, American newspapers from the start were highly politicized; this was a means of encouraging discussions of public policy as well as of conveying information. Newspapers were relatively expensive; the penny daily was still decades away. For all those reasons, newspapers were regularly "broadcast," read aloud by prominent men in public places or by fathers in private dwellings.[33]

> American newspapers from the start were highly politicized; this was a means of encouraging discussions of public policy as well as of conveying information.

To keep its newspaper editors happy and its readers (and their listeners) sated, the triumvirate promised to deliver four essays per week. That would have been a difficult but not onerous task had there been three men to perform it. Unfortunately, after completing just four essays the perpetually sickly Jay fell too ill to continue until the series was almost complete. Thereafter, Madison and Hamilton had to burn the candle at both ends to keep the newspapers full of new installments and the minds and mouths of the Constitution's supporters overflowing with new arguments. They crafted their ideas in the downtime between meetings, trips, and other business and public engagements. Hamilton often worked into the wee hours, snatched six hours of sleep, then reinvigorated himself with strong coffee before putting in six to eight hours of writing interrupted only by his penchant to pace as he waited for the words to flow. Then he would have to work another six or more hours on his law practice.

Aided by the notes he took during the convention and his extensive preparatory reading, Madison had a somewhat easier time of it. Madison was at first ambivalent about the Constitution and hence planned to allow others to defend the convention's work. By late October, however, he joined the fray on the federal side with alacrity, highly motivated to make certain that the document he had breathed life into was fairly portrayed. He worked so hard that a visiting French journalist thought that "he looked tired, perhaps as the result of the immense labor to which he had devoted himself recently."[34]

With two essays due every week from each of the men, there was little time for them to share their incisive analyses with each other before publication, so Madison and Hamilton had to trust each other's judgment, something that a few years later would be unthinkable. Indeed, they rarely had time even to revise their own work. According to Madison, the printers were often already typesetting parts of one of his essays while he scrambled to complete it. Newspaper editor Samuel Loudon would hang about Hamilton's office, waiting for the young savant's quill to rest before snatching the papers and inserting them in the next edition of his paper. Luckily, Hamilton was one of those rare writers whose first drafts were more cogent than many authors' final versions.

In addition to fighting the clock and their own schedules, Hamilton and Madison had to face personal recriminations for their actions. That "Publius" was a pseudonym for Hamilton, Jay, and Madison was soon an open secret. The essays could be seen as breaking a pledge that the members of the convention had made not to disclose the convention's inner workings. This was an era when gentlemen did not break pledges lightly. Whether

Publius broke the pledge at all was questionable, but to protect themselves, they never disclosed who wrote which essays. Scholars have spent two centuries trying to sort it all out. Today, most agree that Hamilton authored 51 of the essays, Madison 29, and Jay, who recovered just in time to write one additional article, 5.

The triumvirate contended with opposing forces in two other camps, outright opponents of the Constitution and sundry scribblers and hacks who mischaracterized the proposed frame of government. The latter group in some ways was as formidable as the former, for what they lacked in vehemence they made up for in confusion. Speaking broadly, the scribblers and hacks were composed of those who supported but misunderstood the Constitution and those who consciously spread lies about it. The liars especially felt the sting of the triumvirate's sharpened quills. In Federalist 42, for example, Madison dismissed claims that the Constitution sought to ban Europeans from emigrating to America. "I mention these misconstructions," he wrote, "not with a view to give them an answer, for they deserve none; but as specimens of the manner and spirit, in which some have thought fit to conduct their opposition to the proposed government."

The Constitution's opponents retorted in newspapers, private letters, and public speeches. When they could not concoct good counterarguments, they resorted to that age-old weapon called calumny. As they toiled for the good of the country, the members of the triumvirate had to suffer personal attacks against their character. "Centinel" wrote that Publius suffered from an "imbecility of judgment" and that his "deranged brain" produced hobgoblins and "myriads of unmeaning sentences." "This writer," Centinel continued, wasted inordinate amounts of time and paper "combating chimeras of his own creation." Ouch! Perhaps the triumvirate was out of its league after all, too harried and outnumbered to make a difference?[35]

The core argument of *The Federalist* held that the Constitution would create a government that would be both powerful and benign, vigorous but not tyrannical, energetic yet not despotic. As Madison pointed out, men were far from angelic, so government was needed to keep the peace. But governments were made of men, so they could act demonically as well, as

The core argument of *The Federalist* held that the Constitution would create a government that would be both powerful and benign, vigorous but not tyrannical, energetic yet not despotic.

anyone with even a passing familiarity of history or Christianity well knew. The "weight of self-government," all knew, was "a burden to which Greek and Roman shoulders proved unequal." Even the Roman Republic had descended into tyranny. "A few will, and must govern" the masses, many Americans believed.[36]

The Bible, the source most frequently cited by the Revolutionary generation, contained additional warnings. Most early Americans were Protestants and hence were encouraged to read and interpret the holy word for themselves. They did so with alacrity, drawing from it many lessons, some moral and some historical. Even those who like Thomas Jefferson eschewed traditional religion for Deism, the Enlightenment belief in an almighty maker who steered clear of involvement in human affairs, or those who like Gouverneur Morris enjoyed secular delights more than regular church attendance, knew the Bible inside and out. From Adam and Eve's fall from grace, which reinforced the notion that men were not angels, to Old Testament stories of tyranny and autocracy (think Pharaoh), to Deuteronomy, an entire book devoted to a description of the formation of a new nation, the Bible's relevance to the Revolution and the Constitution is impossible to deny.[37]

At a time and place in which virtually everyone was swayed by either history or religion, and many if not most were influenced by both, examples of tyrannical government were damning indeed. The lessons of history and revealed religion, many believed, were blazingly obvious. A "disposition … implanted in human nature … [and] confirmed by the unerring experience of ages" ensured that "every man, and every body of men, invested with power, are ever disposed to increase it, and to acquire a superiority over everything that stands in their way." Ergo, America's national government should remain weak. A withered arm, many Americans reasoned, could not strike them down. Switzerland, a loose confederation of cantons, should be emulated.[38]

The triumvirate, too, believed in the importance of religion and history. "Experience," Madison wrote, "is the oracle of truth and where its responses are unequivocal, they ought to be conclusive and sacred." But the authors drew different conclusions from old books. A weak government, they argued, would not be able to stave off foreign predation or the worst types of domestic discord. A strong government would shield Americans from those who wished to do them ill. Moreover, and here was the stroke of genius, the new government would protect Americans from itself. A powerful but heterogeneous government, the authors argued, could be induced to control its own worst urges. "Let ambition counteract ambition," Madison argued in Federalist 51.

With the clarity of hindsight, we know that Hamilton, Jay, and Madison were correct. The Constitution would create a powerful yet nonpredatory government. That government was far from perfect, especially when it came to the treatment of "foreigners" (e.g., Native Americans, Filipinos, suspected terrorists) and even nonwhite citizens (e.g., blacks, during the long period of Jim Crow laws; the Japanese Americans, when they were interned during World War II). Nonetheless, on the whole the freedoms and rights conferred by the Constitution have stood the test of time and remain powerful enough to draw immigrants from around the world. "The U.S. has the worst government in the world," a cold war one-liner aptly asserted, "except for all the others." But in 1788, the bold experiment that came out of Philadelphia appeared to many to threaten a prompt return to a tyranny unseen on American shores since the reign of King George III.

What sort of men feared Leviathan arising out of the Constitution? Most of them were farmers of modest means, the backbone of America's society and economy, 70-plus percent of its workforce. Most owned modest amounts of real estate, some in fee simple (outright), some in long-term leaseholds, others on perpetual ground rents, and yet others by virtue of squatters' rights. Those who owned land were understandably loathe to lose it. Access to land in the late eighteenth century meant life. A man's farm was his fiefdom. From a patch of any decent size or quality he and his family could subsist, could keep themselves warm, dry, and fed until the inevitable, when the plot would also serve as a cemetery. Trade for such farmers was a luxury, not a necessity. They did not mind exchanging any surplus they created on their lands for valuable things—books, clocks, fancy clothes, muskets, and sundry mild drugs (coffee, tea, and sugar)—that they could not make or grow themselves. But they would not willingly risk their farms for them. A distant federal government, particularly one with the power to tax, could prove their undoing.[39]

The tenants had less to lose and more to gain from passage of the Constitution, or more precisely from the economic boom that would possibly follow its ratification. But they also knew what it was like to suffer under the heel of tyrants, their landlords. For many, knowing that their landlords were federalists was enough to make them antis, opponents of the Constitution, although in some areas the oppression was so great they had to remain in the closet for fear of being booted off the land.

Antifederalist leaders tended to be more ideological and self-interested than the rank and file. They were better educated and more articulate than most antis but did not share their aspirations. Some, like George Mason of Virginia, apparently genuinely feared the proposed government. Others, like George Clinton of New York, mostly feared losing their jobs and prestige.

Born and raised on a northern Virginia plantation, George Mason (1725–92) studied under John Mercer. Purported to own the largest library in the northern part of the colony, Mercer was a noted legal scholar who imbued in Mason a deep distrust of imperial government. A friend and neighbor of George Washington, Mason in the mid-1750s built a beautiful home, Gunston Hall, overlooking the Potomac River. He was only slightly active in politics until the imperial crisis drove him to action on the side of the patriots. Poor health prevented him from playing a larger role in the conflict, but he was nonetheless one of the Old Dominion's most prominent rebels. His crowning achievement was his authorship of Virginia's first state constitution and its declaration of rights, both ratified in June 1776.

Mason not only refused to sign the Constitution, because it sought to create a powerful government; he purportedly said that "he would sooner chop off his right hand than put it to the constitution as it now stands."

Mason was to Virginia what Madison was to America. Nevertheless, despite his wealth, commercial orientation, and extensive experience in business, Mason virulently opposed Madison's Constitution. His material interests and experience never overcame the anti-government teachings Mason had been tutored in. Mason not only refused to sign the Constitution, because it sought to create a powerful government; he purportedly said that "he would sooner chop off his right hand than put it to the constitution as it now stands." (Tellingly, the convention in Philadelphia marked the only time in his long life Mason ever left the Chesapeake watershed.) Taken aback by his actions at the convention and his increasing belligerence and stubbornness, Mason's friends began to distance themselves. Unelectable in Fairfax, his home county, Mason barely won a seat in the Virginia ratifying convention by running in nearby but less affluent Stafford County. After his numerous calls for structural changes and an explicit declaration of civil rights in the Constitution went unheeded, Mason withdrew from public life. He refused to serve as a U.S. senator and not even passage of the Bill of Rights cheered him. In 1792 at Gunston Hall, he died a bitter old man but true to his ideology to the last.[40]

Very different forces lurked in the ambitious veins of George Clinton. Born to farmer-surveyor Charles Clinton and Elizabeth Denniston in 1739, Clinton was privately tutored before leaving home in 1757 to serve on the *Defiance*, a privateer sporting 16 cannon. He returned home in 1760, just in time to help seize Montreal from the French. He then studied law under William Smith Jr. and was admitted to the bar in 1764. That was his ticket to the political arena. In 1770, he married Cornelia Tappen, in part to solidify his political base in Ulster County. He supported the Revolution, served in the Continental Congress, and backed Washington for commander in chief of the rebel army. He also headed a militia unit charged with blocking British use of the Hudson River. The stiff defense his troops put up at Fort Montgomery induced the British commander, Sir Henry Clinton, to invade Philadelphia instead of striking northward up the valley as planned.

In 1777, New York's numerous farmers elected Clinton governor over longtime rival Philip Schuyler, who would soon become Hamilton's father-in-law. Clinton brilliantly exploited the patronage powers granted him under New York's constitution (authored, as noted above, by Jay) to forge a powerful political base that ensured his reelection year after year. By 1787, Clinton stood to lose much if a powerful national government came into existence. He therefore mounted a campaign against the Constitution, including a series of letters under the pseudonym Cato, undoubtedly a reference to Marcus Porcius Cato (95–46 BC). Known as Cato the Younger or Cato of Utica, Cato was a staunch republican renowned for his probity. After losing a bitter struggle against Julius Caesar, Cato took his own life rather than compromise with his foes. Clinton would do no such thing, but for the present he was seen as defender of the common man's interests. Thanks to his immense popularity, the antis won control of New York's ratifying convention. For all those reasons, Clinton was Hamilton's biggest rival, far more so even than Aaron Burr.[41]

The antis charged that the new Constitution would soon devolve into a powerful and tyrannical force that would reverse the gains made during the Revolution at the cost of tens of thousands of American lives, massive economic dislocation, and untold psychological devastation. The Constitution, Patrick Henry declared, was an "experiment" that "ought not to be made."[42]

A common antifederalist tactic was to turn federalist arguments on their ear. To the claim that civil war would likely erupt due to the weakness of the Articles of Confederation, for example, "Philanthropos" countered that the Constitution was more likely to lead to domestic discord. "The new constitution," he argued, "is calculated to produce despotism, thraldom and confusion, and if the United States do swallow it, they will find it a bolus, that will create convulsions to their utmost extremities." Civil war would destroy the country as "fathers and sons sheath their swords in one another[']s bowels in the field, and their wives and daughters are exposed to the rudeness and lust of ruffians at home." To the claim that the Articles debilitated America at home and rendered her inert abroad, the antifederalist "Alfred" asserted the opposite. Prices were reasonable, exports enormous, and good land abundant. "When I see these things," he noted, "I cannot be brought to believe that America is in that deplorable ruined condition which some designing politicians represent."[43]

Another tactic was to attempt to frighten the bejesus out of people by raising the specter of evil national tax collectors and armies controlled by a handful of grasping elite politicians safely ensconced "perhaps at several hundred miles distance." "Thus," a "Federal Republican" announced, "will you be fatigued by fruitless attempts into the quiet and peaceable surrender of those rights, for which the blood of your fellow citizens has been shed in vain." State governments would be powerless to stop the national government, another anti explained, because the states would be absorbed into a "grand continental vortex, or dwindle into petty corporations, and have power over little else than *yoking hogs* or determining the width of *cart wheels*"(italics in original). High taxes would be necessary, "A Farmer" claimed, because the new government would overflow with placemen (government appointees of dubious value to the public), sycophants, and other worthless characters clinging tenaciously to sinecures. "When you carry a man's salary beyond what decency requires," he argued, "he immediately becomes a man of consequence, and does little or no business at all."[44]

Some of their arguments were quite practical. An antifederalist who ironically styled himself "A Federalist" complained more about the way the federalists were going about securing ratification than the Constitution itself. The federalists, he claimed, "brand with infamy every man who is not as determined and zealous" in favor of the Constitution as themselves, calling them "bankrupts who wish no government, and officers of the present government who fear to lose a part of their power." Worse, the federalists strove "to overawe or seduce printers to stifle and obstruct a free discussion."[45]

Some antis simply denied that anything was amiss with the Articles of Confederation. Virginia's William Grayson, for example, argued that the federalists spoke only of "phantoms and ideal dangers" rather than actual or even likely problems. No country stood ready to invade America and the denizens of Pennsylvania and Maryland were not about to descend upon Virginia, or any other state, "like the Goths and Vandals of old," nor were "the Carolinians, from the south, (mounted on alligators) … to come and destroy" corn and tobacco fields "and eat up … little children." The foreign loans contracted by Congress were really grants, so repayment was not expected. "Loans from nations are not like loans from private men," he noted. (Perhaps, but the Dutch loans came out of the pockets of investors, not Dutch taxpayers.) Domestic loans, Grayson continued, could easily be repaid through the sale of western lands. (This was a chimera if there ever was one, as it turned out.)[46]

Others took more philosophical stands, arguing, for example, that "quiet is happiness" and "content and pomp are incompatible." "The silence of historians," another argued, "is the surest records [sic] of the happiness of a people." A powerful national government would seek glory and that would bring pain to the common man and his family.[47]

The antis also did quite a bit of special pleading to local audiences. Ratify the Constitution, Patrick Henry argued, and say good-bye to the Mississippi, a frightening thought to western farmers who relied on access to it to get their crops to market. "Agrippa" warned New Englanders that

Ratify the Constitution, Patrick Henry argued, and say good-bye to the Mississippi, a frightening thought to western farmers who relied on access to it to get their crops to market. if the Constitution was adopted, their fine states would be flooded with immigrants. Instead of retaining their pure (blue) blood, they would begin to resemble Rhode Island or, worse yet, Pennsylvania, which everybody knew teemed with rank Germans and hordes of detestable Scots-Irish. The new government would also create numerous corporate monopolies that would enrich a few, probably in Manhattan and Philadelphia, at the expense of many, mostly in Boston and Newburyport.[48]

Some antifederalists concocted clever parodies of federalists and their proposed policies. The efforts of "Montezuma"are worth quoting at some length:

> We the Aristocratic party of the United States, lamenting the many inconveniences to which the late confederation subjected the *well-born*, the *better kind* of people, bringing them down to the level of the *rabble*—and holding in utter detestation that frontispiece to every bill of rights, "that all men are born equal"—beg leave … to submit to *our friends* in the first class for their inspection, the following defense of our *monarchical, aristocratical democracy*. [Italics in original]

The parody, which ran on for three more pages, portrayed the Constitution as chock full of checks and balances against the common man.[49]

The greatest of the antifederalist pen pugilists was "Brutus," after Marcus Junius Brutus (85–42 BC), a nephew of Cato of Utica who sided with Pompey against the machinations of Julius Caesar. After helping to assassinate Caesar (*"Et tu, Brute?"*), Brutus turned into something of a brute and eventually committed suicide after losing a battle. Scholars remain uncertain of the identity of early America's Brutus, but most agree his essays were, ironically enough (*brutus* is Latin for "stupid"), as insightful and well written as the Federalist Papers. In one essay, Brutus accurately predicted that the national government would use the necessary and proper clause of the Constitution (the final paragraph of Article I, Section 8) to greatly extend its powers.[50]

In another important essay, Brutus predicted, echoing the sentiments of Adam Smith, that the new government would "create a national debt, so large, as to exceed the ability of the country ever to sink [pay back]." Here, Brutus was wrong, at least for the eighteenth and nineteenth centuries. The U.S. government indeed paid off the Revolutionary War debt and eliminated most of the debt incurred during the Civil War before the global calamities of the twentieth century made a large national debt a seemingly permanent feature of the nation's economic landscape. What Brutus had to say has more relevance today than it did when he wrote:

> It may possibly happen that the safety and welfare of the country may require, that money be borrowed, and it is proper when such a necessity arises that the power should be exercised by the general government. But it certainly ought never to be exercised, but on the most urgent occasions, and then we should not borrow of foreigners if we could possibly avoid it. The constitution should therefore have so restricted the exercise of this power as to have rendered it very difficult for the government to practice it. The present confederation requires the assent of nine states to exercise this, and a number of other important powers of the confederacy. It would certainly have been a wise provision in this constitution, to have made it necessary that two thirds of the members should assent to borrowing money. When the necessity was indispensable, this assent would always be given, and in no other cause ought it to be.

Some states would later constitutionally limit their ability to borrow, but the federal government's power to do so remains unchecked. We'll leave it for others to argue if restrictions should be put in place now. Clearly, they were not needed before the twentieth century.[51]

The problem with the analysis of Brutus and other antis is that they were way off on the timing and extent of the growth of the national government, usually implying that the states and the people would be overawed within a few years. Over 200 years later, the U.S. government is indeed many times larger and more powerful than it was in the 1790s, but state governments are still vital and important and most Americans desire the services the expanded national government now provides. What the critics missed was that the Constitution was much more democratic than British rule had been, a point that many federalists understood clearly. "Under the present national system," Arthur Campbell wrote in 1789, "the people are an immediate and constituent part, and if they act their part *well*, will increase and render permanent their influences, and of course their liberty" (italics in original).[52]

Opponents of the Constitution made two other crucial mistakes. First, they allowed themselves to be labeled antifederalists. Most people, and early Americans were no exception, react negatively to negative descriptions. Few prefixes in English shoulder more resentment than *anti*. For that reason, those opposed to abortion describe themselves as prolife rather than antiabortion, while supporters of abortion call themselves prochoice rather than antilife. Similarly, antiwar advocates style themselves pacifists or doves. The antifederalists would have furthered their cause if they had been able to brand themselves as *pro* something, perhaps propeople, prostate, or even proconfederation. Some pointed out that they were the true federalists, while the supporters of the Constitution were really nationalists, but they could not make their nomenclature stick.[53]

That brings us to the antis' second problem. The Constitution's opponents never countered with an effective PR campaign of their own. There was no antifederal antidote to *The Federalist*. They would have been more successful if they had set forth a positive vision for America rather than initiating a series of sniper attacks against the federalists. The underlying problem was that the antis had no unified vision to offer and were deeply divided among themselves. Broadly speaking, antifederalist leaders came in two stripes, state politicians who feared a loss of their power, and populist demagogues who equated the right to vote with the absence of predation. The ranks, by contrast, were simply scared witless of a distant, powerful government. As a result, the Constitution's opponents never offered a fully articulated vision of the future that could draw fence-sitters to their side. They had a coherent critique of the Constitution but nothing to offer in its stead. Some wanted nothing whatsoever to do with the Constitution, others wanted to give the government "control over national and external matters only," while still others would accept it if sufficiently amended. The federalists, by contrast, crushed the Articles of Confederation and proffered the Constitution in its place. They had the upper hand, but could they bridge the great divide, the chasm of thought separating them from their foes?[54]

The great strength of the antifederal critique of the Constitution was that it was rooted in fear. In people as in rabbits, fear often results in paralysis, in an utter and complete inability to act. That was a good strategy given that ratification required positive action by many people. The authors of *The Federalist* responded to their foes' fearmongering by showing that Americans had nothing to fear but antifederalism itself. They did so by offering a very different view of the proposed frame of government than that proffered by the antis.

The first essays unleashed a devastating critique of the Articles of Confederation. In four essays, Jay showed that the Articles had made America the laughingstock of the European diplomatic community. Divided and weak, the nation, if it could be called that, would be easy prey for any number of European powers. In the next four essays, Hamilton predicted massive civil strife, a weak economy, and state-versus-state warfare if the Constitution failed to be ratified.

In Federalist 10, Madison, filling in for Jay, destroyed Montesquieu's claim that democracy could last only in small countries, such as the Greek or Italian city-states. Madison's argument, a refutation of an essay, probably penned by George Clinton writing under the pen name Cato, is perhaps the most widely cited of all the Federalist Papers. It held that in larger republics like the United States, competition among interest groups would ensure that no one group could become tyrannical or form a predatory majority. Later called the "tyranny of the majority" by French political scientist Alexis de Tocqueville, the concept of a predatory majority is perhaps best captured by the old joke about two wolves and a sheep voting on what to have for dinner.[55]

Later called the "tyranny of the majority" by French political scientist Alexis de Tocqueville, the concept of a predatory majority is perhaps best captured by the old joke about two wolves and a sheep voting on what to have for dinner.

Hamilton then rejoined the fray, arguing in Federalist 11, 12, and 13 that the Constitution would facilitate economic growth by rationalizing and nationalizing fiscal, monetary, and trade policies. That view he and Madison reinforced through Federalist 22 by recounting how poorly property values (way down) and interest rates (way up) had responded to the

Articles. The national government's inability to tax rendered it so weak that foreign states mocked the country and with good reason. "We have neither troops nor treasury nor government," Hamilton lamented in Federalist 15. In those crucial numbers, the dynamic duo of Hamilton and Madison also disputed the notion that the officials of the national government would be able to ride roughshod over the states.

In Federalists 23 through 36, Hamilton defended the proposed Constitution point by point. He argued that national taxation and a strong military could strengthen the country to the point that no foreign power would dare encroach upon its borders, treaties, or economic interests. As the Revolution had shown, the Atlantic Ocean was not the impenetrable barrier some pretended it to be, but it did raise the cost of messing with America. Professional soldiers and well-equipped sailors were therefore necessary, and only a powerful national government could provide and efficiently coordinate them. Although less adept than professional soldiers, state militias would ensure that the national army fought only external foes. Cannons, cavalry, corvettes, and other military accoutrements would be funded by an efficient national system of taxation.

Starting with Federalist 37 in early January 1788, Madison in a string of 20 essays began to describe the general structure of the new government, paying particular attention to its republican nature. Members of the House were to be directly elected by the people and senators and the president indirectly so. (State legislatures initially elected senators; to this day, members of the Electoral College technically elect the president.) Terms were short, ensuring that the people, the states, and electors would have ample opportunity to oust the venal and incompetent. For those who thought four years too long a period to wait, presidents could be impeached and removed from office. Madison then patiently explained the reasoning behind each of the Constitution's major clauses.

Back in Manhattan after a trip to Albany, Hamilton penned numbers 59, 60, and 61 on the subject of elections. He noted that by virtue of their great numbers farmers would easily control the new government. Some merchants and manufacturers would be elected to Congress, but they would remain a small minority for the foreseeable future. Agricultural interests therefore had nothing to fear.

The next five essays, 62 through 66, concentrated on the Senate. In many ways the most collaborative section of The Federalist, two of the essays were penned by Madison, two by Hamilton, and one by Jay, who finally came off the disabled list. After the discussion of the Senate was finished, so were Madison and Jay. From there on out, Publius and Hamilton were one and the same. In numbers 67 through 77, Hamilton described the executive branch and argued that it could be "energetic" though the powers of its head, the president, were far more circumscribed than those of traditional monarchs like George III. Unlike kings, presidents were "personally responsible" for their behavior in office, were impeachable, and were elected for four years and not born into their position for life. Perhaps even more important, the executive branch was effectively checked by the legislative and judicial branches as well as by the state governments. Provisions of the Constitution dealing with Senate confirmation of judges and ambassadors were key, Hamilton argued. Veto and pardon power ensured that the president could, in turn, check any excesses in the legislature.

Hamilton dedicated numbers 78 through 83 to the proposed national court system. In the first, he introduced the notion, later developed into the concept of judicial review, that the Supreme Court could nullify laws that ran counter to the Constitution. "No legislative act," he argued, "contrary to the constitution can be valid." In the later numbers, he dealt with the thorny issue of jurisdictional disputes between federal and state courts and the proper role of the jury system in different types of court cases.[56]

Hamilton devoted Federalist 84 to a discussion of a bill of rights to protect civil liberties. He argued that an explicit listing of rights might be dangerous. "Why declare that things shall not be done which there is no power to do?" he asked rhetorically. Logically he was right but politically he was wrong. A bill of rights would be one of the new government's first priorities.[57]

In the final essay, 85, Hamilton conceded that the Constitution had its flaws but that it was far better than the existing frame of government, which was no government at all. He also hinted that much of the opposition to the document stemmed from state politicians more interested in protecting their own selfish, narrow interests than in aiding the nation.

The triumvirate gave a virtuoso performance. With one glaring exception, reckoned with below, Hamilton, Jay, and Madison made the Constitution transparent. Intelligent men could still oppose ratification, but they could not pretend to misapprehend the document or the intent of its framers. The claims of antifederalists who complained that "the hideous daemon of Aristocracy" had precluded the people from inquiring about the new frame and extinguished "every spark of liberal information of its qualities" were no longer tenable. The detailed discussions of the convention were still secret, but the reasons underlying most of the choices it had made were not. The American people needed to know what they were being asked to accept, and now they did, except when it came to slavery, that most peculiar of institutions.[58]

Slaves were simultaneously people and property. Like property, they could be bought, sold, mortgaged, insured (like a barn, not like a person), ordered about, and even beaten. Like people, it was unlawful to kill them (unless in self-defense or punishment for a capital crime).

Easily the most divisive issue in the convention, slavery exuded paradoxes from its pores. Slaves were simultaneously people and property. Like property, they could be bought, sold, mortgaged, insured (like a barn, not like a person), ordered about, and even beaten. Like people, it was unlawful to kill them (unless in self-defense or punishment for a capital crime). More telling, they enjoyed certain, albeit limited, economic rights and were liable for their actions under law.

In 1787 and 1788, a few Americans, like the Philadelphia Quakers, thought slavery abominable. A few others, like large slaveholders, thought it a wonderful institution. For most, though, ambivalence reigned. It seemed hypocritical to extol the equality of all men one moment while selling some of them the next. On the other hand, most white Americans were inveterate racists who were quick to rationalize that black people were less than human and hence exempt from the strident assertions of the Declaration of Independence. While the Golden Rule would seem to forbid slavery, many other parts of the Bible seemed to countenance it. All anyone knew for sure was that some powerful men had large sums tied up in human chattel and that they often imagined conspiracies designed to separate them from their hard-earned man-beasts. They were so touchy that the Constitution did not explicitly mention slavery anywhere, instead referring to slaves with euphemisms like "other Persons" and people "held to Service or Labour." The compromises reached in the convention were so well balanced that to this day scholars continue to debate whether the Constitution was a proslavery or antislavery document.

Little wonder, then, that the triumvirate handled the issue of slavery with kid gloves. Only Madison discussed the subject, and only then somewhat obliquely. In Federalist 38 and 42, he notes that the Constitution empowers Congress to outlaw the importation of slaves after 20 years while the Articles of Confederation permitted the traffic forever. In 43, he hints that during periods of civil unrest, slaves ("an unhappy species of population abounded in some of the states … sunk below the level of men") would be inclined to "emerge into the human character" and throw their weight behind the side most likely to aid their emancipation. Finally, in 54, Madison defends the infamous Three-Fifths Clause, the concession that allowed slave states to count each slave as three-fifths of a person for purposes of representation in the House of Representatives.

Although slightly tainted by slavery, Hamilton and Jay ultimately vehemently opposed it; Madison was a large and largely unapologetic slaveholder. Even if the members of the triumvirate had held the same view of the institution, they could not have ended slavery or mitigated its effects. Their goal was to gloss the Constitution, not to perfect a world still plagued by perfidy, pests, pirates, and peculiar institutions. In that, they succeeded.

Patrick Henry once claimed that "no government can flourish unless it be founded on the affection of the people." The Federalist did not evoke much affection but it did garner a great deal of respect. By the time the eighty-fifth and final essay peeled off the presses, the framers' view of the U.S. Constitution had been laid bare for all to contemplate. The essays effectively imbued the document, and the process that brought it about, with a high degree of transparency. The Constitution was not an aristocratic plot to seize the reins of power but rather a device carefully contrived to ensure that the American republic would not suffer the same fate as the Roman. It could not turn men into angels but it could make them behave as if they were. Power and security from tyranny were not necessarily antithetical.[59]

The story of how the Constitution came to be ratified is a complex and interesting one involving political chicanery, a good dose of luck, and stirring harangues and learned speeches by members of the triumvirate and other proponents of the new frame of government. The impact of *The Federalist* on the ratification process was profound, even outside New York and Virginia. In the later conventions, most delegates on both sides of the question appear to have read the treatise, or least picked up the gist of it. Americans accepted the legitimacy of the flawed ratification process largely due to the influence of *The Federalist*. Rabid opponents were not swayed by its perspicacity, inimitable logic, or nuance, but many fence-sitters found the essays persuasive. By the end of the ratification process, most Americans heeded Hamilton's plea in Federalist 85 and decided to give the new frame of government a chance to evolve. As it turned out, that was all it needed.

The federalists quickly gained the upper hand in the ratification process. In December 1787, within two months of the close of the convention in Philadelphia, three states, Delaware (on the seventh), Pennsylvania (on the twelfth), and New Jersey (on the eighteenth), ratified. The following month, two more, Georgia (on the second) and Connecticut (on the ninth), fell into the federalist camp. On February 6, 1788, about the time Federalist numbers 48 and 49 appeared, Massachusetts became the sixth state to ratify. The federalists' success, though, helped to arouse opposition from those who thought that "furious zealots" were "cramming" the document "down the throats of the people, without allowing them either time or opportunity to scan or weigh it." A foreboding lull of almost three months, the rest of February, all of March, and most of April (Maryland ratified on April 28), allowed the trio to complete its mighty tome while granting a reprieve to those who felt unduly rushed.[60]

With the low-hanging fruit already plucked, the federalists began to salivate for the harder-to-reach pieces needed to fill the new government's basket. In several important contests, the triumvirate and its Federalist Papers were important players. South Carolina went federal on May 23 by a vote of 149 to 73. The reasons for the landslide are clear: Charleston was solidly federal and the state's backcountry was politically unorganized.[61]

New Hampshire joined the union on June 21 but only after a close call. Most communities in the state had bound their delegates to vote no. Rather than suffer sure defeat, the federalists won an adjournment so that the delegates could return to their constituents and beg leave to vote as they saw fit. To bind their hands beforehand had turned the election into a plebiscite, which smacked too much of democracy. When the delegates reconvened in June, they voted for ratification 57 to 47.[62]

Virginia ratified on June 25, also by a margin of 10 votes, 89 to 79. Madison and the Federalist Papers played a large role here, in a state where the typical divisions between rich and poor, commercial and subsistence farmers, and rural and urban were not as strong as elsewhere. "It is a little strange," George Washington told a European correspondent, "that the men of large property in the South, should be more afraid that the Constitution will produce an Aristocracy or a Monarchy, than the genuine democratical people of the East." Planters feared the new government because they knew tyrants all too well. They stared one in the face in their looking glasses every morning as they shaved, primped, and preened. Many denizens of Virginia's backcountry backed the new government because they sought a check against the tidewater slaveholders who dominated the state government.[63]

> "It is a little strange," George Washington told a European correspondent, "that the men of large property in the South, should be more afraid that the Constitution will produce an Aristocracy or a Monarchy, than the genuine democratical people of the East."

The final great ratification battleground lay in Poughkeepsie, New York, a bucolic little town on the Hudson's east bank located in Dutchess County. Founded in 1687, its name, like many in upstate New York, derived from the local native language and apparently means something like the place near the water. Although a mere village with fewer than 3,000 inhabitants, Poughkeepsie was chosen to host the convention because it had served as New York's capital since the Revolution and was nestled midway between the state's two leading cities, Albany and Manhattan, on the state's convenient river highway. Known for its whale rendering and brewing industries, the town itself largely supported the Constitution, but most of the delegates that gathered at its spacious and brand-new courthouse on Market Street in the heart of the downtown district assembled for one reason, to keep New York out of the new union until some major changes were made in the Constitution.

At the head of the antifederalist majority stood George Clinton, Revolutionary War hero and longtime governor of the state. The consummate politician, Clinton had very personal reasons for blocking passage of the Constitution: he feared that its implementation would erode his power base. Clinton's first victory against the Constitution had come in 1787, when he handpicked two of New York's three delegates to the convention in Philadelphia. Those delegates, Albany lawyer Robert Yates and John Lansing Jr., Albany's mayor, effectively stymied Hamilton's efforts in the convention. After the pair of antis left the convention on July 10, New York lost its vote. Hamilton bravely soldiered on but seethed at Clinton's perfidy.[64]

Clinton's second victory came in late April 1788, when a larger than usual electorate—all male New Yorkers aged 21 or older instead of only property holders as specified in New York's constitution—voted overwhelmingly for antifederalist delegates at the state's ratification convention. Upstate, Clintonian antis took almost all the seats. Downstate, however, the federalists crushed the Constitution's opponents. In Manhattan, they received some 30 votes for every ballot cast for an antifederalist. When the electoral smoke cleared at the end of May, the antis, who garnered 56 percent of the known votes, had won two-thirds of the seats, thanks in large part to a narrow victory in Albany County, which at the time was huge and mostly rural. Immediately upon achieving a quorum on June 17, the antifederalist delegates, who outnumbered the federalists 46 to 19, gave Clinton his third victory by electing him president of the convention.[65]

Violence in the election period was limited to a bizarre "Doctors' Riot" in Manhattan. An unthinking medical student sparked the riot by waving the severed arm of a corpse at a young Peeping Tom and declaring the arm to be that of his mother. The cruel prank may have ended there had the child's mother not recently passed away. The mob assembled by the child's father raged for several days before the militia put it down by shooting three of its unruly members. During the melee, Jay was struck by bricks, which left "two large holes in his forehead." Luckily, although he "got his scull almost cracked," Jay did not suffer brain damage and was able to attend the convention. Despite the relatively quiet election, feelings on both sides ran high and at times boiled over. In addition to the Albany riot described at the beginning of this chapter, Hamilton almost dueled two of his opponents after a heated exchange on the floor of the New York convention.

Thankfully, the situation was defused before it led to a dawn encounter. The fact that the antis lodged at Poole's Inn and the federalists at Hendrickson's Inn helped to avoid after-hours altercations. The problem was that both sides had their backs to the wall. The antis controlled the convention lock, stock, and barrel, but they could not prevent other states from joining the new union. An impasse appeared inevitable as both sides jostled for position. Ultimately, Hamilton and his outnumbered federalist colleagues carried the day, but only after many setbacks.[66]

The antis expected the federalists to try to orate their way to victory, so they were not surprised when Hamilton and Robert R. Livingston motioned that the Constitution be discussed point by point before the delegates voted on ratification. A postelection shift in public sentiment in favor of the Constitution, undoubtedly aided if not brought about by the appearance of *The Federalist*, helped Hamilton and Livingston's resolution to pass, as did the widespread sentiment that the handsome young Hamilton would eventually embarrass the federalist cause by exposing his supposedly monarchical views. "You would be surprised, did you not know the Man, what an *amazing Republican* Hamilton wishes to make himself be considered," wrote anti Charles Tillinghast. "*But he is known*" (italics in original). The antifederalists, who unanimously supported the resolution, miscalculated. Hamilton did support republican government and wished to do more than hear himself talk. His motion was calculated to stall for time. Hamilton desired the chance to persuade the antis, but more practically, he hoped to gain leverage as news of ratification came in from the east (New Hampshire) and south (Virginia).[67]

Each day thereafter, between 100 and 200 visitors witnessed an oratorical display rarely rivaled before or since. Between 10 in the morning and 2 in the afternoon, and later in the convention for several hours in the late afternoon as well, the crowds heard New York's best and brightest expound, elaborate, and pontificate. Hamilton was called a "political porcupine, armed at all points," who brandished "a shaft to

Hamilton was called a "political porcupine, armed at all points," who brandished "a shaft to every opposer." Jay's reasoning powers were considered "weighty as gold, polished as silver, and strong as steel."

every opposer." Jay's reasoning powers were considered "weighty as gold, polished as silver, and strong as steel." Others, even the few antis who dared to follow the eloquent federalist speakers, won praise. "Mr. Lansing," one newspaper reported, "is often upon the floor, and has that respect paid him by his auditors, which one but men of abilities can obtain: He is heard with attention."[68]

Two men, Hamilton for the federalists and Melancton Smith for the antis, carried more than half of the debate. By all accounts a plain man liked by all, Smith was not impressed with Livingston, whom he called "a wretched reasoner," or with Hamilton, whom he dismissed as long-winded and irrelevant. "Like publius [sic]," he wrote, Hamilton had "much to say not very applicable to the subject." Unlike Hamilton, whose oratory while eminently logical often soared, Smith's debating style was "dry, plain, and syllogistic." According to Jay, neither side influenced the other a single iota. According to Clinton, all Hamilton managed to do was annoy people by repeating parts of the Federalist Papers. But New Yorkers, those in the galleries as well as the huge newspaper audience, were listening intently and many were starting to get it. Nevertheless, the antis remained smug. They had the votes to block ratification, and then some. Their confidence flagged, though, as the convention dragged on, and on, and on. Then came the devastating news that New Hampshire and Virginia had ratified and antis had started a riot in Albany.[69]

Clinton and his delegates tried to hold firm, but in July the nature of the debate shifted away from the merits of the Constitution per se to the expediency of joining the new union and then to the terms under which New York would join. The antis now signaled they would vote in favor of ratification if they were allowed to offer amendments to the Constitution. The federalists listened carefully to all 55 proposed changes but ultimately would have none of them. Any amendment would of course have caused confusion and delay and under one scenario would have led to a new round of ratification conventions. If and when the process would end was not clear. Jay and six other federalists assigned to a subcommittee charged with working out the details deadlocked because the federalists steadfastly refused to support any form of conditional ratification. On July 11 Jay resolved that the delegates unconditionally ratify the Constitution but annex a list of *recommended* amendments.

The federalists argued that the new union would not accept New York's conditional ratification; the antis of course claimed it would. The antis could have voted themselves out of the impasse but chose not to carry the question by weight of numbers. The week of July 14, both sides dickered over language while the federalists hinted that an adjournment was in order. The antis rejected any thought of adjourning because it was clear that sentiment in the state had shifted heavily in favor of adopting the Constitution. Circumstance and Publius had finally turned the tide. The antifederalist ranks began to splinter; Smith rejected one of his own resolutions. Hamilton then threatened that the staunchly federalist downstate region was prepared to secede from the rest of the state and ratify the Constitution unconditionally. Clinton bristled at Hamilton's comments but soon came to realize that they reflected reality. New York federalists then promised that they would seek the desired amendments through the processes prescribed in the Constitution itself.

In Manhattan on July 23, three days before the convention officially acted, federalists held a major procession in support of the Constitution. The festivities began at eight in the morning, on a wet Wednesday no less, at the top of Broadway, then a mile and a half from the parade grounds near the island's southernmost tip. Two horsemen with trumpets and a company of artillery led the way, followed by 10 "divisions" composed of sundry occupational groups—bakers, brewers, hatters, lawyers, merchants, millers, physicians, and students. Each group carried emblems and several rode on elaborate floats. The seventh division's float was the most impressive of all, a 27-foot "frigate" named *The Hamilton*, complete with canvas waves, drawn by 10 horses. Over 6,000 people then feasted on ham, mutton, and bullocks in a series of pavilions connected by a 150-foot colonnade designed by famed French architect Pierre L'Enfant. At 5 p.m. the procession reassembled and retraced its steps, watched by an estimated 20,000 spectators, though most of the city's badly outnumbered antis stayed home.

If nothing else, the pompous parade sent a clear signal to upstate antis that downstate New York was ready, willing, and able to join the new union regardless of the convention's decision. The northern part of New Jersey and most of Connecticut, it was said, were prepared to go to war to ensure that New York, or at least Manhattan, its main connection to international markets, joined the union. The antis may not have believed that war or secession really threatened, but such talk made it clear that the federalists, though technically a minority in the convention, now had the upper hand and were eager to press home their advantage. Along with the stick, the federalists also displayed the carrot, their promise to work strenuously on behalf of amendments. The approach worked. On July 26, enough antis switched sides to ensure a federalist victory, 30 to 27. New York finally became the nation's eleventh pillar, ratifying the Constitution without condition. The victory was not pretty, but for the founding triumvirate it was sweet indeed.

On August 8, 1788, a little over a month after the Green Street riot, Albany's federalists, many festooned in their military garb, celebrated New York's ratification of the Constitution by parading a copy of the document about town on a decorative staff. Eleven ancient citizens, representing the eleven states that had ratified, led the procession, followed by axemen, farmers, brewers, and other occupations, including Indian traders. After dinner in a 154-foot-long "Federal Bower" replete with 11 arches, the federalists drank 13 toasts, each followed by an 11 gun salute. Mobs of antifederalists jeered but no violence broke out, though undoubtedly both sides were as hammered as they had been on the Fourth.[70]

The two remaining holdouts, North Carolina and Rhode Island, could not be swayed by reason, not even the inimitable logic of *The Federalist*. Only after the new government successfully formed and the economy began to flourish did they finally consent to the Constitution. North Carolina joined the union on November 21, 1789. On May 29, 1790, Rhode Island finally capitulated and ratified. The smallest state to this day, Rhode Island was as enigmatic as it was anomalous. Although commercially oriented and located in New England, the state eschewed the Constitution while simultaneously embracing slavery. "Rhode Island has acted a part," one contemporary noted, "which would cause the savages of the wilderness to blush. That little state is an unruly member of the political body, and is a reproach and a byeword among all her acquaintances." Initially, many of its inhabitants believed they could benefit by staying out of the union because independence would allow them to engage in two activities, smuggling and money issuance, that colonial Rhode Islanders had found quite lucrative. Once it became apparent that Hamilton, the newly appointed treasury secretary, would not countenance either form of deviant behavior, Rhode Islanders figured they might as well sign on.[71]

In the meantime, the founding triumvirate worked to fulfill the promise it made at Poughkeepsie to amend the Constitution. Madison, the "father of the Constitution" and the only member of the triumvirate elected to the first Congress, perforce took the lead. Not all of the amendments dreamed up by the New York antis made the cut, but many did. Others were dropped from consideration by Congress or failed to receive the approbation of three-fourths of the states. Those that made it through the winnowing process became the Bill of Rights, the Constitution's first 10 amendments, which officially became a part of the Constitution on December 15, 1791. The antis stuck to their end of the bargain, too, and refrained from arousing animosity. All Americans were on the same team, so to speak, all aiming toward the same goal: political and economic independence. Perhaps George Clinton put it best when he said that antis and federalists alike had "the good of our country in view, though we disagree as to the means of procuring it." Now the means were settled, and so were the antis.[72]

If the national debt played little role at the Constitutional Convention, it played an even smaller one during the ratification debates. The promise of sound money and all that it implied (low interest rates, high land prices, macroeconomic stability) was a major source of support for the new government.[73]

The promise of sound money and all that it implied (low interest rates, high land prices, macroeconomic stability) was a major source of support for the new government.

There could be no doubt that the federalists, and especially the founding triumvirate, supported funding the national debt. Near the end of his presidency of the Continental Congress, Jay beseeched Americans not to soil the new nation's hard-won independence with fiscal profligacy:

Let it never be said that America had no sooner become independent
than she became insolvent or that her infant glories and growing fame
were obscured and tarnished by broken contracts and violated faith,
in the very hour when all the nations of the earth were admiring and
almost adoring the splendor of her rising.[74]

Federalist writers extolled the virtue of restoring public credit by servicing
the existing debt, because public credit might be needed in some future
exigency. "In war," the federalists reminded Americans, "the longest purse
prevails." The threat of an ever-growing debt like that of Britain was distant;
some even intimated that the debt would soon be extinguished.[75]

Federalists at times brandished both the carrot and the stick. Writing while
the convention was still in session in Philadelphia, "Z" made it clear that
America was impoverished despite its vast resources and its citizens mired in
debt despite their hard work and intelligence because the national government was a failure. Strengthen it, he argued, and the economy would grow, to
the benefit of all Americans. That was the carrot. The stick was the claim that
creditor nations like Britain, France, Spain, and Holland would soon swoop
down upon the country in retaliation for its dilatory debt management.[76]

The antifederalists bristled, and rightly so, at such claims. Economic sanctions, particularly by Britain, were possible but armed conflict was doubtful
without further cause. Antis also expressed the fear, a very real one, that the
new national government would contract new, additional debts. Brutus, for
instance, complained that it could "create a national debt, so large, as to
exceed the ability of the country ever to sink." A "greater calamity" could
not "befall this country," he claimed. The government should be allowed to
borrow, he suggested, only if a supermajority (two-thirds) of states agreed.
Another anti likely conversant with Adam Smith's disdain for government
debt, "Sidney," also raised the specter of a large, perpetual national debt
arising under the new government.[77]

Some antis, like Agrippa, argued that the states were making good progress servicing and even paying down the debt and that adoption of the
Constitution would actually arrest progress. "If the new system should take
effect … the increase of expense," he warned, "will be death to the hopes of
all creditors, both of the continental and of the state." Between the tariff and
western land sales, he argued, the states had it covered.[78]

Others thought the Constitution did not go far enough. "Brutus Junior," for example, argued that "a competent provision for the payment of the interest of the public debt is wanting." A dispatch, perhaps a federalist ploy to ease concerns about the secretive Constitutional Convention, laid such antifederalist fears to rest for a time by boldly asserting that the debt would be serviced and a small military funded with a light tariff.[79]

"Light" was the key word. What the antifederalists abhorred was not so much the debt itself as the taxes necessary to pay the interest and principal. In late autumn 1787, for example, "Cincinnatus" railed against federalist James Wilson of Pennsylvania for glossing over the fact that the revivification of national credit would come at a cost to the American taxpayer.

> What the antifederalists abhorred was not so much the debt itself as the taxes necessary to pay the interest and principal.

Like most antis, Cincinnatus exaggerated the tax burden and underestimated the federal government's ability to raise the necessary sums. An honest difference of opinion, yes, but Cincinnatus was so enamored of his cause that he calculated the arrearages on the debt—sums of $1,500,000, $850,227, $500,000, $300,000, and $500,000—as $4,650,227, a cool million too high. A Freudian slip to be sure. He also predicted that imports would "diminish yearly," due to the "nature of things," but unfortunately he did not specify to which things he referred nor did he elaborate on their nature. "With magnificent promises you have bought golden opinions of all sorts of people," he warned, "and with gold you must answer them." But those promises, $1.8 million in specie per year he estimated, "will overhelm the people. It will give immense fortunes to speculators; but it will grind the poor to dust."[80]

⁂

Despite such ominous predictions, the antifederalists did well to keep the peace as they profited from implementation of the Constitution right along with the federalists. For a number of interrelated reasons, the tax burden of the average American likely decreased in the 1790s. For starters, the federal government was more efficient at tax collection. That made it possible, as we will see, for the federal government to fund the national and state debts at a lower rate of interest and for a longer period, both of which reduced the annual debt service.[81]

Like the economies of most states, New York's had sputtered after the Revolution. Fearful of domestic discord or foreign depredations, few risked making extensive investments. People went about their daily business but few strove to better their lot by improving their farms, establishing mills or other types of factories, or opening new channels of trade. Most people were content just to get by, to play wait-and-see. Little wonder the economy stagnated.

But by 1789, Albany, the scene of rioting just the year before, was booming. As one contemporary put it:

> Now we behold Market and State Streets crowded with stores, and rents in those streets enhanced to such a degree as to put houses out of reach of inconsiderable traders. Nor had we any manufacturies of any kind, but depended on importation entirely for every manufactured article. Now we see the citizens stimulated by motives of public spirit, daily promoting them.[82]

That same year, the great American geographer Jedidiah Morse argued that Albany "must flourish, and the inhabitants cannot but grow rich." He was right. In the 1790s and first decade of the 1800s, a burgeoning population, banks, post offices, newspapers, libraries, bridges, and numerous new houses and public buildings outwardly displayed the city's growing affluence. Manhattan, too, blossomed as private credit markets again began to function.[83]

The rest of the country's economy flowered as well. As we will learn in the next chapter, in the early 1790s the young nation experienced a financial revolution complete with sound money (the specie definition of the dollar as the national unit of account and banknotes and foreign coins as media of exchange), a central bank (the Bank of the United States), a system of private banks and insurance companies, and efficient (for the time) markets for foreign exchange, commercial paper, corporate equities, and government debt. Thanks in part to the disruptions caused by the French Revolution, exports boomed. Exports of tobacco from South Carolina, for example, soared from a mere 643 hogsheads in 1783 to almost 10,000 in 1799.[84]

Quite apart from the situation in Europe, industrial production soared. Contrary to common belief, the United States did not experience an Industrial Revolution in the mid-nineteenth century but rather an Industrial Evolution that began circa 1790. By 1795, British author William Winterbotham noted that a gusto for manufacturing had already "taken full possession of the American mind," especially from New England to Pennsylvania.[85]

The root reason underlying the economic boom is clear. After adoption of the Constitution, people's incentives changed. Assured that their lives, liberties, and properties were safe, Americans began to invest in the future. The fence that seemed too much trouble to erect in 1785 looked like a necessity in 1789. In 1786, when interest rates were high and real estate values low, repairing the dam and millrace seemed too expensive. By 1791, with interest rates falling and property values climbing, the repairs would pay for themselves quickly. Impossible tasks in 1782, like connecting Philadelphia and Lancaster with a good road, were in motion by 1792. In short, the Constitution unleashed the nation's latent entrepreneurial energies. Some foreign observers saw this clearly. In 1795, Winterbotham noted that in the United States the "laws and government have for their basis the natural and imprescriptible rights of man: liberty, security of person and property, resistance against oppression, doing whatever does not injure another, ... and an equal chance of arriving to places of honour, reward, or employment, according to their virtues or talents."[86]

The prosperity wrought in large part by implementation of the Constitution soon became a self-fulfilling prophesy. When people find it easy to make money hand over fist, they tend to forget about past problems and concentrate instead on the present and future. Political differences persist but only a few whackos unable or unwilling to partake of the profits contemplate revolution. Political stability and economic growth mate, giving birth to

By the 1830s, foreign observers like Alexis de Tocqueville marveled at America's moneygrubbing, democratic ways. The only thing that could have thrown a wrench in the works was the only thing that did, that damnable institution known as slavery.

another generation of peace and prosperity. By the 1830s, foreign observers like Alexis de Tocqueville marveled at America's moneygrubbing, democratic ways. The only thing that could have thrown a wrench in the works was the only thing that did, that damnable institution known as slavery.

Attitudes toward slavery certainly helped the founding triumvirate to cleave into two, with Hamilton and Jay joining the Federalists and Madison leading the Republicans (called Democrats since the Age of Jackson), but the main cause of the split was closer to the heart of this study, the national debt. As we have seen, the government's debt per se played little role in the framing of the Constitution or ratification debates, because the issue was essentially nonpolitical as almost everyone agreed that the government's obligations should be honored. That was about to change, and dramatically, because what constituted the government's debt, how it should be repaid, and even who rightfully owned it were questions of burning intensity.

5

BIRTH

Alexander Hamilton's Grand Plan

By ratifying the Constitution in 1788, the United States created the crucial home base of its development diamond, an energetic yet nonpredatory government. That new government inherited a national debt that could, and in fact would, serve as a bridge between it and the next facet of its development, a modern financial system. The architect of that bridge was one of the men who had played a large role in the framing and ratification of the Constitution, Alexander Hamilton. The contractors who built the bridge were the tens of thousands of investors who exchanged their Revolutionary War certificates for new federal bonds, then traded those bonds in the emerging capital markets of Boston, New York, Philadelphia, Baltimore, Charleston, and numerous smaller towns.

In 1749, a scribbler described Britain's national debt as a "Gordian Knot" that ached for the sword of "an Alexander to cut thro"' it. No one equal to the task appeared in Britain. After the American Revolution had swelled its national debt to what many contemporaries thought "a hopeless magnitude," Britain initiated reforms, the most important of which was making its sinking fund more difficult for politicians to raid by placing it under the control of a board of commissioners. (Just as Ronald Reagan explained in 1981 that America's $1 trillion national debt was the equivalent of a stack of $1,000 bills 67 miles high, early British commentators tried to convey the debt's enormity. When the British national debt stood at £272 million, for example, it was noted that it would, if laid out in large gold coins, extend for some 4,300 miles!) A long period of warfare with revolutionary France, however, ensured that Britain's national knot would swell in size and complexity until it left the home islands "on the verge, nay even in the gulph of bankruptcy." Even the long period of relative peace between the Napoleonic Wars and World War I, the Pax Brittania, only partially unraveled it. The new United States, by contrast, found its Alexander the Great. Or perhaps he found it.[1]

E ven before the Revolution ended, various evidences of government debt, ranging from loan office certificates to indents to the sundry notes of Robert Morris and his staff to handwritten IOUs exchanged in the field for farm produce and livestock, began to change hands. By 1787 most of the original holders had sold their IOUs at market prices that were a small fraction, from 1 to 30 percent or so, of the debt instruments' face or par values. The reasons why prices were so low are clear: real money, to wit coins and bank liabilities convertible into gold and silver, was scarce and hence dear; when, indeed if, the debts were to be serviced, let alone repaid, was unclear; the markets for the various debt instruments were extremely thin, so purchasers could not be assured of being able to resell them; and prices were uncertain and transaction costs high. For instance, when New York began to accept final settlement certificates as payment for land, their value jumped by one-third. When New Jersey began paying interest on its debt in bills of credit rather than indents (more IOUs), its final settlement certificates increased in price to 20 cents on the dollar. When Pennsylvania funded its debt, prices of its IOUs increased but trading was generally light.[2]

The sheer complexity of the debt was a major problem. Many important traders were not entirely sure what they were trading; Philadelphia's most important securities broker, Matthew McConnell, publicly admitted so much in a pamphlet. New York broker John Delafield also complained about the sorry state of the markets, attributing their "infancy" to the "scarcity of cash" that prevailed most of the time in most places. During the long, lean 1780s, he had to sell a variety of dry goods and alcohol in order to get by. "Even certificates of the state and continent," an observer noted in 1786, "far from meeting with a ready sale, the holders of them find great difficulty in procuring purchasers."[3]

Ratification of the Constitution also increased prices and the volume of trading, but not by much. Risks were still very high and the markets for public securities remained thin and desultory. The Constitution was a giant leap forward but only opened up the possibility of handling the nation's problems in an efficient and respectable manner. There was still the need to form a government, pass laws, and establish administrative mechanisms before any progress could be made on something as massive and controversial as the national fisc and the Revolutionary War debt. Much uncertainty remained. Uncertainty gave way as the government formed and the markets for public debt started to heat up with higher prices and volumes. That increased activity, however, helped to cause a political backlash that almost retied the knot even as the sword of Hamiltonian finance sliced through it.[4]

⇝

The Continental Congress closed up shop peacefully on October 10, 1788, and faded into infamy, though two of its key departmental officers, John Jay as secretary of foreign affairs and Henry Knox as secretary of war, stayed at their posts as the new national government began to form. The Board of Treasury started winding up its affairs, eventually passing along its records, mostly tangled wartime accounts, to the new government. In late 1788 and early 1789, elections were held for president, vice president, and both houses of Congress. For the most part the transition went off smoothly, greatly enhancing the legitimacy of the new order. Virginian and mighty republican warrior George Washington was unanimously elected president and, for geographical balance, John Adams of Massachusetts was selected as his vice president. Both houses of the first Congress were filled with able men, most of whom had supported ratification of the Constitution. In the spring, alone or in small groups, the whole ensemble trundled off to Manhattan, the nation's first temporary capital. Washington's trip from his Mount Vernon plantation took eight days and evolved spontaneously into a processional celebrating the great man's election. Manhattan literally shut down to celebrate his arrival via barge from New Jersey.[5]

By April 1789, the important work of organizing the new government had begun in earnest. Congress got its bearings debating questions relating to titles, ceremony, official etiquette, and the like. In retrospect, the discussions were a colossal waste of precious resources, but at the time they held deep meaning and exposed the extent to which some of America's leaders wished to avoid anything smacking of Britain or her government. Senator William Maclay of rural Pennsylvania, for example, objected strenuously to calling Washington's first inaugural address "his most gracious speech," because the Brits applied that phrase to the king's speeches. Maclay, a bitter pill who at 6 foot 3 inches towered over most of his colleagues, won out. The federal government would strive for the simplicity of the Roman Republic, not the ostentation of European monarchy. The fact that Roman-style finances (to wit, pre-Dutch) would never do for America did not seem to occur to anyone at the time.[6]

After an extensive debate on the tariff, Congress in May 1789 began organizing the executive branch of government. Following some contention between the House and Senate, it was finally agreed that the president would nominate the heads of three executive departments, State, War, and Treasury, but each would have to be confirmed by the Senate before assuming the duties of office. Furthermore, the president could dismiss his appointees at pleasure but the replacement would also be subject to Senate confirmation. Cabinet officers were therefore undoubtedly the president's men but not just anyone could be assigned to the high posts. The hope was that the Senate could prevent the establishment of a British-like patronage system rooted in nepotism and corruption. Ever the careful politician and fearful of running afoul of the Senate and posterity, Washington deliberated carefully on each of the 350 or so federal appointments under his control. "The eyes of Argus are upon me," Washington told his nephew Bushrod Washington as he declined Bushrod's request to join the new government. Argus, by the way, undoubtedly referred to Argus Panoptes, a mythological Greek giant with 100 eyes, only a few of which slept at a time.[7]

Washington first approached Robert Morris, the financier of the Revolution, about taking the top spot at Treasury. Morris was in some ways a logical choice, because in addition to his vast experience and intimate knowledge of the previous government's finances he was well known by Washington, who had lived in his house during the Constitutional Convention. In some ways, though, Morris would have been a poor choice to head the new department because his name and credit were so closely connected with the old government. Moreover, his extensive business dealings made him liable to charges of corruption. Had he taken office, surely one of Argus's eyes would have spotted something amiss and brought censure down upon Washington's head. One suspects Washington sighed with relief when the rotund Philadelphia merchant not only declined the office but suggested that Hamilton should fill it. Washington had met Hamilton in 1776 and came to know him intimately as they experienced the trials and travails of the Revolution together in the field. The two became so close that some speculated they were father and son. (That was utter balderdash.) With Morris's strong recommendation of Hamilton's financial acumen, the general jumped at the opportunity to add his surrogate son to his new team.[8]

By the end of May, if not earlier, Hamilton was confident that he would be the new administration's finance minister. He certainly wasted no time starting to try to put the country's financial house in order. Hamilton realized that the federal government needed to implement a number of important policies, if not all at once then in fairly rapid succession. Foremost were policies having to do with sources of revenue. Without this, the new government would fail as miserably as had the Continental Congress under the Articles of Confederation. On July 4, 1789, of all days, Congress passed its first revenue act. The bill, which was largely the work of James Madison and Thomas FitzSimons of Pennsylvania, imposed specific duties on a wide variety of imported goods. For example, the act laid a tax of 10 cents on "all distilled spirits of Jamaica proof, imported from any kingdom or country whatsoever," a tax of 1 cent per pound on brown sugars, and a duty of 50 cents on each pair of boots. It also levied ad valorem taxes of 15 percent on coaches, chaises and the like; 10 percent on gunpowder, buckles, windows, and other fineries; 7.5 percent on saddles, leather gloves, ready made millinery and clothing, brushes, and other middling goods and 5 percent on "all other goods, wares and merchandise" with a handful of exceptions. Despite numerous claims to the contrary, the measure was a revenue, not a protective, tariff. In other words, its main aim was to raise funds for the use of the government, not to increase prices in order to give domestic producers a competitive advantage. Items with higher duties, ad valorem or specific, were thought to possess inelastic demand. In other words, they were luxury goods demanded mainly by rich people willing and able to pay an extra 10 or 15 percent for foreign fripperies. Domestic producers certainly did gain, especially from the higher ad valorem tariffs, but that was hardly the intent of the legislation. In fact, if the tariff rates had been too high they would have discouraged legal imports, encouraged smuggling, and ultimately decreased government revenues.[9]

Two weeks later, on July 20, Congress passed another revenue act, a tonnage duty, that discriminated heavily in favor of American-built and -owned vessels. Ships built in the United States or wholly owned by U.S. citizens were charged 6 cents per ton per entry in an American port. Ships built in the United States but owned in whole or part by foreigners had to pony up 30 cents a ton, and all other ships were charged 50 cents per ton per clearance. Vessels engaged in the domestic coastal trade and fishing, however, had to pay the duty only once per year rather than with every clearance. Both revenue acts would have been dead letters without an act passed at the end of July that established customs districts and a system of collectors, inspectors, gaugers, measurers, and other officials. Getting the system just right was important because tariff collection was far from costless. Customs men had to be paid, and well at that, lest they turn crooked. Sundry "contingent expenses" also had to be met. Compared with direct taxes the collections costs were low, however, provided merchants and captains cooperated, which they generally did when tariff rates were not excessive.[10]

Passing revenue laws was one thing, but actually collecting significant amounts of revenue was quite another. With little revenue flowing into the new government's coffers in the summer of 1789, Hamilton was eager to assume his duties in order to get things moving. It wasn't until September 2 that the bill creating the Treasury Department finally became law, in large measure because Congress wanted to ensure that the department would be a microcosm of the government itself, energetic but incapable of usurping the sovereignty of the people. Its solution was ingenious. The Treasury would be led by a single secretary with wide-ranging policy powers, but its day-to-day operations would fall to an assistant or vice treasury secretary, a treasurer, a register, a comptroller, and an auditor, each of whom had incentives to monitor the activities of the others for indications of funny business. Shortly after passage of the act, on Friday, September 11, Washington officially nominated Hamilton treasury secretary. The Senate confirmed him that very day and American financial modernization was off to the races. Instead of waiting until Monday to begin work, the Little Lion, as Hamilton was called, roared all weekend. He borrowed $150,000 from two banks to tide over the government until the collection system was humming, penned instructions to his subordinates, and discussed the debt America owed France with her minister, Comte de Moustier.[11]

On September 21, the House of Representatives directed the new treasury secretary to prepare a report on the national debt for its next meeting, in January. Over the ensuing weeks and months, Hamilton handled his quotidian duties while simultaneously penning a massive report on public credit and sketching out a grand plan to reform and reinvigorate the nation's entire economy. He was able to do the equivalent of three jobs at once because he worked hard for long hours and his administrative skills were sublime. Coffee in hand, he had a knack for running large, complex organizations with the utmost efficiency. To this day, administrators could learn from his enlightened policies, which included discovery and implementation of best practices, bilateral information transparency, 360-degree responsibility and evaluation, and just about every other concept to buzz administrative circles in the last two decades. Many Americans were *good* administrators. Hamilton was a *great* administrator and also a first-rate policy maker and statesman, a combination as rare as an albino moose. Most people who can pay meticulous attention to detail can do little else of import; they can't see the proverbial forest for the trees. If thrown into a policy role, they drown

> Hamilton was a *great* administrator and also a first-rate policy maker and statesman, a combination as rare as an albino moose.

in a quicksand of minutia. Not so Hamilton, whose mind and actions constantly flowed between policy and implementation, mundane detail and stroke of genius. A case in point was his survey of October 15, 1789, which solicited information on shipping from customs collectors, merchants, and others in the know. By the time he had digested the flood of responses, Hamilton knew more about that aspect of the American economy than anyone alive, and he put that knowledge to good use in the years to come. Hamilton would soon also come to know more about American governmental finances than anyone else, including Robert Morris himself.[12]

Everybody knew the situation was a mess. Most war debts, inflated to outrageous levels by depreciation of bills of credit, had been reduced to specie values, a fairly simple mathematical chore once a depreciation schedule had been settled upon. Besides that, though, little headway had been made. Left over from the war were two seemingly intractable problems, a mind-boggling array of certificates of different maturities, interest rates, and the like, and state government accounts that were in utter disarray. It was not clear who owed what to whom or why. Consider, for example, the claims of Samuel Wood of upstate New York:

> Some Time in May 1781 Genl. Deportale Quartered at my House two Months with his aides. [How many aides? What did the quartering entail? Food, drink, and horse forage? Cleaning and cooking? How can someone stay for two months in May?]
>
> Last Spring I had a Field of about ten Acres laid open by the Army, five of which were Meadow which I lost. [Does that mean that the other 5 acres were undamaged? Was the meadow destroyed forever or was just that year's crop damaged? What was the economic value of that loss at that time and place?]
>
> I supplied Saml. Evans Forrage Master with Ten Cords of Firewood during the Time he was at my House as P Certificates. [How long was he at Wood's house? Did the market value of the firewood vary over that time?]

Other problems, like the "place where the Debt was contracted," were also sticky given faulty memories and incentives to lie. Rather than try to sort out all the details as a simple administrative mind might, the big-picture, policy-making statesman side of Hamilton urged the more radical path laid out in his *Report on Public Credit*. Dated January 9, 1790, but communicated in writing to the House of Representatives, which insisted that Hamilton not personally address them because that would seem too

British, on the fourteenth, the report was so long and complex that the House ordered it printed. Soon after, excerpts appeared in newspapers nationwide.[13]

Broadly speaking, the Revolutionary War debt came in three flavors, foreign, national, and state, each of which had its own unique requirements. Almost everyone agreed that the foreign debt had to be repaid, as Hamilton argued in his report, "according to the precise terms of the contracts." The national government did not have the resources at present to do so, Hamilton explained, unless it could negotiate new foreign loans, on better terms, to give it breathing room for a decade or so. This part of Hamilton's plan was an unqualified success. Between 1790 and 1794, the Treasury borrowed millions of dollars, mostly in Holland's capital market, and used it to pay off its wartime obligations to France, Spain, and earlier Dutch investors. It serviced the new bonds religiously, paying them off when due in the first decade of the nineteenth century. By raising America's credit abroad, the operation made possible the purchase of Louisiana in 1804.[14]

Through the years some people had hinted that the national and state governments should repudiate their domestic debts. Hamilton demurred on the basis of both expediency and morality. "States, like individuals, who observe their engagements, are respected and trusted," he argued, "while the reverse is the fate of those, who pursue an opposite conduct." Moreover, if the government could not borrow, or could only borrow small sums on ruinous terms, it would not be able to defend the people from foreign invasion or domestic insurrection. "Loans in times of public danger, especially from foreign war," he reminded the members of the House, "are found an indispensable resource, even to the wealthiest" of countries. The defaults that had occurred under "a defective constitution" were to be regretted and rectified as quickly as possible due to "immutable principles of moral obligation." Repudiation was expropriation, plain and simple.

It was also in the country's economic self-interest to pay its debts in an honorable fashion, Hamilton argued. Proper servicing and repayment of the national debt, he explained, would lead inexorably to "great and invaluable ends" including promotion of "the encreasing respectability of the American name" and the restoration of justice. Funding the debt would also "furnish new resources both to agriculture and commerce … cement more closely the union of the states … add to their security against foreign attack," and last but not least "establish public order on the basis of an upright and liberal policy." Increasing the value of public securities would enrich their current holders—Hamilton steadfastly refused to countenance discrimination in favor of original holders—but also everyone else because it would drive interest rates lower. That, in turn, would "restore landed property to its due value" and allow "both the public and individuals to borrow on easier and cheaper terms… . From the combination of these effects," Hamilton concluded, "additional aids will be furnished to labour, to industry, and to arts of every kind."

The mouths of the antifederalists were already agape, but Hamilton unleashed a bombshell. "An assumption of the debts of the particular states by the union, and a like provision for them, as for those of the union," he claimed, "will be a measure of sound policy and substantial justice." And then another: a final settlement of accounts between the national and state governments would be made. And another: unpaid interest, the "arrears of interest" in the lingo of the day, ought to be "provided for on an equal footing with the principal." And then, in a final bombshell, the treasury secretary advocated reducing the interest due to domestic creditors from 6 (generally) to about 4 percent. So, not only did Hamilton want the national government to begin to pay interest and principal on the $11.7 million it owed to foreign potentates and investors at full interest, he wanted to service, at about 4 percent, $40.4 million worth of IOUs, including national Revolutionary War certificates and the back interest due thereon, and another $21.5 to $25 or so million in state obligations, including principal and interest.

The rationale for assumption of state debts by the national government Hamilton laid bare. First, assumption would "contribute in an eminent degree to an orderly, stable, and satisfactory arrangement of the national finances" by reducing uncertainty and information requirements and increasing the liquidity of federal bond markets. Second, it would prevent the states and federal government from competing for revenue. Third, assumption would impose, if not lower taxes, more uniform ones. Finally, in arguments privately made, Hamilton said that economies of scale would allow the national government to service the unified debt at less total expense than the states could.[15]

The payment of about 4 percent to domestic creditors owed 6 percent, Hamilton pointed out, was, though not strictly necessary, highly prudent. The interest due on the foreign debt was over $500,000 per year and that on the domestic debt, national and state, exceeded $4 million per year. The government could raise that much revenue, Hamilton hinted, but quickly added that he believed "that, to make it, would require the extension of taxation to a degree, and to objects, which the true interest of the public creditors forbids." In other words, he didn't want high taxes because he knew that they would hurt an economy still reeling from war, trade disruption, and an absolute dearth of cash. High taxes could have negative political repercussions, too. Of course, the government's necessity did not make the reduction just, even if it was for the common good. But, Hamilton argued, the reduction of interest would not be a partial repudiation of the debt because conversion of the old certificates to his new bonds would be entirely voluntary "in fact, as well as in name." He therefore proposed new loans that would be payable in the old certificates at ratios that would reduce the government's overall interest payments to about 4 percent.[16]

Hamilton realized, shrewdly, that most certificate holders would give up some interest to own new bonds that traded in liquid markets, punctually paid interest quarterly, and were not redeemable at the government's pleasure rather than hang on to the old stuff, which was difficult to trade, paid interest less frequently, and could be redeemed at the Treasury's whim. "Those who are commonly creditors of a nation," Hamilton knew, "are, generally speaking, enlightened men." "When a candid and fair appeal is made to them," he continued, "they will understand their true interest too well to refuse their concurrence."[17]

To ensure that interest would indeed be paid punctually, Hamilton in his report urged Congress to lay some additional taxes on commodities, like wines, spirits, teas, and coffee, for which demand was relatively inelastic, or as Hamilton put it, "luxuries [that] lay the strongest hold on the attachments of mankind, which (especially when confirmed by habit) are not easily alienated from them … . It will be sound policy," he correctly noted, "to carry the duties upon articles of this kind as high as will be consistent with the practicability of a safe collection." In addition, the consumption of large quantities of "ardent spirits" was "pernicious" because it injured "health and morals," creating negative externalities that injured "the economy of the community." To discourage a shift to domestic production of hard liquors, Hamilton suggested the imposition of an excise tax on spirits. To discourage smuggling, he suggested establishing a second line of defense, at the dealer level. Traditionally, an import that was successfully brought ashore was safe from further scrutiny or risk. Internal controls would increase the risk to smugglers and decrease their exertions proportionally.

> "The proper funding of the present debt," Hamilton concluded, "will render it a national blessing."

"The proper funding of the present debt," Hamilton concluded, "will render it a national blessing." Hamilton then added a big qualification that many scholars have missed, noting that the maxim that "public debts are public benefits" was "liable to dangerous abuse" and should not invite "prodigality." Careful administration of taxation was so instrumental to "rendering public credit immortal," Hamilton argued, "that he ardently wishes to see it incorporated, as a fundamental maxim, in the system of public credit of the United States, that the creation of debt should always be accompanied with the means of extinguishment." In other words, no borrowing without taxation. (Aye. This seems like a joke today.) Far from desiring to render the national debt perpetual, as his critics often claimed, Hamilton encouraged Congress to establish a sinking fund out of the revenues of the post office, which was expected to run a substantial surplus. (Another cruel joke today!) Unlike the British sinking fund, Hamilton's would be inviolably applied to purchase government bonds trading below their "true value." Such purchases were win-win-win because the seller received cash, the government paid off some of its debt cheaply, and the remaining public creditors benefited from the price support. Once the debt was funded and at par, foreigners would make large purchases, freeing up domestic resources for higher-risk but also higher-yielding investments in "agriculture, commerce, and manufactures." Finally, Hamilton argued that the faster Congress acted on his recommendations, the better it would be for public credit and the national economy.

❧

Hamilton would be proven right about most of this, but not before a fight, or rather a series of them. In January 1790, his report was still just that, a report. It could not become policy unless Congress and the president gave their assent and there were no assurances that they would, especially given that the report caused an immense amount of commentary, some positive and some negative. Maryland gentleman farmer and lawyer John Beale Bordley, for example, published a little pamphlet backing Hamilton's funding scheme. "Under this efficacious, mild, and free government," Bordley wrote, "we have now before us a report of the price of her freedom, and of the means for satisfying her creditors which is … clear, and promising … [and] honorable to the abilities and integrity of the Secretary of her Treasury." "Scarce a head in New York that is not ready to burst with a plan," one politician noted in early February. By mid-month, Manhattan was, according to another observer, "all in a flame about funding, nothing else heard even among women and children." That flame soon engulfed the bridge between Hamilton and the other major half of the Publius team, James Madison.[18]

By mid-month, Manhattan was, according to another observer, "all in a flame about funding, nothing else heard even among women and children." That flame soon engulfed the bridge between Hamilton and the other major half of the Publius team, James Madison.

The main battle lines were drawn even before Hamilton's report was made public. Soon after the Constitution's ratification, rumors began to swirl about precisely when and how the new government would handle the nation's debt problem. Sentiments were largely bullish. In his report, Hamilton noted that securities prices had almost doubled over the course of 1789 and that "the intelligence from abroad announces effects proportionably favorable to our national credit," claims verified by careful scholarship. Appreciation of public securities caught everyone's attention, but what some heralded as great news others viewed with horror. Massachusetts yeoman William Manning, apparently an average

Joe in every way save that he ruminated deeply on matters of political economy, proclaimed that he could not "but view with abhorrence all the arguments that have as yet been offered in favor of paying the whole sum of the debt to its present holders." In fact, the failure of Hamilton's plan to endorse discrimination, to forsake "widows, orphans, soldiers, and other distressed public creditors" and favor the greedy speculator, was the single most potent criticism directed against it.[19]

According to proponents of discrimination, securities had moved from south to north, west to east, rural to city folk, the poor and uninformed to the rich and well-connected, from, in a word, the deserving to the undeserving. Ownership of the debt certainly became much more concentrated after the war, the cumulative effect of many small sellers and a relatively few large purchasers. Like many other Americans, Manning worried that speculators would reap windfall profits if they were paid in full. That was an awful prospect given that speculators were considered by many to be vile critters, a prejudice that became imbued in the American mind during the colonial period. "A Crisis of public distress is the proper time for this kind of vermin to swarm," scowled Pelatiah Webster, a Yale-educated Philadelphia businessman and author, then in his sixties, "like flies about a sore, or crows around a carcase [sic]."[20]

Speculators, another critic of Hamilton's plan claimed, "strike at the roots of industry and economy, create habits of idleness, and open wide the door to knavery." To see speculators "set up their carriages, and run into other courses of idleness and pleasures, luxury and dissipation," wailed Webster, while the soldier and sailor went essentially unpaid would incite civil unrest and actually undermine public credit. One critic went so far as to call for national bonds to be inscribed with "1. The bloody arms of a soldier. 2. The wooden leg of a soldier. 3. A soldier's heart pierced with a bayonet," all to remind speculators of those "grossly defrauded and injured" by the funding system. Stories, presumably true, of shysters who defrauded soldiers of their Revolutionary War IOUs found wide circulation. In one such story, a master of scam lies to a war hero struggling to feed his wife and four children in order to bilk him out of his pay certificates for a mere $11. Although a staunch supporter of the Constitution and a nationalist, Webster also moaned aloud about the plight of the "soldiers and other public creditors who really and actually supported the burden of the late war," and whipped Congress with the Golden Rule. "Gentlemen, please do as you would be done by," he pleaded. A moving sentiment that was, to be sure, but a far cry short of the mark, because the rights of subsequent holders also had to be considered.[21]

"The original creditors of the government," Manning argued, "acted more like persons beset with robbers and prudently delivered up their purses rather than their lives." True enough, but the culprit was the government, not the purchasers of the securities (at least not those who acted lawfully and ethically by offering pecuniary relief to the sellers). For example, Thomas Jefferson argued in December 1781 that the government of Virginia would "never enter on account" due to the "multiplicity & intricacy of the accounts" and the "immense crowd of private losses by depreciation incurred while the treasury was without money." Wronging the current holders, who did no wrong, would only further undermine the government's credibility. As one observer noted, speculators were not the evil. Rather, the real villains were anemic government, low money supplies, and high interest rates, 25 to 30 percent for many types of loans. "Devoid of national credit," explained Pennsylvania jurists James Wilson and Thomas McKean, "we saw our public securities melt in the hands of the holders, like snow before the sun." In fact, the speculators were great patriots for showing faith in the government when others valued a few coins—and speculators did pay in specie—over its bonds. "We differ exceedingly on the head of Public Securitys," Manhattan securities broker and speculator John Delafield explained to a correspondent in early 1784. "You have no confidence, I a great deal." In the end, Delafield was rewarded, one of at least three New York speculators thought to "have made very great Fortunes" in return for their support of government credit at its lowest ebb. Casting blame on speculators was worse than blaming the ocean for a tsunami; it was more like chastising the levees. "A Speculator is a man," noted one contemporary, "who profits by his experience and foresight. Is it criminal to possess these qualities?"[22]

Casting blame on speculators was worse than blaming the ocean for a tsunami; it was more like chastising the levees.

A critique of nondiscrimination that hit closer to the mark was set forth by Pelatiah Webster, who argued convincingly that soldiers and other original creditors should not be understood to have been paid because the certificates they received were worth little in the market at the time of issuance and the "universal practice among all men" was to credit the market value of payments, giving "no regard at all ... to the nominal value." Webster's reasoning suggested that both the original and subsequent holders should be paid off in full, but nobody, including Hamilton, wanted to augment the debt that much. There was also the problem of moral hazard. As Edward Carrington tried to explain to Madison: "After one instance of a discrimination, since you are still to give out paper, is it to be expected that a depreciation will not take place again upon an apprehension that the same thing will be done again?" Who would buy the government's new bonds if they believed the government might again make ex post contractual changes?[23]

Another problem was the practical one of how discrimination would work. It was a much more intractable problem than proponents of the policy, including Webster, admitted. Who could prove who sold what to whom, when, and on what terms? Even if the information was cheaply available, on what basis should different types of holders be compensated? Not all speculators, it turns out, were winners. In the Deep South, for example, many certificates had already changed hands by 1783. Speculators who bought in then, though at low prices, earned less than the market rate of return. Market interest rates were very high in the 1780s and the debts were often not serviced until much later, in some cases not for a decade, so speculators would have been better off if they had not purchased at all. Indeed, one observer in 1786 noted that many speculators "are obliged to submit to a very considerable loss."

By 1787, most original holders nationwide had given up their IOUs for whatever they could get, which was not much given high market interest rates and the government's poor credit. After passage of the Constitution, speculators—securities traders of all stripes, really, including rich foreigners—mostly fed off each other, not the downtrodden. For example, wealthy plantation owner William Lee of Virginia willingly took his Continental loan office certificates to New York for sale in 1789 before embarking on an extended tour of Europe. (It is difficult indeed to feel for Lee, especially given that later he was one of Virginia's most active investors in federal bonds.) And of course in the process of buying, purchasers of Revolutionary securities furthered the nation's credit and aided the economy by driving interest rates downward.[24]

Nevertheless, many critics of Hamilton's report pulled out old-country party critiques of the British national debt, arguing that the proposed funding system would create a system of political corruption and avaricious placemen who defrauded the poor of their last farthing. That many congressmen were involved in securities speculation did not help matters. Stories of legislators with purses grown fat on public securities induced Philadelphia physician Benjamin Rush to call Hamilton's funding plan "highway robbery." In seven years, he predicted, the system would turn America into Britain and prove "that revolutions ... are the *rage* of the many for the benefit of a *few*" (italics in original).[25]

Nor did it help that some Northern speculators swept through the South in late 1789 and early 1790, before news of funding and assumption had reached the region, buying as many of the remaining government IOUs for as little as they could. For example, 79 nonresidents owned $837,660 worth of Virginia state debt in 1790. Only 2 were from states south of Virginia. The rest were foreigners, Marylanders, New Yorkers, or Pennsylvanians. It was much the same story in North Carolina and South Carolina, where by 1790 $1.51 million and $2.2 million worth of state IOUs, respectively, were held by nonresidents, including foreigners and Americans from Georgia to Massachusetts. All told, 249 nonresidents owned $4.6 million of the securities of those 3 states. The vast majority of those nonresidents, who owned almost three-quarters' worth of that $4.6 million, hailed from New York and Pennsylvania. The flow of securities to New York, Philadelphia, and to a lesser extent Boston is not surprising, as those cities had the most liquid markets. That means that securities were worth a little more there because they could be sold more quickly and cheaply than elsewhere. As political economist Henry C. Adams later noted: "Debt paper will naturally flow to that market where there is free capital to absorb it." Nevertheless, the misuse of inside information was widely suspected and was particularly infuriating to southern sensibilities, at least when they had hold of the smelly end of the stick. (Fifteen years later none other than Thomas Jefferson used his inside information regarding the embargo to successfully speculate in the Richmond tobacco market, but no one proclaimed the republic at an end due to his timely sales.)[26]

Another old-country party canard, that the debt would become perpetual, seemed obvious to many because, as Manning pointed out, it was "always the art of the Few so to manage" the debt "as to take the whole of the revenues (let it be more or less) to pay the interest and support government" rather than pay down the debt. Instead of funding the debt, Manning argued, the government ought to monetize it by paying off domestic creditors with bills of credit. Given the dearth of money in circulation, that plan may have worked had Americans not so recently and strongly felt the sting of the death of their colonial, state, and national bills of credit.[27]

Hamilton's funding plan faced other objections, some made in public discussions, some in Congress, some in both. Some critics thought the plan went too far, that the debt could be, if not repaid, then reduced by issuing bills of credit, while others thought that it fell short because the terms of original contracts were not strictly kept. Both bulls (those who wanted securities prices to rise) and bears (those who wanted them to decline) trembled because they could not discern what would happen if the plan was implemented. Land speculators were aghast because the plan would ruin their favorite game, buying hundreds, thousands, and in some cases hundreds of thousands of acres of frontier lands with depreciated Revolutionary War certificates. Others saw in Hamilton's plan nothing but national power mongering, higher taxes, the enrichment of idle speculators, and some, strangely enough, a plot to abolish slavery. An empowered national government was a threat to the peculiar institution, a point brought home by petitions from Quakers and the Pennsylvania Abolition Society asking for abolition of the slave trade and slavery itself.[28]

James Madison essentially sided with Manning and other populist critics, fighting Hamilton's plan in Congress at every turn. Why he did so is not entirely clear.

James Madison essentially sided with Manning and other populist critics, fighting Hamilton's plan in Congress at every turn. Why he did so is not entirely clear. In fact, he had originally opposed discrimination and the schemes of discrimination and assumption that he proposed, if implemented, would have enlarged the national debt considerably, a position difficult to reconcile with his conviction that "a public debt is a public curse." New Jersey representative Elias Boudinot said that Madison's support of discrimination did more credit to his heart than to his head. Indeed, Madison's sense of justice may have interceded. Perhaps, though, he merely wanted to support the desires of his constituents in central Virginia, who, like most agrarians, for some reason got upset when others' wallets grew fat, even if it wasn't demonstrably at their expense. Maybe Jefferson, who was an idiot when it came to economics and finance but a savant when it came to almost everything else, corrupted his thinking. But then again, maybe not. For all his nationalist pretensions, Madison may have feared the power that funding and assumption would give the national government and presumably sap from his "native country," Virginia.[29]

Surprised, betrayed, and concerned at his friend's turn, Hamilton essentially disowned Madison, whom he claimed showed a "womanish attachment to France and a womanish resentment against Great Britain." Those were harsh barbs pointed at a man who as late as the summer of 1789 had ambled about Manhattan with Hamilton, playing with pet monkeys. Fisher Ames of Massachusetts also had choice words for Hamilton's erstwhile friend. Madison, Ames claimed, "is so much a Virginian; so afraid that the mob will cry out, *crucify him*; sees Patrick Henry's shade at his bedside every night … and perhaps thinks it unpleasant to come in as an auxiliary to support another's plan" (italics in original).[30]

Although now effeminate in the eyes of Hamilton and his friends, little Jemmy managed to induce the House to debate discrimination for two weeks before his antidiscrimination motion met defeat, 36 to 13, with 9 of its supporters hailing from Virginia. Madison "kept himself wrapt up in mystery," Ames complained, "and starts new objections daily." Through a series of shrewd parliamentary ploys and, as John Adams called them, "stupid motions," Madison managed to stall passage of a funding bill through the end of July. Speculators rejoiced because the delays allowed them to buy largely of depreciated certificates, taking full advantage of temporary dips occasioned by the twists and turns in the debate. Hamilton, readers may recall, urged Congress to act quickly but thanks to Madison it did anything but. According to historian Forrest McDonald: "Before he was through Madison would put more profits into the hands of speculators than Hamilton could have done by inviting them to help themselves to the Treasury."[31]

Hamilton, who often sat in the gallery during the debates on funding, and his allies, like Ames, responded to the criticisms of Madison and others in measured terms. There was much good in the nation's indebtedness, though Hamilton readily conceded that there existed a tipping point beyond which

Hamilton readily conceded that there existed a tipping point beyond which additions to the national debt would be economically and politically deleterious. "Where this critical point is cannot be pronounced; but it is impossible to believe," he assured, "that there is not such a point."

additions to the national debt would be economically and politically deleterious. "Where this critical point is cannot be pronounced; but it is impossible to believe," he assured, "that there is not such a point." While Hamilton clearly wanted to repay the debt eventually, he saw no need to rush because repaying it sooner than later would necessitate ruinous taxes and deprive the economy of liquid capital. Unlike Adam Smith and his followers, Hamilton and his backers believed that the issuance of bonds by government augmented rather than destroyed capital. Government received cash from the loan, while purchasers received a bond that they could easily and cheaply convert back into cash by selling it to another investor. Moreover, the debt helped to create positive net present value projects:

> Though the funded debt is not in the first instance, an absolute increase in Capital, or an augmentation of real wealth; yet by serving as a new power in the operations of industry, it has within certain bounds a tendency to increase the real wealth of the Community, in like manner as money borrowed by a thrifty farmer, to be laid out in the improvement of his farm may, in the end, add to his Stock of real riches.

Importantly, Hamilton drew a distinction between the effects of a funded debt and of an unfunded one. Only the latter, he claimed, created "a pernicious drain of our cash from the channels of productive industry," by contributing "to the scarcity of money." A funded debt, by contrast, increased the money supply by serving as a close substitute for cash in "the principal transactions of business."[32]

During the debates, Madison had managed to get assumption, the nationalization of state debts, removed from the funding bill, and Hamilton's friends never were quite numerous enough to get it reinserted, so the whole measure hung suspended. Opposition to assumption came from many quarters. Ideologues opposed it for the same reasons that they opposed any sort of funding plan, because they foresaw iniquity rather than prosperity springing from it. Robert R. Livingston, for example, feared "a careless assumption of new debts before we have complied with our present engagements" and an expansion of the pernicious practices of "stock-jobbing." Land speculators were against it because it would ruin their plans to obtain huge tracts of western lands on the cheap. Those who owned mostly federal obligations did not want assumption because it might impair the national government's ability to pay them their due. Large owners of Pennsylvania's well-funded state debt, like manufacturer and securities speculator John Nicholson, saw in assumption a heavy-handed attempt to aggrandize the federal government at the expense of the states. Still others wanted assumption tied to the sticky issue of the final settlement of state Revolutionary War accounts with the national government. Virginia in particular felt slighted because it had already repaid a large portion of its debt. And yet Virginians trembled because the Old Dominion's accounts were in such disarray the state might be found a debtor to the nation, or not as large a creditor as her politicians hoped.[33]

Had assumption been the only thing that members of Congress cared about, it might never have passed. But another issue, the permanent location of the national capital, interceded. Some wanted it in Manhattan, others in different parts of Pennsylvania, and still others along the Potomac in Virginia. Sixteen sites in all, from Annapolis to Trenton, jockeyed for position, much like modern contests for hosting the Olympics. Gridlock as tight as that over assumption ensued. To break both impasses, which some believed were becoming dangerous daggers pointed at the breast of the young union, various vote-trading schemes were attempted. "Without a firm basis for public credit," Fisher Ames warned in May, "I can scarcely expect the government will last long." George Washington, too, was "dangerously sick," casting additional gloom over the scene. Finally, in late June a series of compromises and vote swaps brokered by Thomas Jefferson and involving, among others, Senator Robert Morris, Hamilton, and Madison, made assumption a reality, declared Philadelphia the temporary capital, fattened Virginia's settlement balance, and placed the permanent capital on the banks of the Potomac.[34]

"An Act for Making Provision for the Debt of the United States" finally became law on August 4, 1790. In its final form, the law inviolably appropriated specific taxes for the repayment of the principal and interest of specific debts, established a sinking fund out of the proceeds of western land sales, authorized the president to borrow $12 million to consolidate the foreign debt, and, effective October 1, opened a new domestic loan payable in Revolutionary War certificates of a national character, including loan office certificates; indents; bonds issued by the Register of the Treasury (registered debt); IOUs issued by various commissioners for adjusting the accounts of the quartermaster, commissary, hospital, clothing, and marine departments; sundry miscellaneous types of notes; and Continental bills of credit. The last-named item was received at 100 to 1, their official market value in April 1781; all others were taken at their specie value on their date of issuance. In return, subscribers to the loan received new bonds. For every $100 principal value of old IOUs subscribed, they received $66.67 (two-thirds) of new bonds that paid 6 percent interest on a quarterly basis effective at the end of March 1791 and $33.33 (one-third) of bonds that would pay the same effective at the beginning of 1801, an implicit yield of about 5.1 percent (assuming a 6 percent discount rate). The law also gave the government the option after one year of paying 8 percent per year, 2 percent being applied to the principal, a point to which we shall return. For the interest component of old IOUs and subscriptions made in indents, which were issued en masse in lieu of interest payments in the 1780s, investors received new bonds that paid 3 percent per annum quarterly, effective the last day of March 1791, and were redeemable at the government's pleasure. (Interest on the old certificates was to be capitalized through December 1790.) Old state IOUs were funded at different ratios, yielding investors 4.4 percent on par value. For every $100 in principal and interest, state creditors received $44.44 (four-ninths) of 6 percent bonds, $22.22 (two-ninths) of deferred 6 percents, and $33.33 (three-ninths) of 3 percent bonds. The law further stipulated that subscriptions were to be received by a commissioner in each state who would cause to be recorded the details of each subscriber's account, including transfers and interest payments.[35]

Thus were legally created the Sixes, Deferred Sixes, and Threes that formed the backbone of the first national debt and the records that allow their histories to be detailed. Actual creation of the bonds, however, was left to market forces. As Hamilton had requested in his report, the new loan was voluntary. "Nothing in this act," read section 9 of the law, "shall be construed in any wise to alter, abridge, or impair the rights of those creditors of the United States who shall not subscribe to the said loan ... but the said contracts and rights shall remain in full force and virtue." The only caveat was that old certificates had to be registered before interest could be paid on them. The registration process reduced the old IOUs to specie value and helped to decrease the chance of counterfeiting, which apparently was quite common. Many investors took full advantage of the voluntary aspect of the law, confirming Hamilton's claim that they were uncoerced de facto as well as de jure. Early on, many prudent holders of old certificates undoubtedly waited to see how the market would value the new bonds, exercising an implicit call option when prices were high enough to induce them to get into the game. Others may have paused because Virginia's House of Delegates in November 1790 resolved that assumption was unconstitutional and that the funding system was dangerous. (There was more backroom political smoke than fires of rebellion in those resolves but that wasn't immediately clear.)[36]

> Many investors took full advantage of the voluntary aspect of the law, confirming Hamilton's claim that they were uncoerced de facto as well as de jure.

Other early holdouts were upset at the interest reduction. Holders of Pickering notes, issued by Quartermaster General Timothy Pickering, could for example point out that their IOUs plainly stated that if not paid on their due date the principal "shall afterwards bear an Interest of Six per Cent. per Annum until paid." Still others were likely just plain stubborn or dilatory. The original law stipulated that the new loan would close after a year but subsequent acts extended the subscription period until the end of 1797, though the vast majority of the old debt had been subscribed to the new loans by the beginning of 1795. All told, the national government assumed $22.5 million worth of state debts, $18.3 million in bonds paid to individuals, and $4.2 million in bonds paid to the seven states determined to be net creditors to the national government. The six debtor states, in the tradition of the Articles of Confederation, never paid up and the federal government never forced them to. Some state debts, including outstanding bills of credit, still existed but for the most part they were small and readily paid off. For the next several decades, the states were free of long-term debt, save for a few issues during the War of 1812, the aftermath of the Panic of 1819, and New York's financing of its famous canal. Low government expenditures, low taxes, and significant revenue from state-owned assets prevailed until the early 1830s.[37]

On August 12, just eight days after passage of funding and assumption, Congress beefed up the sinking fund with a law entitled "An Act Making Provision for the Reduction of the Public Debt." Designed to repay the debt, save the government finance charges, and raise the value of public securities, the sinking fund was by this law endowed with any funds left from tariff and tonnage duties after interest payments on the debt had been made. Those funds it was empowered to use to purchase government bonds "at its market price, if not exceeding the par or true value thereof." Composed of the chief justice of the Supreme Court, the secretaries of state and treasury, the president of the Senate, and the attorney general, the sinking fund committee could, with the approbation of the president, make purchases "in such manner, and under such restrictions as shall appear to them best calculated to fulfill the intent of this act" so long as the purchases were made "openly, and with due regard to the equal benefit of the several states." In addition to helping to sink or pay down the principal of the debt, the sinking fund served, as we'll soon see, an important secondary function during periods of financial distress.[38]

❦

Most of the rest of Hamilton's grand plan also met staunch resistance in the legislature but eventual widespread acceptance by investors. A few days after passage of the funding and assumption bill, Congress adjourned but not before the House instructed Hamilton to make yet another report on public credit and have it ready when the House reconvened in December. Hamilton again obliged, in spades, by working hard and smart. He produced not one but three reports, the first on raising additional taxes, the second on establishing a national bank, and the third on creating a national mint.

The tax report that Hamilton submitted on December 13, 1790, reiterated earlier proposals, including an excise on distilled spirits, while also providing Congress a lecture on theories of taxation. To take the bite out of the excise, which many Americans feared would lead to the creation and perpetuation of British-like placemen, Hamilton suggested limiting their powers of search and retaining trial by jury. He suggested paying tax collectors a 5 percent commission instead of a salary to ensure that they did their jobs diligently. He argued that excise taxes were necessary because tariffs could be raised only so high before they began to encourage smuggling and to result in decreased revenue as people imported fewer goods. Moreover, international trade was highly cyclical, so a steady domestic source of income was imperative. The other major potential source of domestic tax revenue, federal taxes on land, Hamilton wished held in reserve. And the final line of defense, the sale of government lands in the west, still lay largely untapped, like, as a contemporary called it, "a precious mine of national wealth." Prices for the lands were low and demand weak, so they produced "no present profit" but nevertheless helped to secure the nation's credit.[39]

The very next day, Hamilton submitted his famous report on a national bank. His comments on the unreliability of tariff revenues helped to set the stage. The national government, he argued, needed an institution that would lend it large sums for short terms to help it over temporary imbalances between revenues and expenditures. Existing banks had been helpful but they were too small and their interests were too distinct from those of the government to be relied upon during emergencies or financial panics. When flush, the Treasury would need a safe place to store its money. It also needed an efficient way of making interest payments on the domestic national debt four times a year. A new bank, partially owned by the national government and beholden to it for its charter, could meet all those needs and more, Hamilton argued. Capitalized at $10 million, $2 million of which would be owned initially by the federal government, the national bank would be far larger than the other three banks then in existence *combined*. It could therefore easily regulate them and spread its own branches around the nation. Best of all, stockholders could pay for

> Capitalized at $10 million, $2 million of which would be owned initially by the federal government, the national bank would be far larger than the other three banks then in existence *combined*.

part of their shares with government bonds. That would have the double virtue of increasing demand for Hamilton's new Sixes, Deferred Sixes, and Threes and endowing the bank with liquid and remunerative secondary reserves. To ensure that the bank, which he styled the Bank of the United States, did not become a behemoth monopoly, the treasury secretary was allowed to examine its books and place the government's deposits elsewhere if he saw fit. Foreign stockholders could not vote in its elections, director rotation was mandatory, and the bank's charter was limited to 20 years. Finally, state governments were free to charter as many competing banks as they wished. Genius is not a strong enough word for this plan.[40]

His third report, on the mint, Hamilton sent to Congress on January 28, 1791. The mint was not truly necessary, because Americans were accustomed to using foreign coins and banknotes and deposits were increasingly in use. Nevertheless, a national mint was a symbol of fiscal orthodoxy for European countries, so Hamilton was loathe to go without one. The most important part of the report, and the act, which passed into law on April 2, 1792, was that it defined the U.S. dollar in terms of gold and silver and made the dollar the government's unit of account. (A subsequent act passed February 9, 1793, rated foreign coins in terms of the U.S. dollar unit of account.) The U.S. Mint itself was a nonstarter, an inconsequential institution that produced a mere trickle of coins until well into the nineteenth century. "Every cent coined at the mint," it was said, "cost the government half a dollar." That was partisan hyperbole, to be sure, but most observers conceded that the mint's expenses were "very great; without a corresponding benefit."[41]

Somewhat ironically, the mint was uncontroversial, eliciting little response in Congress other than the usual legislative torpor. The liquor excise, on the other hand, exercised many an oratorical blowhard, with which Congress, then as now, was overendowed. Opponents had the wind, but not the votes. The House tried to cap the amount collectors could receive but the Senate demurred. The upper house also added its own wrinkle, one that Hamilton approved but that rankled defenders of states' rights, collection districts that transcended state boundaries. Stalemate ensued and the bill became entangled with the national bank issue and, once again, the question of the location of the permanent federal capital. Apparently, plans were afoot to ensure that the government would never move from Philadelphia, the new temporary capital. Outraged, Jefferson and Madison worked behind the scenes to squelch the bank, which was to be headquartered in Philadelphia, or at least to gain leverage for additional assurances that the government would move to northern Virginia on schedule. When those were not forthcoming, Madison attacked the bank as unconstitutional in two long speeches delivered in early February 1791. The Constitution, he argued, did not explicitly grant the federal government the right to charter a bank, or any sort of corporation for that matter. To cajole such a power from the implied powers or "necessary and proper" clause at the end of article I, section 8 was to go too far. Further, he claimed that the bank was inexpedient and played to Americans' hatred of corporations and anything smacking of Britain, but his protests were to no avail.

Although Madison was an avowed expert on the Constitution, plenty of members of Congress had been at the convention too and came away from it with a much looser interpretation of the powers it granted. The bill sailed through but of course needed Washington's approval before it could become law. Troubled by the claim that the bank was unconstitutional, Washington asked his cabinet for their opinions on the matter. Attorney General Edmund Randolph and Jefferson both voted thumbs down. Hamilton of course voted thumbs up and explained himself so convincingly that Washington signed the bill into law. A series of simultaneous maneuvers in Congress that assured the removal of the capital to the Potomac and broke the excise impasse also helped. That another grand bargain had been struck is likely but is not as well documented as the one that assured passage of funding with assumption of state debts by the federal government.[42]

The Bank of the United States proved a smashing success. Its initial public offering of stock, held on July 4, 1791, was largely oversubscribed. The market price of the shares, which had a par value of $400 each, three-quarters of which were payable in public debt, soared so high, so quickly, that it caused Jefferson and his ilk to groan in agony. "The delirium of speculation," Jefferson complained in late July, "is too strong to admit sober reflection." Madison told friends that "stock [public securities] & script [bank shares] continue to be the sole domestic subjects of conversation." "Merchants, grocers, shopkeepers, sea captains, and even prentice boys have embarked in the business," Benjamin Rush complained to his wife in August. Allegedly, men involved in the speculative fever relinquished women as well as their usual business pursuits, a sure sign to critics that society hung together by a thread. That 30 members of Congress, more than half the number that had voted the bank into existence, made a killing with the stock only fanned the flames of discontent. Despite much criticism, the new bank formed as planned. Ably led by the nation's first commercial banker, erstwhile president of the Bank of North America Thomas Willing, the BUS, as it came to be known, soon blossomed into a highly profitable central bank largely owned by private investors. It kept the federal government so well greased with loans that by 1796 it had to urge a scale-back from the $6.2 million that the government owed it. Throughout its existence, the BUS provided the Treasury with valuable assistance in the collection, safe storage, transfer, and disbursement of the government's monies, including interest payments on the national debt. It also smoothed the Treasury's cash flow, allowing it to spread tax collection over months and even years, rendering taxation less onerous. Finally, the B.U.S. also enhanced the new government's legitimacy domestically and overseas. "This bank," wrote historian Thomas Goddard in 1831, "tended greatly to establish not only stability of character at home, but to command respect abroad."[43]

The record of the excise, which became law on March 3, 1791, and was amended in 1792, was mixed. It was not an important source of revenue, was much more expensive to collect than tariffs and tonnage duties, and eventually fomented a minor tax revolt, the so-called Whiskey Rebellion of 1794. If nothing else, that revolt ensured that excises on nonluxury items would remain minor during peacetime.[44]

Riding high on the success of his funding program and national bank, Hamilton, in conjunction with his second-in-command at the Treasury, a Philadelphia merchant-manufacturer-political economist named Tench Coxe, took up the subject of manufactures, the final pillar of his grand plan. If, as some suppose, Hamilton's goal was to turn the American economy into an industrial juggernaut overnight by means of a protective tariff and a national manufactory, he failed miserably. If, on the other hand, Hamilton merely sought to provide an object lesson in manufacturing entrepreneurship, he succeeded, though not as spectacularly as usual. Asked for a report by Congress in January 1790, Hamilton and Coxe undertook significant data collection before drafting and revising the report over the course of 1791, finally delivering it to Congress in December. Although a theoretical as well as empirical tour de force, the report met with silence in Congress and derision from many private quarters. Undeterred, Hamilton and Coxe obtained a charter of incorporation from the New Jersey legislature authorizing them to establish a factory on the falls of the Passaic River by the name of the Society for the Establishment of Useful Manufactures or SEUM. Like the BUS, much of the SEUM's capital stock was composed of public securities. Unlike the BUS, the SEUM fell at first into unscrupulous hands and later into incompetent ones. It went moribund for a while before struggling to its feet. It eventually found more success as a landlord and power supplier to small manufacturing firms than as a manufacturer itself. The SEUM's lack of success, though, did not injure America's credit or forebode the failure of domestic manufacturing. As we'll see, the U.S. manufacturing sector experienced strong growth in the 1790s despite the SEUM's difficulties. We'll also see that one of the beautiful things about the entrepreneurial capitalism that Hamilton and Coxe modeled with the SEUM was its resilience and flexibility.[45]

Hamilton was able to implement the great bulk of his grand plan for two reasons. Madison's views, though strongly held in some quarters like his native central Virginia, were simply not as popular as Hamilton's. Most Americans were small businessmen, artisans, farmers, and professionals, with aspirations of material success. To achieve their lofty goals, they needed just what Hamilton offered: an adequate supply of cash; a stable unit of account; low rates of interest; low taxes; entrepreneurial gusto; and security of life, liberty, and property, in short, economic opportunity aplenty. "I will venture to assert," Henry Knox wrote in 1792, "the most unexampled instances of prosperity are exhibited that ever was presented to the human view [sic]." The prosperity of the early 1790s was proof positive of the wisdom of the new system of government and finance. Hamilton was definitely helped here, as he anticipated in his 1790 report on public credit, by low interest rates in Britain. People in France and the

Low Countries invested "immense sums" in British public securities in the late 1780s and early 1790s, bidding up their prices (and bidding down their yields) to record levels. That induced many investors to seek out more remunerative but still low-risk investments. U.S. government bonds fit that profile to a T, encouraging a flood of foreign investment that could not help but stimulate growth in a free country with a tolerably low tax burden.[46]

❧

Despite the prosperity and the obvious influx of foreign capital, vociferous opposition to Hamilton and his financial system continued throughout the 1790s. If William Findley (1742–1821) was not the biggest critic of Hamilton's financial program, he was certainly the most vocal. An ardent Jeffersonian farmer who represented western Pennsylvania in the House of Representatives for over two decades (1791–99; 1803–17), Findley was a native of Ulster, Ireland. In his lengthy *Review of the Revenue System* (1794), he portrayed the Constitutional Convention as a thinly veiled attempt to reestablish monarchy. Having failed to impose its designs during the convention, the aristocratic element looked forward to the day that it could twist the new Constitution in its favor. In the "prodigious mass of unfunded public debt," the sinking fund, the national bank, and the whiskey excise tax, Findley asserted, the monarchists saw the vehicle of their salvation.

The main problem, Findley quickly revealed, was that some 90 or 95 percent of the original debt certificates had changed hands, most for just a few shillings on the pound (pennies on the dollar). The purchasers, Findley claimed, were mostly foreign and domestic speculators, whose occupation, as we have seen, was charged with negative connotations. According to Findley, the sellers were at best the "poor" and "meritorious" and at worst simple folk swindled out of their property for a "trifle." Hamilton's financial program therefore did not aid the common weal or even promote national honor. Rather, it was

> The moneyed aristocrats were much worse than the aristocrats of Europe, though, because instead of owning productive assets like land, they owned property that produced nothing and that drove them to wish for only one thing, "oppressive taxes."

designed to "aggrandize the treasury department," to increase Hamilton's power, and to "promote a new monied interest." The moneyed aristocrats were much worse than the aristocrats of Europe, though, because instead of owning productive assets like land, they owned property that produced nothing and that drove them to wish for only one thing, "oppressive taxes."

To aid in the creation of this inimitable monstrosity, Findley asserted, Hamilton leaked information about his funding plan to a favored group of speculators. Those speculators immediately canvassed the southern states, buying up any remaining securities on the cheap. Findley admitted that the evidence to support his claims was only circumstantial, but he raised the specter of Treasury employee William Duer, the infamous speculator. Hamilton essentially cashiered Duer, but Findley purported that Duer left of his own accord "as soon as ... more open speculations" became possible.

Hamilton managed to implement his evil plans, Findley claimed, because the first elections were essentially rigged in favor of the monarchical party. "Many procured seats in Congress," he argued, "who had an interest of their own, incompatible with disinterested views for the public good." To ensure passage of the reforms, Hamilton's measures were rammed through Congress without giving the meager opposition adequate time to prepare its case. Even then, the measures passed only with "a great deal of art and intrigue."

Findley saw the national debt only as a burden on taxpayers, so he was appalled at assumption, particularly the way that it served to augment the debt and to increase the powers of the national government at the expense of the states. He also lamented that the government had not discharged the national debt by selling government lands in the trans-Appalachian west. He also clearly viewed Hamilton's funding plan as an unconstitutional usurpa tion of power. His political persuasion clearly colored his views of Hamilton's state papers and the actual functioning of the debt markets. It also induced him to resort to provocative language like the "rape on the Constitution."[47]

James Callendar, a radical Jeffersonian newspaper editor of Scottish extrac-tion, also poured invective on Hamilton and his system. Callendar's techniques were worthy of Karl Rove—slash, burn, slander, exaggerate. His pen turned expenditures of $8 million into $80 million, increased interest rates of 1 or 2 percent per month to 5, transformed banknotes into "a bundle of old rags," raised minor battlefield setbacks into causes of disunion, and transmogrified indifferent orators into geniuses or boobs, depending on their political pose.[48]

Thankfully, Hamilton and his allies could easily dismiss or answer such calumny, ultimately rendering it harmless for everything except Hamilton's historical reputation in some circles. More important were legislative attempts to damage the funding system, like calls for taxation of government bonds. Hamilton managed to fight those off, too, with help from his friends in Congress and his indomitable logic. "Is there a right in the Government to tax its own funds?" Hamilton asked rhetorically in his final report on public credit. Absolutely not, he responded, because "to tax the funds, is manifestly either to take, or to keep back, a portion of the principal or interest stipulated to be paid." (To this day, interest on some bonds is not taxed. Our progressive income tax structure, however, rendered it necessary to tax interest on government bonds, but not retroactively.)[49]

Despite all the vituperation, praise for Hamilton's financial system was not wanting. In July 1791, for example, the New York Chamber of Commerce threw Hamilton a dinner party. "I have no doubt," one contemporary conversant with the party animal side of Hamilton's persona jibed, "but that his heart as well as those of many others will be somewhat dilated with the generous effluvia of the Grape." In other words, Hamilton and the leading men of Manhattan planned on getting smashed to celebrate the success of the grand plan. Their celebration was not premature. In 1795, French foreign minister Talleyrand asserted that U.S. bonds were "safe and free from reverses," because they were "funded in such a sound manner" and American prosperity was "growing so rapidly that there can be no doubt of their solvency." About the same time, British observer William Winterbotham argued that "the Americans are in a fair way not only to pay their interest, but to sink the principal of their debt, and that without direct taxation." Reality interceded to delay that day but Winterbotham was essentially correct. Little wonder that Daniel Webster would later say of Hamilton: "He smote the rock of the national resources, and abundant streams gushed forth. He touched the dead corpse of the public credit, and it sprung to its feet."[50]

In the next chapter, we'll see precisely how Hamilton's brainchildren developed. But first, we need to joust. Hamilton's critics, then, now, and in the ages between, oft dismissed or at least discounted his achievements by claiming that he slavishly copied the British financial system. Jefferson called Hamilton "the servile copyist of Mr. Pitt," the famed British prime minister, and Jeffersonians ever since have deprecated Hamilton's policies as too British, aristocratic, and oppressive. In 1794, John Taylor of Caroline, a proslavery Virginia firebrand who made Jefferson's most vitriolic anti-Hamiltonian comments look tame by comparison, rhetorically asked if it was not time "to enquire, whether the constitution was designed to beget a government, or only a *British* system of finance?" (italics in original). According to Taylor, Hamilton's reforms were "literally copied from the monarchical system of Britain."[51]

On the surface, the financial system that rapidly took form in early 1790s America did look like that of Britain. The resemblance, however, was largely an illusion consciously created by Hamilton. A long-term funded debt and central bank surrounded by a growing network of private banks and insurance companies as well as markets for business debts and equities were the state of the art, what modern business management gurus call "best practices." In other words, to accomplish his goal of raising American credit to the highest level, Hamilton had to keep up appearances, to walk the walk and talk the talk of modern finance. But Hamilton went well beyond British precedents in many important ways. American finance, like other Old World institutions transplanted to the New, underwent profound changes before it took root and flourished.

American finance, like other Old World institutions transplanted to the New, underwent profound changes before it took root and flourished.

One major difference was that America's central bank, the Bank of the United States, could and did form branches. Its British progenitor, by contrast, was London bound. Hamilton had reservations about the Bank of the United States' branches, but he did not blanch at these apprehensions. Ultimately, he realized that the branches would allow the bank to fulfill more effectively several of its functions, including collecting and making payments for the national government and ensuring that state banks did not issue too many notes. And unlike the Bank of England, the Bank of the United States was mostly a commercial bank with a large portfolio of loans to merchants and other large businesses, not a pseudogovernment bond mutual fund. As a for-profit institution, it was largely independent of government control, which is today recognized as an important characteristic of successful central banks.[52]

Hamilton's critics claimed that he wished to render the U.S. national debt perpetual like that of Britain. For example, Albert Gallatin, the Swiss-born financier turned Pennsylvania democrat who served as treasury secretary under Jefferson and Madison, insinuated that Hamilton did everything he could, especially with his liberal treatment of state debts during the assumption process, to keep the nation mired in debt. Free nations, Gallatin believed, should repay their debts with all due haste lest interest payments rob the poor and further enrich the wealthy.[53]

The national debt indeed increased slightly in nominal terms during the Washington and Adams administrations but that was largely due to the Quasi-War, several years of undeclared naval war with France, rather than by design. In fact, by Hamilton's grand plan the national debt would slowly be paid off during peacetime. The contrast with the British system is marked. The British issued Consols, which were indeed perpetual obligations, while U.S. Threes were redeemable at the government's pleasure, a huge difference. Threes in fact were not redeemed in significant quantities until the 1820s, because it was obviously in the government's interest to first redeem bonds that paid higher rates of interest. Hamilton pushed for higher taxes whenever he thought the economy could carry the burden. On December 3, 1792, for example, he issued yet another report on public credit calling for additional taxes to help pay down the principal of the national debt, the result of which were taxes "upon carriages for the conveyances of persons," on liquor and wine retailers, and on domestically manufactured snuff and refined sugar, all passed on June 5, 1794. Before the month was out, additional tariffs and a federal auction tax also became law. On January 16, 1795, just before leaving office, Hamilton submitted his final report on public credit, which sought to identify and rectify "whatsoever may remain unfinished of our system of public credit, in order to place that credit, as far as may be practicable, on grounds which cannot be disturbed, and to prevent that progressive accumulation of debt which must ultimately endanger all government."[54]

At the end of this last great public report, Hamilton made a plea as important and moving as that made by George Washington in his Farewell Address. (Which, by the way, Hamilton played an important role in writing.) The following, in my opinion, should be added to the oaths of office of all U.S. federal officials:

It will be the truest policy of the United States to give all possible energy to public credit, by a firm adherence to its strictest maxims; and yet to avoid the ills of an excessive employment of it by true economy and system in the public expenditures; by steadily cultivating peace; and by using sincere, efficient, and persevering endeavors to diminish present debts, prevent the accumulation of new, and secure the discharge, within a reasonable period, of such as it may be, at any time, matter of necessity to contract.

Specifically, Hamilton urged Congress to make provision to repay a large portion of the debt by continuing the sinking fund's occasional purchases of government bonds in the open market and by invoking the government's annuity repayment option. As noted above, Hamilton built a clause into Sixes and Deferred Sixes giving the government the option of turning them into annuities in which the principal could be reduced 2 percent per year. Hamilton created that "hidden sinking fund," because, unlike some observers in Britain and America, he did not think that a sinking fund could magically pay off debt through the power of compound interest. Although it complicated matters somewhat for investors, the government exercised the annuity option in an act passed on April 28, 1796, by the terms of which much of the national debt was whittled down like a modern amortized home mortgage. Sixes and Deferred Sixes were fully paid off at the end of 1818 and 1824, respectively.[55]

Hamilton also realized that he could use the sinking fund to conduct what are today called "open market operations," to in other words buy bonds during financial panics and other emergencies. Those purchases infused the economy with money and supported the price of government bonds, both of which helped to restore confidence and private credit. Hamilton's use of the sinking fund to stymie the Panic of 1792, though rarely appreciated by scholars, was nothing short of masterful.

The events of early 1792 have been chronicled elsewhere. Here is the short version: Some securities speculators borrowed too much and at precisely the wrong moment, just before the nation's handful of banks began contracting their loans. Some of the speculators, including William Duer, went bankrupt owing large sums to numerous lenders, including "shopkeepers, Widows, orphans—Butchers, Cartmen, Gardners, market women, & even the noted Bawd Mrs Macarty." A chain reaction ensued as lenders furiously began to call in debts. Interest rates spiked and the prices of government bonds, other securities, and land plummeted, evoking panic on Wall Street, Main Street, and every street in between. "The crash has been tremendous," and "bankruptcies continue to encrease," Jefferson and Rush reported to their correspondents. "The Mississippi and South Sea schemes, will shortly be realized among us," one newspaper proclaimed, "to the mortification of all men," including "the Butcher, and Baker, the Barber and Truckman," who lent "their hard earnings, at 4 per cent per month, to a celebrated Speculator," to wit Duer, who had no money but plenty of depressed securities. "Commerce has for some time past been diverted from its regular course, into an improper channel," another observer complained, due to "the great field, for various kinds of speculation." The dire end predicted by Jefferson and his ilk appeared to be at hand.[56]

Although some counseled to let matters run their course—"If folly is let alone it will tax itself to death," it was said—Hamilton responded to the "madness" quickly and decisively, much as Federal Reserve chairman Alan Greenspan did in 1987 and 2001. First, he persuaded the banks to increase their lending, slowly and safely, to anyone who offered good collateral, including U.S. government bonds. To ensure that borrowers were truly distressed, the banks, Hamilton counseled, should lend at a higher than usual rate. Second, he ordered the sinking fund to purchase bonds in the open market. That would give distressed security holders an out and pump money into the system. Third, he eased up on the collection of debts owed to the government and sold government assets, including bills of exchange drawn on a timely Dutch loan, on easy credit terms. The techniques worked like a charm. Much to the chagrin of Jefferson and other critics, the panic quickly abated as soon as securities prices in the U.S. markets fell to the levels prevailing in Europe. At the end of April, the Bank of the United States claimed not to have "met with the loss of one dollar" because it foresaw "the evils of the late wild speculations" and "took early precautions." The other banks also pulled through largely unscathed. The panic certainly diminished the quantity of securities trading and arrested prices but hardly decimated the markets.[57]

Within a few months, the young American economy began to roar again, mocking Jefferson's hyperbolic claim that the panic had been tantamount to Manhattan's utter destruction. One creative writer described the panic and its aftermath in terms any seafaring man could grasp:

STOCK MARINE LIST

THE Six-per Cent, a first rate, belonging to the fleet commanded by Admiral HAMILTON, notwithstanding several hard contrary gales, and a strong lee current setting out of the Hudson and Delaware is still working to windward; and bids fair to gain her destined port.

The Three per Cent, a frigate belonging to the above mentioned fleet, in sailing through Speculation Straights, received a land flaw, which threw her on her beam ends— She has, however, since righted, and is pursuing her voyage.

And so forth for most of a column![58]

With his actions, Hamilton invented one of the pillars of central banking theory, the doctrine of lender of last resort. The doctrine was certainly not a British financial import. In late 1792 and early 1793, for reasons that many contemporaries admitted they did not fully understand, "a species of pecuniary distress, unparalleled as to its extent," struck "the commercial and manufacturing interests of Great Britain." Some 100 of the 350 "country bankers" in England and Wales stopped payments, half of those were "ruined," and 22 declared formal bankruptcy. Had the Bank of England acted decisively much of the pain could have been avoided, or so early-nineteenth-century economic historian John Ramsey McCulloch would later assert. "Had the bankers possessed adequate funds to meet the claims upon them," he argued, "the contraction of their issues could not have caused any panic or run, and would have been effected with very little difficulty." Some country banks did request aid from the Bank but, for reasons that remain unclear, it refused. After flailing around for some months, the Bank of England and Exchequer (British treasury) eventually thwarted the panic

It isn't clear if the British copied Hamilton or merely hit upon the same doctrine, but it is crystal clear that Hamilton's reaction to the panic was no slavish imitation of the British, or anyone else for that matter.

using Hamilton-esque techniques. It isn't clear if the British copied Hamilton or merely hit upon the same doctrine, but it is crystal clear that Hamilton's reaction to the panic was no slavish imitation of the British, or anyone else for that matter. The British might have imitated Hamilton again in 1810–11 and, again belatedly, in 1825–26. But they forgot about the importance of the doctrine of the lender of last resort during subsequent panics and weren't reminded of it again until late in the nineteenth century when financial journalist-cum-central bank theorist Walter Bagehot rediscovered it. Bagehot's Law, the policy prescription that the lender of last resort should lend during crises on good security at penalty rates, should rightly be called Hamilton's Law.[59]

For many, the Panic of 1792 and the surface resemblance to Britain's financial system forever stained Hamilton's grand plan. For others, though, with success came acceptance. "If the funding system, (tho' it originated in injustice) and the banks, are found of *public benefit*," "A Republican" asked rhetorically in 1800, "who is to controul [sic] the people from continuing and supporting them?" (italics in original). The public would continue to find the debt useful, as we'll learn in the next three chapters.[60]

6

YOUTH AND MATURITY

The Public Debt Grows Up, Then Slims Down

Given the amount of ink spilled on the clashing political ideologies of the Federalists, led by Hamilton, and the Republicans, led by Jefferson and Madison, it's rather amazing that so little has been written on what Hamilton's policies actually wrought. Perhaps advocates of both sides feared what they would find. Even if they were curious, the vast majority of scholars did not realize that records exist that would allow them to examine the first national debt in minute detail. The few who did know about the records apparently found the enormity of the task before the advent of cheap computing daunting. Even though I was armed with a laptop, several small grants, and a research assistant, this chapter and the next took several years to research and write, which was longer than the rest of the book combined. It was well worth the effort as they show, beyond all doubt, that by the early 1790s America possessed a modern, active market for the public securities composing its national debt. The markets were broad and liquid. In other words, many investors, both domestic and foreign, owned Sixes, Deferred Sixes, and Threes and those bonds could be, and were, bought or sold quickly and cheaply. As Hamilton foretold, although ownership of government bonds was extremely fluid, enough people in enough places owned enough of the debt to help bind the young nation together. Also as Hamilton predicted,

> As Hamilton foretold, although ownership of government bonds was extremely fluid, enough people in enough places owned enough of the debt to help bind the young nation together.

161

foreign investment was large enough to keep the economy growing, and domestic investors benefited enormously from owning government bonds.

Given all this, why have so many scholars assumed the debt remained in the hands of an elite few? Late in the nineteenth century, policy wonk Henry C. Adams underestimated for political gain the dispersion of the national debt as it then stood. He examined only the registered debt, ownership of which was probably considerably more concentrated than ownership of the government's bearer bonds. He also downplayed the importance of holdings by banks, insurance companies, and other intermediaries. In 1880, out of a population of about 50 million, 71,587 different individuals directly owned registered government bonds and untold others possessed bearer bonds (unregistered bonds owned by the person holding them) or the liabilities of intermediaries that owned public securities. That, however, was not the story Adams wished to tell. Opponents of Hamilton's funding system also grossly underestimated the number of Americans who owned public securities for political purposes. For example, Robert R. Livingston of New York claimed that only .025 percent of the population (1 out of every 4,000) owned federal securities, prompting him to mock Hamilton by asserting that "this supposed cement will appear to consist of untempered mortar." Livingston underestimated the number of bondholders, offered a mere snapshot at one moment in time that failed to account for the constantly shifting ownership caused by active securities trading, and was clearly a partisan source hostile to Hamilton. Nevertheless, scholars latched onto his estimate and didn't let go. Apparently, the notion that the first national debt was highly concentrated was perpetrated for partisan purposes and proliferated because it matched the views of historians with radical political agendas hostile to corporate capitalism.[1]

Readers may recall that federal bondholders were not required to swap their old certificates for Hamilton's new bonds, only to register them with the Treasury. Despite the lower interest rate paid on the new bonds, most eventually made the exchange. By January 1, 1794, the funded domestic debt stood a shade under $39.7 million, and the assumed debt a tad less than $18.3 million. At the end of that year, the total of assumed debt was the same, but the funded domestic debt had grown to just under $44.8 million, "nearly the whole" of that portion of the national debt. The new bonds were superior to the old for two reasons. First, interest payments on them were well secured by federal taxes and paid promptly each quarter. Second, highly liquid markets for them arose and flourished throughout the country. The total dollar volumes and the number of trades were impressive by the standards of the day. In fact, foreigners claimed that seemingly every American was "a stockjobber by nature" and newspapers reported that "small tradesmen, shopkeepers, clerks of all degrees, operatives of town and country, members of the learned professions, students in the offices, beginners in the world without capital, or with a little, all frequent the exchanges." Nor was this a passing phenomenon. "Speculation," opined British financial analyst David Morier Evans in 1859, "is known to be one of the permanent maladies of the transatlantic republic." Clearly, some of the 60,000-plus transactions my research assistant and I recorded were family affairs, like estate transfers. Most, though, were arm's-length sales conducted via broker-dealers. The register books themselves reveal that, as do prices reported in the newspapers, which in the major markets usually showed at least weekly movements indicative of market activity. Prices bounced around with interest rates, which in turn vacillated with the speculations of bulls and bears, both foreign and domestic, trends in foreign trade, and the likelihood of war.[2]

There was quality as well as quantity in the early U.S. financial system. The market for public debt grew sophisticated quite quickly. By the summer of 1791, time bargains, attempted corners, interstate and international arbitrage, and other modern moneymaking machinations were commonplace, especially in the New York market but elsewhere as well. Fancy finance waxed and waned over the years but never completely disappeared from the American scene.[3]

There was quality as well as quantity in the early U.S. financial system. The market for public debt grew sophisticated quite quickly.

Trading levels were substantial in most states. Unfortunately, due to the nature of the sample it is not possible to draw firm conclusions about rankings. Massachusetts is not represented at all, the New York sample includes trading in only relatively unimportant types of government bonds issued in the late 1790s, of which more below, and the records for New Jersey, Georgia, and North Carolina are incomplete. Nevertheless, it is clear that debt holders lived throughout the land actively buying and selling federal bonds.[4]

Interestingly, the volume of trading, though still impressive, fell off dramatically after the Panic of 1792. As the quantity of public debt trading declined, some speculators shifted their focus to land. (Sound familiar?) "Speculation in Land seems to engross the whole conversation in this quarter among the monied men," John Remsen told his brother Henry in 1794, "and they appear to be very sanguine that Lands will rise considerably higher than they at present sell for." The shift in speculative focus was actually good news for the securities markets, which for over two decades were not regularly roiled by massive price fluctuations or the political fallout that accompanied bubbles and panics.[5]

Trading volumes are flows. What about the stocks (no pun intended)? In other words, how many people owned federal bonds at a given moment? Based on admittedly sketchy evidence, financial historian E. James Ferguson estimated that "there were probably at most no more than 15,000 to 20,000 holders of public securities in the nation" circa 1790. Based on a much more careful analysis of the records, I think that was a good guess. I estimate that on January 1, 1795, about 21,500 different entities (individuals, business corporations, municipalities, nonprofit organizations, and estate trusts) owned U.S. national bonds. That works out to about .47 percent (1 out of every 212) of the population. The number of different places where bondholders lived is astounding, especially given that the Massachusetts and New York loan office books were not examined. The wide diversity of occupations also bolsters the view that the debt was held by people across the socioeconomic spectrum.[6]

The ownership of federal bonds in the January 1, 1795, sample was highly concentrated in dollar terms but most federal bondholders owned only between $10 and $1,000 face value (i.e., principal) of Sixes, Deferred Sixes, and Threes in total. Large bondholders, though, those with holdings exceeding $1,000, owned most of the debt by value. Due to a few very large holdings over $10,000, the average holding was $3,437.75, but the median was only $571.19.[7]

Those general characteristics appear to have held up over time. Ownership of the federal debt on June 30, 1803, by states and by category is also known in some detail. About half the domestic debt was then owned by foreigners, mostly English and Dutch investors. Most of the debt that was domestically held was on the books of the Treasury in Washington, D.C., and in the registers of the loan officer commissioners of Massachusetts, New York, and Pennsylvania, but substantial sums, in per capita terms, were still held in all the states except North Carolina, Georgia, and Delaware. The number of entities that owned federal bonds dropped, though, to about 14,000, suggesting ownership of the debt became more concentrated after 1795.[8]

Interestingly, in the early nineteenth century more than 2 percent of Britons (1 out of every 50) owned British government bonds, a figure much higher than that of the United States. Two factors were likely at play here. First, the British national debt was much higher in per capita terms, requiring higher levels of market penetration. Second, the British had more investment capital and yet fewer high-return investment outlets. They therefore had more to invest in relatively safe securities like government bonds. In fact, as we've seen, they purchased considerable sums of U.S. bonds. Although the level of foreign investment in the U.S. national debt, and American securities in general, waxed and waned with market conditions, foreign investors were always significant players in the markets during peacetime. Trading in U.S. bonds in London was active enough by early 1792 that some British and American newspapers periodically quoted their prices and continued to do so for almost two decades until regular quotations began in 1811. Beginning in the mid-1790s, European investment manuals regularly included descriptions of U.S. government bonds and gave advice about when, where, and why to purchase them. "Many purchasers of the domestic debt," Hamiltonian critic James Callendar noted in 1798, "reside in … Europe." In the nineteenth century, foreign investment continued hot and heavy in government bonds and bank stocks. "The whole stock of the bank of North America," Samuel Blodget claimed in 1801, "has been thus sold twice in Europe." In 1815, Daniel Dulany of Downing Street, London, owned 2,763 shares in the Bank of the Manhattan Company and used his dividends to purchase yet more shares in the bank. Though politicos like Callendar, the Lou Dobbs of the late eighteenth century, lamented any economic interaction with foreigners (save selling them our stuff), clearer minds saw that foreign investment could only help the American economy.[9]

⚜

The U.S. national debt could be said to have matured in early March 1797. Alarmed by the possibility of a French invasion, farmers in the marine districts of England ran on their local banks and sold government securities to "get cash into their hands." Both actions had the effect of pulling gold reserves out of the Bank of England, which responded by stopping the conversion of its liabilities into specie. That induced other British investors to sell off Consols, perpetual British government bonds, making their price "vibrate" between 50 and 52 percent of par. That much was not unusual. Unwelcome shocks always made government bond prices droop. For instance, when in 1745 Bonnie Prince Charlie, the young pretender to the throne, landed in Scotland and pressed an army south toward London, Consols fell from 93 to 84.25 percent of par. What was different in early 1797 was that as British investors sold Consols, they purchased U.S. securities, the prices of which leapt skyward. "American Stock," the *London Times* reported in early March, "has risen near 7 per Cent. within the last 10 days." In just a week, shares in the Bank of the United States trading in London increased in price from £103 to £117, while the prices of U.S. Sixes and Threes jumped from 80 to 90 and 49 to 55 percent of par, respectively. So for a brief moment, the 3 percent bonds of the U.S. government had a higher credit (lower yield) than the substantially more liquid (over £200 million outstanding) 3 percent bonds of the British government, *in London*! At that moment, the old revolutionary Tom Paine, who the year before had prognosticated that the

"English funding system … will not continue to the end of Mr. Pitt's life, supposing him to live the usual age of a man," seemed prescient. The Brits kept a stiff upper lip, though, and managed to claw their way clear of invasion and default. The risk premiums on American bonds returned, but when peace and prosperity prevailed they remained low. Peace, however, was a rare commodity in the late eighteenth and early nineteenth centuries, and prosperity was occasionally beset upon by commercial crises. Luckily, the tender young republic was able to keep its wars and its panics small, until 1812 and 1819, that is.[10]

In February 1795, Oliver Wolcott of Connecticut took over for Hamilton as treasury secretary, but Hamilton continued to provide the Washington and Adams administrations with consulting advice, whether they wanted it or not (as was the case with Adams). Wolcott was a pretty sharp guy but the nation's finances were still young and hence somewhat precarious, so gracious acceptance of his former boss's expert advice was prudent, to say the least. As shown in Chapter 5, critics continued to snipe away at Hamilton's grand plan, but for the most part they were naught but annoying gnats. Above, we saw that the secondary market for public securities was an active one, and that the debt was owned by a geographically and occupationally diverse set of investors. The one remaining problem was the government's budget. Due to a series of miniwars, the federal government had to spend more than it would like to have done. At the same time, periodic commercial crises threatened its revenues. Both problems conspired to render additional government borrowing necessary.[11]

In running up its nominal national debt in the last decade of the eighteenth century and the first two decades of the nineteenth, the early United States was hardly alone. In 1714, the public debt of all the nations of the world totaled about $1.5 billion and was largely confined to Britain, Holland, and a handful of other countries. By 1793, those same countries, joined by a few others, including America, had debts of about $2.5 billion. Thanks in large measure to the Napoleonic Wars, public indebtedness worldwide stood at $7.75 billion by 1820.[12]

Where America differed from most of its contemporaries was that it managed to keep its national debt in check, especially given that its population and economy were growing quickly. More people and more prosperity meant more government revenues with which to meet larger interest payments on the increased nominal debt. The Treasury, with help from the Bank of the United States, made its payments each quarter without delay or cavil. Detractors, though, concentrated on minor increases in the nominal debt, speaking in grave tones about its growth and perpetuation. Some, like the vituperative anti-Hamiltonian James Callendar, even disparaged the amortization feature of the Sixes added in 1795. Callendar also claimed that the Treasury was slow to pay its other creditors, proof positive, he asserted, that the federal government had been seized by public creditors who ensured that they were paid first, a palpable threat according to the republican constitutional theory espoused by Jefferson, Madison, and Gallatin. Hamilton denied that the Treasury dillydallied in its payments and in fact made a point of ensuring that it could always meet all its obligations promptly because "an hour's distress or embarrassment ... would be baneful to public credit." (Truth be told, the Treasury probably was a little slow making payments, as anyone who has ever waited on an IRS refund or government contract check can testify. Unless there was an explicit due date the practice then, as now, was to put off payment until "dunned." The check has been "in the mail" for over 200 years!)[13]

⟨⟨⟩⟩

The nominal national debt crept upward in the latter half of the 1790s because the government found it necessary to borrow some fairly sizable sums. In addition to obtaining numerous loans from the Bank of the United States and other banks, the government issued new bonds when necessary. The national government found it expedient to borrow anew in the mid- and late 1790s for several reasons. From its founding, the new government found itself embroiled in an Indian war that remained at a low boil for decades. Barbary Coast pirates were another vexation that required the use of minor force at times and bribes or concessionary payments at others. Minor tax rebellions in 1794 and 1799 were double blows, because they increased expenditures while simultaneously reducing revenues. The Quasi-War with France in 1798 did likewise. Upset with the Jay Treaty, which strengthened Anglo-American

> Minor tax rebellions in 1794 and 1799 were double blows, because they increased expenditures while simultaneously reducing revenues.

commercial ties in 1794, and torn asunder by the internal power struggles that erupted after the downfall of the Ancien Regime, the French tried to extort bribes from American diplomats. When news of this gaffe, known as the XYZ Affair, broke in April 1798, many outraged Americans called for war. Thankfully, the Adams administration did not satiate their bloodlust as the country was not well positioned for a big war. "At present," James Callendar argued in 1798, "the United States neither enjoy the tranquility of peace, nor the animation of war. Equally despised and hated by both France and England, this country must remain the helpless spectator of her own commercial ruin." Though a formal declaration of war was never made and the anticipated French invasion never occurred, de facto warfare broke out on the high seas "with very great virulence." From July 1798 until the fall of 1800, U.S. Navy warships like the *Constellation*, *Enterprise*, and *Merrimack* pounded French privateers, capturing 85, with nary a loss on the U.S. side, though French depredations on American merchant ships were at times heavy.[14]

Two minor commercial crises also somewhat crimped government revenues. In 1797, a liquidity crisis caused some Philadelphia and Baltimore businesses to fail and caused a monetary stringency in Virginia. The shock injured trade, and hence government revenues, a bit. A few years later, chaos again struck Baltimore and threatened to spread to the commercial centers of the north, because its root causes, plummeting tobacco prices and the failure of some European merchants, had negative implications for the entire U.S. economy. The crisis struck Baltimore with particular force, in part because many of its firms were highly leveraged and very sensitive to tobacco prices. Interest rates soared and the quantity of lending plummeted as people and institutions sought to reduce their outstanding debts and maintain a strong cash position. Not everyone could get liquid quickly enough, so some had to suspend payments. Apprehension quickly turned into panic. The Baltimore branch of the BUS responded by following Hamilton's Law, i.e., prudently extending credit to solid companies adversely affected by the panic. Unable to discern the solid from the flimsy loan applicants, the directors of the branch required a "Deposit of Merchandize" to collateralize the loans. Headquarters chastised the branch for turning the BUS into an oversized pawn shop:

A greater share of responsibility ought to have been attached to the Negotiation, by requiring additional names of respectable Characters, as

Indorsers on the Paper that may be offered: – which Species of Security is more consonant to the Spirit of Bank operations, & more agreeable to the Provisions of the Charter.

The committee charged with reviewing the branch's actions, however, lauded the Baltimoreans for understanding the BUS's overall mission:

> At the same time, we are not inclined to press hard upon any commercial Establishment, whose operations may be paralyzed by the unfortunate State of Commercial Credit. – On the contrary where Solid & unquestionable Security can be obtained, we recommend a friendly hand to be extended towards them, by affording them a temporary Relief from Such Embarrassments, as arise from the Pressure of Sudden unexpected Casualties; – always aware, that in the dispensation of your favors the best Customers of the Bank are entitled to a decided Preference.

Government bonds remitted to Europe in lieu of specie also helped to relieve the pressure on interest rates. Panic quickly gave way to normalcy but the crises and Quasi-War had a negative impact on government receipts.[15]

To bolster its sagging revenue, the government increased customs duties. More controversially, it also turned to a direct tax on dwelling houses, lands, and slaves assigned to the states on the basis of population, as specified in the Constitution. Although progressive—the rates increased as the value of houses increased—the tax proved unpopular and unremunerative, especially in eastern Pennsylvania, where cooper-turned-auctioneer John Fries led a tax rebellion in 1799. As famed economist John Kenneth Galbraith once quipped, early Americans objected to taxation with representation as much as they objected to taxation without it. Much like the Whiskey Rebellion five years earlier, Fries' Rebellion was quickly put down, its ringleaders captured, convicted, sentenced to death, then pardoned. Nevertheless, the revolts were politically successful. The taxes didn't net much and, in 1802, the Jefferson administration eliminated all forms of federal excise (except the levy on salt,

Much like the Whiskey Rebellion five years earlier, Fries' Rebellion was quickly put down, its ringleaders captured, convicted, sentenced to death, then pardoned.

which it did away with in 1807) and property taxation, substituting in their stead higher customs duties.[16]

Although some, like Virginia rep John Stratton, believed it would have been better to maintain the luxury excises on carriages, stamps, and refined sugar and reduce the imposts on "the necessaries of life," the repeal of excise taxes was a very good move politically. Increased taxes and debt, wars and rebellions, legislation seemingly inimical to civil liberties, tight restrictions on entry into banking, and a variety of other grievances drove urban artisans and other groups out of the Federalist fold and into the arms of Madison, Jefferson, and the Republican Party, which carried the presidential and congressional elections in 1800 and decimated the Federalists' ranks thereafter.[17]

Debt reduction was a major goal of the new administration and Congress. "The propriety of pursuing measures for the final extinguishment of the public debt is a position too obviously true," the Committee of Ways and Means declared in 1801, "to require any illustration." The committee then proceeded to lay out the reasons for debt reduction! It was then a time of peace and prosperity but war and desolation lurked, the committee intimated. Like the ant in Aesop's fable, the nation that worked hard in the summer would survive the long, cold winter to come. They were right, but what came along first was not war but a once-in-a-lifetime opportunity to buy not one but millions of anthills, and a whole lot more, for a paltry $15 million. The seller was France, the nation that helped America to win its independence only to turn on it after its own revolution. The U.S. government paid $3.75 million of the purchase price to Americans on behalf of France, reimbursement for the sundry "spoliations" on American commerce by French vessels in the 1790s. The balance of $11.25 million the U.S. government could not pay in cash, so it issued bonds for that amount to Napoleon, who promptly sold them to British investors via Dutch investment bankers. Known as Louisiana Stock or Louisiana Sixes for the territory they allowed the United States to acquire and the interest they paid each year, on a semiannual basis, the bonds were repaid on schedule between 1812 and 1823.[18]

Hamilton and his policies were now completely vindicated. Just as he predicted, his funding system, in conjunction with the modern financial system wrought by it and the rest of his grand plan, helped America to defeat a

European power on the high seas and other, albeit lesser, adversaries, in land and amphibious battles, and enabled it to more than double its size on the cheap. The Little Lion, however, was not long for this world. On July 11, 1804, the vice president of the United States, Aaron Burr, shot Hamilton in a duel. The father of America's national debt and financial system died the next day. Many were truly grief stricken. "Must the sod, not yet cemented the tomb of WASHINGTON, still moist with our tears," moaned Harrison Gray Otis, "be so soon disturbed to admit the beloved companion of WASHINGTON, the partner of his dangers, the object of his confidence, the disciple who leaned upon his bosom! ... He was a planet, the dawn of which was not perceived; which rose with full splendor, and emitted a constant stream of glorious light." When Hamilton assumed the office of treasury secretary, Otis reminded the old and informed the young, "the treasury of the United States ... existed only in name, unless folios of unsettled balances, and bundles of reproachful claims were deserving of the name of a treasury. Money there was none; and of public credit scarcely a shadow remained." The national debt "was not only unpaid," Otis continued, "but its amount was a subject of uncertainty and conjecture." By the time Hamilton left office, and because of the "comprehensive vigour of his mind, ... a dormant capital was revived, and with it commerce and agriculture awoke as from the sleep of death."[19]

> By the time Hamilton left office, and because of the "comprehensive vigour of his mind, ... a dormant capital was revived, and with it commerce and agriculture awoke as from the sleep of death."[19]

With Hamilton gone and the Republicans ensconced in power, it was the Federalists' turn to gripe about the debt. On the eve of the 1804 presidential election, for example, "Hume" attacked the Jefferson administration's record on the debt, claiming that its policies "may continue it forever .... They passed an act," he claimed, "entitled an 'Act for the Redemption of the Whole Public Debt of the United States,' trusting that the country would look only at the title, without regarding its provisions." Hume completely ignored that the law greatly reorganized, simplified, and beefed up the sinking fund to the tune of $7.3, and soon $8, million per year. Thus was yet another perfectly good, if overly optimistic, statute sullied for partisan purposes.[20]

Treasury Secretary Albert Gallatin, in fact, well performed the functions of his office. "Gallatin is a treasure," Madison once noted, because he was "sound in his principles, accurate in his calculations, and indefatigable in his researches." During his long tenure in Congress and as secretary, Gallatin helped to make the national accounts more transparent, induced Congress to exert more control over the budget, and made it clear to all that there was only one way to pay off the debt—keep revenues up while slashing expenditures. "I know," he explained to all, "but one way that a nation has of paying her debts; and this is precisely the same which individuals practice. Spend *less* than you receive" (italics in original). This was more than just talk; Gallatin and his party actually reduced government expenses, and not just a little for show.[21]

One of the most difficult aspects of national finance in the first decade of the nineteenth century, besides dealing with Jefferson's financial naïveté, was remitting money to Europe each year to pay the interest and principal on the Dutch loans in Holland's own money, called guilders. Shipping specie would have been expensive, dangerous, and unpopular, but finding enough bills of exchange at good rates was tough, too. "The difficulty and risks attaching to the purchase of remittances, which can only be obtained at a distance from the treasury department, and without any immediate controul [*sic*] of any office of government," Gallatin explained, "may not perhaps be obviated by any means." Hamilton and Wolcott had also found making remittances to Europe inconvenient. "Payment of interest and installments of our foreign debt in the countries where it was contracted," Hamilton argued, "is found by experience to be attended with difficulty, embarrassment, some loss, and a degree of casualty which occasionally puts in jeopardy the national credit." So the government had tried, in 1795, to pay off the loans due and payable in Europe by issuing domestic bonds, to wit, bonds denominated in dollars and payable in the United States, bearing 4.5 and 5.5 percent. France agreed to the terms of the conversion but, somewhat ironically given that France occupied the Low Countries at the time, the Dutch did not, so remitting guilders remained a thorn in the Treasury's side until 1809. To meet its payment in 1802, for example, the government resorted to selling its last 2,220 shares in the BUS to British banker Alexander Baring, who paid a 45 percent premium for the shares at the favorable exchange rate of 41 cents per guilder.[22]

Another difficulty that Gallatin and subsequent treasury secretaries had to contend with was mismatches between balances in the sinking fund and the value of bonds eligible for redemption. Sometimes, the sinking fund could do nothing but purchase government bonds in the open market, at times enough to drive up their price to levels that made further purchases imprudent or illegal. Again in the 1820s, federal government surpluses sometimes exceeded the value of the bonds that the government could legally redeem. (At other times, however, the sinking fund was insufficient to pay off the value of bonds becoming redeemable. On January 1, 1826, for example, $19.5 million worth of the Sixes of 1813 became redeemable but the Treasury anticipated paying off only $7 million of them. [This was not a default, as the bonds were only redeemable, not payable, on that date.] It actually did slightly better than that. The same thing happened the following January, when $13 million worth of the Sixes of 1814 became redeemable. The mismatches were due mostly to fluctuations in imports resulting from world economic trends and changes in U.S. tariff laws.)[23]

To help make it easier for the sinking fund to pay down the debt, Congress in February 1807, at Gallatin's prompting, passed a law authorizing the exchange of Sixes, Deferred Sixes, and Threes for 6 percent ordinary bonds payable at the pleasure of the government. Gallatin believed that the market priced the first two species of bonds too low due to the clunky operation of their repayment terms, the 2 percent of capital returned each year, and feared that future bond issues would suffer because of it. He hoped that investors would prefer to receive their principal in one lump sum upon redemption rather than in small dribs and drabs and that they would find the exchange of Threes at 65 percent of par advantageous. He was wrong. Investors exchanged only $8.154 million of the $31.8 million worth of bonds covered under the law. The failure of the exchange was in a sense self-reinforcing, because as it became clear to investors that few exchanges would be made, the safe bet was to stick with the original bonds because they enjoyed a much more liquid market. The markets for the new "exchanged" and "converted" Sixes (the former was the term for old Sixes and Deferred Sixes and the latter for old Threes) were thin compared with the older issues. Another exchange program implemented in 1812 converted an additional $2.98 million of old Sixes.[24]

Gallatin and the government soon faced much greater difficulties. During their ongoing titanic struggle for world supremacy, Britain and France rode roughshod over American neutrality. Impressment (forcible seizure) of American sailors on the seas, blockades, outright naval battles, and over 900 ship seizures portended war. Rather than join the fray, Presidents Jefferson and Madison opted instead for economic warfare in the form of sundry embargoes and nonintercourse acts. The problem with the tactic was that it hurt the United States much more than either Britain or France. The depredations plus "Our Bullying language and demands on Great Britain without the smallest preparation even for Defense," Richmond merchant Robert Gamble predicted in late 1807, "must parryalize [*sic*] all enterprise and commerce." Gamble couldn't spell very well but his prediction was right. Low levels of international trade also reduced government revenues, which sagged from $17 million in 1808 to $7.8 million the following year and $9.4 million in 1810. The dip forced the government to borrow $2.75 million in 1810. Repeal of the trade restrictions allowed revenues to rebound to $14.4 million in 1811 and the 1810 loan to be repaid.[25]

With the international crisis deepening and economic sanctions discredited, hawks began to beat the war drums. For example, in an 1810 pamphlet successful Philadelphia doctor, chemist, and brewer Robert Hare deplored the "present humiliated condition of the United States. ... Our ships plundered or burned—by the cruel mandates of the insatiate Napoleon;—our commerce subjected to constraint of vexation—by the unnecessary and impolitic restrictions of England:—our honour tarnished by the most tame endurance of aggravated insult;—and our prosperity arrested by the most abject submission to accumulated injury." According to Hare and others, a naval buildup was warranted. However, warned Hare, the country was not as well prepared for an arms race, let alone an extended battle, as it might be, due to the "aversion of the majority of our countrymen from national debt." Although the nation's "greatest obstacle," this aversion to debt was difficult to extirpate because it was rooted in ignorance. If only more people could be brought to see that the national debt not only afforded "all those advantages which flowed from our glorious revolution" but also "became a most productive source of wealth" that facilitated "commercial interchange," Hare lamented. Complicating matters, hawks who thought war with France was preferable and doves who opposed war with anyone flew about, too. Meanwhile, a strange coalition of westerners, southerners, and others who hoped to acquire Canada, Texas, and/or Florida gained strength seemingly with each passing month.[26]

The anti-British hawks, aided by President Madison, finally won out in June 1812 when the United States declared war on the former mother country. The war was in many ways a strange one, with the United States losing most land battles but winning many of those at sea. British forces stopped American incursions into Canada cold and, after defeating Napoleon, the Brits counterattacked with vigor. Only with their backs against the wall at Baltimore, where "The Star-Spangled Banner" was written, and New Orleans, where Andrew Jackson's reputation was made, did U.S. land forces regain their lost honor.

The Second War for Independence, as it was sometimes called, began as the first had, with the credit of the U.S. government "very low." One problem was that in 1811 the government had decided, over Gallatin's protests and by a razor-thin margin, to allow the charter of the Bank of the United States to expire. The nation therefore had to enter the war without a central bank or a sure source of short-term financing. The other problem was that the Treasury, already weakened by the trade embargoes, was heavily dependent on tariffs and tonnage duties. Sharp curtailment of foreign trade during the war therefore wreaked havoc on government finances as revenues plummeted from $14.4 million in 1811 to $9.8 million in 1812. Revenues rebounded to $14.3 million in 1813 but dropped back to $11.2 million in 1814.[27]

> Sharp curtailment of foreign trade during the war therefore wreaked havoc on government finances as revenues plummeted from $14.4 million in 1811 to $9.8 million in 1812.

The Republicans' failure to follow Hamilton's admonishment to maintain the direct tax collection apparatus intact also injured public credit. Rather than move quickly to reinstate direct taxes, Congress dithered, a costly delay considering that the new excises could not be assessed, laid, collected, and remitted in less than a year after congressional authorization. Due to the disruption of trade, tariffs slid in importance in terms of both their absolute and their relative contribution to federal coffers during the war. All told, taxes paid for less than half of the war's expenses. Sinking fund appropriations were diverted to expenditures, as it made little sense to pay down low-interest debt with one hand while borrowing at high rates with the other. Thankfully, the war was short, and, outside of New England, popular. Moreover, the armed forces used a contract system similar to that developed during the first war for independence, which placed much of the risk on mercantile contractors. That meant high profits at times, but large losses too. "Until the last year," reported a Richmond merchant in early 1815, the Virginia contractor's "profitts [sic] were large" but his losses in the last year of the war were estimated at $50,000.[28]

Most of the burden of war finance fell upon the nation's banks and money and capital markets. Contemporaries knew that the government had two types of needs, long-term capital and short-term liquidity loans. To meet the latter

> Most of the burden of war finance fell upon the nation's banks and money and capital markets.

it issued Treasury notes, short-term (usually one-year) bonds that paid interest of 5.4 percent. Gallatin and others had considered issuing Treasury notes as early as 1811, to supply the country with a uniform medium of exchange and the government with short-term loans, but decided against it due to "the prejudice which exists on the subject of paper currency." In other words, the public was still not ready to accept anything that looked like bills of credit. Instruments that bore interest, however, were palatable. During the war, the government issued some $36 million worth of the notes, including $5 million issued at its outset. State banks, which numbered 125 at the war's outset and 181 at its close, also supplied funds when government long-term bond issues faltered, as they often did, and made short-term loans to the Treasury as well.[29]

Hamilton had not thought it prudent, lawful, or moral to sequester or confiscate government bonds in time of war and the Republicans, who increasingly appeared to be Hamiltonians mugged by reality, apparently agreed, because payments to British investors holding U.S. bonds were maintained throughout the war. Nevertheless, many British investors were not thrilled to hold American bonds, the prices of which sagged in the London market. Wartime conditions apparently prevented arbitrageurs from buying the debt cheap in London for resale at much higher prices in America. In any event, early in the conflict British investors remitted large numbers of U.S. bonds purchased before the war and clearly were in no mood to purchase large sums of new American bond issues. Dutch and other European investors, exhausted from over a decade of war, were in no position to offer aid, as a botched attempt to sell Sixes in Europe in 1814 verified. American investors would have to go this one alone.[30]

The first test came in 1812, before war was officially declared but after mobilization had taken its first tentative steps. Investors bought at par about $8 million of the $11 million worth of 6 percent bonds (Sixes of 1812) the government offered. Banks took up another $2.15 million on special redemption terms; for other investors, the bonds became repayable at the government's pleasure any time after the first day of 1825. To help maintain the prices it could procure on the sale of new bonds, the government worked to keep up the prices of the old debt in the secondary markets. To raise Louisiana Sixes to par from their usual 99 to 99.5 percent, for example, Gallatin urged Congress to make them transferable on the books of the various state loan offices instead of just in Washington, because the transaction costs, to wit "the delay, and the necessity of employing an agent," were the cause of the lower price for the bonds that prevailed "in the commercial cities." It was a good thought, but offered far too little to prevent the chaos to come.[31]

In 1813, the government went back to the capital markets again, this time for $16 million. Although vigorously opposed by congressional doves seeking peace, the measure, which created a 6 percent bond (Sixes of 1813) redeemable at pleasure after January 1, 1826, passed. But investors nationwide were reluctant to buy on the government's terms, which did not include convincing permanent increases in taxation. Moreover, many moneyed men, particularly New Englanders, were outright hostile to the conflict, the government, and its bonds. The initial subscription, taken on March 12 and 13 at 19 banks in 11 cities across the nation, hauled in less than $4 million. The Treasury was at this point virtually broke. Induced by a commission of .25 percent and, some say, a good dose of patriotism for his adopted country, longtime Philadelphia resident Stephen Girard, a half-blind merchant-turned-banker born in France, stepped in to help. Along with two other European-born capitalists, wealthy Philadelphian David Parrish and New York fur and real estate mogul John Jacob Astor, Girard purchased the remaining bonds, over $10 million worth in all. The syndicate members kept some of the bonds for themselves, but retailed most of them off to institutions and small investors. In fine, $15.469 million worth of the issue sold, but only at 88 percent of par. Later that year, another issue of $7.5 million sold, with the help of Girard and the other early investment bankers, at a discount of 11.75 percent. Bank loans and another $5 million of Treasury notes supplied the balance of the government's financing needs for the year.[32]

The Treasury, headed by George W. Campbell between February 9 and October 6, 1814, when he was replaced by Alexander J. Dallas, issued notes and bonds again in 1814 and 1815 and again encountered reluctant investors. The government and the investment bankers could not agree to terms, however, so the Treasury went it alone. One major consequence of the government's poor credit was that it had to pay more than it otherwise would have for war material. In his memoirs, New York City sailmaker Stephen Allen relates the following telling story about the government's efforts to build a fleet on the Great Lakes:

> As the goods in my store at the time were insufficient to supply the order, and as the parting with the whole of them would have left me destitute of the means of supplying the calls of my regular customers, I declined selling, unless the article was unattainable elsewhere. I proposed to the agent therefore, that he should authorize me to purchase on the credit of the government such quantities as could be bought of the holders of small parcels, not to exceed the number of pieces wanted. To this he assented and I was accordingly authorized to purchase on a credit of ninety days, paying in Treasury Notes at the market price of the notes on the day the money should become payable; but, so low was the credit of the government at this period that but few of the holders of the commodity would sell at any price and those who consented to sell added eight or ten per cent to the fair price of the article before they would part with their goods on the terms proposed.

Although unaided by investment bankers this time, the Treasury received
$17.895 million from sales of the Sixes of 1814, but ultimately at only
80 percent of par. The Treasury here
made the major blunder of promising

> The Treasury here made the major blunder of promising early investors that they would receive the best terms obtained during the year.

early investors that they would receive
the best terms obtained during the
year. That provided investors with the
incentive to depress securities prices
instead of support them, as they typically would have. As a result, the 12 per-
cent discount on government Sixes early in the year swelled to 20 by the end!
Still hungry for cash, late in 1814 the Treasury borrowed $1.45 million from
banks under special contracts and issued another $8.318 million worth of
Treasury notes.[33]

Although the war ended officially in December 1814, but in reality in January 1815 after General Andrew Jackson's stunning victory at New Orleans, the
government's needs still far outstripped its means. Public buildings ravaged
by the British raid on the capital on August 24, 1814, had to be rebuilt, soldiers
paid, existing government contracts fulfilled, and temporary loans repaid. So
in 1815, the Treasury issued $12.288 million more worth of long-term bonds,
some at 6 and some at 7 percent interest. The average discount on the former,
which varied widely among locales, was 4.80 percent. The government also
issued more Treasury notes, and a new type of note designed to circulate as
money. Although at peace, the nation's economy was considerably deranged
by the suspension of specie payments by the banks outside of New England.
The British raid on the capital had caused hoarding and large shipments of
specie to New England and Canada that, according to Dallas, "considerably
diminished the fund of gold and silver coin" elsewhere in the country. With
"no adequate circulating medium, common to the citizens of the United
States," large *domestic* exchange rates arose, making it costly and at times
impossible for the Treasury to transfer funds from one part of the country
to another. As a consequence, "the moneyed transactions of private life [we]
re at a stand, and the fiscal operations of the Government labor[ed] with
extreme inconvenience." "The difference of Southern money and money
here," banker Henry Remsen explained to John P. Van Ness, "is so great,
that you will not be able to remit the sum you intend ... without sustaining

considerable loss. If you have U.S. stock, and can afford to sell it for 5 or 6 percent under par, that will prove a good remittance," he said, adding that "specie can be remitted at 9 or 10 per cent above par at the present moment. The present," Remsen concluded, "is truly a most unfavorable period, as regards commercial intercourse and remittances between our great cities."[34]

The derangement also injured public creditors, who had to "accept whatever the treasury [was] able to offer" at its various offices. The State Department could not pay its stationery bill, it was said, and the War Department could not meet a bill for $30. Secretary Dallas thought it best to keep that fact on the q.t., as they say. "The state of the business," he explained to North Carolina congressman Bartlett Yancy, "is better to be explained at the treasury, than to be announced in an act of Congress." As a temporary expedient, the government in 1815 rendered some of its new Treasury notes more liquid, more moneylike, by issuing them as bearer instruments, in small denominations, and without interest. In other words, the federal government issued what members of the Revolutionary era called bills of credit.[35]

The politically motivated failure of the federal government to recharter the Bank of the United States had come home to roost. In 1816, therefore, the government incorporated a new bank of the same name and paid for $7 million worth of its stock in new 5 percent bonds. The bank's notes soon provided the country with a widely accepted medium of exchange. By January 1817, businessmen instructed their agents to recoup sums due them in the notes of a local bank *or* the "UStates Bank." The bank also provided government with a wide range of financial services and, like the first BUS, it sopped up large amounts of public debt because three-fourths of its $35 million capital was payable in it at par (Sixes at 100, Threes at 65, and Sevens at 106.51).[36]

❧

The first U.S. debt topped out at the beginning of 1815, during the administration of a man whose mouth it was said could not utter the word "debt" without also uttering "evil," at $127.335 million. Although "the public credit was depressed during the war," as Treasury Secretary Dallas admitted, the country, its economy, and its financial system had performed much better than during the Revolution. There were inconveniences and losses, but no

The first U.S. debt topped out at the beginning of 1815, during the administration of a man whose mouth it was said could not utter the word "debt" without also uttering "evil," at $127.335 million.

repetition of the scenes at Valley Forge, Morristown, or Newburgh. Even more impressive was the rapidity with which the national government rebounded. The war had cost some $88 million to prosecute, but before the end of the decade the government had reduced the total debt, including the remaining Revolutionary War debt, well below the $100 million mark, despite sizable pension payments made to Revolutionary War veterans beginning in 1818. (That the government could finally be generous to those men in the wake of a second war against the erstwhile mother country was another sign of the maturity of the nation's government and economy.) A surge in imports after the war was a leading cause, as was the increase in the permanent sinking fund appropriation to $10 million per year, a deft maneuver ascribed to Albert Gallatin and William Lowndes. Tax reforms helped too. Government revenues increased from $15.8 million in 1815 to an incredible $47.7 million in 1816. Revenues in 1817, 1818, and 1819 remained strong at $33.1, $21.7, and $24.6 million, respectively. In 1819, however, a commercial crisis and financial panic, by far the worst in the nation's history to that point, placed the "monetary concerns and trade of the country … in a depressed state" as interest rates on private paper soared and the price of lands plummeted, in some areas by 50 percent.[37]

The ensuing recession prompted some deep soul-searching and hurt the public treasury more than a little. Imports slacked off and over $3 million in merchants' bonds pledged to pay customs duties went to suit, by far the largest sum of such bonds ever to default. Government revenues shrank to $17.8 million in 1820 and $14.6 million the following year, causing the impressive postwar debt paydown to cease, and then, with the issuance of new 5 and 6 percent bonds in 1820 in 1821, to temporarily reverse. The good news was that the recession brought with it lower interest rates, so the Treasury in 1820 was able to sell its Sixes, and in 1821 its Fives, at a premium rather than a discount.[38]

In 1824, the Treasury successfully sold $5 million worth of new 4.5 percent bonds at par, the proceeds of which were used to satisfy the terms of a treaty negotiated with Spain in 1819 that gave the United States title of, and control over, Florida and portions of the Gulf Coast. That same year, the Treasury sold another $5 million worth of 4.5 percent bonds at par and used the proceeds to repay Sixes that became redeemable after January 1, 1825. A similar batch of Sixes about to become redeemable were voluntarily exchanged by investors for 4.5 percent bonds redeemable in 1833. In 1825, another exchange loan program faltered, however, attracting subscriptions of only about $1.5 million. Although market interest rates had risen, the Treasury again offered only 4.5 percent interest and moved the redemption date up to 1831, which together conspired to kill investor interest in the conversion. Thereafter, the Treasury drew lots to determine which bonds would be redeemed as the monies to do so became available.[39]

Part of the reason why the government was able to borrow on such good terms was that, after a rocky start, the second Bank of the United States assumed the same central banking role that the first BUS had played. Especially under the leadership of president Nicholas Biddle, the BUS was "the great regulator of the entire machine which prevents too violent shocks from taking place." In 1825, for example, Biddle employed Hamilton's Law to thwart the spread of a financial panic that lay Britain's economy prostrate. Thus cloistered from commercial shocks, the Treasury, investors believed, would have little difficulty meeting its obligations in a timely matter.[40]

Even British investors were impressed. "The heavy fall of stocks in England towards the close of 1825," Secretary Richard Rush later remembered, "affected those of this country less than might have been anticipated from the connexions of business between the two countries, and serves to show the value of those of this government, even under untoward occurrences, in that great centre of the commercial world." Continued political support for stiff revenue tariffs further strengthened the nation's credit. Experimentation with protective tariffs in the 1820s and early 1830s was given up after the Nullification Crisis, South Carolina's refusal to enforce high federal tariffs in 1832–33. After a testy confrontation that nearly led to armed conflict, tariff levels were prudently and slowly phased down until by 1846, with the Walker Tariff, levels were as low as they had been in 1816.[41]

The repayment of the national debt exacerbated the Nullification Crisis because it weakened the ties between wealthy South Carolinians, who no longer owned federal bonds, and the national government. During the Missouri Crisis a dozen or so years earlier, the national debt had helped to bind the union together because southerners believed that "the free states which hold two thirds of the National debt and of the National Bank stock" would not allow the South to secede "till we have paid our just debts. They will hold our Noses to the grindstone as we hold those of our slaves. For, after all, a Debtor is no better than a slave. His creditor is to all intents and purposes his Master, till by the payment of his debts he is set at liberty from his fetters and Bonds."[42]

A strong political commitment to debt repayment also bolstered government credit. Many public creditors found repayment inconvenient because, as Treasury Secretary Richard Rush noted in 1828, "his reliance upon the faith and resources of the nation is so unbounded, that he prefers to let his capital stock remain in its [the government's] hands, subject only to his calls for the interest." Other investment opportunities abounded, but none so safe. Most Americans, however, wanted the debt paid off as quickly as prudently possible. In 1820, erstwhile Federalist treasury secretary (1795–1800) Oliver Wolcott, then governor of Connecticut, suggested that government debt should be paid down rapidly because it was crowding out private investment in manufacturing. He also wanted to strengthen and extend the country's "system of internal revenue" so that the government was not so reliant on tariff revenues. Presidents Monroe, Adams, and Jackson heeded the former but ignored the latter suggestion. All pushed for debt repayment as rapidly as the state of the economy and federal treasury allowed. And pay off the debt they did, until it shrank so low in per capita terms, and as a percentage of aggregate output, that it became economically possible to eliminate it.[43]

The transfer books of all the bonds issued during and after the War of 1812 have not been examined in detail, but by all accounts the markets for the bonds were very similar to those of the old Sixes and Deferred Sixes.

(And the old Threes were still around and well until the very end.) Women, men from a wide range of occupations, and sundry institutions—including banks, insurance companies, and charitable organizations—owned the bonds, transferring them at will. Trading volumes were sufficient to induce many newspapers in the bigger cities to quote their prices. Prices of U.S. bonds were also regularly published in European newspapers by the early 1810s. Foreign investment in U.S. bonds continued in the 1820s, thanks in part to bullish commentary by analysts like Bernard Cohen in his *Compendium of Finance*. In October 1824, for example, British investors owned $18.5 million worth of U.S. bonds, while Dutch investors owned a cool $3.4 million, and sundry other foreigners owned a total of $2.1 million. Despite the wartime hiatus, Britain throughout this period was "notoriously a large holder of the stocks of this country." Government bonds served the same role as specie in the international commercial system, i.e., as a means of settling balances due when a country's imports exceeded its exports. That role was a particularly important one for the early United States, which possessed no large gold or silver mines and ran trade deficits in all but seven years between 1791 and 1840, inclusive. Acting as a substitute for specie was but one of the many benefits of the first national debt. In the next chapter, we explore its other benefits in considerable detail, from the standpoint of some of Virginia's federal bondholders.[44]

7

LIFE

The Life and Times of Federal Bondholders in Virginia

"I find" that Hamilton's report is much disapproved of here; and of all things the assumption of the State debts under any modification whatever is dreaded as the greatest of evils. Let Congress do this and remove to Philadelphia and a schism in the nation must happen." So wrote Charles Lee from Richmond in June 1790. He was far from alone but perhaps not as representative of the Old Dominion as generally believed. Although a hotbed of political sentiment against funding, assumption, banking, and finance in general, Virginia was home to a surprising number of holders of federal bonds. Between October 20, 1790, and June 14, 1834, at least 1,781 different entities, 120 of whom were women, registered bonds on the books of Virginia's federal loan office commissioner. Each major area of the state, from the Tidewater, to the Piedmont, to the Valley, and from No. Va., to Central Virginia, to the Southside, was home to federal bondholders. A wide variety of occupations were represented as well, including administrators and executors of estates, agents, attorneys, brokers, corporate directors and officers, doctors, esquires-gentlemen, guardians, merchants, politicians, planters, printers, clergymen, spinsters, tax collectors, trustees, and widows.[1]

Most Virginia federal bondholders left little trace in the historical record other than census, probate, and tax records. Tantalizing clues, however, abound for some, and for a few biographies have been, or could be, written. In the sections that follow, I generalize from an in-depth study of 100 of them. We cannot consider these people typical in any rigorous statistical sense but nevertheless their stories can help us to understand the role that federal bonds played in the lives of Virginians and indeed all early American federal bondholders.

Augusta County farmer John Bowyer first appears in the historical record in 1753, as a poor young schoolteacher. A year later, though, he married into financial independence. Soon thereafter, he became justice of the peace and a militia captain. Later, he acquired a large tract of land near the James River and became county sheriff. He sat in the House of Burgesses from 1770 until 1776, when he was a member of the convention that voted for independence and adopted the state's famous Declaration of Rights. He served in the House of Delegates in 1776–78, 1782, 1784–86, 1789–96, and 1799–1802. Not that serving in the Virginia legislature was a big deal at that time. According to one account, the early House of Delegates was an amateurish affair that once adjourned at Christmastime because almost all the members were sloshed on eggnog. "The members from their copious potations of the beverage of the season" were in a "helpless condition," it was later recalled. In a more sober time, 1781, Bowyer led 200 men against the British invaders. Likely because of that service, he obtained over $1,800 worth of federal bonds in January 1792. In May, just after the Panic, he sold his holdings. That same year, Bowyer became a brigadier general in Virginia's Thirteenth Brigade. A staunch Jeffersonian, Bowyer died in 1806, the proud owner of some 1,325 acres of land.[2]

William Cabell (1730–98) was part of the large and influential Cabell clan that dominated colonial central Virginia just east of the picturesque Blue Ridge Mountains. As befitting a large plantation owner (he owned 25,000 acres by his death), Cabell was Amherst County's first lieutenant, surveyor, and coroner. From 1761 until the Revolution, Cabell represented Amherst County in the House of Burgesses, colonial Virginia's legislature. Although not influential at first, as the imperial crisis with Britain deepened his power rose; he was several times unanimously re-elected to office.

He was an extremely active legislator during and after the war. During Virginia's Ratification Convention, Cabell and his son Samuel J., also a delegate, remained staunchly antifederalist. In addition to his plantation, he owned an interest in an ironworks and the James River Company. His federal securities ownership was extremely limited, just over $200 of Sixes and Deferred Sixes between February 1791 and February 1792.[3]

Obviously, then, one need not have been a federalist (a supporter of the Constitution) or a Federalist (a supporter of the Washington and Adams administrations) to own federal bonds. But it helped. As shown above, some bondholders were antifederalists and/or Jeffersonian Republicans. Like Bowyer and Cabell, however, they tended to divest quickly and thereafter stay out of the funds. At any given time, then, many, perhaps most, Virginia bondholders were outright Federalists or had Federalist sympathies. Many were former Revolutionary War officers driven to nationalist views during the war and its ugly aftermath. Others were merchants or professionals, occupations that harbored large numbers of Federalists and fellow travelers. Even Virginia's planter class contained its fair share of Federalists, particularly planters who had served in the Revolution, or who feared attacks from foreign enemies, be they seaborne or indigenous.

> At any given time, then, many, perhaps most, Virginia bondholders were outright Federalists or had Federalist sympathies.

Consider, for example, Accomack County tobacco planter John "Jack" Cropper. Although born rather late (1755), Cropper as a stripling youth served as a captain, then a major, in the Continental Army. He barely survived the pummeling Washington's army took at the Battle of Brandywine Creek in September 1777, during which he took command of his unit, as surviving ranking officer, though wounded in the thigh by a bayonet. Exhausted, his men could not retreat with the rest of the army so Cropper hid them in a nearby field for the night, rejoining Washington the next morning. Cropper also lived through the Germantown debacle and the cruel winter that followed at Valley Forge. Later, when back home on furlough, men from a loyalist privateer plundered his house, which lay just a few yards from the sea on Virginia's Eastern Shore, and "savagely threatened" his wife. Caught by surprise in the middle of the night, Cropper managed to escape to a neighbor's house several miles distant, where he borrowed some muskets that he used to feign an attack by a large number of men. The ruffians, their minds by this time thoroughly drenched with Cropper's wine, fell for the ruse and fled, just before they were about to blow up Cropper's house with gunpowder. Understandably fearful of leaving his wife, young daughter, and slaves unattended and sick of the lack of pay and the dearth of hard money, which even his wealthy friends had difficulty obtaining on his behalf, Cropper resigned his commission in August 1779 and returned home, where he led local militia units not just until the end of the war but to the end of his life in 1821.[4]

While serving in various official state offices in the 1780s and 1790s, Cropper suffered much personal pain, including the death of his first wife and the loss of three infant daughters, each of whom he had named after his mother. Despite those personal setbacks, Cropper's crops thrived. By 1820, Cropper owned a new, large mansion, 20 adolescent and adult slaves, and almost 1,300 acres of land. In September 1791, Cropper converted about $300 of his old federal securities into Sixes, Threes, and Deferred Sixes. The following January, he did likewise with over $7,000 worth of state securities. He sold the whole lot of them on July 25, 1792. He held on to his military lands in Ohio, some 6,666.67 acres, and Kentucky, however, perhaps because he acted too slowly to get them properly located and surveyed. In any event, he bequeathed those lands to his heirs in his will.[5]

Like many Virginia federal bondholders, Cropper was a Federalist, and recognized as such in 1799 by none other than soon-to-be U.S. Supreme Court chief justice John Marshall. Cropper was a recipient of William Austin's 1800 campaign missives on behalf of the Federalist American Republican Ticket and later was courted by John Patterson, who as late as December 1819 proclaimed himself "proud in being denominated a Federalist." In 1817, Cropper was made Accomack County's commissioner for the receipt of donations to erect a monument to George Washington, "the Father of His Country" and the figurehead of Federalism.[6]

Cropper also received the circulars of Burwell Bassett (1764–1841), who, though eventually elected to Congress as a Republican was hardly a true-blue Jeffersonian. Bassett, who grew corn and wheat on his plantation, opposed the recharter of the Bank of the United States on constitutional grounds but proclaimed to his constituents that he would rather slow or even cease repayment of the national debt than see Navy expenditures cut. He knew that a weak navy would threaten his constituents, most of whom, like Cropper, lived a short distance from the Chesapeake Bay, with foreign predations. A graduate of the College of William and Mary, Bassett narrowly lost election to Congress in April 1813 by just 57 votes. Due to voting irregularities, including votes cast by people with dubious qualifications and a questionable polling time extension, he appealed. Numerous votes on both sides were disallowed but when all was said and done his opponent, Thomas Monteagle Bayly (1775–1834), still prevailed by 5 votes. Bassett recuperated and won election to Congress on and off again into the early Jacksonian period. By then, though, his aristocratic bearing and old-fashioned "small clothes and powdered hair in a queue" many found more offensive than quaint. Extant accounts with his tailor, Anderson McCandlish, suggest that Bassett was indeed a proper *eighteenth-century* gentleman.[7]

Despite having inherited a large fortune from his father, also Burwell Bassett (1734–93), Bassett owned Sixes and Exchanged Sixes only as the guardian of Burnett Lewis, one of at least a half-dozen orphans, likely his godchildren, that he aided. On behalf of Lewis, he purchased the bonds in 1802, 1803, and 1807 and sold them off in 1807 and 1811. His own money Bassett appears to have invested in his neighbors, likely for political advantage.[8]

The Thomas Bayly who narrowly defeated Bassett in April 1813 was born and raised in Accomack County. After graduating from Washington Academy in Somerset County, Maryland, and the College of New Jersey (now Princeton University), Bayly became a planter and Federalist politician. He served in Virginia's House of Delegates and Senate before defeating Bassett for a seat in the U.S. House of Representatives, running on an antiwar platform and, as we've seen, with a good dose of luck. Despite his opposition to the war, Bayly helped to defend his native state by serving in its militia. He did not seek reelection to Congress in 1815, concentrating instead on his plantation and law practice. He did, however, serve a few more terms in the House of Delegates and was a delegate to the Virginia constitutional convention of 1830. He died in January 1834 deeply in debt. Bayly's bond ownership history was straightforward: he obtained a few hundred dollars of Threes, Sixes, and Deferred Sixes in April 1793 and sold them in August 1806.[9]

John Blair was another prominent Federalist bondholder, and one of eighteenth-century Virginia's legal legends. Born in 1731 in Williamsburg, the son of a longtime member of the governor's council and four-time acting governor, Blair attended the College of William and Mary and studied law in the Middle Temple in London. He returned to Williamsburg to practice law and run his plantation shortly after marrying his cousin, Jean Blair, in Edinburgh, Scotland in 1756. Blair became clerk of the governor's council in 1770. During the Revolution, he helped to prepare the Virginia Declaration of Rights and its first constitution and sat on its highest courts. In 1787, he attended the Constitutional Convention in Philadelphia on behalf of Virginia. Although he made no recorded speeches, he signed the document and supported its unconditional ratification. As thanks for his support, Washington in 1789 appointed him to the U.S. Supreme Court, where he served with distinction. He resigned in 1795 due to poor health ("A strong disorder of my head," he wrote Washington, possibly the first of several strokes) but remained active in local Federalist politics. Blair also remained an active federal securities trader. Between late September 1791 and June 1794, Blair in 19 transactions bought over $16,000 in federal bonds and sold, in three transactions, about $9,500 worth. Between 1795 and his death in 1800, he made nine more purchases, totaling just over $2,200, and one sale, for $2,800 and some change. About a month after his death, the balance of his holdings was transferred to other parties.[10]

On March 13, 1724, Cornelius Calvert was born of Cornelius Calvert the great merchant of colonial Norfolk, Virginia. After an obligatory stint at sea, the young Calvert, like his daddy before him, got married and settled down in Norfolk as a merchant. By 1776, when his house and warehouse burned along with much of the rest of the city, Calvert lost over £2,300, a small fortune at the time. Active in city politics, Calvert served as mayor and alderman as well as in lesser offices. After the Revolution, he also led a movement to reform the colonial city charter, which he deemed unrepublican and conducive to corruption. He was no democrat, though, as he showed in 1798 when he called the Alien and Sedition Acts "excellent bills" because they kept foreigners at bay and the "unruly mob" away. On his own account, Calvert accumulated about $5,000 worth of federal bonds between May 1793 and February 1804. He owned all of them in November of that year, when he died. His executor sold off his portfolio the following April. The executor also sold the bonds, worth over $5,000 all told, that Calvert owned as administrator of the estate of William and Mary Walk.[11]

In 1754 in Augusta County was born Robert Gamble, another Federalist and big federal bondholder. Educated at Liberty Hall Academy, the forerunner of Washington and Lee University, Gamble set up as a merchant but soon after closed his business to serve his country in the Revolution, first as a lieutenant and later as a captain. Before the long struggle was over, he had seen action at Princeton, Monmouth, and Stony Point and "acquired great applause for his bravery and good conduct." After the war, Gamble became a lieutenant colonel in the militia. He also again took up mercantile pursuits with his brother-in-law, Robert Grattan, at a store in Staunton in the Shenandoah Valley. In the early 1790s, Gamble retained a summer home in Staunton but moved his mercantile operations to Richmond, where he conducted a wholesale business as "Gamble and Temple," "Robert Gamble & Co.," and, finally, "Robert Gamble & Sons," from a large building at Main and Fourteenth Streets. Gamble lived in a commodious brick building at Third and Byrd Streets, atop what came to be known as Gamble's Hill.[12]

Like many merchants, Gamble was a Federalist, though he professed to rarely having time to "hear any of the debates" himself. He distrusted Republicans, especially when it came to financial matters. He should have distrusted everyone. He was liberal with trade credit, far too liberal, in fact. Gamble frequently found it difficult to collect small sums advanced to people like Dr. William Gross; "a likely well made Dutch man," Jacob Woland, "by trade a rough carpenter"; another "Dutch man," who skipped town before paying his bill; and "an active sprightly looking little man" named Eliot Brown. Gamble was also on the lookout for James Fisher, a middle-aged man of "middle size inclined to be corpulent" who owed Gamble for a consignment of butter worth about $200. As Gamble's business grew, so too did the magnitude of his accounts receivable, until by the late 1790s a single person owed him over $3,400, a princely sum at the time. Some debtors looked for any excuse not to pay, including claiming a dearth of "safe conveyances" by which to send money. Gamble knew that that excuse was lame because as a final resort banknotes could be cut in half and enclosed in different letters sent by post, then reattached "with a bit of paper & a wafer" by the recipient.[13]

Delinquent accounts were a real problem when Gamble was "in great need of money," as he often was. In 1797, for instance, he noted that he was "under a present embarrassment for money" due to a "train of harassing debts." In 1800, he lost a bundle when "the credulity of a well meaning young man, that I unfortunately confided the management of my affairs to in my absence," was, he claimed, "unexampled in this part of the Country." So once again Gamble was "in extreme need of every dollar." In 1803, Gamble was in trouble again, complaining that all he had on hand was a "large stock of *refuse*" and goods, like butter, that glutted the market (italics in original). April 1804 was another "distressing time for money" because all merchants had "large quantities of produce on hand." In 1808, Jefferson's embargo and its zealous execution caused yet more financial problems. "All is astonishment and alarm," Gamble wrote, "and God knows when the evil is to subside."[14]

Although a firm believer in punctuality of payment, Gamble, try as he might, was not always able to oblige. That probably induced him to mock the spoiled brat of a rich planter for bragging about his punctuality. After sending the youth $55 in BUS notes and eight half-Joes (Portuguese gold coins worth £19.7.4 Virginia pounds or about $65),[15] Gamble remarked that he "can't help *smiling* at the prodigious outcry you make on account of the deplorable situation you are placed in. *Poor fellow*," he wrote sarcastically, the youth ought to thank God for providing for him "so bountifully ... by the agency of your parents" and friends (italics in original). "You know little about difficulties," Gamble scoffed. Despite his rough handling of the young dandy, Gamble was generally a charitable man and in fact helped to found the Amicable Society of Richmond, an early charity.[16]

Gamble left the partnership with his sons by degrees in 1805 and early 1806 after complaining that mercantile pursuits had made him a "Drudge & Slave" and that he needed time to attend to "old business"—all those uncollected debts. Nevertheless, he was only semiretired at best, continuing to do some commission, exchange, and bank stock business on his own account. Bank stock he thought at that time offered a much better investment for men "who can occasionally share part of their funds to be invested" than keeping monies "in hands whose circumstances will not enable them to hold it." Purchases of bank stock at par he thought a great, if temporary, deal occasioned by rising interest rates and merchants' dire need for cash. In 1806, he was offered a directorship in a bank. Gamble also ran his sons' business when they were away, which was a rather frequent occurrence, and guaranteed their debts "as if my name was publickly announced therein."[17]

Despite the occasional illness, Gamble was in good health in 1810, remitting a large sum of banknotes to flour miller Thomas Massie on April 5. Just a week later, on the morning of April 12, Gamble was reading the newspaper atop his steed when some buffalo hides thrown out of a window frightened the poor creature, who threw the old merchant on his noggin. Gamble died a few hours later, though a good doctor had quickly trepanned his head to relieve brain swelling. Although he had some bank debt, Gamble died a fairly wealthy man, the owner of eight slaves and four horses, including the one that accidentally killed him. Unsurprisingly, Gamble was one of Virginia's most important federal securities investors. Between March 1791 and March 1795, Gamble bought over $10,000 worth of federal bonds in 15 transactions, selling during that period only once, $942.35 of Sixes during the Panic of 1792, presumably because he needed the cash. (He later told correspondents to invest in bank shares when they could because like government bonds they were "an article from which by sale money can be always raised in an emergency.") Cash constraints probably also explain why he sold over $9,000 worth of bonds from early April through July 1795. (Some trading activity in March 1795, by contrast, was likely motivated by a desire to swap Deferred Sixes for interest-bearing bonds.) From then until his trading activity ended in 1804, a total of 10 transactions, Gamble gambled, buying and then selling the same security within a few months.[18]

Gamble's son Robert married into a prominent Scots Irish family when he took one of Federalist attorney and planter James Breckinridge's daughters as his bride. Breckinridge was born in 1763 and, due to his youth, fought in the Revolution as a private and an ensign. After his duties, he did some surveying in Kentucky but he returned home to Botetourt County, ostensibly because while he found Kentucky women attractive none was rich enough for his tastes. Tutored privately before the war, after it he attended Washington and Lee and then took up law at the College of William and Mary. In 1788, he watched the Virginia Ratifying Convention debates from the gallery and found them "elaborate, elegant, eloquent and consequently entertaining and instructive." In early 1789, Breckinridge returned home, where he did some surveying work, practiced law, and collected federal taxes. He also acted as a private debt collector for distant creditors desirous of chasing down wayward debtors in the south-central valley while, at other times, he served as counsel to insolvent debtors.[19]

Also in 1789, Breckinridge began a long stint in the House of Delegates, where he soon became a leading Federalist. He supported Hamilton's financial program by voting against a resolution in the Virginia legislature that called assumption "repugnant to the Constitution" and "dangerous to the rights and subversive of the interests of the people." In 1799, the Federalists ran Breckinridge for governor, but he lost to future U.S. president James Monroe. As a delegate, Breckinridge backed internal improvements, like the James and Kanawha River projects and a turnpike over the Blue Ridge Mountains at Rockfish Gap, likely to help his constituents (and himself) get their agricultural surpluses cheaply to market. He was delighted to learn that steamboats had begun successfully plying the mighty Susquehanna.[20]

Between 1809 and 1817, Breckinridge served in the House of Representatives, gaining election, his friend Joseph Lewis claimed, because "the people are honest" and "they will always act right" if provided "with correct information," presumably about the hardships caused by Jefferson's trade strictures. Specifically, the prices of flour and tobacco were low, trading was dull, and "the holders [we]re seriously uneasy" because the freights were "so high" due to the nonintercourse law "as to make shipments very hazardous." It helped, too, that Breckinridge ran unopposed! There was no sense running against him, a fellow Federalist noted, because there was no one worthy. "A federal seventy four," he wrote, alluding to warships, "was never afraid of a Democratic gun boat."[21]

Breckinridge rarely spoke on the floor of Congress but like most Federalists he made it clear that he feared France more than Britain. "Within the last year," Breckinridge reminded his constituents in a circular letter dated February 27, 1811, the French had seized $30 million of Americans' property and thrown "several hundred of our seamen ... into the Dungeons of France, many of whom were destitute of the means of subsistence." As a matter of course, Breckinridge opposed the War of 1812, going so far as to vote against federal direct taxes and emissions of Treasury notes, both of which, as we've seen, were necessary to prosecute the war. Nevertheless, he led militia troops to Maryland during the British invasion of the Chesapeake in 1814. He returned to the House of Delegates in 1819, where he served on committees for finance and on schools and colleges, from which platform he helped to obtain funding for the nascent University of Virginia. He also continued to support improvement of the James River and voted in favor of chartering the Chesapeake and Ohio Canal Company. His successor in Congress, John Floyd, tried to lure him back into the Washington fray in the mid-1820s, but Breckinridge, who was getting on in years, declined. He died in 1833.[22]

Robert Gamble Jr., who was also a Federalist, solicited his father-in-law for any juicy but nonsecret information he wished to divulge that would help his brother George and him to "make a fortune." "In the event of War with England," the Gambles asked Breckinridge in 1812, would the national government "repeal the non-importation act and admit British Manufactures, either directly or indirectly in neutral Ships?" Breckinridge indeed supplied his son-in-law with some valuable information on the eve of the war, but it was not enough, as we will see, to render the Gambles independent.[23]

Breckinridge was as savvy financially and in business generally as he was politically. He employed an overseer to monitor the activities of the several score slaves (at least) who worked his 4,000 acres of land on which grew a

wide variety of food crops and hemp. The plantation also boasted a brick-
yard, tannery, forge, and mill. Breckinridge explicitly added those improvements because he believed that they would be profitable. "I believe my mill &
tannery," he wrote Henry Lee one Sunday, "in the hands of a careful honest
man a sure fund tolerably productive at first & encreasing annually." Moreover, diversification smoothed his income because when the prices of some
of his crops were depressed, the prices of other of his productions, like iron,
tended to be elevated. Like most big plantation owners, Breckinridge also
bought and sold land as necessary.[24]

Breckinridge astutely insured his home with the Mutual Assurance
Company after helping to prepare its charter in the House of Delegates.
Including the kitchen and stables, his new mansion, which unsurprisingly
was Federalist in style, was thought worth $12,100, far too costly to risk
losing. Fires regularly consumed entire blocks in America's early cities, and
sometimes consumed entire districts, because many houses were of wood
and firefighting technology ranged from primitive to archaic.[25]

In November 1815, with American monetary conditions still in a confused
state following the British sack of Washington and the subsequent suspension of specie payments by banks, Breckinridge astutely instructed one of his
agents, Fleming Saunders of Franklin County, to hold the proceeds of a land
sale "until an opportunity of sending it to me occurs or I draw for it." Breckinridge said that he would divide it between two creditors and wanted to
make certain that he paid them in their preferred medium of exchange. The
following June, by contrast, when monetary conditions were more stable, he
instructed Saunders to send money "by Mr. Cook or any other safe conveyance." At the same time, though, Breckinridge lost on other transactions due
to the inland exchange disparities then prevalent. "I am much deceived if
your friend Colo. J.," wrote his son-in-law Robert Gamble in January 1816,
"is not availing himself of the exchange upon this place [Richmond] instead
of paying you what he can in Va. money of what he owes."[26]

In February 1794, Breckinridge acquired $666.67 worth of Sixes, which
he sold three months later. In 1813, despite his opposition to the war, he
bought over $5,300 worth of the Sixes of 1813. He sold those bonds in April
1816, but briefly reinvested $1,600 of the proceeds in the Sevens of 1815.
He did this on the investment advice of Richmond merchant John Gamble,
his son-in-law Robert's brother, who advised him to sell his shares in the

Farmers and Mechanics Bank of Georgetown, which then commanded $110 (specie) per share, and buy "the State Stock bearing an interest of Seven Per Cent payable half yearly." Each share would purchase $117.77 worth of the stock, producing a yield that Gamble estimated at 8.25 percent. Going further, Gamble, who had gambled on specie price fluctuations, offered to trade $12,000 in Virginia Sevens for $11,000 in specie. Breckinridge apparently declined but used the hint to purchase U.S. Sevens.[27]

Breckinridge also owned other bank stocks, $3,581.59 of the proceeds from the sale of which were deposited in the Bank of Virginia on his behalf in late January 1816. He contemplated investing that money in bank stock again, but Robert Gamble urged him not to as he was "well satisfied that Bank stock will decline during the summer much below what it is at present," and in fact would drop all the way back to par. In mid-May, shares in two of the three major Virginia banks traded in Richmond indeed dipped below par, and the third hit par, a drop of some 10 percent in each case. The stocks then appreciated a few points "in consequence of an expectation ... that a dividend will be declared as usual," Gamble explained. Even with that bounce, Gamble had saved his father-in-law a bundle. Breckinridge reciprocated by acting as Gamble's banker, lending him shares in the Bank of Alexandria and other banks for him to sell or use as collateral, and making outright loans to him during a large tobacco speculation. Gamble, for his part, acted as Breckinridge's agent with the Richmond banks, depositing checks in his accounts for him and keeping track of their directors' and stockholders' meetings and the like. He also tried to buy some $30,000 worth of Virginia Sixes on Breckinridge's behalf in December 1826 but bid three points too low.[28]

Gamble's numerous business connections were in fact very valuable to Breckinridge. In 1817, for instance, Gamble arranged a large, eight-year contract for Breckinridge's pig iron, reminded Breckinridge that an iron furnace was an "excellent mode of clearing" his land due to its high demand for charcoal (made from trees), and even suggested a convenient source of ore. Later that year, Gamble encouraged Breckinridge to produce as much flour as possible and get it to market in the early spring when, it was thought, it would command a high price. Ironically, Gamble's business sputtered badly while Breckinridge's plantation gushed forth, 2,500 bushels of wheat in 1819 alone, so much that Breckinridge thought it wise to purchase larger millstones if they could be gotten on good terms. Gamble also informed Breckinridge of a new millwheel–powered "wheat machine" that cost only $50 but could thresh about 200 bushels a day. And in 1823, he advised Breckinridge to bring his cattle to market early, in October and November, because the price then was likely to be just as high as later "and much expence in feeding avoided."[29]

Interestingly, Gamble's trading losses induced him to enter farming and to aspire to become a Florida planter. Breckinridge worried that his loans to Gamble would be endangered by the career switch, but Gamble noted that Breckinridge would be "as well secured upon my land & negroes as if invested in Bank Stock." Gamble later hit him up for more cash, $10,000, complaining that to establish himself in Florida "upon a scale that would leave little doubt of success will require more funds than my own means, or the aid my mother can furnish" and that he would otherwise be forced to "raise money in the mode usually resorted to, i.e., by paying high interest." Breckinridge declined but Gamble made the move anyway. Breckinridge probably hesitated because Gamble was not born and bred to farming. In fact, in 1809 he ran Breckinridge's estate while the statesman was away to make sure the overseer and negroes were working hard rather than hardly working. Gamble admitted that this, his "first assay in farming," was rather embarrassing due to the number of "obsticables," like rain for days on end, thrown in his way. Gamble prospered in Florida, though, growing cotton, tobacco, and sugar and managed to live through the Civil War.[30]

A Federalist lawyer like Breckinridge, Daniel Call came into the world in 1765 and left it in 1840. In between, he studied and practiced law in Petersburg and Richmond, and married into several important families, including that of Virginia state treasurer Jacquelin Ambler, of whom more below. Although related to John Marshall by marriage and close to him personally, professionally, and geographically (residing just a few yards from Marshall's house in Richmond), Call kept his politics to himself until June 1798, when he took "so active a part of all the violent and abusive speeches against France, against any farther connections with that Republic, in favor of a reliance upon G.B. and of a war with France" at a rally held in Richmond. "He is at this time so federal," one of his friends complained, "that he cheerfully offers up our Lives & our fortunes to be devoted to Executive uses." It may have been for patriotic or political reasons, therefore, that Call purchased a Navy Six in late October 1799 and held it until April 1801, his only known federal securities ownership. Given that he specialized in real estate law, it is not surprising that he invested most of his considerable legal and later legal publishing fortune in land in Richmond, neighboring Henrico County, and the west. He was also, logically enough, a director of the Mutual Assurance Society Against Fire on Buildings.[31]

As Call's experience suggests, while many major federal bondholders in Virginia were Federalists, not all Federalists owned large amounts of U.S. government bonds. Richmond wholesale merchant William Austin, for example, was an active Federalist who campaigned hard against Jefferson in 1800. In February of that year, Austin,

> As Call's experience suggests, while many major federal bondholders in Virginia were Federalists, not all Federalists owned large amounts of U.S. government bonds.

acting as secretary of an exploratory committee, lambasted a new Virginia law that changed "the antient [sic] usage of this country in elections, by substituting, in the place of viva voce suffrage, a ballot by a general ticket.... The acknowledged object of this alarming innovation," Austin declared, "is to annihilate, in this instance, the rights of the minority as citizens of the United States, and thereby produce such a change in the government thereof, as may involve, at this period, extreme hazard of the peace, union, and independence of the American people." Soon thereafter, Austin became secretary of the "American Republican Ticket," a Federalist slate with a strong Virginia tinge. The group's campaign pitch was basically "It's the economy, stupid." "The increasing prosperity of our happy country," especially contrasted with the "severest calamity" afflicting "almost the whole of the civilized world," made it clear that voters should "be satisfied with our present government." "To the adoption of our constitution, to the sage maxims of the administration established by the immortal WASHINGTON," Austin's missive continued, "may fairly be ascribed our present prosperous situation." Ever the realist, Austin knew the American Republican Ticket would likely meet defeat, but he soldiered on anyway, in the belief that arousing a "respectable minority in the ensuing election" was "very important."[32]

Despite his impeccable Federalist credentials, Austin's federal bond trading was slight. In February 1797, he purchased almost $3,000 worth of

Sixes. He sold them in mid-June of that year, likely because he was "hard pushed for money," including a cool grand owed him by his friend and land speculation partner Henry Banks, who had the temerity to run off to Philadelphia for an extended stay without settling up. "I was in great hopes to have had the pleasure of receiving a remittance from you long before this as you promised," Austin chided his buddy on June 16, the day after selling his Sixes. Banks's perfidy was troubling, but the root of Austin's financial troubles was systemic. "These are the worst times I ever saw in this place," he complained a month later, adding that he believed that interest rates were "higher here than any other place in the world." (They were certainly high. Austin himself charged Banks over 50 percent for short-term funds.) His federal bonds long since sold, Austin complained that "nothing will command money except Tobacco." Thankfully, it sold at "a good price," but Austin's finances remained "cramp'd" into early 1798. By October 1799, Austin was ready to buy federal bonds again, but not in a major way. He purchased a Navy Six with a $100 par value, which he sold in March 1802.[33]

❦

Many of Virginia's professional men, its doctors, lawyers, ministers, and college professors especially, were fond of owning federal bonds, because they were a remunerative but not troublesome form of property. Unlike professional fees, federal bonds provided predictable income that could be counted on quarter after quarter.

Born in Caroline County in 1748 or 1749, William Baynham followed his father John into medicine by apprenticing to Thomas Walker of Albemarle County, then studying at Saint Thomas's Hospital, London. An extremely skilled anatomist and surgeon, Baynham taught and practiced medicine in London throughout the Revolutionary War. In 1785, however, he removed to rural Essex County, Virginia, where he practiced with considerable national reputation, though later was slowed down by a shoulder injury incurred in an "unfortunate accident" in the winter of 1804–5. For reasons unknown, the irascible yet quiet Baynham specialized in more exotic forms of federal bonds, Converted and Exchanged Sixes. He bought and usually quickly sold tens of thousands of dollars' worth of them between 1807 and 1812. Baynham died in 1814.[34]

Thomas Chrystie was born in Scotland in 1753, give or take a year or two. At some point early in his life, he went to America, where he served as a surgeon during the Revolution. After the war, he started a private practice. The great surgeon William Baynham endorsed Chrystie's work, assuring one Mrs. Garlick that although her "disorder" and "present situation" were grave, he had "great hopes of a favorable termination from the judicious mode of treatment" that Chrystie adopted in her case. Unlike Baynham, Chrystie was not a medical innovator, but as his surviving accounts, which are copious, show, he was skilled in a wide variety of treatments and remedies typical of the period, including amputations, anodyne drafts, bark elixirs, blisters, castor oil, cooling powders, "curing a person of a Gonorrhea," imposthume lancings (which is fancy medical jargon for pus bag popping), laxatives, laudanum, mercurial purges, salt and snake root doses, spirits of lavender, sundry mixtures and ointments, volatile drops, vomit inducements, and worm powders. Also typical of the period, Chrystie often took payment for his services, which included short-term visits, long-term attendance, and medical advice, in livestock fodder and other agricultural products.[35]

Chrystie was happy to get paid at all, in fact. In the period between 1794 and 1802, his patients, most of whom actually survived his treatments, ran up unpaid bills to the tune of $3,476.52! That posed quite a problem given that Chrystie had bills to pay. He subscribed to the *Universal Gazette*, drank port, sherry, rum, tea, coffee, and the occasional whiskey, and enjoyed relieving himself in a nice chamber pot when it was inconvenient to use his spacious 6-by–8-foot outhouse. Moreover his business, which at times included the local postmastership, required a horse and chair, candles, paper, ink, and the like, as well prodigious amounts of medicines and linens for dressings. The good doctor brought some of his cash flow problems on himself, by not charging interest for sums due on book account and hiring wimpy debt collectors.[36]

Chrystie attended to slaves as well as their masters, which may explain why in his will he intimated that he would have emancipated his own six slaves if state law allowed it. Instead, he willed that his slaves "be at liberty to chuse their master or mistress, but they are not to be sold contrary to their wish or carried out of the state unless they desire it." Chyrstie's heirs received 625 acres in Ohio allotted to Chrystie for his war services. They also received the proceeds of the $4,613.23 worth of federal bonds that Chrystie obtained between February 1791 and January 1792. (Before that, in the late 1780s, Chrystie had paid some of his taxes with indents and Revolutionary War warrants, strongly suggesting that he held on to the IOUs he received during the war.) Chrystie was a long-term investor, likely because his bonds were the only assets he owned, besides eight bank shares, that paid him cash on a regular, reliable basis. That was important, because while Chrystie patiently awaited payment from his patients, tax collectors in Virginia and Ohio pressed hard and reappeared each year.[37]

Shortly after Chrystie's death, his executor drew up a short "things to do" list that included depositing Chrystie's cash—$590 in banknotes, an English crown, an English guinea, a U.S. gold eagle and 10 half eagles — in the bank and inquiring into the sale of his securities. He soon sold Chrystie's federal bonds to provide the estate with yet more cash. The money was quite necessary because Chrystie was laid to rest in style, in a mahogany coffin lined with flannel and covered by a large, flat gravestone, with a long inscription that asserted that Chrystie "distinguished himself for humanity, skill and assiduity in his professional duties, possessing a cultivating mind and a benevolent disposition." Thanks to that benevolent disposition, his slaves also had to be clothed and fed while the long probate process played out. Chrystie's other assets, which included about $3,000 in troublesome debts, like that owing from the great Virginia jurist Spencer Roane, were reeled in only slowly. Even the tools of his trade, which included a large medical library, sold only slowly and on credit.[38]

Like Chrystie, James Currie was born in Scotland, in Annadale, circa 1742. He emigrated to Virginia before the Revolution, ran a "medicinal shop" and became an eminent Richmond doctor, and before he died in 1807 was noted for his skill. "Dr. Currie of Richmond," it was said, "practiced through his life with great reputation. He seemed to possess intuitively the faculty of distinguishing the character of disease and of discovering the remedy." Also like Chrystie, Currie was well versed in the medical practices of the era, such as they were. Unlike Chrystie, Currie was more circumspect in his accounts when referring to venereal diseases, particularly with married men, and was more apt to bleed his patients both literally and financially. During the Revolution, Currie and other doctors, including George French, advertised that they would charge their prewar fees but expected to be paid in coin or marketable commodities at the rates that prevailed in the colonial period. Currie, whose business practices were considered somewhat sharp but very astute, was a major investor in federal securities, all told engaging in 27 federal securities transactions. He bought up exactly $11,678 worth in the first seven months of 1792 and held them until 1794, when he sold off almost $8,000 worth. In 1795, 1797, and 1799, however, he again added to his portfolio, to the tune of $3,700.45. In August 1802, he began slowly divesting, a process finished in October 1806, not long before his death.[39]

Currie was lucky to live so long because in July 1785 he came close to being challenged to a duel by Archibald Cary (1721–87), whom one biographer described as "handsome, strong, tall, and pugnacious," with emphasis on pugnacious. Although little known outside of Virginia, Cary was a leading planter and politician. He was upset because he believed that Currie had besmirched his daughter's character and that "the Lye is pretty well circulated." Cary assured Currie that if the matter was not "instantly cleared up," he thought it his duty to his family to "make a very serious matter" of the situation. "I will at the risk of my life defend my family from insult," he told Currie in terms that could not be misunderstood.[40]

Born in 1743, George Gilmer, son of the Williamsburg doctor of the same name, graduated from Edinburgh's famed medical program. Gilmer returned to Williamsburg, where he practiced medicine and midwifery until moving to Albemarle County, where he became an active politician. In the early stages of the Revolution, Gilmer formed a militia unit that marched on Williamsburg but arrived after Patrick Henry's men had already taken care of business. His scrapbooks are suffused with the stump speeches he gave early in the Revolution, which Gilmer liberally peppered with telling quotations that revealed the Lockean underpinning of his political and constitutional theorizing. "Allegiance is one thing," he declared, "obedience another. Allegiance is due to the King," he continued, "so long as in his executive capacity he shall protect the rights of the people." Laws were to be followed, but only "when founded on the constitution." Otherwise, "disobedience instead of obedience is due, and resistance becomes the law of the land." In June 1779, Gilmer stopped talking and started working, aiding some 120 sick soldiers stationed near Charlottesville and giving directions for the construction of a hospital and the procurement of medicines. The following year, in response to the nation's monetary crisis, he advertised a list of medicines for sale and notified customers that he would accept only cash or commodities in payment.[41]

Interestingly, Gilmer was close friends with Thomas Jefferson, whose famed plantation lay across the Rivanna from Gilmer's "Pen Park," and often managed his affairs while he was away on public business, as he often was. His close association with Jefferson did not stop Gilmer from acquiring over $5,000 worth of Threes, Sixes, and Deferred Sixes in January 1791 and holding those bonds until his death in 1795. (The executors of his estate finally liquidated his holdings in October 1801.) Gilmer could hold the bonds in his portfolio because his own credit was good enough that his personal bonds were sometimes purchased by third parties. One of Gilmer's daughters married U.S. attorney general William Wirt but she died young. (Wirt later replaced her with one of the daughters of Robert Gamble, the Richmond merchant discussed above who died of a concussion after being thrown from his horse.)[42]

> His close association with Jefferson did not stop Gilmer from acquiring over $5,000 worth of Threes, Sixes, and Deferred Sixes in January 1791 and holding those bonds until his death in 1795.

That Federalists, merchants, and professionals held U.S. government bonds in early Virginia is interesting but perhaps not surprising. That many planters owned such assets is intriguing and, given that nary a biography mentions their holdings, unexpected indeed. Consider, for example, George Buckner, who arose from the midst of a large and complex clan in Caroline County in 1760, just in time to serve in the Revolution as a captain. By the late 1780s, Buckner owned some 1,300 acres and eight slaves. He inherited his father's slaves in the mid-1790s, increasing his total to 31. He died in 1828 a widower and without issue. His will reveals that, in addition to his "Braynefield" plantation in Caroline County, by 1807 he also owned land in Fredericksburg and Culpeper Counties in Virginia, and Kentucky, respectively. Touchingly, he forbade his estate to be appraised, so that "those to whom I have given my slaves will treat them with humanity and kindness particularly the old ones." There is no mention of his bonds and for good reason. He sold the $200-odd worth he earned in the Revolution on February 28, 1792, just before the Panic struck.[43]

Some big planters, especially Federalist ones, were also bondholders. Paul Carrington (1733–1818) was the firstborn son of George Carrington, an Irish-Barbadian (that's right, got a problem with that?) who emigrated to Virginia in 1727 and became one of the Ancient Dominion's most prominent politicians. (Federalist attorney Edward Carrington was one of Paul's younger siblings.) Paul read law under Clement Read from 1750 to 1755, in which year he married Read's daughter and received a license to practice. The young couple set up housekeeping on Mulberry Hill in what became Charlotte County. Extremely active in the colonial militia, Carrington was also the clerk of Halifax County, a position he relinquished to his son in 1776, presumably so he could play a more prominent role in the Revolution. Carrington served in the Virginia Senate and General Court during the war and voted for the U.S. Constitution in the 1788 Ratification Convention, because he was, in his brother Edward's words, "much discontented with our present situation and thinks that no change can be against us." In 1792, after the death of his first wife, he married a 15-year-old young lady and had at least 3 children by her. Also in 1792, he bought a 332.5-acre tract of land paying for it partly with cash and partly with a promissory note for $291.38 due October 8, 1793. He paid off the note early, on April 20, 1793, saving himself a little over $6.67 interest. In addition to that purchase, by January 1, 1793, Carrington owned 1,992.5 acres on the Little Roanoke and Staunton Rivers alone. At his death, he owned only 1,600 acres in that area due to several sales. He left the bench in 1807 very old but very rich.[44]

Carrington acquired almost $1,000 worth of federal bonds in mid-January 1792. He sold his entire portfolio at the end of October 1800. That was not the only foray he made into the brave new world of finance, as he also owned at least one $200 share in the James River Company. Carrington likely found government and corporate securities better investments than the many private loans that he made as many of them defaulted, and badly at that. Other debts had to be handled gingerly lest offense be taken. Making such loans was virtually impossible to avoid, however, as most arose in the course of land deals and other trades.[45]

Carrington may have embraced finance because in the colonial period he was a major loser because of the lack of it. In 1772, he feared for the success of a large business venture, so he signed on three partners to assume two-thirds of the risk. Carrington advanced the money for the property, sold it off, and collected the debts due. His partners did nothing but were still entitled to the majority of the profits. In effect, they were Carrington's insurer, and their premium was a whopping one! "PC might have saved [that large premium]," a contemporary noted, "if he had not been afraid to risk so large a capital alone." (Now that I have made the point, I'll divulge that the property Carrington speculated in was human, "a cargoe of negroes" as a contemporary put it.)[46]

Carrington's son George was born in 1758. He probably attended William and Mary before succeeding his father as the clerk of Halifax County, an office he held for 21 years, except for the years 1780 to 1783, when he served in the cavalry regiment led by Henry "Light Horse Harry" Lee. Captured by British forces while reconnoitering near Dorchester, South Carolina, Carrington spent a year in captivity before rejoining his unit. Due to his service, he received 2,666.67 acres of western land and enough securities to allow him to acquire over $2,800 worth of federal bonds in mid-March 1791. He sold his entire portfolio in early February 1792, just before the Panic. Interestingly, given that he was a former military officer and that his father was a staunch Federalist, Carrington voted antifederalist in the 1788 Virginia Ratifying Convention. He later became a militia brigadier general and a Virginia state senator and member of the House of Delegates. When he died in 1809, he owned more than 2,850 acres of land and some 50 slaves.[47]

In 1765, gentleman planter George Corbin graduated from Princeton, where he was known to associate with other young men on the make like

William Paterson, Oliver Ellsworth, and Luther Martin. He pledged his loyalty to the king in September 1773, but a little over a year later he joined a committee created in response to the imperial crisis engulfing the continent. He appears to have been inactive militarily early in the war but from 1779 to 1781 he served as the Accomack County militia's lieutenant before turning his duties over to his nephew, John Cropper. Corbin nevertheless remained actively interested in the defense of the Eastern Shore, ever fearful of attack, even after Yorktown. William Davies of the War Department commiserated with him, noting that "the very circumstances of perpetual apprehension is one of the most disagreeable ingredients to embitter human life." After the war, Corbin was a man of major means, especially after inheriting his father's lands. Corbin purchased over $2,800 worth of federal bonds in seven transactions in April through October 1791. In December of that year, perhaps reeling from the price gyrations of the fall, he liquidated almost his entire portfolio. But he was a buyer again in 1792, picking up almost $5,300 worth in January and another $2,800 in July. Between September of 1792 and May 1795, Corbin, who died in 1793, and his executors liquidated his portfolio over nine transactions.[48]

Like most members of his generation, planter Isaac Hite of Frederick County had, after the Revolution, tremendous difficulties adjusting and repaying prewar and wartime accounts. His records even include a manuscript copy of the scale of depreciation used to reduce inflated wartime values to their specie equivalent. Hite accumulated almost $6,500 in federal bonds between June 1791 and April 1793. Over the course of 1796, he liquidated his entire portfolio in six transactions.[49]

> Like most members of his generation, planter Isaac Hite of Frederick County had, after the Revolution, tremendous difficulties adjusting and repaying prewar and wartime accounts.

Joseph Eggleston was born in Middlesex County in 1754. At the age of four, he moved to his father's plantation in Amelia County, where he studied under private tutors until he was ready to attend William and Mary, from which institution he graduated in 1776. During the Revolution, he served first as a captain then as a major in the cavalry and was reportedly one of the horsemen's most brilliant officers. After the Revolution, Eggleston managed his plantation, endeavoring to rid it of the dreaded Hessian fly. He also served in the House of Delegates and the U.S. Congress in the House of Representatives. A Republican, he was said to be "violently opposed" to paying British creditors. He wasn't opposed to getting paid his due, though, which included certificates for pay, depreciation of pay, and commutation certificates (five years' pay instead of half pay for life). Eggleston exchanged those IOUs under the terms of Hamilton's funding plan but was a federal bondholder for just five days in November 1791, when he sold his $169.18 worth of Sixes, $126.89 of Threes, and $84.60 of Deferred Sixes. He died in 1811.[50]

Lest readers be led astray by the likes of Robert Gamble and Paul Carrington, it should be pointed out that not all federal bondholders in Virginia were big shots. In fact, most were not. It is difficult to say much about the common bondholder, however, because few narrative records of their lives survive. For example, William Woolfolk (1752–1822) of Caroline County bought over $350 worth of federal bonds in April 1793 and sold them all almost exactly two years later. He later moved to Kentucky. His surviving correspondence, scant as is, indicates that he was neither well off nor well educated. Thomas Willock moved from England to Norfolk, Virginia, in 1784. In 1787, he married a Virginian and at some point became a naturalized American citizen. Willock bought $2,000 worth of Deferred bonds in July 1797. In late November of that year, he added $500 of Navy Sixes to his portfolio. He sold his Deferreds Sixes in January 1801 and his Navy Sixes that December. Junius K. Horsburgh of Williamsburg bought almost $550 worth of federal bonds in November 1818, shortly after graduating from William and Mary College. He sold out the following March. Although considered "among the most distinguished of our youths for Talent and Genius," he never made much of himself.[51]

At least Horsburgh did not go bankrupt. The same could not be said of Fauquier County resident Thomas Chilton, who acquired a little over $200 in federal bonds in early February 1792 and sold them in early January of the following year. The record on Chilton is pretty bare but it looks like he was imprisoned for debt for a time in the mid–1820s and then filed for bankruptcy under Virginia law claiming that he owned no real or personal estate. Similarly, Richmond's Thomas Hooper bought $100 worth of Navy Sixes in late October 1799 and sold them in May 1800, undoubtedly due to financial difficulties. By February 1802, he noted that "my misfortunes [and] my heavy losses compeld me to surrender my affects in order that all my creditors should share and share alike."[52]

A number of federal bondholders were artisans of means ranging from moderate to minor. In the colonial period, for example, James Anderson was a Williamsburg gunsmith and Virginia's public armorer. A patriot, during the war he continued to serve his native state as armorer, moving his shop to Richmond and, after Benedict Arnold's raid destroyed eight of his bellows, rural Fluvanna County. His men repaired as many as 150 muskets per week, but the state never adequately compensated him for his losses or his work. Nevertheless, he managed to establish a blacksmith shop in Richmond in 1782 and turned his business over to his son and namesake in 1794. In September 1791, Anderson received $21.78 worth of Threes, $32.48 of Sixes, and $16.25 of Deferred Sixes, probably for old Revolutionary certificates. He sold the Threes and Deferreds 11 months later and the Sixes in January 1795. Anderson died in September 1798.[53]

Another artisan bondholder was John Beale. Born in France in 1749 and raised in Pisa, Italy, Beale migrated to Maryland in 1771, served under Pulaski in the Revolution, and then settled in Virginia, living first in Petersburg, then Lynchburg, then Alexandria, and, finally, Richmond. Along the way he worked in copper, tin, gold, silver, and jewels and also repaired clocks, watches, and mathematical instruments on the side. In Richmond, he established a dry goods and grocery store and ran it until 1817. During the last two decades of his long life, which ended in 1837, he apparently lived off his savings and his son James. In 1791 and 1792, Beale speculated heavily in all three types of federal bonds, alternatively buying and selling with the market's gyrations. Undoubtedly, he was one of the people Jeffersonians had in mind when they lamented the effects of Hamilton's funding system on the working classes. Interestingly, the Panic of 1792 did not ruin Beale but instead was a profit opportunity for him, as he greedily bought bonds at its nadir and thereafter. He took some profits in late 1792 but held on to over $3,600 in governments until March 3, 1803, when he sold out for reasons unknown.[54]

Born in England, Benjamin Bucktrout emigrated to Williamsburg by September 1765. At first Anthony Hay's journeyman cabinetmaker, Bucktrout soon established his own shop on Main Street, near the capitol. In addition to making fancy chairs, Bucktrout repaired musical instruments, engaged in paper hanging, and conducted funerals. He aided patriot hospitals during the war but also mysteriously disappeared for two years before returning to Williamsburg to continue his trades in 1781. He was city surveyor for a time. In 1791, Bucktrout obtained over $2,900 worth of Threes, Sixes, and Deferred Sixes. He sold his Deferreds in 1799 and his Sixes in June 1802 but apparently kept his Threes until his death sometime in late 1812 or early 1813.[55]

Myer M. Cohen acquired about $40 worth of Sixes and Deferred Sixes in March 1791. He sold his holdings in late July of that year. A watchmaker by trade, Cohen was by no means a wealthy man. When he died in 1798, he owned one female slave (his most valuable asset at $100), the tools of his trade, and a small inventory of parts, which in all was worth $455.83. Lord knows how much debt he owed. The apparently unrelated Jacob J. Cohen, the proprietor of Cross Keys Tavern near the courthouse in Richmond, was a much wealthier man than Myer. His buildings, which included a dwelling 26 by 16 feet, a blacksmith shop 20 by 16 feet, and a detached kitchen were insured for $500, and the tavern itself, including its stable and large lot, for $900. Cohen accumulated over $1,200 worth of federal bonds between March 1795 and June 1800. He did not sell any of his bonds until late 1806, when he disposed of all of them. At some point, while maintaining ownership of the tavern, he moved to Philadelphia, where he died in 1823, aged 80.[56]

Born in Scotland in 1759, Charles Cameron came to America with Samuel Woods and settled in the western part of Virginia. He served the patriot cause in the Revolution as a lieutenant and saw action at Brandywine and Germantown. Later, he was promoted to captain. Likely due to his services in the Revolution, Cameron acquired over $2,600 worth of federal bonds in May 1791, about the time he became the clerk of Bath County, newly carved out of Augusta County in the far western portion of the state. For reasons unknown, he sold all his holdings in early November 1791. He held his clerkship for 23 years and after he died in 1829 (some say 1839), his widow received a pension for his war service.[57]

A native of Bucks County, near Philadelphia, William Darke (1736–1801) moved with his family to Berkeley County, Virginia, in 1741. Darke's family was not well off, residing in a log cabin, so Darke received little formal education. He was bright, though, and reportedly of "herculean proportions," so he was a fine farmer who eventually was able to purchase his own land and add to it. He also owned considerable lands in the west due to his service in the Revolutionary War, first as a captain, then a colonel. He likely attained such rank because he'd had significant military experience during the French and Indian War, serving as a corporal in a company of rangers in 1758 and 1759. During the Revolution, Darke was wounded and captured at Germantown and held as a prisoner in New York until his exchange three years later. It is said that he literally walked home to western Virginia! He then formed a company of militia and witnessed the horror of his son, Captain Joseph Darke, being butchered by Indians. The incident caused Darke's dark side to come forth, which urged him to join the Indian Wars of the early 1790s. Darke saved St. Clair's defeated army from massacre and was promoted to brigadier general for his valor. He represented Berkeley in the Virginia Ratification Convention in 1788 and was elected to the Virginia legislature. In 1794 and 1795, Darke in six transactions bought a little over $4,500 worth of federal bonds, which he held until his death. His estate sold his holdings on February 19, 1802.[58]

Unfortunately, even less is known of Virginia's female bondholders, most of whom could not be located in the historical record. Of those who could be tracked, little was found. Hannah Fleisher of Richmond acquired $31.75 in Threes in November 1793. She sold out the next month. In late February 1794, though, she picked up almost $150 worth of Threes and Sixes. In November of that year, she sold out again and thus ended her stint as a federal bondholder. Born circa 1762, Fleisher died in May 1830 and was

> Unfortunately, even less is known of Virginia's female bondholders, most of whom could not be located in the historical record.

buried at Saint John's Church, Henrico Parish. Mary J. Lee of Westmoreland County purchased a little less than $200 worth of Threes and Deferred Sixes in April 1819 and sold them in late January 1821. She apparently ran her own plantation. In 1801 and 1802, Elizabeth Macauley of Yorktown purchased almost $2,800 worth of Threes, which she clung to until her death in early 1830. Her tangled estate led to a court case that made it all the way to the Virginia Supreme Court of Appeals. Macauley devised her slaves, various effects, half of her lands (a big lot in Yorktown and 452 acres in Warwick County), and "all the ready money, shares of bank stock, and stock of any kind whatsoever, which at the time of my death I may possess" to her daughter, Helen M. Anderson, to enjoy "subject to her own individual control." Her daughter sold the stock in June 1830 but the lands became ensnared in a sequence of ill-fated events, including the destruction of deeds during the Civil War, too arcane to detail here. Finally, Martha Miller of Rockbridge County acquired $17.66 in Threes, Sixes, and Deferred Sixes on January 27, 1792. There is no record of those bonds ever being sold, perhaps because Miller held them until they were redeemed. She was clearly involved in some sort of business, selling a mare and a colt in November 1787, then drawing for the proceeds.[59]

Regardless of their gender, occupation, or political affiliation, many federal bondholders owned bonds for different reasons and in different capacities. In the latter instance, cross-fertilization appears likely. Exposed to the virtues of federal bond ownership in one context, Virginians found in Threes, Sixes, Deferreds, Navy Sixes, Eights, and other U.S. government bonds solutions to multiple problems. Executorships, trusteeships, and the like sometimes introduced federal bonds to neophytes, who then invested on their own account. Other times, people with experience trading U.S. government bonds for their own emolument later used them to help them to fulfill the obligations of various positions of trust. Executors and executrixes, administrators and administratrixes, guardians, and generally trustees of all types often invested the sums in their care in government bonds because they were remunerative, safe, and liquid relative to private investments. Just as executives in the 1950s and 1960s bought IBM computers because they could never be fired for going with such a strong brand, many trustees bought government bonds because they could not be faulted for doing so. They could be faulted, though, for investing other people's money in riskier investments. In April 1821, for example, Henry Edmundson worried about investing a deceased man's fortune in the dead man's own company, the Prestonville Company, a joint-stock corporation chartered in 1817 to make lower Tinker Creek in Roanoke County navigable, because he did not think it safe "to pay it to the promotion of a scheme … the principal object of which has failed." Rather than pay the capital calls on the stock, therefore, he suffered it to be sold at auction. (For a variety of reasons I address elsewhere, most early corporations called their capital in over time rather than taking it all up front.)[60]

One example of a Virginian who owned federal bonds in several capacities was John Baylor, who was born in Caroline County in 1750. At age 12, he was sent by his parents, John and Frances Walker Baylor, to Putney Grammar School in England. As early as 1770, Baylor planned to attend Cambridge University's Caius College but in 1772 he had to return to Virginia due to his father's illness. One of his relatives in England was happy Baylor left because he "drank so plentifully" and was "glutted with all those pastimes that are now in Vogue." Baylor's father died just before his son's ship completed the long passage home. A good deal of young Baylor's inheritance, including the mighty steeds Fearnought and, ironically enough, Sober John, had to be sold to meet the debts of his elder's estate. To complete his degree, Baylor returned to London, where in 1778 he married Frances Norton, his cousin. The following year he returned to Caroline County, where he later laid the foundations for a mighty mansion, which neighbors dubbed "Baylor's Folly." Folly, indeed! Baylor died in 1808 and the stunning edifice was never completed.[61]

Baylor owned federal bonds on his own account and as one of the executors of the estate of George Baylor, likely a brother or uncle who, though indebted to some, apparently died owning more than he owed. Baylor purchased first as executor, obtaining over $5,000 worth of Sixes, Threes, and Deferred Sixes on February 7, 1792. The estate sold some of the Sixes in March and September of that year and disgorged the rest, along with the other bonds, in June 1793. Exactly a year later, Baylor bought over $1,600 of federal bonds on his own account, selling them all on July 22, 1794, possibly to help fund construction of his giant folly of a mansion. Whatever the case, Baylor was clearly in no position to own many bonds as, like his father before him, he was deeply indebted to his friends and neighbors. In 1800, for example, Doctor Robert Wellford wrote to Colonel John Spotswood in Orange County that he had "exerted all my eloquence to prevail upon Baylor to give you a new Note including the interest, but he has most obstinately denied it" though the debt was clearly just and long past due. Wellford concluded that Baylor had become "Mean and Dishonest" (underscore in original). To his credit, Baylor and his family were quite ill at that time, racking up almost $300 in doctor's bills between July 1799 and December 1801.[62]

Robert Andrews was born in Pennsylvania circa 1747. After receiving his BA from the College of Philadelphia in 1766, he moved to Virginia to tutor and preach. He served as a chaplain and private secretary during the Revolution, and also assumed a professorship at the College of William and Mary in Williamsburg, where he continued to reside after the war. Also a gifted astronomer, cartographer, and mathematician, Andrews, who served in the House of Delegates from 1790 to 1799, aligned himself with the Federalists. Although he denounced the Jay Treaty, he voted against the Virginia Resolutions in December 1798 and opposed Thomas Jefferson for the presidency in 1800. Finally free of political life, he served as president of the Dismal Swamp Canal Company in 1802.[63]

Andrews certainly had no problem trading in federal bonds. As executor for the estate of Samuel Beall, Andrews bought over $1,200 worth of Threes, Sixes, and Deferred Sixes in November 1795. He sold those bonds in 1798 and 1799, ostensibly to make payments to Beall's legacies. In the late 1790s and early years of the 1800s, Andrews also bought federal bonds on behalf of a fund for the relief of clergymen's widows, of which he was treasurer. Andrews was even more active on his own account. From May 1791 until January 1807, three years after his death, Andrews (and his estate) made 65 different purchases of federal bonds totaling $44,154.55. A fairly active trader who bought and sold bonds several times each year until just before his death in January 1804, Andrews never owned more than $10,000 worth of bonds at one time, buying and selling as his personal finances allowed and his whims dictated.

In the first half of the eighteenth century, John Heth emigrated from Ireland to Pennsylvania where, in 1750, his son William was born. Little is known of William's early years but by all accounts he was well educated, artistic, and extremely literate. As a lieutenant colonel, Heth took part in the failed invasion of Canada early in the Revolution and paid for it with more than six months as a POW. He later became a major, then a colonel, though he lost an eye in battle. In January 1788, he and David Henley were selected to head a commission to settle Virginia's account with John Pierce, the federal government's commissioner of army accounts. Later, he was federal tax collector for the ports of Richmond, Petersburg, and the Bermuda Hundred, in which capacity thousands of dollars passed through his hands each month. (This was one of the monetary capillaries that allowed the federal government to pay its bills, including interest and principal on the national debt.) The job was complicated by the government's allowing merchants to pay their duties with bonds, forcing Heth to monitor the often over $100,000 due from importers to the government. Apparently, Heth was pretty good at his job, but he was eventually ousted from office by degrees after Jefferson's election to the presidency, which induced the outspoken collector to publicly mock the Sage. The stout Heth did not need the gig, as by that time he owned three plantations and numerous slaves. Interestingly, his brother Henry was the U.S. commissioner of loans for Virginia and a coal miner. Well, an owner of coal mines, not a hard hat.[64]

Heth owned federal bonds in three capacities, as treasurer for the Society of the Cincinnati in Virginia (16 transactions over 16 years), of which he was a founding member; as a trustee for the Sinking Fund of the United States (5 purchases totaling $63,616.15 in March 1791 turned over to the Sinking Fund commissioners in June); and on his own account. Between late December 1790 and early March 1792, Heth accumulated over $17,000 of federal bonds in 6 transactions. From late May 1792 until May 1810, Heth (or his estate; he died in April 1807) was involved in another 14 transactions, 3 purchases totaling almost $5,000 and the rest sales that in the end completely liquidated his holdings.[65]

Jacquelin Ambler wore four different hats when trading federal securities: Virginia state treasurer, trustee, private trader, and cashier of the Mutual Assurance Company Against Fire. Unsurprisingly, his trading as trustee was straightforward: he purchased $450 worth of Threes at par value on June 15, 1793, and sold them on October 14 of that year. On his own account, he bought $450 worth of Threes (from himself, as trustee) and $740.47 worth of Deferred Sixes in June 1793, only to sell them in October of that year. He also bought $66.66 and $2,568.08 worth of Sixes on March 6 and 7, 1795, respectively, and sold them on July 7 and 10, respectively, of that same year. On account of the Old Dominion, Ambler accumulated $4,792.19 in Sixes, $28,318.67 in Threes, and $2,396.11 in Deferred Sixes stock through 1795. In April 1798, after his death, the bonds were transferred to the credit of his successor, William Berkeley. Finally, as cashier of the insurance company he bought $37,785.20 worth of Sixes in 11 transactions between November 23, 1796, and February 5, 1798. After his death, the bonds were transferred to his successor, Andrew Dunscomb, of whom more below. Ambler had other financial investments too, most notably four shares in the James River Company with a par value of $800, all told.[66]

Ambler was born in Yorktown, Virginia, in 1742 and educated at William and Mary and the College of Philadelphia. He clerked in his father's mercantile house for two years before becoming a partner. Due to the deaths of his father and elder brothers, he and his two younger brothers inherited the considerable family estate. A patriot, Ambler served in various political capacities in the colonial, war, and postbellum years. Most important, he served as Virginia's state treasurer from April 1782 until his death in January 1798. A Federalist sympathizer, Ambler kept his job because of his diligence and effectiveness as an administrator.[67]

Born in Manhattan circa 1757 and the son of a merchant, Alexander Dunscomb was a member of the New York Committee of Safety in 1775 and served in the Continental Army. After the war he moved to Richmond, where he helped to settle the Revolutionary War accounts of Virginia and the United States. He resigned in 1790 after attacks on his work. Soon after, Dunscomb became one of Virginia's few securities broker-dealers. As a broker, Dunscomb merely arranged transactions between bond buyers and sellers for a commission. As a dealer, he bought bonds for later resale at a slightly higher price, taking the difference or spread as compensation for his services. Between December 1790 and November 1803, Dunscomb (and his estate) engaged in 175 such transactions, in which over $105,000 worth of bonds were involved. Dunscomb also invested in government bonds as a trustee for William Reynolds and, as noted above, as the cashier of the Mutual Assurance Society, an insurance company he helped to found. Between March 1798 and August 1802, Dunscomb on behalf of that fire insurance corporation engaged in an additional 48 transactions, buying and selling bonds worth almost $201,000. His activities slowed after the mid–1790s, for good reason: he became mayor of Richmond and a militia major. He died in 1802.[68]

Some Virginia federal bondholders were speculators, people who hoped to buy low and sell high, or sell high and buy low. Others were liquidity junkies who were happy to collect interest until they had to sell to make payments. Other investors were in it for the long haul. They bought and held, for years, decades, an entire lifetime. Not usually big planters or extensively engaged in risky mercantile pursuits, the last-mentioned type of investor had little need for quick cash but they did need to own a type of asset that provided a reliable income and would not easily lose its value. Then as now, government bonds were the ticket. Like the old nag that looked and smelled kind of funky but provided reliable transportation, government bonds were not spectacular investments, but they were tried-and-true.

> Then as now, government bonds were the ticket. Like the old nag that looked and smelled kind of funky but provided reliable transportation, government bonds were not spectacular investments, but they were tried-and-true.

One such long-term investor was George Weedon, who was born in Westmoreland County in 1734, the son of a farmer of the same name. Weedon received a few years of formal schooling but was largely self-taught. He served extensively in the French and Indian War, rising to the rank of captain. After that war, Weedon remained active in the militia. He also married and with his wife ran a tavern in Fredericksburg said to be among the most popular in all Virginia. George Washington admitted that he often played cards there, and usually lost. By 1774, Weedon was already "very active and zealous in blowing the flames of sedition." Little wonder, then, that Weedon fought in the Revolution with alacrity, first as a colonel and later as a brigadier general. He fought in all the early major engagements except Princeton, and took a particularly brave stand at Brandywine. He later quit and returned to his tavern after being passed over for a promotion but stayed active in the Virginia militia and helped to besiege the British at Gloucester, across the river from Yorktown. After the war, Weedon, suffering from the gout and perhaps a touch of alcoholism, retired, living off the rents from his tavern and, eventually, interest on federal bonds. He acquired over $11,200 worth of them in October 1790 and another $1,161.10 the following April. He sold the last batch the following month but by June 1791 he was buying again, $19,595.10 in six transactions. Weedon (and his estate—he died in 1793) sold his huge portfolio in batches in December 1792, March 1794, and January 1797. He bequeathed his bonds to his nephews John Mercer and Hugh T. W. Mercer, and his wife, who also received his numerous urban lots and their home, the "Sentry Box." Weedon gave his Kentucky military lands to his brother-in-law.[69]

Another Revolutionary War hero, John Blackwell of Fauquier County, was also a long-term investor. Blackwell saw action around New York in the late summer of 1776 and in 1778 he was a captain in charge of a company in the Virginia Third Regiment. In March of that year, he received $40 for his services, while the 32 enlisted men under his command each received between $6.67 and $8.83. (As discussed above, later in the war soldiers would go for long periods without pay.) In 1796, Blackwell sold off 72.5 acres of his land to Thomas Keith, another Fauquier resident, who acquired $685 of federal bonds in April 1791, but was not a long-term investor. (Keith sold off $166.67 worth that July and the rest in December. He died in 1805.) Blackwell obtained almost $4,000 in Threes, Sixes, and Deferred Sixes in April 1791, almost certainly due to his service in the Revolution. He purchased some $2,500 more in late January 1792, just before the Panic, but held tight until he sold off some $1,200 worth of Sixes in 1798. He later bought some Exchanged and Converted Sixes but began divesting about the same time, selling off the last $575.50 worth of his federal bonds in February 1814, over two decades after making his first purchases.[70]

Robert Bolling of Petersburg appears to have been a generous man. In 1808 he allowed Townsend Stith, a young man in his employ, to take his horse to Kentucky to search out "a new plan of life." Bolling also ceded an entire acre to the town of Petersburg so that it could erect a courthouse, jail, and public wharf. But every man has his limit. In 1814, Bolling sued the town. The parties agreed to arbitration but it fell through and tensions remained high for over a decade. The problem was that the town subdivided the land and rented lots thereof to private parties "for the purpose of creating an emolument for the benefit of the Town," raising Bolling's ire. His blood began to boil when the town removed about a third of the soil for use as fill elsewhere in the city. The last straw was when the town moved the jail from the northwest corner of the grant to the northeast corner, where it created "an oppressive nuisance, to the great annoyance" of Bolling and his tenants. Having a jail across the street was a shame, as contemporaries considered Bolling's brand-new house, which was said to cost upward of $50,000 to build, a "superb, fine palace." Bolling's suit lumbered on into the 1830s. In the end, the courts denied Bolling's claim but apparently gave him the wharf. The town then sued and won because it expended $6,796.66 more on the wharf than it received in wharfage rents, and the court charged $4,899.63 of that to the section of the wharf claimed by Bolling. Bolling survived the blow, living long enough to console Dolly Madison on the loss of her husband in the summer of 1836.[71]

Of course, Bolling was not idle while that long drama played out but instead played an active role in attempts, including the Roanoke and Appomattox River canal, to keep Petersburg alive as a commercial entrepot amid Virginia's internal improvement craze following the War of 1812. He also maintained a portfolio of government bonds. Bolling acquired about $825 worth of Threes, Sixes, and Deferred Sixes in January 1792 and $500 worth of Navy Sixes in November 1799. He sold off those Navy Sixes and some of his other holdings in October 1807, and converted and exchanged most of the rest, which he divested in 1809, 1812, and 1814. In December 1815, however, he purchased a portfolio worth over $1,000 of federal bonds, about half of which he sold off in 1816, when interest rates reached 50 percent in northern Virginia, and 1817.[72]

Another long-term federal bondholder was Charles Dabney (1745–1829), whose long life was one of the more interesting of Virginia's early federal bondholders of any stripe. The son of a prominent planter, he served his parish as a vestryman, his county as a justice of the peace, and his colony on important commissions. By the late colonial period, he was already a prominent Hanover County planter and copartner in a blacksmith shop. Dabney

Another long-term federal bondholder was Charles Dabney (1745–1829), whose long life was one of the more interesting of Virginia's early federal bondholders of any stripe.

conceived of Virginia, not Britain, as his homeland and so was an ardent patriot, first as the captain of a company of minutemen, then as the lieutenant colonel of his own eponymous legion. (A "legion" was bigger than a company but too small for a regiment.) In 1778 his legion joined the Continental Army in the Virginia State Regiment just in time to take part in the important battle at Monmouth. That epic struggle was so energetic and took place on a day so hot that many soldiers expired from heat exhaustion. Dabney and the other soldiers fighting under the unusually cool General Smallwood were almost killed when at the end of the day a Frenchman claiming Washington's authority ordered them to attack the British along a narrow causeway near a swamp. Although the mission was clearly suicidal, Smallwood pressed forward saying in effect that it was not a soldier's duty to question why but to do and die. Luckily, the Frenchman's overzealousness was uncovered and Smallwood was recalled just before his unit made contact with the well-ensconced enemy. Dabney and the others, it was said, "retreated with much more alacrity than they had advanced."[73]

Later, Dabney and his men fought under Anthony Wayne at Stony Point, said to be "one of the most daring and hazardous enterprises undertaken during the war." During that engagement, Dabney's legion stormed a well-garrisoned fortress in a brilliant and bloody bayonet attack. They also served under Putnam, who put them to work pressing apples and, more important, under Lafayette at Yorktown, where Dabney's bravery reconnoitering the British breastworks came to the attention of Alexander Hamilton

In September 1782, the large and athletic Dabney put down a small mutiny, probably by brandishing his trademark weapon, a large bore rifle that bore his name.

and others. Dabney stayed in service after that, trying desperately to hold his ragtag little army together without the aid of bills of credit, clothes, medicine, supplies, or regular payroll and without enraging the local populace. In September 1782, the large and athletic Dabney put down a small mutiny, probably by brandishing his trademark weapon, a large bore rifle that bore his name. Dabney neverthe-less wrote that "unless the troops get money soon, I fear it will be out of my power to keep them in service." He somehow succeeded until they mustered out at war's end in April of 1783.[74]

Soon after that, Dabney headed west to locate the lands his military ser-vice entitled him to. He sold those lands for a pittance, some immediately and some in the 1790s, probably because he had encountered too many hostile Indians and too many empty acres and un-bridged rivers during his trip. Besides, by 1785 he was already, if not affluent, at least of easy enough circumstances that he could afford to turn down a commission as county lieutenant in the militia. He declined the job, he said, because he spent so much time away from home, presumably lobbying in Rich-mond for payment for himself and his fellow Revolutionary War officers. When that came to naught he sued the state, winning in 1791 some $6,327 worth of state IOUs, which he wasted no time converting under the terms of Hamilton's assumption plan. By that mechanism and further purchases, Dabney accumulated federal bonds between January 1791 and September 1802—amounting to $14,434.01 in Sixes, Threes, and Deferred Sixes in 21 transactions, some of which he stashed under the books in his bookcase. (He kept his gold in the bookcase, too, and also a trunk, and stashed his silver coins in a desk drawer and a shot bag. Dabney was an avid hunter.) The money for his 1795 bond purchases came directly from the proceeds of the sale of some of his western lands: "The above £300 [$1,000] left in the hands of Micajah Crew, who is to deliver it to William Dabney in Rich-mond. I have wrote to him, to lay the above money out in 6 pr ct. Stock." Dabney converted $1,500 of his Threes into Converted Sixes in October 1807 but held tightly to the rest of his portfolio. In 1812, he began to divest by selling his Converted Sixes. In 1818, he sold almost $9,000 of his Sixes, and in 1824 the balance of his portfolio was redeemed. Dabney also invested in bank stock, including at least one share in the Bank of Virginia purchased in April 1806 for $100.[75]

A Federalist, the immorality Dabney saw in Virginia's cities, particu-larly Williamsburg and Richmond, disgusted him to such an extent that he refused to leave the area around his home in Hanover. (He had one of his young relatives, William "Billy" Dabney, draw the interest for him in Richmond.) Nevertheless, Dabney consented to run on the American

A Federalist, the immorality Dabney saw in Virginia's cities, particularly Williamsburg and Richmond, disgusted him to such an extent that he refused to leave the area around his home in Hanover.

Republican Ticket in 1800. He was defeated, in part because he refused to engage in "the brawls, the intrigues, and the debasing scenes" that were said to "disgrace our popular elections" at the time. (The more things change.) Just as he would not court public favor, Dabney would also not court women; he never married.[76]

Although not highly formally educated, Dabney had in the words of a contemporary an excellent "natural understanding" and a "large stock of valuable knowledge," a claim that Dabney's scrapbooks certainly bear out. For instance, he knew of a simple cure for piles (hemorrhoids) that entailed applying a $3/4$-inch-long piece of cold, wet, strong British alum to the affected area "morning and evening" for seven days. Those attributes—the knowledge and understanding, not the piles—made him a natural leader in war as well as in peace, so his neighbors frequently consulted him on weighty matters, though Dabney was not above taking advice from them as well, as in April 1816 when another federal bondholder, Dr. Carter Berkeley, recommended several books to him. Dabney was also said to possess "a thorough knowledge of human nature" and nowhere did that show more than in his unusual relationships with his slaves. He understood that slaves did not respond well to physical punishment, so instead of whipping them, he credited them wages for the year, making deductions whenever they slacked or misbehaved and settling balances due in cash each Christmas season.

He understood that slaves did not respond well to physical punishment, so instead of whipping them, he credited them wages for the year, making deductions whenever they slacked or misbehaved and settling balances due in cash each Christmas season.

His descendants claimed that his tactic did not work, but then again they had ideological reasons to reject it. His plantation certainly did not seem to suffer. On May 26, 1792, for example, Dabney owned 44 cattle plus 7 calves, 61 pigs including 6 sows and 1 boar, 18 sheep and 11 lambs, and 10 horses. That fall his fields yielded 88 bushels of wheat, 120 barrels of corn, and Lord knows how much

tobacco, all harvested and processed with the aid of 63 tools of a dozen varieties, likely made in Dabney's sizable blacksmith shop. In December 1793, he
had on hand 49 cattle, 29 sheep, and 66 pigs, which he recorded by size and
type. For decades, his plantation produced such bounty.[77]

Dabney's business acumen and sterling character shine through the many
records he has left us. For instance, he was not averse to experimentation in
crops or techniques and was unafraid to heat his home with good Virginia
coal instead of wood. He used subcontractors, providing raw wool to local
ladies for them to process (wash, spin, etc.). Also, he paid his overseer on a
salary plus commission basis rather than paying him a salary only, a tactic
used by astute planters to mitigate slacking by overseers. He immediately
sacked one overseer he caught engaged in "usury, and an infamous traffick
in slaves" for fear that people would think him in league with the scoun-
drel. Dabney frequently, liberally, and often secretively assisted friends and
relatives financially by slipping a large banknote into a handshake or letter,
thereby helping them to stave off the usurer or shaver ("cormorants that
fatten on the miseries and misfortunes of their fellow men"), or, in more
extreme cases, the wolf of hunger and want. Despite his munificence, at his
death Dabney possessed assets assessed at $22,730.45, some $9,000 of which
was the value of his slaves. Rather than emancipate them, which he was constrained from doing by law, the deeply religious but nondenominational
Dabney ordered that they be rented out and allowed one-third of their rental
price, and under no conditions were families to be rent asunder.[78]

∾

Other Virginians hoped to profit from federal bonds through price speculation, by buying low and soon after selling high. One such speculator was
Richmond merchant Nathaniel Anderson, who drew in his business horns
in 1792 "on account of his ill state of health." In 1795, he purchased a country estate (which he named "Asylum") in rural Albemarle County, where
he "intended to spend the Balance" of his days provided he was "not forced
to sell it." To stay active, he entered into partnership with Thomas Reeves.
On his own account and in partnership with Reeves, Anderson at times
speculated in federal bonds, buying only to sell again a few days, weeks,
or months later. His profits were modest at best. He bought Threes at the
end of January 1794 when they sold in Philadelphia at 51.25 percent of par

and sold them a few days later, just before the Philadelphia price slipped to 50.42. (Prices of government bonds in the Virginia markets of the late eighteenth century are rarely available. The price differences among the major markets were usually negligible, especially when the banks were paying specie, as they did most of the time.) The interest earned on the few days he owned the bonds would not even have covered his brokerage costs. During another speculation, Sixes slid from 91.67 to 91.25 percent of par, but Deferred Sixes rose in price, from 56.25 to 56.67. All told, though, it must have been a wash, or worse. The same could be said of a speculation in Sixes later in 1794, in June and July. Sixes purchased above par (100) by the partnership in January 1793 sank below 90 percent of par before recovering, but unfortunately not before the company found it necessary to liquidate some of its holdings. (The Threes the company bought at the same time also lost about 10 percent of their value.) It sold the rest late in 1794 much closer to the price it had originally paid for the bonds. With interest payments safely received, the speculation may again have broken even. Rather than buy and hold, Anderson and his company thereafter shied away from federal bonds, investing instead in loans to neighbors and friends, though such bonds never appreciated and often had to be put to suit.[79]

Another Virginia speculator was Charles Johnston. Born in 1769, too late to see action during the Revolution, Johnston nevertheless nearly lost his life in battle, in the Indian wars of the early 1790s. "The war is now raging with great fury," he wrote in 1792, "& I fear many valuable lives will be lost before it comes to a conclusion." He was one to know. He surprised his friends when he returned to Virginia from a business trip to Kentucky because they had "considered me lost & had not known that I was alive" after receiving word that he had been captured by unfriendly Indians. The hero was a French-Canadian trader named Duchouquet who paid the Indians' ransom of 600 silver broaches in exchange for Johnston's life. Several of Johnston's party who survived the initial barrage were also eventually released unscathed, but one man was "so unfortunate as to fall a sacrifice in the nation of the Miamis, to whose towns he was carried and then tortured to death in a most cruel manner." Johnston recovered from his ordeal and soon set on foot "a scheme of matrimony ... with a Girl from whose merits & fortune I have the highest prosperity of future happiness. If I can obtain her," he wrote, "I shall immediately give up the idea of all profit and happiness except what is to be reaped from a private retired life."[80]

Despite his early optimism, Johnston remained active in business affairs. In the 1820s, he invested in the Prestonville Company, losing a bundle when it went under. Johnston recovered, though, by establishing a hotel and summer resort, the famous Botetourt Springs. He operated the resort until his death in 1833, shortly before the first national debt itself expired. Johnston bought his first federal bond, a Six with a $150 par value, on November 13, 1792. He sold said bond a few months later, on February 2, 1793. Although he probably lost a bundle on that one, buying in at 105 or higher and selling out at 95 (in other words, he paid $150 \times 1.05 = \$157.50$ for an asset he sold a few months later for about $150 \times .95 = \$142.50$, collecting only about $150 \times .015 = \$2.25$ interest in the meantime), Johnston initiated a series of small-scale speculations that continued through 1800. All told, Johnston bought (and subsequently sold) $4,376.22 worth of Threes, $2,371.59 of Sixes, $100 of Navy Sixes, and $3,905.43 of Deferred Sixes. He repaid a debt of his own, to Duchouquet, in 1802.[81]

Mace Clements of Tappahannock, Essex County, acquired over $5,000 of federal bonds in December 1790 and immediately disposed of them. In May 1793, he bought in again, but only to the extent of $1,083.07. He sold those holdings off in three transactions in May and October 1795 and December 1797. In July 1799, he bought in yet again, this time about $750 worth. He sold out again, part in January 1800 and the balance in late July 1801. Clements died in 1806 or early 1807 after stating in his last will that he was "sick and much indisposed" and ready to meet his maker. Clements may have had a love child by the name of John. In any event, he emancipated and bequeathed 200 acres of his Kentucky land to "my mulatto boy John." That may have just been an expression, though, as Clements also emancipated his slave Sam, but gave him only 30 acres and a horse. His unenumerated Virginia estate he gave to his pregnant wife during her widowhood, with various contingencies dependent upon the unborn child's gender.[82]

Another Virginia speculator was Samuel Beall, who by January 1780 had set himself up as a merchant in Williamsburg and immediately revealed himself to be an astute player capable of juggling guineas, silver dollars, sterling bills, and land deeds, and someone willing and able to lend large sums to the public, including Virginia commercial agents Benjamin Day and Duncan Rose, for the right price. In late 1781, he also endeavored to invest Continentals in land for his friends, but apparently could get no more than 10,000 to 1 for the discredited currency. In terms of specualting on federal bonds, he played the Panic of 1792 just right, selling out in early January 1792, when prices were high, and buying back in late in April, when prices were low. He sold out all of his holdings over several weeks in May 1794, ostensibly so as not to rattle Virginia's relatively thin markets.[83]

> In terms of specualting on federal bonds, he played the Panic of 1792 just right, selling out in early January 1792, when prices were high, and buying back in late in April, when prices were low.

Alexander Buchanan was a major securities speculator. On October 29, 1791, he bought $39,804.46 worth of Threes, Sixes, and Deferred Sixes. Less than two weeks later, he sold over $3,400 worth, but a few days after that added almost $6,000 to his portfolio. In late November and early December, though, he disgorged over $28,000 of federal bonds in 6 trades. He bought back over $13,000 before the end of January 1792, however. He sold about $1,300 worth in late February but held strong during the Panic and bought another $6,000 worth of bonds, Sixes, in June. He then took a breather before launching into a five-year-long buying spree. In 45 transactions between May 1793 and February 1798, he purchased over $20,500 worth of federal bonds and sold none. Between then and March 1800, he sold a few bonds but on net added bonds worth almost $6,400 to his portfolio. From October 1800 to December 1802, Buchanan sold off his holdings, worth almost $58,500 in total, in 11 transactions, including over $38,000 on May 28, 1801.

Based in Richmond, Buchanan had other interests as well, including making loans on the collateral of slaves and/or land. He also speculated in lands directly, selling in 1798, for instance, 2.5 lots of prime Richmond real estate to John Cringan. Buchanan also had ties to the James River Company. He wasn't all about business, though. In 1788, Buchanan and six other Richmond gentlemen established the "Amicable Society of Richmond," a charitable organization that quickly grew in numbers and fame for its good works. Buchanan was the organization's treasurer for a time but apparently the society never purchased federal securities.[84]

Educated at home, Archibald Blair replaced his cousin, famed jurist John Blair, as clerk of the Council of State in July 1776, a post he would hold for nearly a quarter of a century. After being dismissed from his post in 1800, likely for political reasons, Blair stayed in Richmond and became a merchant, land speculator, and a director of the James River Canal Company. Blair was also a major federal securities speculator. Between March 1791 and May 1793, he was bullish on bonds, buying over $6,250 worth in 15 transactions while selling only about $2,700 worth in 4 trades. In 1793, 1794, and 1795, Blair sold his portfolio in 14 transactions. In 1798, 1799, and the first half of 1800, he turned bullish again, buying over $2,000 of federal bonds, including Navy Sixes, in 17 transactions, and making only 1 small sale. Between August 1800 and the end of October 1801, Blair again sold off his entire portfolio, save for about $600 worth of Deferred Sixes he finally jettisoned in October 1808. Blair died in Richmond in October 1824 after a long illness, having come into this life circa 1753.[85]

William Galt was an even bigger player. Born in 1755, Galt fled his native Scotland to Richmond in 1775 due to a little misunderstanding over British customs laws. (Apparently, Galt was a smuggler.) He never married but lived for a time with John M. Gordon, whom he sometimes sent out to collect debts from laggards like Washington merchant Robert Preston. Late in his life Galt adopted three close relatives orphaned in Scotland. He died in 1825 one of the richest men in Virginia, the proud owner of urban real estate in Richmond and Lynchburg, five plantations, hundreds of slaves, numerous mills, and a big chunk of the Bank of Virginia. From July 21 to November 22, 1791 he acquired over $18,000 of federal bonds. Later in November and in early December, he sold over $4,500 of his holdings but clung to the rest through the Panic. In 20 transactions between May 1793 and August 1802, he added another $3,143.87 to his portfolio. He changed over $10,000 of his bonds into converted and exchanged Sixes in March 1808 but sold them off in late October and early November of that same year.[86]

⁂

Federal bonds were outstanding investments because they paid interest punctually, could be quickly sold to raise emergency cash, and their value, while hardly fixed, was relatively stable. Their value decreased during the

Federal bonds were outstanding investments because they paid interest punctually, could be quickly sold to raise emergency cash, and their value, while hardly fixed, was relatively stable. Their value decreased during the Panic of 1792, but they held up well during the Panic of 1819 because investors took the "flight to quality," to assets they knew to be good in the most uncertain of times.

Panic of 1792, but they held up well during the Panic of 1819 because investors took the "flight to quality," to assets they knew to be good in the most uncertain of times. For example in New York in June 1819, "where the failures are innumerable … nothing but U.S. Stock commands money." In more tranquil times, bank stocks and corporate bonds were fairly close substitutes, but personal bonds and mortgages were not, as they often could not be sold quickly for cash and because they suffered from high rates of default.[87]

Government bonds were in some respects superior investments to physical assets. Land could always be worked, but it could quickly plummet in value. "Splendid country seats, that cost large sums," Peter Beverely told his brother in 1819, "are in market for a song." And even then they moved only slowly and almost always on a long credit. Slaves and at times certain commodities were easily saleable for cash *compared with real estate*, but their liquidity should not be overestimated. Slaves were less liquid than financial securities for a number of reasons. Most important, they were idiosyncratic, not uniform like most financial securities. So they had to be inspected before purchase but even the most thorough looking over could not reveal some diseases or undesirable personality traits. Slaves were also human, so they had to be fed, insured, and guarded while in transit. Some slaveholders also blanched at the thought of breaking up families, selling friends, and the like. Finally, slave prices trended upward most of the time, so the best investment strategy was to "buy and hold" rather than to short sell them. All in all, then, slaves were better used as collateral for loans than as saleable assets. Federal securities could be more quickly, easily, and cheaply sold and were also easily used as collateral.[88]

Many Virginians therefore bought federal bonds to help see them through liquidity pinches, collecting a decent and safe stream of revenue from them until they were needed to meet pressing exigencies. Norfolk merchant Richard Blow was a typical Southern merchant of the period, with his fingers in a thousand pies, including banks, canals, a plantation, private lending, slaves, insurance, ships, bills of exchange, lawsuits galore, and, to a limited extent, public securities. Blow owned an 8 percent bond for a brief period in the late summer and early fall of 1800, perhaps disgorging it because he feared what Jefferson's impending election to the presidency might do to its price. Then again, he held a Navy Six he purchased in November 1799 until September 1807, apparently selling it in distress. In August 1807, troops billeted in his house "on account of the unfortunate affair that took place betwixt the British Ship Leopard & our Frigate Chessepeak [sic]." As a result, trade, except for the exportation of tobacco, temporarily ceased. By mid-August, Blow beseeched creditors to not draw on him, "for these bad times unless Carolina Bank Notes" would answer their needs.[89]

One of Richard Blow's friends, merchant William Barksdale, often resided in London but as early as 1783 sometimes ran his business out of Petersburg, Virginia. After Napoleon announced his blockade of England in 1807, Barksdale commiserated with Blow over insurance rates, which had soared to 10 percent, enough to "ruin any Voyage." ('Twas nothing compared with the 50 percent premium during the War of 1812, but it was high by peacetime standards.) Nevertheless, Blow continued to send him tobacco in London by the boatload via Rotterdam, Hamburg, or other Continental ports if necessary. Barksdale was lucky, smart, or well informed, or perhaps all three. He acquired Threes, Sixes, and Deferred Sixes in July and November 1791 only to sell them off again in December 1791 and January 1792, on the eve of the Panic of 1792. After the Panic, he bought back in, purchasing almost $2,700 worth of Sixes, which he held until August 31, 1802.[90]

Henry Haxall was a Petersburg merchant, sometimes on his own and sometimes in partnership with his brother William. Like other merchants, the Haxalls' business suffered through periods, like the fall of 1797, when "money is very hard to get" and the years leading up to the War of 1812, when "the times are so pregnant with unforeseen events." In November 1813, Haxall bought over $3,500 worth of federal bonds. He managed to hold them through the war, and the horrific fire of July 1815, in which he and his brother were reportedly "heavy sufferers." He sold a few hundred dollars' worth in

January 1819, almost certainly to raise cash during the financial panic, but kept the rest until April 1824. Haxall knew what could be gotten for his bonds at all times because he subscribed to *Ming's New York Price Current* and likely other early forerunners to the *Wall Street Journal*.[91]

Well known to Haxall was Norfolk merchant Conway Whittle. Whittle bought $300 worth of Navy Sixes in November 1799 and $1,000 of Eights in August 1800. He sold his Navy Sixes in September 1802 and his Eights that November, almost certainly to raise the needful. He was interested in Navy Sixes because those bonds helped to fund the Navy, which as a merchant was important to him. He had marveled in 1798 about the USS *Constitution*'s seizure of a French privateer of 20-plus guns taken near the American coastline and at the same time hit Haxall up for a loan so he could pay his customs duties. Again in February 1801, Whittle was "distressed in money matters," this time because of the loss of the ship *Jane* "that had funds on board to pay for two former Cargoes." Luckily, Whittle's warehouse was flush with rum, sugar, coffee, and molasses, which were "very scarce" in the market, so they could "command cash." Like the Haxalls and other Virginia merchants, Whittle was involved in a wide variety of lines, from foreign exchange to domestic produce to West Indian drugs to foreign luxuries.[92]

Virginians who sold their federal bonds (or comparable liquid assets) often paid a heavy price in terms of lost liquidity, especially if they could not obtain bank loans. Joseph Carrington Cabell got lucky. In 1819 he was able to borrow money from one bank to repay loans falling due in another until he was able to sell his flour. Merchant Harrison Allmand of Norfolk, Virginia, had no such luck. He purchased a $100 par value Navy Six on November 22, 1799. The purchase and sale price of the bond is unknown, but Allmand sold his bond on August 3, 1802, just before Navy Sixes reached their apex price of $102 in Boston, the market where they traded most heavily. Thereafter, Allmand stayed away from government bonds, preferring to invest in Norfolk rental properties, slaves Tom, Pluto, Willis, Richard, Joanna, Betsey (who he claimed was a "very good look") and others, and his mercantile business, including a ship called

The Thomas, a bake house, a warehouse on Maxwell's Wharf, inventory, and scads of accounts receivable, individually small but in sum enough to bankrupt him if delinquent.[93]

Allmand later regretted not holding more of his wealth in the form of government securities. In the bloody aftermath of the Panic of 1819, he had to inform the Bank of Virginia that "Various Loises [*sic*] & some recently to a considerable amt. & others expected … with other misfortunes & distressing circumstances" made his financial situation "hopeless & in vain to struggle any longer." His notes at the bank would have to be protested as he could not raise the money needed to meet them. The problem, he explained, was the "continued decline in the value of this kind of property" and the inability to sell commodities for cash had rendered him temporarily insolvent. Allmand learned the hard way that it was essential to own some sort of asset that was quickly saleable at something close to its value. Defeated by events and 65 years of age, Allmand fell ill and died in April 1822.[94]

Warren Ashley, a wholesale grain and tobacco merchant based in Norfolk, also learned about risk the hard way. In November 1799, Ashley purchased $300 par value Navy Sixes, probably at something less than par. In September 1800, he added $1,000 par worth of Eights to his portfolio, which then were selling for 109 in New York. When Ashley sold all of his federal bond holdings on April 7, 1802, Eights were selling for 110.50 in New York and Navys were selling at par, so in addition to the interest received he earned modest capital gains. But losses on the personal bonds he later invested in far exceeded those profits. For example, he had to sue people he'd lent thousands of dollars to, after they sold to unknown persons the slaves that they'd posted as collateral.[95]

Rawleigh Colston was born in Northumberland County, Virginia, in 1749. Orphaned at an early age, he lived with a guardian who had him well tutored before apprenticing him to his brother, a Williamsburg merchant. By his own admission, Colston learned but little there as he spent much of his time hanging out with William and Mary students, "most of whom at that time were more celebrated for their vices than their literary accomplishments." (William and Mary a party school? Imagine that!) When his master died, Colston moved in with an indulgent relative near Richmond. After enjoying his "dissipated" lifestyle for another year or so, Colston, disgusted with himself, moved back to Williamsburg to study law under

George Wythe. His law practice foundered, however, so when the Revolution came he used it as an excuse to sell his estate. Unfortunately, he did so on credit, so most of it "was lost by depreciation." Passed over for an officership, he became a commercial agent for the collection of military stores from abroad, and settled in Saint Domingo and Curaçao for the purpose. The gig made Colston an "easy fortune" and in 1784 he returned to Richmond, where a year later he married. He then went into farming, settling near Winchester, Frederick County. In 1801, he removed to a new plantation called Honey Wood near Martinsburg, Berkeley County.[96]

Contemporaries considered Colston learned, religious, and commercially astute. Indeed, Colston bought over $26,000 worth of federal bonds between September 1791 and May 1792, buying even during the Panic, when they were relatively cheap. He liquidated some $10,000 of his bonds in August 1792 and the balance of his portfolio in July 1793. He also bought up lands given to officers for their services during the Revolution. In 1807, he wished that he still owned some federal bonds because he was "most cruelly disappointed in the receipt of money" that he "expected with the utmost certainty." He therefore "contracted to pay money which it" was impossible for him to do unless he could collect from his debtors, always a tenuous proposition in this period. Colston died in 1823.[97]

⮾

Some Virginians shifted their investments from federal bonds to other financial securities, many almost as liquid and safe as government bonds, at least during good times. For instance, Norfolk's John Cowper (1763–1847) purchased $1,000 worth of Navy Sixes in November 1799 and sold them in March 1800. In September of that year, he bought $1,000 worth of Eights but sold them in December. He then abstained from federal bond trading until July 1816, when he bought $2,560 of Threes, which he sold exactly three days later. After the Panic of 1819, when Cowper was an insurance broker specializing in finding shippers insurance with marine insurers, especially the big corporate ones that had come to dominate the market, he again considered buying federal bonds, comparing them to bank stocks. Interestingly, he leaned toward the banks, especially the Bank of the United States and the Virginia banks in which the Virginia government owned significant stakes. Although he failed to account for the governmental and political meddling that had sometimes hurt the Virginia banks, his reasoning was astute. Banks, he intimated, were almost as secure as government bonds because the federal and state governments, respectively, "must support them by every means" in their power. Bank stock was almost as liquid as government bonds and often much more remunerative. He realized, too, that his decision must ultimately hinge on both current prices and the prices likely to be had on each type of security in the

> Bank stock was almost as liquid as government bonds and often much more remunerative.

future, but ultimately admitted that much guesswork was involved. "The man who has sagacity to perceive what will be … [in] twelve months hence, I believe does not live," he noted. Foreseeing the future was particularly difficult in the wake of a financial panic. "The sudden change of fortune in so large a portion of the community," he argued, "must produce very injurious effects on Society, not only in their own industry lost, but the industry of an infinitely greater number, who depended on them for employment. Men who have been accustomed to active lives, suddenly thrown out of employment, become at first depressed, afterwords [sic] desperate." That desperation, he reasoned, much like a modern economist, increased moral hazard (fraud for example), making predictions even more difficult. By the 1820s, Cowper was employed by the Marine Insurance Company of Norfolk, where one of his duties was to correspond with foreign consulates regarding ship seizures, insurance claims, and the like.[98]

As early as 1784, James Bruce of Halifax County considered establishing a store as well as a plantation. By 1793, he was indeed engaged in a mercantile way, buying tobacco from his neighbors and complaining of the scarcity of money. Bruce obtained about $135 worth of federal bonds in September 1791 and sold them ahead of the Panic on January 5, 1792. Later, he donated $1,000 to form a school in Halifax County, purchased a second plantation in Albemarle County, was heavily involved (277 shares by 1836) in the Roanoke Navigation Company, and complained bitterly about the "extravagant salaries" of Virginia bank directors. The reason became clear when he drew up his last will in October 1836—he owned 594 shares in the Bank of Virginia and 773 shares in the Farmers Bank of Virginia. His will also reveals that he owned Wolf Island in Caswell County, North Carolina, and much other real estate besides and the slaves necessary to work them. Much to his son's chagrin, he died with too much of his fortune loaned out to Virginia elites, like Edward C. Carrington (1790–1855) and Colonel James Madison, who were slow to pay up. The city of Richmond, to which he had lent $35,000, was a better bet.[99]

The process also worked in reverse, with people accustomed to other types of financial securities buying government bonds when they became frustrated with high default rates. James Boyce, who rented lot 26 of the Town Point Company tract in Norfolk for $12.50 per year, may have invested $200 in Navy Sixes in November 1799 because he was sick of dealing with his fellow Virginians, who often "paid" their debts with personal bonds and court judgments, particularly when money was tightest and hence most needed. Boyce sold his holdings in September 1801.[100]

Whatever the specific reasons early Virginians owned federal bonds, they saw them to be of value, as did Americans in every other state, to a greater or lesser extent. Over time, the debt tended to migrate northward, where the lure of easy slave plantation riches was nonexistent. A catch-22 soon developed—the most liquid federal bond markets were in the north, so the bonds were often worth slightly more there than in the thinner southern markets. That, over time, drew yet more bonds northward. Regardless of who owned them, federal bonds provided investors with safety, liquidity, and, at times, an object of speculation. In the next chapter, we'll see how the national debt, via the development diamond, also aided America's overall economic and political development.

8

BLESSINGS

American Economic Growth

A
t the dawn of the nineteenth century, Samuel Blodget Jr., a gifted entrepreneur and architect from New Hampshire, predicted that the United States would "become hereafter THE GREATEST AND MOST POWERFUL NATION OF THE UNIVERSE" (emphasis in original). Although his pronouncement was bombastic and his methodology, projecting recent trends into the distant future, was simple, Blodget wasn't far off the mark. "You all know," he began, "the comparatively miserable state of our country, when, in the years 1787 and 1788, our wharves were destitute of shipping, our poor in rags, their houses in the most ruinous state, their farms fenceless, and the low prices of our produce were scarce sufficient to defray the cartage to market." Since the "commencement of the funding system," however, "the country prospered beyond all former example. New villages, towns and cities sprang up as if by magic: our agriculture flourished, and our commerce extended to all parts of the globe: our public and private credit became universal." The American economy certainly received a boost in the 1790s due to the series of wars that enveloped Europe following the French Revolution. But it is equally true that Hamilton's reforms made it possible for American merchants, manufacturers, and farmers to take full advantage of the opportunities that those wars afforded. Why did Blodget see the causal connection among funding and finance and economic growth so clearly, while others, then and now, saw theft and penury?[1]

"Only our familiarity blinds us to the marvelous nature of the system." So wrote British banking theorist Walter Bagehot in his famous treatment of London's money market, *Lombard Street*. A similar familiarity with the wonders of America's current financial system may blind readers to the blessings wrought by Hamilton's funding system. So, too, may partisan rage, a fervent desire to score ideological points rather than to gain historical understanding. To this day, scholars occasionally emerge from the underbrush to snipe at Hamilton, particularly his assertion that the national debt could be a national blessing. The snipers talk big but proffer little of substance and much in the way of innuendo, misinformation, and misunderstanding. In the past, I have chastised them and moved on. Here, I shall simply move on, tempting as it is to mock the claim that Hamilton was *not* "the architect of America's economic 'take-off,'" and remain content to tie all the strands of the development diamond model together into a rope of sufficient strength to hang any future snipers.[2]

Above, I presented a mountain of new evidence that shows that Hamilton was right: the national debt was, *in the case of the early United States*, a national blessing. In the simplest terms, the interest paid on the debt did not exceed its usefulness to the nation, so the country gained by it. Or, as British observer William Winterbotham noted in 1795: "While the European governments draw annually from their subjects at least one fourth of their bona fide property to defray the interest of their public debt, the citizens of the United States are scarce sensible of any burthen arising therefrom; nay, on the contrary, in its present state, it is to them a real national advantage." In addition to helping the nation to achieve and maintain its independence, preserve itself whole under intense domestic centrifugal pressures, and more than double its physical size, the public debt served as the bridge between the nation's nonpredatory government and its emerging financial system. That financial system, in turn, spurred the crystallization of the rest of America's development diamond, its entrepreneurs, managers, and the business firms they ran. As Treasury Secretary Richard Rush put it: "A State whose natural resources and territory are abundant, whose institutions are free, and whose interests are diversified, may witness occasional and temporary pressure upon some of those interests ... but transient inconvenience is lost in the aggregate prosperity, and must, in the end, participate in that prosperity."[3]

The development diamond described in Chapter 1 is not a chimera, the fanciful creation of modern ivory-tower intellectuals. Rather, it traces its roots to the Enlightenment. By the early nineteenth century, its main outlines were a fixture in political economy textbooks. "A principal cause of national wealth is a constitution of government, or establishment of political liberty, and equal rights," asserted one anonymous textbook author in 1805. "The invention of the greatest consequence in the production of wealth," he noted, "is that of *money* .... Public securities," he continued, "contribute to the national wealth, by causing capital and labor to flow into the state, from abroad" and by acting as a money substitute (italics in original). "The admirable effects of commerce" combined with "national skill in finance," Samuel Blodget observed in 1801, had turned a marsh (Holland) and a sterile clay island (Britain) into world superpowers and would turn wild expanses (North America) into one in turn. Blodget went so far as to assert that trade and finance could make a wealthy country of "even a barren rock." (Before dismissing this as hyperbole, consider Iceland.) "The means" of American national wealth, Blodget continued, would be "principally these: increase of population, extension of commerce, and a compleat system of finance, supported by public credit and an increased CAPITAL STOCK" (emphasis in original). That capital would help finance everything from insurance to factories to transportation systems. In May 1831, for example, 101 different stockholders owned 1,436 shares in the Albany and Schenectady Turnpike Company, which was then considering improving its road and laying railroad tracks. Tens and perhaps hundreds of thousands of other investors, from Maine to Georgia and the Mississippi to the Thames, did likewise, providing thousands of U.S. corporations with the long-term external financing they needed to make profits and, in the process, valuable goods, public and private.[4]

> "The admirable effects of commerce" combined with "national skill in finance," Samuel Blodget observed in 1801, had turned a marsh (Holland) and a sterile clay island (Britain) into world superpowers and would turn wild expanses (North America) into one in turn.

Blodget proved remarkably prescient. The combination of nonpredatory government and a variety of external financing options provided the milieu in which much vaunted American characteristics, like Yankee ingenuity and Mid-Atlantic enterprise, could thrive. Increasingly, foreigners traveling through America, especially the northern states, remarked that "all is activity, enterprise, speculation, hazard." By the 1830s, even haughty European observers recognized the United States as "one of the richest countries on the earth" because its economic efficiency increased by leaps and bounds even as its population and geographical extent did likewise. Far from remaining wed to agriculture, as many Jeffersonians desired, the American economy, slathered in entrepreneurial endeavors, evolved into a potent mix of agricultural, commercial, financial, and manufacturing endeavors.[5]

Finally, it is also possible that the financial system, and the national debt in particular, aided economic growth indirectly by fortifying America's nascent democracy. We're on less certain grounds here, but the argument is intriguing and has been proffered by several serious scholars. Here is the gist of the story: Governments suffer from credibility problems because they can say one thing but do another (or nothing at all). Why should people trust them with their money? Or with the power to kill in their name or, what ultimately amounts to the same thing, to tax? Checks and balances, separation of powers, and so forth go only so far. What matters is what governments actually do, not the way they are nominally structured. One way for a government to show that it is capable of sticking to its commitments is to sell negotiable bonds, then service them as promised. Every trading day, the market, which is to say the collective wisdom of everyone, assesses the likelihood of the government's ability and *willingness* to meet its promises. Creditworthiness becomes a proxy for credibility. If the government can prevent the masses from defrauding public creditors, and vice versa, then it can probably also be trusted to maintain the rights of other minorities. This view works nicely with Hamilton's idea that "credit is an entire thing. Every part of it has the nicest sympathy with every other part; wound one limb, and the whole tree shrinks and decays," and with his conviction that restoration of public credit was necessary "to preserve the government itself by showing it worthy of the confidence which was placed in it."[6]

The best way to test the contention that the Constitution, the national debt, the financial system, entrepreneurs, and managers spurred American economic growth would be to run carefully controlled experiments in lab petri dishes. That is clearly impossible but occasionally social scientists can examine "natural experiments," real-life cases that approximate the rigor of laboratory controls. The hypothesis that communism creates poverty, for example, received much support from natural experiments in Germany and Korea, formerly unified countries that shared much in common until one part became communist with command economies and the other became democratic with free markets. Both communist areas stagnated while the free market areas flourished, providing strong evidence that communism was the cause of the poverty.

I strongly suspect that William Ouseley, attaché to the British Majesty's legation in Washington, D.C., had it right when he argued that "doubtless the adoption of the form of the United States would not have *alone* caused" America's population and economy to flourish (italics in original). Nor would the absence of a national debt have prevented the country from creating "such a maritime force and commercial navy as now exist … . But, on the other hand," he conceded, "all the favourable circumstances to which we have alluded would not, under an opposite system, have produced similar prosperity." He then urged readers to "look at Mexico" as an example of a country richly endowed by climate and natural resources but which nevertheless showed "little promise … of such proportionate aggrandizement as the example of the United States might lead us to expect." Much the same could be, and in fact was, said of Canada. And because Canada's roots were northern European (French and British), cultural differences loom less large in comparisons of the United States and Canada than in comparisons of America and Mexico. In short, early-nineteenth-century Canada and the United States, particularly anglicized Upper Canada (Ontario) and New York, can be seen as a natural experiment that bolsters the view that the development diamond underlay America's economic growth.[7]

Today, by some estimates, Canadians enjoy a higher standard of living than do Americans. Such was not always the case. In the early nineteenth century, the Canadian economy was clearly inferior to that of the United States and even to that of New York, with which it shared much in common. In 1822, Canadian Robert Gourlay argued that the comparison of New York and Ontario was a fair one. "The neighbouring state of New York," he wrote, "furnishes a fair comparison and example. The northern and western districts of that state resemble the adjacent districts of Upper Canada in respect to soil, climate, and markets." Despite those similarities, Gourlay intimated, Canadians envied New Yorkers because "land of similar quality and corresponding situations, although once very cheap there [in New York], now bears a price four times as high among them as among their neighbours in this province." Indeed, in 1825 New York State boasted some $273 million worth of real and personal property, while that same year Canadian tax assessments arrived at a total of only $9 million. Even adjusting for differences in population sizes and assessment techniques, Gourlay's claim was clearly no hyperbole. Nor was it a transient phenomenon. In the early 1840s, Lord Durham noted that Canadians envied New Yorkers because otherwise comparable farms fetched "*several hundred per cent*" more in the Empire State (italics in original). Like Gourlay, Durham did "not believe that the universal difference in the value of land can any where be fairly attributed to natural causes."[8]

Before the American Revolution, Canada looked very much like the American colonies both politically and economically. Yet by the nineteenth century, even those parts of Canada similar in resources as neighboring portions of the United States, like the Niagara Peninsula, had fallen behind.

The enormous differences between Ontario and New York puzzled many observers. Before the American Revolution, Canada looked very much like the American colonies both politically and economically. Yet by the nineteenth century, even those parts of Canada similar in resources as neighboring portions of the United States, like the Niagara Peninsula, had fallen behind. By 1830, for example, the population density on the American side of the Niagara River was 30 persons per square mile, while the density on the Canadian side was only six.[9]

Numerous eighteenth- and nineteenth-century observers pointed to Canada's corrupt governments and relatively backward financial system as the main reasons it fell behind. John Duncan traveled through Canada and the United States in 1818 and 1819. He pointed out that in America "scarcely has an infant settlement numbered a hundred houses, till a corporation for the manufacture at least of bank notes, if it be nothing more, is immediately set on foot … . The commercial capital of Canada, on the other hand, with a population of about twenty thousand, and a trade employing annually about 150,000 tons of shipping," he noted, had just formed its first bank. Duncan thought the Americans more commercially precocious than the merchants of Montreal but noted too that high illiteracy rates made banking in Quebec a challenge. "As an expedient to assist those who cannot read," Duncan continued, the new Canadian bank "exhibited a row of dollars upon the margin of each of their notes, corresponding in number to its amount." Canada's banks were extremely cautious early on too, so they rendered little aid to the government during the country's fiscal crisis in the mid–1820s.[10]

Also in the 1820s, James Buchanan, the British consul in New York, lamented Canada's relative "torpidity, and indolence" and explicitly attributed the difference to Canada's immature financial system. About the same time, an English farmer named Joseph Pickering visited Canada and the United States with an eye toward immigration. He noted the paucity of banks in Canada, adding that "it is the numerous banks in every part of the States, that have given such a stimulus to enterprise among the Americans." In 1833, George Hebert, another British observer, also lamented the sorry state of Canada's economy. He, too, considered the dearth of intermediation facilities a major cause of the north country's economic backwardness. "Bank notes circulate very little beyond the towns in Lower Canada [Quebec]," he noted, adding that by forbidding interest payments "the Catholic clergy" induced the faithful to hoard specie rather than to suffer "the risk of lending it for nothing." Steep discounts of 20 to 25 percent for cash payments indicated high implicit interest charges on book accounts, Hebert noted. "Money is so scarce in Upper Canada [Ontario]," he further explained, "that most of the farmers are obliged to pay their labourers with grain." Indeed, another source indicates that the money supply of Upper Canada in 1825 was only £135,000 Canadian currency (i.e., $540,000,[11] or $3.58 per capita[12]). Another traveler, one who resided in Canada for five years, noted that "for want of current coin in Canada, a system of barter exists," a pernicious and inefficient one at that. The system was prevalent through the 1830s at least.

> Before the mid–1830s Upper Canada was but, in the words of one contemporary, "a limb of the monetary system" of the United States.

Before the mid–1830s Upper Canada was but, in the words of one contemporary, "a limb of the monetary system" of the United States.[13]

An early 1840s traveler, William Thomson, also observed that Canada lagged behind New York in "wealth, cultivation, and internal communication," but argued that the colony compared favorably with "the western and more recently-settled States" in matters of wealth cultivation and internal communication. John Robert Godley thought that foreign investment made all the difference: the United States could attract it but Canada could not, not even from the mother country. "The prosperity of America, her railroads, canals, steam navigation, and banks, are the fruit of English capital," he argued. "England," he claimed, "has sunk nearly £40,000,000 in the States ... . On the other hand," Godley lamented, "hardly a shilling of English capital has found its way into this province."[14]

To explain the embarrassing differences between colonial Canada and independent America, Lord Durham also blamed the province's backward government and weak financial system. He fingered French influences in Quebec as the major barrier to development, a popular argument. In his famous *Report on the Affairs of British North America*, Durham argued:

> The English population ... looked on the American provinces as a vast field for settlement and speculation ... . They wished to form themselves into companies for the establishment of banks, and the construction of railroads and canals ... . The applications for banks, railroads and canals were laid on one side ... . In all these decisions of the Assembly ... . the English population perceived traces of a desire to repress the influx and success of their race.

Indeed, influential French-Canadian politicians like Louis-Joseph Papineau regularly attacked banks as tools of anti-French political forces. French-Canadian politicians may also have slowed the proliferation of other Anglo-American financial innovations, including insurance companies, savings banks, and building societies, all of which appeared in Canada soon after their introduction to New York, but in much smaller numbers. Not until 1835 did the first French-controlled bank appear.[15]

Due at least in part to the French antibank influences, Canada's early banking system remained stunted and corrupt. Durham took special note of the "evils of the banking and monetary systems" of the colony, especially the corrupt practices of the "all-powerful" cliques that controlled its few chartered banks. Durham advised Canada to try to emulate the United States, marveling that the state of New York was able to construct "its own St. Lawrence from Lake Erie to the Hudson, while the Government of Lower Canada could not achieve, or even attempt, the few miles of canal and dredging which would have rendered its mighty rivers navigable almost to their sources." Ultimately, Anglo-Canadians had only themselves to blame for not bringing the French to heel. In a stunning passage, Durham pointed out that Americans had quickly co-opted the French indigenous to Louisiana. He also noted that New York State, too, had successfully absorbed the laws and human capital of a Continental people, to wit the Dutch. Nonpredatory governments summoned forth the energies rather than the jealousies of all.[16]

New York enjoyed far more commercial banks than did Canada, and did so far earlier. Canadians, backed by British merchants, attempted to establish banks of issue and deposit in 1792, and again in 1808 and 1811, but all their efforts quickly failed. Not until 1817 did the Bank of Montreal form, but its success did not usher in a flood of entry into the sector. Canadian banks enjoyed branching privileges, a right denied to most New York banks, so the number of banks per se is not as telling a statistic as the per capita bank capital, money supply, and credit figures. Canada severely lagged behind New York in each of those measures. The lack of a central bank analogous to the Bank of the United States, or a financial center like Wall Street, also hamstrung the Canadian banking system, rendering it during the insurrections and financial panics of 1837 and 1838 something of a joke to domestic and foreign observers alike.[17]

The recession that followed the panic and rebellion of 1837 slowed Canada's development but the Union of 1840, the long-awaited political ascendance of Ontario, and Britain's trade liberalization policies finally tipped the balance in the 1840s, when Canada's economy began to show signs of development. Political unity indeed brought improved public credit and more foreign investment, likely because it also ushered in an era of less predatory government. In 1843, the new colonial government issued bonds in London guaranteed by the mother country, using the proceeds to jump-start internal improvement projects, which fueled expansion of the commercial sector. Improved infrastructure, further development of the financial system, and movement out of the relatively inefficient agricultural sector spurred growth in manufacturing in the 1850s.[18]

The Canadian financial system improved in the 1840s and 1850s but continued to trail that of New York. Only after Canada adopted a nonpredatory government did it thrive economically, its rate of economic growth accelerating from a likely average of well under 1 percent per year to modern levels, 3.38 percent on average, between 1850 and 1870, when it finally threw off the yoke of direct British rule. In the second half of the nineteenth century, Canada's financial sector continued to develop, and growth proceeded apace. By the early twentieth century, Canadians enjoyed one of the world's wealthiest economies in per capita terms.[19]

❧

> The economic changes wrought by the Constitution, Hamilton's financial revolution, the revival of public credit, and the birth of American capital markets affected the North more deeply than the South.

Differences within the United States were also evident. The economic changes wrought by the Constitution, Hamilton's financial revolution, the revival of public credit, and the birth of American capital markets affected the North more deeply than the South. Nevertheless, the South was not immune to the salubrious effects of the development diamond, as the case of South Carolina demonstrates. Slavery was doubtless the single most important facet of South Carolina's economy before the Civil War. The peculiar institution rightfully deserves the attention that scholars and the public have bestowed upon it for the last century or so. A portion of South Carolina's economy, however, was able to transcend the shackles of slavery and foster entrepreneurship via corporate capitalism, a network of financial intermediaries, corporations, and other firms that raised long-term external financing in the form of equities and bonds via capital markets. The cradle of nullification and the birthplace of secession possessed an economy that was, in part, structurally similar to that of the

North. Corporate capitalism suffused the entire Palmetto State and waxed strong as the Civil War approached.[20]

Corporate capitalism—in the original sense of the word as the existence of capital markets, as opposed to the much broader notions of capitalism used by some scholars today—intertwined intimately with slavery in South Carolina. For example, some slaveholders invested in corporations and some corporations used slaved labor. All corporations used goods tainted with slave labor and all slaveholders purchased goods manufactured, financed, and/or transported by corporations. Ultimately, however, corporate capitalism and slavery represented distinct ways of organizing production and distribution. Although corporations sometimes relied on force and political favoritism, corporate capitalism ultimately rested on market competition and long-term financial contracts. Conversely, although slaveholders competed in a variety of markets, slavery in the final analysis rested on physical violence, state power, outright ownership of factor inputs (land and labor), and short-term financial contracts.[21]

Corporate capitalism required four basic components: investors, borrowers, banks, and securities markets. Investors ranged from individuals to nonprofit organizations to businesses with earnings in excess of expenditures. Consumers were sometimes borrowers but by far the largest sums went to governments and businesses, including new, entrepreneurial firms. Savings flowed from investors to entrepreneurs in two ways, via intermediaries like banks and insurance companies and via markets for stocks and bonds. Before the Civil War, South Carolina enjoyed in per capita terms significant numbers of investors with substantial savings, corporations and other businesses, banks, and securities that traded in the Charleston market.[22]

Like planters in Virginia, South Carolina planters often invested their savings in additional slaves and plantations. Nevertheless, considerable numbers of planters and other South Carolinians invested some of their savings in financial securities to hedge against adverse weather conditions and volatile prices for land, slaves, indigo, rice, cotton, and other agricultural products. Financial securities were also valued, because, as noted above, in many instances they were more liquid (easily, cheaply, and quickly saleable) than plantations, slaves, and commodities. South Carolina was also home to a major international seaport, Charleston, and, by the Civil War, dozens of inland commercial centers, all of which teemed with merchants who also saw the value of holding some of their assets in the form of financial instruments. The governments of Charleston and the state also invested in corporations, especially railroads, banks, and combinations of the two, by purchasing their equities and/or providing them with long-term loans. The total value of investment in financial securities by South Carolinians will never be known with precision. The extent of federal bondholding in South Carolina, however, is now known with some certainty and reveals a considerable level of investment in that important asset class.[23]

Between November 1790 and January 1797, 854 different entities registered their federal bonds in South Carolina's transfer books, records kept by a federal official in Charleston so that the owners of the Three, Six, and Deferred Six bonds created by Hamilton's funding system would receive the interest due them each quarter. That is not to say that 854 South Carolinians owned federal bonds in that period, however. For whatever reason, some South Carolinian investors registered their bonds elsewhere, including Pennsylvania. Also, some accounts listed several people as owners and some people controlled several accounts. The former were generally partners in mercantile firms; the latter were typically attorneys who held bonds in trust for minors, the estates of the deceased, and so forth. Finally, those 854 accountholders hailed from at least 87 different places, from Amsterdam to Bermuda, from Bordeaux to Bristol, and from Massachusetts to Georgia. Most, however, resided in Charleston or its environs. The accountholders included members of at least 48 different occupations, including bricklayers, gunsmiths, innkeepers, and housepainters.

Federal bonds registered in South Carolina actively traded hands in the 1790s. The size of transfers ranged from sums of $1.40 to almost $804,000. The average sale, of which there were 2,148 over the period, was for $1,359.10. The median transaction size was only $540.07, however, and 25 percent of the transactions were for bonds the face value of which was $173 or less, a sum well within the reach of "middling" households. Merchants were major participants in the market, being both numerous and geographically dispersed. In aggregate, however, various miscellaneous holders (females, estates, trusts, partnerships, and organizations) were more numerous than merchants and purchased a greater amount of the bonds. The market for government bonds was quite active both in terms of the number of trades and the face value traded.[24]

By the early nineteenth century, federal bonds were by no means the only financial securities regularly traded in South Carolina. A variety of companies began operations by selling shares to the public. Some of those DPOs (direct public offerings, as opposed to initial public offerings intermediated by investment banks) were quite hot affairs, as was one in 1834 in which investors offered to buy 894,000 shares in the Bank of Charleston, which was offering for sale only 20,000. On the other hand, like some other companies the South Carolina Canal and Rail Road Company was not able to sell all the shares it wanted to at its DPO but managed to begin operations anyway, and for a time was the longest railroad in the world. The number of financial securities listed in South Carolina newspapers, a good sign that many investors were interested in their prices, peaked at 15. Although far below the number of corporations listed in newspapers in Boston, New York, Philadelphia, or Baltimore, that was a respectable number given the state's relatively small white population. Listed securities included federal, state, and municipal bonds, banks, insurance companies, and a few transportation, utility, and miscellaneous corporations. Trading in some of the listed securities was probably thin, because prices changed only intermittently. Frequent price changes in other listed securities, by contrast, suggest relatively brisk trading, and there is ample narrative evidence of Charleston investors "playing ... at bulls and bears." Price changes and presumably trading activity could change over time for the same security. Trading in securities was relatively thin until after the War of 1812, then slowed again after the onset of the recession of 1819–22.[25]

Judging by changes in their prices, trading in government bonds, first federal and later state, was relatively heavy, and trading in bank securities was usually heaviest of all. Extant balance sheets—Warren Weber, a researcher at the Minneapolis Fed, has discovered 322 of them for antebellum South Carolina banks—provide glimpses into the importance of those institutions to the state economy. On January 1, 1850, a dozen South Carolina banks employed a capital stock of over $13 million, a circulation of bank-notes approaching $9 million, and deposits and other liabilities of about $6 million to provide borrowers with some $20.6 million worth of loans, over $20 per capita.[26]

South Carolina was also home to building and loan associations, which made mortgage loans to members, and savings banks like the Provident Institution for Savings in the city of Charleston. Established in December 1843, the latter institution by January 1849 boasted of 1,184 depositors and over $160,000 worth of deposits, which it invested in stocks and bonds. Unfortunately, the composition of the loan portfolios of the state's commercial banks is not known with precision, but they almost certainly were similar to those of other early U.S. banks, particularly in the South. That means that most if not all of their loans were structured as discounts on promissory notes or commercial paper maturing in less than a year. Such loans could be, and often were, renewed if both the bank and the borrower agreed on terms. Planters and their factors likely received many of the loans, as did merchants, retailers, and larger urban artisanal firms. Many of South Carolina's numerous corporations appear to have received their share of loans as well. Prior to the war, only two South Carolina banks failed, a very good record likely aided by the state's stringent usury laws and its state-owned bank, both of which gave South Carolina bankers incentives to maintain a safe portfolio of loans and an adequate cushion of cash reserves.[27]

South Carolina before the Civil War was home to a surprising number of corporations, almost all of which took the joint-stock form, which is to say that they obtained their initial financing by selling shares of themselves to investors. In exchange for supplying the corporations with cash, investors received dividends. The year-by-year account of the number of new corporations chartered in South Carolina and the amount of capital that they were authorized to sell is impressive. As in other states, incorporation activity fluctuated over time, due mostly to macroeconomic conditions. When times were bad, as in the first half of the 1840s, chartering activity fell off along with other forms of entrepreneurial business activity. When times were good, more people sought to establish new, large businesses and the state legislature, which in the absence of a general incorporation act had to approve each new charter, proved more receptive. Unsurprisingly, a political cycle tied to logrolling or quid pro quo arrangements among legislators also appears to have existed. The totals, 262 corporations capitalized at over $76 million, are impressive given the state's relatively small free population and pockets of agrarian Jeffersonian and Jacksonian antipathy toward the granting of "exclusive privileges on certain persons," and bastions of "Old Fogyism" or antientreprenuerial attitudes in the Upcountry.[28]

The range of corporate activity was impressive as well. The most capital-intensive businesses in the economy, banks and railroads (which were sometimes one and the same company), accounted for a full three-quarters of the authorized capital though they represented only slightly more than a quarter of all charters granted in the period. That does not mean that other types of corporations, from bridge and insurance companies to cemetery and manufacturing concerns, were pinched for long-term investment funds but simply that they required less capital. Although a few of the corporations were well-established businesses before they received state charters, most of the corporations were entrepreneurs in the sense of being start-ups. Many of the companies, including the banks, building and loans, bridges, ferries, hotels, railroads, canals, and steamship companies, were extensive entrepreneurs, businesses that pushed existing technologies and processes to new geographical areas. Others, like the plank road, theater, ice, telegraph, and many of the manufacturing and construction companies appear to have been the creations of innovative entrepreneurs that brought new technologies and processes to market, although not always successfully.[29]

Clearly, then, the American development diamond deeply penetrated even the Deep South during the height of its slave system. By the 1830s, if not before, Americans were world-renowned entrepreneurs, prepared to risk all on untried products, markets, and techniques. Many failed, but therein lay the genius of the American economy. It was not so much that everyone owned financial securities, had a bank deposit, or could obtain loans directly from intermediaries. Rather, the important thing was that everyone who wanted to be involved in the financial sector could be. Even women, Native Americans, and free blacks had bank accounts, used banknotes, borrowed on mortgage, and the like. (Only slaves were systematically excluded.) So the financial system did not restrict capital to entrenched incumbents but rather spread the love widely, especially

Even women, Native Americans, and free blacks had bank accounts, used banknotes, borrowed on mortgage, and the like. (Only slaves were systematically excluded.)

compared with what was available in other countries at the time. And that is what mattered most.[30]

Much the same could be said of the patent system, which was much cheaper and more accessible in the early United States than in Britain, France, or elsewhere. Although before 1860 fewer than 100 people per year per million Americans actually obtained a patent, any free person could, and that is the point. Patenting rates generally far exceeded those of Britain, which, though it enjoyed a hefty technology head start, was soon eating America's technological dust. Property rights institutions like patent systems can add, as Abraham Lincoln famously noted, "the fuel of interest to the fire of genius." But they alone are insufficient to drive systemic development. Long-term growth in per capita income must be tied in part to an economy's ability to discover and introduce new technologies and industries. The driving force of any dynamic enterprise system is therefore what economists call "innovative entrepreneurs," individuals who launch new firms with the aid of a novel product, process, or approach. Most innovative entrepreneurs ultimately failed to turn a monetary profit sufficient to allow them to continue operations, but while failure may have caused personal tragedy it was not a problem *for the economy*. Entrepreneurs essentially test the economic margin and in the process create valuable information about production and distribution costs, consumer preferences, market structures, and political sentiments. The production of such information can be expensive in terms of opportunity and sunk costs but it is voluntarily paid and is much less costly than government forays, which tend to turn into large-scale blunders financed by plunder.[31]

As English farmer, North American traveler, and wannabe immigrant Joseph Pickering put it, the American financial system "may cause rather wild speculations, and some bankruptcies occasionally." However, he continued, "these speculations are, at all events, public benefits, and cause great undertakings with little or no capital" at the cost of only temporary losses to individuals.

The failure of American beet sugar manufacturing, which experienced a short-lived boom at the end of the 1830s, is therefore actually an example of success, a point not lost on contemporaries.

As English farmer, North American traveler, and wannabe immigrant Joseph Pickering put it, the American financial system "may cause rather wild speculations, and some bankruptcies occasionally." However, he continued, "these speculations are, at all events, public benefits, and cause great undertakings with little or no capital" at the cost of only temporary losses to individuals.[32]

How and why did the beet sugar companies arise? What became of them and why? Their story is an interesting blend of international technology transfer, tariffs, abolitionism, market structure, and capital markets. It begins at the turn of the nineteenth century when future U.S. president John Quincy Adams, already recognized as "a man of genius and observation," toured Europe, where he encountered beet sugar enterprises (perhaps Count Wrbna's factory in Korzovitz, Bohemia, but most likely Frederick William III of Prussia's works on his Cunern estate near Steinau, Silesia) and thought them inspired by the region's protective-mercantilist predispositions. "They are no converts to the opinions of Adam Smith and the French economists, concerning the balance of trade," he noted, "and always catch with delight at any thing which can prevent money from *going out of the country*" (italics in original). A committee of the Academy of Sciences, however, called early claims that "one square mile of beets would furnish sugar for the whole Prussian dominions" a pipe dream. "Since this report," Adams wrote, "we have heard little or nothing of beet-sugar." That the method for crystallizing the sugar using alcohol developed by German chemists was "much too expensive to answer commercial and general purposes" also helped to squelch the movement. As late as 1818, observers still lamented that known processes for crystallizing sugar from beet syrup had not "been yet found more applicable to general use."[33]

In France, beet sugar found a major patron in Napoleon and his infamous Continental System, which, with aid from the British Navy, largely shut off continental Europe from tropical sources of sugar. "In the space of two years," a British observer noted, "more than two hundred manufactories of sugar, from the beet, furnished to the refineries, or brought directly into the market, vast quantities of sugar, which was made use of, without the nicest judge perceiving the difference." Most of those enterprises, however, experienced "great losses" due to the "uncertainties in the process of [beet sugar's] manufacture ... [and] the imperfection of the instruments employed in rasping the roots, so as to extract the juice." Then peace broke out and restored trade and imports of cheap cane sugar. Most of the new companies "were so discouraged, that they abandoned the pursuit." The remaining firms persevered but with "great difficulty" because they "were scarcely in a state to profit." Only about 5 percent of the companies, those that used steam engines and other capital-intensive technologies to extract the juice, survived the postwar shakeout.[34]

One of the surviving companies was owned by Count Chaptal, who claimed that beet sugar cultivation and manufacture "might enrich French agriculture more than sixty million of livres annually." To bolster his claim, Chaptal published his factory's inputs and outputs, figures that would later greatly impress American beet advocates:

Tillage, sowing, weeding, carriage	7,000 francs
Labor	2,075
Fuel	4,500
Animal charcoal for clarifying	1,100
Repairs, interest of capital, etc.	4,000
Total expenses:	18,675
Raw sugar	29,132 pounds weight
Sugar from second boiling	10,960
Total weight of sugar:	40,092[35]

The beets also produced 158,000 pounds of livestock fodder and other valuable ancillary products and improved the quality of the land when properly rotated with other crops. A tariff on sugar imports protected Chaptal and other French beet sugar producers in the late 1810s and through the 1820s, but by the 1830s they were strong enough to threaten colonial cane producers, who began to cry foul. In 1843, beet and cane sugar were finally put on an equal footing; the beet industry survived, many believed, only because slavery had been recently abolished in many cane-producing areas. German beet sugar production also benefited from tariff protection. By contrast, the British government, likely as a sop to

> In 1843, beet and cane sugar were finally put on an equal footing; the beet industry survived, many believed, only because slavery had been recently abolished in many cane-producing areas.

its colonial cane producers, discouraged the production of beet sugar by laying upon it an excise of 24 shillings per 112 pounds.[36]

As early as 1788, Americans noted privately that European beets like the Mangel Wurzel, or "root of scarcity," were great forage for animals, good eats for humans, and friendly to the soil, but they were unaware of its potential for producing sugar. By the late 1820s, however, beet sugar caught the attention of American farmers. William Johnson of South Carolina opined that "Ohio will, in time, sell sugar to Louisiana" because beet sugar would trump cane. Johnson predicted that beets would prove a profitable crop for farmers throughout the country and publicly discussed their conversion to sugar in some detail. Enthusiasm for the industry faded in the South, though, after abolitionists came to see beet sugar as a way of weakening slavery economically by reducing demand for slave labor. "The project is not a bubble," one abolitionist paper chimed. "We had thought so in ignorance," the editor admitted, but the success of the industry in France induced him to call on "every good and true abolitionist" to "gain and circulate as much information on this subject as he can." David L. Child (1794–1874), America's greatest early beet sugar producer, was at least partially motivated by abolitionist sentiments. The husband of famed abolitionist Lydia Maria Francis, Child was an important voice in the fight against slavery in his own right, authoring tracts such as *The Despotism of Freedom, or Tyranny and Cruelty of American Republican Slave-masters* (1832) and *The Taking of Naboth's Vineyard, or History of the Texas Conspiracy* (1845) and serving as a vice president of the Massachusetts Anti-Slavery Society (1835). A lawyer by training, he saw in beet sugar a practical way of decreasing demand for cane sugar and hence slaves.[37]

Beet sugar also became a bone of contention between American protectionists and free traders. The editor of *The Banner of the Constitution* mocked Ohioans for contemplating the manufacture of beet sugar, urging them instead to manufacture flour from their wheat fields and trade it for cane sugar. Making sugar from beets would make no more sense, the editor claimed, than it would for Pennsylvania farmers "to raise all

> The editor of *The Banner of the Constitution* mocked Ohioans for contemplating the manufacture of beet sugar, urging them instead to manufacture flour from their wheat fields and trade it for cane sugar.

their tobacco, instead of buying it in Maryland or Virginia, where they can get double the quantity at the same sacrifice of labor." Similarly, Henry C. Carey lambasted the French colonial system for forcing French peasants to grow beets at home instead of importing cane sugar.[38]

Free trader Condy Raguet also castigated the French government for wasting that nation's resources by giving beet sugar artificial support. "Beet sugar manufacture in France is a losing business," he explained, "unless refined sugar is worth twenty-one cents per pound. But refined sugar could not be kept up at twenty-one cents, but by means of a high duty upon raw sugar." French consumers, he calculated, paid over $1.2 million in taxes annually "for the purpose of enabling one hundred beet sugar makers to produce a quantity of sugar which could be procured in the West Indies or Brazil, in exchange for French wines, silks, and other productions, *for less than half the amount of this tax alone*" (italics in original). France would be better off, he concluded, if the government would pay the beet sugar interests $1 million in exchange for "stopping their works" and dropping the tariff. By the same reasoning, Raguet continued, the U.S. government should stop protecting Louisiana sugar planters with a tariff on imported sugar that had been considered "a most oppressive tax" since 1816, when it became avowedly protectionist. Louisiana sugar interests countered with a "big country" or monopsonistic analysis that concluded that foreign producers ultimately paid the tax. "Reduce the tariff," Louisiana senator Bullard claimed, "and you relieve the foreign planter, without benefiting your own citizens."[39]

With that tariff in place and beet sugar a close substitute for cane, Louisiana sugar interests opened the door to domestic competition from American beet sugar manufacturers. In 1836, information on beet sugar production poured in from Europe. A technical treatise translated from French called *A Manual of the Art of Making and Refining Sugar from Beets* appeared from the Boston press of Marsh, Capen & Lyon and the Beet Sugar Society of Philadelphia reached a not trivial audience with the publication of its report on beet sugar cultivation and manufacture in France. James Ronaldson was the moving force behind the society. Born in Edinburgh, Scotland, in 1768, Ronaldson visited Philadelphia in 1791 before taking up permanent residence there in 1794. After his Philadelphia biscuit bakery was destroyed by fire in 1796, Ronaldson, in partnership with Andrew Binny, established America's first permanent foundry for the making of type for printing presses. A serial entrepreneur, Ronaldson turned the successful business over to his younger brother Richard in 1823 in order to devote himself to starting another manufacturing enterprise, Hillsburgh Mills on Ridley Creek, about 15 miles from Philadelphia, the purpose of which was the spinning and weaving of cotton. In 1827, he was at it again, establishing Ronaldson's Philadelphia Cemetery and building a string of row homes overlooking it. Ronaldson was clearly an independent and innovative thinker. Although a Whig, he was a personal friend of Andrew Jackson. Both hated banks and their notes, ostensibly because both were burned by banks in the financially bloody aftermath of the Panic of 1819. Specie at that time went to a premium of 12 percent and interest rates soared, regulated "according to circumstances, the magnitude of the object, the pressure of the moment, and the nature of the transaction and security, and the person who wants it." A protectionist, Ronaldson was nevertheless willing to countenance freer trade. "As for politicks," he wrote his brother Richard in 1820, "I frankly express my persuasion of the manufacturing system being the best. But declare I hope Congress will reduce the import duties 50 p[er]cent that we may try the effect and if it proves beneficial stick to it."[40]

Due to his extensive and varied background, Ronaldson had both the general technical expertise and the ideological convictions to appreciate the potential value of beet sugar manufacturing. His Beet Sugar Society engaged James Pedder to visit France on a fact-finding mission. Born on the Isle of Wight in 1775, Pedder moved to America around 1832. He would later work for Joseph Lovering, proprietor of one of Philadelphia's largest cane sugar manufactories, before becoming an editor of various agricultural journals. Thanks to Pedder's report, the pirated French treatise, and a slew of articles in the agricultural press, Americans soon knew everything they needed to in order to begin beet sugar production. Samples of fine French beet sugar and the society's activities, which included importing 600 pounds of beet seed from France and distributing it at cost, excited "great interest ... in every portion of the country, from Louisiana to Maine."[41]

Samples of fine French beet sugar and the society's activities, which included importing 600 pounds of beet seed from France and distributing it at cost, excited "great interest ... in every portion of the country, from Louisiana to Maine."

Sanguine expectations of high profits or, failing that, government aid provided further inducements to action. Beets were a triple play as one could profit by manufacturing the sugar, by growing and selling the beets, or by selling prime beet lands at high prices. Some beet promoters expected revenues of some $240 to $320 per acre from the best beet-growing lands, a tidy sum at the time, and well in excess of the expected cost of raising the crop, which amounted to $40 to $140 per acre. Combined, those figures meant that beets would be more profitable to grow than "grass and grains." "There is an end to all question and doubt as to profit," the editor of the *Farmer's Register* proclaimed in 1836. "No crop can produce more money than the sugar beet," another claimed in 1838.[42]

Although Pedder and others described French farm families that made sugar in small rooms in their houses, most analysts conceded that the work was most profitably conducted on a large scale. The roots had to be cleaned, crushed, pulped, dessicated, evaporated, clarified, and finally concentrated. Steam engines, hydraulic presses, huge pots, and other expensive but efficient pieces of physical capital proved invaluable for completing several of those operations economically. Few individuals in America could afford to risk the huge sums required to establish such a large, capital-intensive operation from scratch. But that presented only a minor barrier, because Americans by the 1830s had over 40 years of experience creating joint-stock companies, the bulk of which formally incorporated under general incorporation statutes or, what was more common, a specific act of legislature. The time and cost of obtaining a charter varied according to time, place, and the political connections and savvy of the incorporators but was generally low. Shares in joint-stock companies were sold through direct public offerings (DPOs), unintermediated sales of stock by the company to investors. Because shareholder liability was usually limited to the par value of the stock owned, subscription books often filled quickly, but DPOs of weak companies held at unpropitious times could falter. Governance of stockholder-owned companies was as difficult then as it is today, but early Americans understood the principal-agent problem (e.g., employees stealing from owners), strove to mitigate it, and often successfully did so.[43]

Governance of stockholder-owned companies was as difficult then as it is today, but early Americans understood the principal-agent problem (e.g., employees stealing from owners), strove to mitigate it, and often successfully did so.

By December 1836, the nation's first beet sugar manufacturing company had organized in Northampton, Massachusetts. Composed of chairman Edward Church, secretary Samuel Wells Jr., and 50 others, the company employed Maximin Isnard, the French vice consul in Boston and a pioneer of the French sugar beet industry, to return to France to procure seed and up-to-date technical know-how. The European-educated Church was the enterprising son of a merchant. Born in 1779 in Boston, he served under Napoleon during the Peninsular War. After his return to the United States, he fell in with Robert Fulton and spent a decade and a half establishing steamship lines in Europe, where he learned of beet sugar cultivation first-hand. He later moved to Kentucky, where he befriended Henry Clay. Church moved to Northampton in 1834. Under his ostensibly effective leadership, the company received a charter from the state of Massachusetts in March 1837 and began to take orders from area farmers for seed, which it promised to sell at cost, and sought to raise a capital of $50,000, $100,000, even up to $200,000.[44]

After a year of experimentation, the Northampton factory churned out sugar "not inferior in flavor or appearance to the finest West India musco-vados." Despite the 3-cent per pound state bounty passed in early 1837, the Northampton factory's output was only about 300 pounds in 1838. By the fall of that year, however, the company announced that it was preparing to "operate on a large scale." In 1839, 1,300 pounds of sugar (one source claims 107,000 pounds but appears to be in error) came out of the factory, which won a silver medal for raw and refined sugar at the Massachusetts State Exposition. David Lee Child, who appears to have taken operational control of the company after learning the business firsthand in Europe in 1837, won the $100 prize the Massachusetts Society for Promoting Agriculture offered to the person or corporation that raised the greatest quantity of sugar beets per acre and another prize of like size to any person or corporation that manufactured beet sugar of the "greatest quantity and of the best quality." Child also won a silver medal related to beet sugar from the Boston Mechanic Association. In 1840, Child published a book detailing what he and the company had learned. Via process and machinery improvements, several of which he reportedly patented, Child claimed to drive the cost of production down to 11 cents per pound, the value of "the pulp and manure not being taken into account," and predicted that costs could be reduced to about 4 cents per pound. The Northampton company folded in 1841, however, due to unspecified financial difficulties. Little is known of its precise situation, but other beet sugar manufacturers utilized standard corporate finance practices like selling commercial paper into the money market to meet their liquidity needs if bank loans dried up, so it is unlikely that the closure was due to a temporary cash constraint. Church moved back to Kentucky, where he died in 1845, and Child continued his abolitionist activities.[45]

Other beet-sugar-manufacturing companies met the same fate. On December 20, 1836, a group of people in Lebanon, Pennsylvania, petitioned the legislature for a charter. The Lebanon Sugar and Silk Company resulted, but it too quickly faded. In New Jersey, a group based in Bergen and Essex Counties sought to establish the Beet Sugar Manufacturing Company with banking and trust powers capitalized at $500,000. In upstate New York, experiments with beet horticulture were also afoot. "In the flourishing and extensive nurseries and gardens of Rochester," one observer claimed, "may be found abundant proof" of the fact "that no part of the United States can equal the Genesee Valley in the growth of that root." In the remote reaches of Maine, pundits claimed, beet sugar would complement maple and free the region from cane, where it was particularly dear due to "the expense arising from the transportation." The same was claimed for remote regions of Tennessee.[46]

> In the remote reaches of Maine, pundits claimed, beet sugar would complement maple and free the region from cane, where it was particularly dear due to "the expense arising from the transportation." The same was claimed for remote regions of Tennessee.

In late March and early April 1837, the legislature of the state of Ohio chartered three corporations for the production of beet sugar, the Stark County, Franklin, and Hamilton County beet sugar companies. Each of those companies was authorized to sell 2,000 shares of stock at $100 per share, for a total capitalization of $200,000 each. In February 1839, Ohio also chartered the Middlebury Silk and Beet-Sugar Company in Middlebury, Portage County, and authorized a capital of $50,000 composed of 2,000 shares of $25 each. Also in 1837, a corporation capitalized at $200,000 formed in Illinois for manufacturing sugar from beets and oil from poppies and culturing silk.[47]

By 1838, entrepreneurs throughout the old northwest were attempting to profitably produce beet sugar because the cane variety was especially costly there due to high transportation costs. The agricultural press reported that in Michigan "several companies had formed for the purpose" and "some wealthy individuals are planting largely on their own account." Egged on with a state bounty of two cents per pound, at least one company of significant size began operations in 1838 but folded in 1840. In early 1839, a beet sugar manufactory began limited operations in White Pigeon, Michigan. "Farmers and other enterprising men" pumped about $5,000 into it before seeking a loan of $5,000 more from the state legislature, citing the current "scarcity of money" and novelty of the operation to "the western world" as reasons its prayer should be granted. With a promise to manufacture 200,000 pounds a year, which would keep in the state some $20,000, it got its money out of the state government. According to one report, Michigan factories in the early 1840s churned out 240,000 pounds of beet sugar. But they failed anyway.[48]

The American Beet Sugar Refining and Manufacturing Company incorporated in Maryland in early 1840 and successfully organized later that year. It too failed. As interest in beet sugar began to sag, two prominent Europeans with American connections, Michael Chevalier of France and Charles L. Fleischmenn of Bavaria, reported process improvements that promised lower manufacturing costs. S. S. Cowles in Hartford, Connecticut, and others continued to schlep copies of Child's *Culture of the Beet* but by the end of 1840 the bloom was off the rose. "The subject went out of vogue," an editor noted in a postmortem several years later. "The history of beet-root sugar," the editor pointed out, "affords us an excellent illustration of the effect of prices upon commercial productions."[49]

America's first beet sugar forays failed for several reasons, none of them strictly technical. The factories and farms were for the most part situated in an ideal climactic band for sugar beets, which extended from western Massachusetts to Philadelphia, then westward along the Great Lakes, subsuming large portions of Ohio, Michigan, Indiana, and Illinois. By the late 1830s, Americans had successfully engineered, built, and operated a variety of factories more sophisticated than beet sugar mills and, as shown above, ample technology diffusion from Europe regarding the specifics of beet sugar manufacture had taken place.[50]

Why then did early beet sugar factories fail? First, they formed and began operations at the onset of the nation's worst economic recession up to that time. Nominal per capita GDP in current dollars, which had jumped from $88 in 1835 to $97 in 1837 and 1838 before peaking at $99 in 1839, sank to $82 by 1843. Most directly, recession brought with it lower prices for all sugar, including cane, which dropped from about 10 cents per pound in 1835 to approximately 6 in 1838 to about 4 in 1841. The recession also made it difficult to launch new ventures in novel areas. After returning from a trip to France to learn the state of the art, for example, Charles P. Bosson refused to begin manufacturing, citing the "unfavorableness of the times, and the general prostration of business and enterprize." Higher average short- (from 7.00 percent in 1835 to 13.22 in 1839) and long-term interest rates (from 4.43 percent in 1835 to 6.07 in 1842) were a leading cause of that "prostration" as was the concomitant downturn in bank lending, which dropped from about $525 million in 1837 to $251.5 million in 1843.[51]

Other factors were at play as well and help to explain why the industry did not revive with the nation's economic fortunes in the middle of the 1840s, when interest rates receded and bank loans and per capita incomes again swelled, or the generally buoyant 1850s. One major blunder was that beet sugar enthusiasts sought only to convince consumers that beet sugar was indistinguishable from sugar made from cane. (Chemically speaking, it was in fact identical.) That meant that they had to go head-to-head with cane manufacturers on price alone. As economist William Baumol has recently shown, to be successful in a competitive environment innovative entrepreneurs usually need to find ways to engage in some form of price discrimination, to segment the market by differentiating their product from other goods. One obvious way to price discriminate would have been to market beet sugar as a product untainted by slavery, as some companies today sell environmentally "green" or socially conscious goods. Why producers of beet sugar did not wave the banner of abolition more effectively is unclear, as many noted that the success of beet sugar would "be another blow to slave-labor." The entrepreneurs' failure may simply have been bad luck. The beet sugar craze occurred just as two major schisms erupted, both having to do with the issue of slavery. The first schism was between the adherents of the older, gradualist view of abolition and the proponents of the newer, immediatist doctrine. A second rift also developed between those who sought to end slavery by any means and those who wished to end it through moral reformation. As an advocate for the latter put it: "When beet-sugar is cultivated in order to make cane-sugar unprofitable, it is no longer an argument addressed to the 'understanding and conscience' of any body, but an argument addressed solely to the *pockets* of the Louisiana and Florida planters." That was directly inimical to the constitution of the American Antislavery Society, the goal of which was to "bring about a full and thorough emancipation, as the result of *conviction*" (italics in original). In short, abolitionists were not unified and abolitionism was just an umbrella term for a wide range of groups seeking to eliminate, or at least weaken, the institution of slavery. So, not all abolitionists cooperated with the "free labor produce" movement, of which beet sugar was a part. Besides, a successful movement against cane would have barely affected U.S. chattel slavery, as fewer than 10 percent of America's slaves worked on sugar plantations.[52]

Beet sugar advocates could also have urged their product on Americans as a way to improve the nation's trade balance by reducing imports. "Two millions of dollars annually paid out of a state for a foreign product, which for aught we know, can and eventually will be raised cheaper with us than with them," opined Charles P. Bosson, "is certainly matter for the grave consideration of legislation."[53]

Bosson's comment points to another shortcoming of beet sugar entrepreneurs, the fact that they were too quick to turn to government for aid. No sooner had the Northampton, Massachusetts, company formed than its head, Edward Church, noted that it looked "with confidence to our legislature for every support and encouragement which our infant enterprise can fairly ask." Within a few years, both the early cost and

Many still thought beet sugar production could be a profitable venture, however, even though beet cultivation was labor intensive and hence expensive due to the relatively high wages prevalent in North America.

revenue estimates were discredited as too sanguine. Many still thought beet
sugar production could be a profitable venture, however, even though beet
cultivation was labor intensive and hence expensive due to the relatively high
wages prevalent in North America. But rather than try to adapt French practices to local circumstances, many of the beet men used up valuable time and
resources rent-seeking, trying to obtain what Senator Henry Clay called "the
liberal patronage of Government." Although father of the "American System,"
a policy of high tariffs, federally sponsored internal improvements, and a
national bank, Clay immediately conceded defeat when beseeched to obtain
aid for beet sugar producers from the national government. "The diversity of
opinions which exist as to the powers and duties of the General Government,"
he noted, rendered direct federal assistance to beet interests highly unlikely.
Clay was right. Except for some words of encouragement from the Committee
on Agriculture and a report by the Committee on Manufactures, the federal
government paid little heed to the new industry.[54]

At the state level, some attempts to procure government aid were successful but others foundered on the rocks of laissez-faire ideology and the
self-interest of cane growers and West Indies merchants. Duplicity may have
played a role too, as American beet sugar advocates often spoke out of both
sides of their mouths, pronouncing a desperate need for government largesse
while simultaneously claiming that "the climate and soils of our country are
better adapted to the growth of beets than those of France," and making
other sanguine predictions.[55]

It was all too little, too late. An 1848 report on world sugar production
prepared for Treasury Secretary William M. Meredith included cane sugar
from Louisiana, Mauritius, and elsewhere as well as French and Belgium
beet sugar but did not bother to include American beet sugar production
as it was too trivial. That same report made clear that in America, brown
sugar, including some 20 million pounds per year of maple sugar, was king.
It showed, too, that planters in Louisiana and other parts of the world were
churning out increasing amounts of sugar made from cane. Unless it could
be sold as cheaply as cane, or urged on people who opposed slavery or cared
deeply about the country's balance of payments, American beet sugar could
not take root.[56]

In 1851, American cane and maple sugar was on display at an exhibition in London, but American beet sugar was absent. By the late 1850s,

America's early foray into beet sugar was all but forgotten in most places, even as major strides were made in the manufacture of sugar from cane. France's beet sugar industry was derided as a "hollow and worthless sham, devised by an unscrupulous military dictator, as a measure of safety in a war" and urged as a "warning" for a "young nation" with a "scanty" population and "dear" labor costs. "Let us not be seduced into devoting millions of precious capital, and years of toil," warned the editor of the *New York Times*, "to the cultivation of every outlandish root which enthusiasts recommend to us, to the neglect of our legitimate productions, and our real sources of wealth and greatness."[57]

After its early failure, the American beet sugar industry sputtered along for decades, cropping up here and there when world sugar prices and local climactic, labor, transportation, and entrepreneurial conditions made it possible that beet sugar could be produced for less than cane could be imported and shipped. For example, the Mormons tried beet sugar production because they had to pay a hefty $1 per pound for cane in remote Utah. But they too failed at first.[58]

The American beet sugar industry finally began to thrive in the late nineteenth century behind a tariff wall, federal and state bounties, and tax breaks that helped it to compete with cheaper sugars made from German beets and tropical cane. The demise of the last vestiges of slave-produced cane sugar also helped, and a new wave of technological diffusion from Europe, boosterism by Edward H. Dyer, George Washington Swink, and numerous other "beet sugar cranks," along with the inclusion of beet sugar manufacturers in the "sugar trust," ensured that the industry would swell. By 1900, the center of the industry had shifted well west, to Colorado, which dominated domestic sugar production for nearly four generations, though California, Utah, and other western states were also major producers. The beet sugar industry prospered in the first three quarters of the twentieth century, when some 165 factories operated at various times in 26 states. In 1933, the United States became the world's largest producer of beet sugar despite Hawaiian, Puerto Rican, and Philippine cane sugar by then being able to be imported duty free. The industry faded after the mid–1970s, however, due to a technological breakthrough that rendered corn sweetener the most economical source of industrial sugar. Some sugar beet factories still operate but by 2002 the industry was again inconsequential, composed of only 35 factories spread over 10 western states on a payroll of 5,697 and revenues of only $2.26 billion.[59]

Without a doubt, sugar equal to that of cane *can* be produced from beets. But that does not mean that it *should* be. America's antebellum beet entrepreneurs failed, but in so doing they learned that given the technological, tariff, and transportation constraints of that time, American consumers felt they were best off buying maple and cane sugar. The failed beet bubble does not tell us if consumers were indifferent to the continued existence of slavery or merely felt that the purchase of beet sugar would be unlikely to bring the "peculiar institution" to an end, but it does indicate that few Americans were willing to pay a premium for sugar produced by free, as opposed to slave, labor.

It is also important to recognize that the antebellum beet sugar fiasco was only one of many failed agricultural crazes to strike America's agricultural sector, which of course was then its largest. Before the Civil War, manias for merino and Saxony sheep; mulberry trees and silk; sundry varieties of chickens, cows, and hogs; superpotatoes; and a wide assortment of different corns, wheats, and other grains, also erupted and went down in flames. Such speculative episodes seemed wasteful to many observers when they were occurring, as they do now, and it would be more efficient if no new business enterprise ever failed. We live, however, in a world haunted by the specter of bounded rationality, asymmetric information, nontrivial transaction costs, and uncertainty. In such a world, economists can estimate margins but outcomes will be in doubt until real world trials are made. Countries, like antebellum America, that allow such experimentation more cheaply and readily through liberal policies of entry and exit have more vigorous and dynamic economies than those that do not. Although most individual entrepreneurs fail, entrepreneurial economies generally do not.[60]

The essence of all this is that by the time Andrew Jackson became president in 1829, the United States possessed a development diamond composed of nonpredatory government, a modern financial system, entrepreneurs, and, increasingly, professional managers. We know that the diamond was likely the cornerstone of America's economic success because that other Anglo-American nation, Canada, stagnated until it emulated its southern neighbor. The development diamond story is a compelling one. The government protected Americans from foreign and domestic threats to their lives, liberties, and properties, giving them incentives to try to improve their lot. The financial system enabled those attempted improvements by linking savers to borrowers, investors

> The government protected Americans from foreign and domestic threats to their lives, liberties, and properties, giving them incentives to try to improve their lot.

to entrepreneurs. Many of those entrepreneurs failed but those that thrived made the economy more efficient. The managers who took over for the entrepreneurs after their businesses grew too large and unwieldy did likewise. The entire magnificent edifice was strengthened by the national debt, which served as the bridge, the direct connection between the establishment of nonpredatory government in 1787–88 and the financial revolution of the early 1790s. By the 1820s, however, the debt's role was less pronounced. As it dwindled rapidly, other uses were found for the financial capital it represented. It would eventually be extinguished, only to rise from the dead shortly thereafter, though more like a zombie than a messiah.

9

DEATH AND REINCARNATION

Jackson's Triumph and Failure

On January 8, 1835, Andrew Jackson's supporters throughout the country met to celebrate the twentieth anniversary of their Old Hero's victory at the Battle of New Orleans and to celebrate the repayment of the first national debt, which met its official demise at the end of 1834. The day was marked by cannon salutes, resolutions, speeches, suppers, toasts, and other solemnities and festivities, all of which exuded pride in paying "the last cent of a debt" that once exceeded $127 million and praised Jackson for the outcome. "Our Revolutionary Debt," went one particularly mushy toast, "It produced our National Independence. Public virtue has extinguished the former, and preserved the latter." The celebration held in Washington, D.C., was of course the largest and most lavish of such affairs. After dinner at Brown's Hotel, the hall of which was "fitted up in a superb style," including full-length portraits of Washington and Jackson, the 250 men in attendance, every important Democrat except Jackson himself, applauded a bombastic speech by hard-money blowhard and Missouri senator Thomas Hart Benton. The irony of the situation was not lost on Benton, who explicitly noted that "wars create debt." Jackson, in short, had helped to create that which he destroyed. But that, in Benton's mind, only rendered Jackson's deed all the more extraordinary.[1]

Jackson deserves some, but not all, of the credit for eliminating the debt. Near the top of the long list of his enemies, right up there with Redcoats, Indians, and the Bank of the United States, was the national debt. In 1824, Jackson went so far as to call the public debt "a national curse" because he believed that it, like the BUS, gave ascendancy to a "monied aristocracy"

In 1824, Jackson went so far as to call the public debt "a national curse" because he believed that it, like the BUS, gave ascendancy to a "monied aristocracy" bent on destroying individual liberty with what one of his supporters called "harpy fangs."

bent on destroying individual liberty with what one of his supporters called "harpy fangs." How he came to harbor such views is quite beyond my comprehension, so I'll leave the matter to his many biographers. Suffice it to say here, people often hate, or at least deeply mistrust, that which they do not understand. It's not that Jackson was dumb—far from it—just that, like Jefferson, when it came to financial matters he was quite ignorant. Little wonder both Jackson and Jefferson faced severe financial problems throughout much of their lives. It's more than a little ironic, then, that, with the aid of able counsel in the Treasury Department, both were able to do so much to extinguish the nation's debt. In any event, no one was surprised that as the debt shrank, Jackson smelled victory and pressed home the attack, just as he had countless times before against foes on the battlefield and dueling grounds.[2]

According to historian H. W. Brands, "the Jacksonians had been good stewards of the budget." That's a bit of a whitewash. For starters, as Jackson's many enemies were quick to point out, the long string of federal budget surpluses began during the administrations of James Monroe and John Quincy Adams, not Andrew Jackson. All that Jackson did was to execute "the plan long since adopted for the payment of the public debt." Worse, the panics of 1837 and 1839, which if not caused directly by Jackson's policies were certainly exacerbated by them, ended the budget surplus streak by reducing government receipts much more quickly than expenditures could be slashed. The nation was soon in hock again and has been ever since.[3]

Moreover, the United States paid off its national debt at a time when governments worldwide were keeping a fairly close lid on their debts, the aggregate rising from $7.75 billion in 1820 to only $8.65 billion in 1848. Thereafter, however, the indebtedness of countries worldwide soared, to $26.97 billion by 1882. The number of countries borrowing also blossomed, from just a handful early in the century to over 100, including China, Japan, Persia, Siam, Egypt, Liberia, Orange Free States, and Zanzibar, by its end. Those borrowings paid for wars but increasingly they were also used to finance social programs like public schools, factory acts, compulsory insurance laws, public parks, and government railroads. By delaying the ultimate payday, governments were able to win political support for those and other novel policies, much as Adam Smith and others had forewarned.[4]

> By delaying the ultimate payday, governments were able to win political support for those and other novel policies, much as Adam Smith and others had forewarned.

For that reason, the fiscal constraint the U.S. government showed in its early decades, in terms of both the tight lid it kept on spending and the level of taxation it maintained, continues to astonish observers. As economist E. Cary Brown noted in 1990: "The elimination of a public debt by a central government is a rare happening in fiscal history." What makes the episode even more amazing is that the final, dramatic rundown after the War of 1812 began during a period of deflation, a time, in other words, when the public creditors received more purchasing power than they lent.[5]

The tariff played a major role on the revenue side. Many, especially in the North, supported tariffs because they thought they aided the economy, or at least their particular industry. So they did not mind the taxes, which on many goods could be increased to pretty high levels before negatively impacting imports and hence government revenues. Many in the South didn't much like the tariffs but they had their own little subsidy, the government's continued toleration of slavery, and besides, tariffs were less onerous than other forms of taxation. The tariff was almost the only game in town until the Civil War.[6]

On the spending side, most Americans believed that government, especially the national government, ought to limit itself to the supply of a few essential public goods, like defense. So there was no great demand for government to increase spending in peacetime, and what demands there were could be shunted aside fairly easily because most were essentially local calls for "internal improvements," to wit, infrastructure projects. The success that corporations and states like New York had creating bridges, turnpikes, canals, steamboat lines, and eventually railroads rendered massive federal logrolling, where everyone in the country got something in exchange for their support, unlikely, especially given that the old prejudices against enlarging the national debt remained virulent. In fact, in his failed national infrastructure plan of 1808, Gallatin apparently had just such a quid pro quo orgy in mind. Another such movement was afoot, some claimed, until Jackson vetoed the Maysville Road bill and in the process made it clear that "extravagant appropriations for internal improvements" would not meet his approbation, whether they entailed government construction projects or federal investments in corporations. Jackson and his followers did support infrastructure improvements funded by the federal government but only where it had a clear Constitutional mandate to do so. A toast at one of his fetes made that point clear: "Internal Improvements—We cherish them, and they will increase, without any construction of the Constitution to aid them by exhausting the National Treasury."[7]

The political desire to redeem the debt was so strong that politicians established a "Committee on Retrenchment" and engaged in whizzing matches to show that they understood the mechanics of the federal budget better than the next guy. Behind all the politicking lurked something almost as dastardly, scholarly pretensions. After declaring banks a cheat on labor, Philadelphia political economist Stephen Simpson argued that "unhappily modern nations have not only used public credit to a most wonderful extent, but they have abused it to a ruinous one." The British were in particularly bad shape, Simpson argued, because of "the immense amount of their public debt held by foreigners, who draw the interest in bullion." "Foreigners" also bought heavily of U.S. bonds, Simpson lamented, "and thus impose upon us the tribute of interest, to be abstracted from the metallic currency of the country, to its impoverishment and degradation." The national debt of the United States also imposed on its economy "a most onerous and calamitous burden" that was "beyond calculation pernicious and destructive" by diverting millions of dollars from "the mass of producers" to a few "idle" bondholders and "luxurious" capitalists, a critique that dated back through Gallatin to early theorists in Britain. "Its operation upon labor," Simpson claimed, "is to depress, harass, and impoverish." And the effect was a large one, he argued, because at 5 percent simple interest, total interest payments equaled the principal sum borrowed in just 20 years.[8]

Supporters of the debt counterattacked, arguing that foreign ownership was a great boon to the country, not a loss. Robert Hare, the Philadelphia scientist who deplored the state of the U.S. Navy on the eve of the War of 1812, again entered the fray in the early 1830s. "When the government, with the funds borrowed from foreigners, purchases produce of the farmer or landholder, for defence or improvement," he argued, "the nation in the first place gains by the excess of the advantage resulting annually from the improvement or defence, over the interest paid to the foreign creditor." It also gained, he claimed, "by the superior efficiency of the property borrowed, over that which is consumed; or by the advantage of exchanging those raw materials of which we have a superabundance, for articles in which we are greatly in want." In other words, borrowing, even from foreigners, for positive net present value projects was a win-win scenario. Only by borrowing to defray the "ordinary expenses of government" was a national debt a "robbery of posterity." To that end, Hare argued that "the public credit should only be resorted to under circumstances, where the permanent character, or prosperity of that nation may be at stake."[9]

As the debt dwindled, there was some talk in Congress that southerners were particularly eager to repay the national debt *"to weaken the ties which bind the people to the Union"* (italics in original). Daniel Webster, for example, thought he perceived "a morbid fervor on that subject; an excessive anxiety to pay off the debt; not so much because it is a debt simply, as because, while it lasts, it furnishes one objection to disunion. It is a tie of common interests while it lasts."[10]

> As the debt dwindled, there was some talk in Congress that southerners were particularly eager to repay the national debt *"to weaken the ties which bind the people to the Union."*

Those fearful of disunion need not have worried, for there was still plenty of economic glue cementing the union together. As we'll see shortly, as the federal debt shrank state government borrowing ballooned, and was widely held in both Europe and across state borders. Moreover, the federal surplus that arose after repayment of the national debt ironically acted as a sort of debt as the states, to which it was promised, came to see it as their due. Finally, the national debt's demise was rather short-lived, if you'll forgive the expression. As noted above, Jackson himself was largely responsible for its reincarnation. In addition to repaying the debt, which arguably spurred economic growth by freeing up capital for productive uses, Jackson implemented several other economic policies that were, well, kind of goofy. He vetoed a bill that would have extended the charter of the BUS and soon after that ordered the treasury secretary to yank the government's deposits out of it and spread them across numerous state banks. He also ordered that federal lands had to be paid for in actual gold and silver and not bank liabilities. When London caught financial cold in the late 1830s and sneezed on the American cotton trade, the U.S. financial immune system, greatly weakened by Jackson's policies, could not resist. The U.S. economy became phlegmatic, suffering for five long years before recovering. Wealth long in the making "melted like the snows before an April sun," according to New York bigwig Philip Hone. The federal government's revenues suffered, too. Bank dividends disappeared with the BUS, and public land sales plummeted due to the general depression and the Specie Circular, the federal government's policy of requiring buyers of federal lands to pay in gold or silver (rather than on credit). Moreover, custom revenues did the belly flop. Soon the debt, puppy that it was in per capita terms, reappeared.[11]

Predictably, the rapid revival of the national debt became a political football in presidential election years, with each side accusing the other of running it up and/or not doing enough to pay it down. "Pending the presidential canvass of 1840," Democrats later complained, "the Whig party laid great stress upon the vast debt, which they charged, before the people, that the administration then in power [that of New Yorker Martin Van Buren] had contracted and thrown upon the country." The $40 million that they claimed was greatly exaggerated but that hardly mattered. "Was there ever a cooler piece of official hypocrisy," William G. Rives asked a correspondent, "than the *last words* of this *condemned* President [Van Buren]? To preach economy, in the face of the most lavish expenditure of the public Treasure by himself—to deprecate and denounce a *public debt*, when he is the only President who ever *created* one, in time of peace" (italics in original). The Democrats had their turn in 1844, after the debt almost touched $33 million in 1843, at the pit of the recession. That was nothing compared with the $68 million debt achieved in 1851, in the aftermath of the Mexican-American War, a sum not again reached until the horrors of the Civil War.[12]

After the federal government assumed their debts under Hamilton's funding plan in the early 1790s, state governments borrowed but little, financing their modest expenditures with low taxes and income from investments in banks and other corporations. Starting around 1820, three of them, New York, Pennsylvania, and Ohio, began borrowing extensively, some $26 million by 1830. In the 1830s, many states went on borrowing binges. By 1838, they had borrowed over $170 million and by 1843, $231.6 million. American cities about that time, by contrast, owed only about $25 million; the larger ones, like New York and Philadelphia, were of course the biggest borrowers but even little cities like Petersburg, Virginia, were in the game in a small way. Of the $172.3 million owed by state governments in 1838, $54.1 million had been borrowed to fund banks, $60.2 for canals, $42.9 for railroads, $6.6 for turnpikes, and $8.5 for miscellaneous purposes.[13]

The states borrowed because, with the federal government out of the internal improvement game, many believed they had to make investments in large public works. Cheap funds were available because as the federal debt dwindled away, the millions it had tied up for decades were returned to investors, many of whom sought to keep their money relatively safe, yet at interest. State bonds looked like a good alternative, even to foreign investors. In the early 1840s, British investors owned some $150 million of U.S. state bonds. States also borrowed because it was easier politically to do so than to tax.[14]

Predictably, some states borrowed too much, too fast. The same recession that revived the national debt put a severe strain on state budgets too. In 1841, Mississippi and Florida defaulted, as did Arkansas and Indiana. The following year, Illinois, Michigan, Maryland, Pennsylvania, and Louisiana also stopped making interest payments on their bonds. Four of the states, Arkansas, Florida, Michigan, and Mississippi, repudiated all or part of their debts. The other five managed to refinance and eventually extricated themselves, though bondholders of course suffered a "haircut."[15]

Calls for the federal government to assume state debts as it had in the early 1790s went unheeded. The movement for a second federal assumption of state

The movement for a second federal assumption of state debts was afoot by the end of 1839 and made its appearance in the presidential campaign of 1840.

debts was afoot by the end of 1839 and made its appearance in the presidential campaign of 1840. The Democrats painted their opponent, Whig William Henry Harrison, as a Hamiltonian bent on re-creating the potent antirepublican engine, "A National Bank Founded on a National Debt." The tactic failed; Harrison won. He died soon after assuming office, however. Meanwhile, the Treasury Department found it could not sell U.S. government bonds in Europe, because investors there blamed it for the state defaults. The House of Representatives considered federal assumption again in March 1843. Although a 600-page report favorable to assumption was read out of committee, it was tabled and the movement faltered. That was probably a good thing, because it would have raised the moral hazard by giving state governments incentives to make a beeline toward fiscal profligacy safe in the knowledge that Uncle Sam would come to their aid.[16]

Although American banker Thomas Cary and others tried to explain that the national government could not be expected to pony up for wayward state governments, and that European investors knew that because they had demanded a risk premium for state bonds, foreigners remained wary of U.S. government bonds for a few years. In late 1846, the federal government sold £1 million worth of new bonds in London only with difficulty, and at 6 percent. That was certainly a sign of discredit, because at the same time first-rate British railroads could raise that much at 4.5 percent and America was "teeming with abundance" and receiving "large returns in specie." The damage was only short-term, though. By the late 1840s, some foreigners were again buying U.S. bonds in sizable quantities, ostensibly due to the uncertainty caused by the 1848 revolutions. Foreigners also still held large sums of state bonds, over $36 million worth in early 1849 according to one source, and formed an association to agitate for payment of arrears.[17]

Nevertheless, due to the defaults and repudiations many states began to amend their constitutions to prevent future fiscal fiascos. Rhode Island and New Jersey, though largely free of debt themselves, were the first of a wave of 19 states to restrict their state government's borrowing powers. States that joined the union after 1845 also invariably constrained the ability of their governments to borrow. Some banned it outright while others included a referendum provision. Only seven states never restricted their legislatures in this respect, though in two of those, Massachusetts and Delaware, supermajorities were required to authorize bond issuance.[18]

> Rhode Island and New Jersey, though largely free of debt themselves, were the first of a wave of 19 states to restrict their state government's borrowing powers.

Predictably, borrowing by local municipalities blossomed in the 1850s and soon in aggregate exceeded the federal debt until, of course, the Civil War. Equally predictable, in the twentieth century many of the state debt provisions lost their teeth as state legislatures found court-approved ways of circumventing them through the issuance of revenue (as opposed to general obligation) bonds, the establishment of public corporations, and sundry other devices. By the early post–World War II era, such methods were so refined and ubiquitous that observers believed that most states could "incur debt in any amount for virtually any purpose" though at rates of interest higher than they would have to pay were the restrictions not in place and the workarounds not necessary.[19]

⤫

The dynamics of the paydown of the Civil War debt were similar to those of the payoff of the first national debt. To wit, a desire for high tariffs, small government, and rapid economic expansion ensured that the federal government ran budget surpluses most years. Again, the Treasury sometimes found that it had more money than it knew what to do with. Those poor souls! The United States government was able to pay off the debt incurred during its revolutionary wars entirely, and later took a huge bite out of the Civil War debt, in large part because of the nation's extremely rapid economic growth, its "national industry" in the words of a contemporary, and its "industrial vigor and expanding wealth of its inhabitants" in the words of one late-nineteenth-century student of the subject.[20]

Bully for our distant ancestors. The record of our more recent ancestors and ourselves, however, is not so strong. The debts of our many twentieth-century wars—World War I, World War II, Korea, Vietnam, the cold war, the "wars" on poverty and drugs, and the war on terror—are still with us and waxing ever more ominous due to the power of compound interest. Precedent here is of no consequence. Simply because a country did something in the past does not mean that it will, or indeed can, do it again. America's economic growth rate has slowed somewhat since its heyday and it is not likely to ever again approach its earlier level, which was achieved during a time of relatively little international competition due to the widespread prevalence of tyrannical governments. In short, the United States might not be able to grow out of its obligations this time.[21]

Moreover, the U.S. government over the twentieth century morphed from being the protector of life, liberty, and property into a nanny state that must tell its citizens what not to eat and drink, what to eat and drink, when, where, and how to save for the future, how to raise their children, and on and on and on. Many citizens either like the government-as-nanny model or don't know any better. Either way, both major political parties today appear bent on winning votes by creating or perpetuating popular programs that extend the government's power, scope, and budget. At the same time, politicians know that taxes are as unpopular in America as ever, so they finance their pork-laden projects by borrowing instead of raising taxes, just as Smith and Brutus foretold.[22]

> Many citizens either like the government-as-nanny model or don't know any better. Either way, both major political parties today appear bent on winning votes by creating or perpetuating popular programs that extend the government's power, scope, and budget.

Politicians borrow because taking on debt is less likely to cost them votes than increasing taxes would. Unfortunately, they no longer have an obvious, relatively popular, and economically viable tax to turn to. Some Americans call for the return of high tariffs, but only to protect their own industries. Were those interests to log roll or vote swap and get tariff rates increased across the board, the ameliorative effect on the federal deficit (hoping perhaps against hope that politicians could cap pork barrel legislation and the extension of the nanny state) would probably be offset by the tremendous harm such duties would cause the economy. Tariffs likely hurt America's economy in the nineteenth century, too, but not as much as similar levies would today because the world then was much less open to trade. Tariffs were optimal policy in the second-best world of empires and sailing ships but would not be in today's world of trade liberalization and the Internet.

What, precisely, is the problem with increased government borrowing? Jefferson's qualms about saddling our descendants with massive debts aside (the atmospheric carbon we've left them may prove burden enough), government borrowing could trigger a nasty shock that would cause widespread economic pain. Several doomsday scenarios are possible. One entails a rapid depreciation of the U.S. dollar, say a 40 percent decline in a month or two. Unlike most nations, the United States borrows in its own currency, so a rapid depreciation would not, unlike various Southeast Asian nations or Russia in the late 1990s, increase the risk of default. The Federal Reserve could always print more money, more bills of credit. But that would cause high levels of inflation, which would raise nominal interest rates, which, in turn, would induce companies to stop investing in new physical capital and inventory and, sooner rather than later, to lay off workers. Or, foreigners could panic and sell U.S. government bonds and other U.S. dollar-denominated assets en masse. That, too, would force up interest rates and hurt the American economy, perhaps severely. A weaker dollar would make American exports more competitive, and foreign imports less so, so the economic troubles would not necessarily be permanent. During the years it would take the economy to adapt, however, many Americans would suffer, perhaps enough to foment civil unrest, tax rebellions, protectionist programs, or other aftershocks that could slow, or even prevent, the necessary restructuring. America has been blessed with a virtuous cycle of domestic peace and economic prosperity for a long time. Assuming claims about God's agency in America's prosperity are unfounded, the virtuous cycle could reverse itself and become vicious, as some think it almost did during the Great Depression. If that happens, all bets are off and your best investment will be water, food, and ammunition.[23]

Over the years, numerous books have portended the end of capitalism, the demise of a vibrant U.S. economy, and the like. Thus far, all have been wrong. As Larry Kudlow likes to say, economic pessimists have predicted nine out of the last zero recessions. But we should not dismiss pessimists as financial cranks. When storied economists like Will Baumol and Robert Solow publicly announce that "a fiscal disaster seems inevitable" and that the sky is not yet falling but is definitely "growing darker," it is time to take notice. Like the recent movie version of the old Chicken Little story, economic pessimists may have simply spotted a trend before the rest of the world has. Nevertheless, it is easy, much, much too easy, to forecast doom by casting aspersions on the intelligence of those who see not the gathering gloom. In a pamphlet predicting the imminent demise of the British funding system, for example, Thomas Paine mocked speculators: "Go, count the graves, thou ideot [*sic*], and learn the folly of thy arithmetic."[24]

> Instead of choosing sides, we should instead admit that nobody can foretell the future but that sometimes people can glimpse it.

Instead of choosing sides, we should instead admit that nobody can foretell the future but that sometimes people can glimpse it. The pessimists' glimpse of it, if true, is frightening. You owe $30,037.75. I owe $30,037.75. George Bush and Tom Cruise each owe $30,037.75. So, too, do the panhandler, the soldier maimed by a car bomb in Iraq, and the newborn child still dripping amniotic fluid. As of December 1, 2006, that is the share of each citizen (man, woman, child, or transsexual, just over 300 million in all) of the explicit U.S. national debt, which currently stands at $9.1 trillion, give or take a few billion bucks. The figure may not frighten you, but it should because it is growing, and much faster than the economy, the population, and personal incomes. The calculation assumes that we'll all shoulder the same amount of the burden, but many Americans cannot help out very much because the median income in the United States is only about $45,000 per *household*. That means that half of American families could not pay their share even if they turned over to the government every dollar they made for an entire year. Moreover, many Americans have large personal debts of their own to tackle.

And it gets worse. Most of the explicit national debt falls due within the next few years. Presumably, the government will pay the obligations as they mature by borrowing yet again, much like a profligate college student juggling credit cards. The government might have to pay higher rates of interest and conceivably may not be able to find enough purchasers to roll the entire debt over. The risk is palpable because much of the debt is not owned by penny-pinching grandparents or even domestic financial intermediaries but rather by foreign potentates, including the communist government of China.

So we can't dismiss the problem with the old canards that we owe the debt to ourselves or that bondholders need to lend more than the government needs to borrow. China now finds it convenient to buy U.S. bonds, but it may not always find it so, especially if either country is racked by internal dissentions or other shocks, like a war or major terrorist attack.[25]

As if that was not depressing enough, the explicit national debt represents only a small fraction of the U.S. government's total liabilities. The social safety net, including Social Security and the various health care entitlements, also imposes a severe strain on the national economy. Already, Congress has no control over the bulk of the federal budget. Most taxes have been spent before they ever make it into the Treasury; they are earmarked to pay interest on the explicit national debt and to keep the safety net aloft. The latter debt we do owe to ourselves, in a sense, but that will be small consolation to children born after the year 2000 who will have to support elderly Americans nearly as numerous as they.

Here is the most terrifying fact of all: these are not the intoxicated ravings of a few madmen on the periphery of public discourse but rather the sober warnings of David M. Walker, the comptroller general of the United States. For the last few years, Walker has argued forcefully that the national government will soon face a major debt crisis due to the combined effects of the explicit national debt, Social Security, and health care liabilities. The size of the latter two liabilities is unknown and to a large extent unknowable. They may turn out to be less burdensome than projected, but they could also turn out to be veritable budget monsters. Even if current projections hold true, a crisis looms. When it will occur and how it will manifest remain unclear but something is going to have to give at some point. Scholarly researchers have also begun to sound the alarms by publishing tales of fiscal caution and prudence.[26]

This book of history cannot prevent or even delay the crisis. It can, however, help scholars, policy makers, and the general public to prepare for and mitigate its effects. After all, this fiscal crisis is not America's first. The United States was born in debt, a debt so deep that it threatened to rend the young nation asunder. Thankfully, its most important policy makers found in history, precedent, and powerful market forces a way out of the morass. Their solution turned out to be merely temporary, however, because the founding generations, from the administrations of George Washington to those of Andrew Jackson, never found a way to reconcile America's Jeffersonian heart with its Hamiltonian mind. Thomas Jefferson considered the national debt a monstrous fraud on posterity, while Alexander Hamilton called it a national blessing that would cement the young nation together and help it to prosper. Both, as it turns out, were right. The national debt greatly aided the early nation's economic and political development. The national debt's subsequent history, however, including its rapid revival after Jackson left office and the crisis that looms before us now, shows that Jefferson's view was also prescient. Money borrowed today to fund the consumption of the elderly, currently the nation's most powerful political lobby, is indeed unfair because the people who will have to pay it back, the unborn and generations just born, do not benefit from it and hence may not feel obliged to pay it back. America's first national debt, by contrast, paid for something of immense value, the nation's independence and the people's liberty.[27]

If we take history as our guide, we should pay our current debts down as much and as quickly as we can without making taxation onerous. As Henry C. Adams put it: "The rate of taxation should at no time be so excessive as to act like a dead weight on the spirit of enterprise." The first debt was paid off without grievous taxes, a point of pride to Treasury Secretary Levi Woodbury. "It is an additional source of gratification," he wrote, "that this has been effected without imposing heavy burdens on the people, or leaving their treasury empty, trade languishing, and industry paralyzed; but, on the contrary, with almost every great interest of society flourishing, with taxes reduced, a surplus of money on hand, valuable stocks and extensive lands still owned by the government, and with such various other financial resources at command as to give our country, in this respect, a very enviable superiority."[28]

What America needs most of all is tax reform. Americans worry about the percentage of their income they turn over to the government but they are also concerned with the numerous, grasping ways government obtains what it claims is necessary. Income taxes have grown onerous, unfair, and far more intrusive than any early American's worst nightmare. The plethora of different types of taxes Americans pay induce many to overestimate just how much the government

> The plethora of different types of taxes Americans pay induce many to overestimate just how much the government takes.

takes. Fewer, simpler taxes, be they income, value-added, and/or capital levies would enable the government to increase its total net haul by reducing tax collection costs, tax avoidance strategies, and outright tax evasion.

Increased revenue would help to reduce the nation's debt only if expenditure growth can be stopped cold. One way to do that would be to find a way to rein in the sprawling and expansive federal bureaucracy. Protected from popular criticism and even politicians by a maze of union and civil service rules as well as the size and complexity of the agencies and departments they run, federal bureaucrats enjoy tenures almost as secure as those of university professors. Unsurprisingly, their productivity is almost as low. Attempt to make them accountable for their actions (and budgets), and they raise the bloody flag of the nineteenth-century patronage system. Something must be done about this but I won't venture to say what. As some of the antifederalists predicted, we've allowed a seemingly uncontrollable and unelected Leviathan to arise in our midst but have no harpoon at hand to smite it.[29]

It would be better still if expenditures somehow could be trimmed. Construction, education, and health care are ripe for reforms that could cut billions from the federal budget. The biggest barriers to such cuts are, ironically enough, politicians. "Parties will arise in free governments," Henry Knox reminded Edward Carrington in 1792, "and party prejudice is proverbially blind." Given the permanence of parties, and the fiscal problems they cause or exacerbate, perhaps the best way to protect the people's pockets is to do as the Swiss have done and separate the power to tax from the power to spend. Let one house of Congress decide how much the government will collect in taxes and let the other house decide how to spend it. Constitutionally limit the government's ability to borrow. That would give government a true budget constraint, thereby forcing politicians to make difficult decisions regarding taxation and expenditure, rather than bequeathing that inevitable trade-off to future generations by borrowing to the hilt today to ensure reelection tomorrow. Or, as economist

Brad DeLong and others have suggested, Congress could delegate its fiscal powers to an independent agency, much the way it has outsourced monetary policy to the Federal Reserve System. Better still, in my opinion, let individual Americans determine the discretionary part of the federal budget by allowing them to allocate their taxes as they see fit. In a sense, that would be the ultimate in democratic decision making and would provide people incentive to pay more rather than fewer taxes.[30]

Anything that would reintroduce "republican simplicity," in Treasury Secretary Woodbury's apt phrase, to our government councils would help immensely. History suggests, however, that important reforms are unlikely to take place until a crisis occurs. It is difficult to see the Constitution or Hamilton's grand plan passing without the political, military, economic, and financial difficulties of the 1780s. The second BUS, too, was born of a crisis of military and economic weakness and debt. Let us hope that the reforms we appear to need now gain traction before Manhattan (September 21, 1776) and Washington, D.C., (August 24, 1814) burn again.

APPENDIX

TABLES

TABLE 1: Issuance of Loan Office Certificates by Year, 1776–81

Year	Loan Office Certificates	Number of Bonds	Loan Offices
1776	$52,400	171	Pa.
1777	$4,291,500	8,398	Conn., Del., Md., N.H., N.J., N.Y., Pa.
1778	$8,134,200	17,300	Conn., Del., Md., N.H., N.J., N.Y., Pa.
1779	$24,927,100	32,974	Conn., Del., Md., N.H., N.J., N.Y., Pa.
1780	$12,851,000	15,124	Conn., Del., Md., N.H., N.J., N.Y., Pa.
1781	$1,687,500	2,576	Md., N.J., N.Y., Pa.
TOTALS	$51,943,700	76,543	

Source: Record Group 53, Records of the Bureau of the Public Debt, National Archives and Records Administration

TABLE 2: **Issuance of Loan Office Certificates by State, 1776–81**

Loan Office	Loan Office Certificates	Number of Bonds	Number of Purchasers	Percent Women	Years
Connecticut	$9,377,900	19,323	2,639	7.65%	1777–80
Delaware	$538,000	715	181	14.92%	1777–80
Maryland	$3,931,800	6,432	967	9.00%	1777–81
New Hampshire	$971,600	1,951	534	6.18%	1777–80
New Jersey	$5,909,800	9,060	1,857	9.59%	1777–81
New York	$3,327,500	6,070	1,381	7.46%	1777–81
Pennsylvania	$27,887,100	32,992	5,614	8.41%	1776–81
TOTALS	$51,943,700	76,543	13,173	8.37%	

Source: Record Group 53, Records of the Bureau of the Public Debt, National Archives and Records Administration

Note: The dollar value figures for most states are close to the official ones provided in Cochran. Some, though, are vastly different (Connecticut, for example, is listed at only $4,293,200) for reasons unknown. Cochran also provides dollar values for Massachusetts ($8,092,907), Rhode Island ($1,866,800), Virginia ($2,957,800), North Carolina ($1,209,800), South Carolina ($3,846,405), and Georgia ($951,000). Thomas Cochran, *New York in the Confederation: An Economic Study* (Philadelphia: University of Pennsylvania Press, 1932), 189.

TABLE 3: **Foreign Loans of the U.S. Government, 1777–1794**

Source	Amount in $	Issue Year(s)	Redemption Year(s)
France, Farmers General	181,500	1777	1778–79, mostly 1793
France	3,267,000	1778–82	1791–95
Spain	174,017	1781–82	1792–93
France	1,815,000	1781–82	1792–95
France	1,089,000	1783	1795
Holland, 1782	2,000,000	1782–86	1793–97
Holland, 1784	800,000	1784	1801–7
Holland, 1787	400,000	1787–88	1798–1802
Holland, 1788	400,000	1789	1799–1803
Holland, 1790	1,200,000	1790–91	1800–1804
Holland, Mar. 1791	1,000,000	1791	1802–5
Holland, Sept. 1791	2,400,000	1791	1802–5
Antwerp, 1791	820,000	1791–92	1803–5
Holland, Dec. 1791	1,200,000	1791–92	1803–7
Holland, 1792	1,180,000	1792–93	1803–7
Holland, 1793	400,000	1793	1803
Holland, 1794	1,200,000	1794	1805–9

Source: Rafael A. Bayley, *The National Loans of the United States, from July 4, 1776 to June 30, 1880* 2nd ed. (Washington, D.C.: Government Printing Office, 1882), 5–28

TABLE 4: Theodosius Fowler's Bond Trades, 1792

Date	Security	Face Value ($)	Exchange Value ($)	Price (% of par)
1792.0107	6s	895.93	1,119.91	1.2500
1792.0107	3s	671.94	470.35	0.7000
1792.0107	Deferred 6s	447.97	313.57	0.7000
1792.0107	3s	5,580.00	3,627.00	0.6500
1792.0111	Deferred 6s	5,000.00	3,291.66	0.6583
1792.0111	3s	5,000.00	3,208.33	0.6417
1792.0111	6s	3,750.00	3,750.00	1.0000
1792.0111	6s	3,180.28	3,816.43	1.2000
1792.0123	3s	18,375.50	13,781.20	0.7500
1792.0124	3s	20,000.00	13,333.33	0.6667
1792.0126	6s	20,000.00	23,500.00	1.1750
1792.0131	6s	803.70	892.00	1.1099
1792.0131	3s	523.19	345.30	0.6600
1792.0110	6s	4,000.00	4,458.33	1.1146
1792.0110	6s	10,000.00	9,375.00	0.9375
1792.0110	6s	739.26	850.14	1.1500
1792.0126	6s	5,000.00	6,250.00	1.2500
1792.0110	3s	554.44	401.96	0.7250
1792.0110	Deferred 6s	369.62	267.97	0.7250
1792.0110	South Carolina excess	263.93	164.95	0.6250
1792.0110	6s	500.00	575.00	1.1500
1792.0110	6s	5,000.00	4,666.66	0.9333
1792.0111	6s	10,000.00	9,333.32	0.9333
1792.0111	6s	7,666.66	7,701.72	1.0046
1792.0124	6s	572.58	701.41	1.2250
1792.0126	6s	1,000.00	1,093.75	1.0938
1792.0126	6s	5,000.00	6,291.66	1.2583
1792.0131	Deferred 6s	10,000.00	7,250.00	0.7250
1792.0131	Deferred 6s	286.29	207.56	0.7250
1792.0124	3s	589.23	427.19	0.7250
1792.0204	6s	10,000.00	12,062.00	1.2062
1792.0204	6s	10,000.00	12,083.33	1.2083
1792.0210	Deferred 6s	8,753.31	6,564.97	0.7500
1792.0220	South Carolina excess	3,402.76	2,389.02	0.7021

(Continued)

Date	Security	Face Value ($)	Exchange Value ($)	Price (% of par)
1792.0220	South Carolina excess	4,073.87	3,259.09	0.8000
1792.0228	6s	6,000.00	7,302.60	1.2171
1792.0228	6s	1,500.00	1,800.00	1.2000
1792.0228	Deferred 6s	6,000.00	4,525.00	0.7542
1792.0228	6s	10,833.34	13,037.99	1.2035
1792.0228	6s	7,833.34	9,422.37	1.2029
1792.0229	3s	1,883.46	1,283.42	0.6814
1792.0229	3s	4,296.29	3,007.40	0.7000
1792.0201	Deferred 6s	10,000.00	7,750.00	0.7750
1792.0204	Deferred 6s	9,687.42	6,861.95	0.7083
1792.0216	Deferred 6s	6,407.06	4,805.30	0.7500
1792.0218	Deferred 6s	10,000.00	7,500.00	0.7500
1792.0201	Deferred 6s	8,417.21	6,242.76	0.7417
1792.0223	Deferred 6s	6,000.00	4,708.33	0.7847
1792.0226	Deferred 6s	23,000.00	17,345.83	0.7542
1792.0201	3s	12,685.82	9,153.71	0.7216
1792.0227	3s	9,257.21	6,480.04	0.7000
1792.0227	3s	5,000.00	3,062.50	0.6125
1792.0226	3s	12,056.59	8,489.85	0.7042
1792.0226	3s	2,500.00	1,760.41	0.7042
1792.0203	New York debt	500.00	730.31	1.4606
1792.0210	New York debt	135.70	211.43	1.5581
1792.0216	New York debt	500.00	810.00	1.6200
1792.2010	Unfunded debt	17.50	27.93	1.5960
1792.0211	6s	1,500.00	1,807.81	1.2052
1792.0215	6s	10,500.00	12,797.39	1.2188
1792.0226	6s	4,000.00	4,816.66	1.2042
1792.0226	6s	2,500.00	3,026.04	1.2104
1792.0226	6s	2,500.00	3,018.21	1.2073
1792.0226	6s	2,500.00	3,022.43	1.2090
1792.0226	6s	15,000.00	18,000.00	1.2000
1792.0301	6s	1,000.00	1,200.00	1.2000
1792.0301	Nourse's certificate	617.46	—	—
1792.0301	Loan office	44.01	44.01	1.0000
1792.0301	6s	670.26	770.80	1.1500

Date	Security	Face Value ($)	Exchange Value ($)	Price (% of par)
1792.0303	3s	4,556.59	3,208.59	0.7042
1792.0305	3s	3,333.33	2,347.22	0.7042
1792.0305	Deferred 6s	5,666.67	4,273.61	0.7542
1792.0305	3s	3,333.33	2,347.22	0.7042
1792.0305	Deferred 6s	5,666.67	4,273.61	0.7542
1792.0308	6s	911.80	931.90	1.0220
1792.0308	South Carolina debt	970.37	539.14	0.5556
1792.0308	6s	35.00	23.50	0.6714
1792.0308	3s	17.50	11.75	0.6714
1792.0308	Continental money	15,085.00	411.50	0.0273
1792.0308	Georgia debt	32.75	14.73	0.4498
1792.0310	3s	20,000.00	14,000.00	0.7000
1792.0314	6s	15,463.50	20,618.00	1.3333
1792.0319	6s	5,000.00	6,125.00	1.2250
1792.0314	6s	1,200.00	1,800.00	1.5000
1792.0330	6s	478.06	418.62	0.8757
1792.0330	3s	358.99	314.12	0.8750
1792.0330	Deferred 6s	239.32	209.63	0.8759
1792.0330	South Carolina debt	170.96	149.59	0.8750
1792.0302	Deferred 6s	8,500.00	6,516.66	0.7667
1792.0308	6s	1,000.00	1,200.00	1.2000
1792.0313	6s	35.00	42.00	1.2000
1792.0317	6s	5,017.06	5,455.78	1.0874
1792.0313	South Carolina debt	970.37	775.92	0.7996
1792.0313	3s	17.50	13.12	0.7497
1792.0302	6s	5,000.00	6,125.00	1.2250
1792.0302	3s	10,000.00	7,125.00	0.7125
1792.0331	Deferred 6s	2,500.00	1,625.00	0.6500
1792.0405	6s	5,386.03	6,921.04	1.2850
1792.0405	3s	7,524.82	5,963.42	0.7925
1792.0405	Deferred 6s	9,975.56	7,980.44	0.8000
1792.0405	New York debt	500.00	727.50	1.4550
1792.0412	Deferred 6s	1,600.00	1,000.00	0.6250
1792.0417	3s	666.66	389.48	0.5842
1792.0417	6s	4,318.91	4,318.91	1.0000

(Continued)

Date	Security	Face Value ($)	Exchange Value ($)	Price (% of par)
1792.0417	3s	6,390.90	3,838.14	0.6006
1792.0417	Deferred 6s	5,429.14	3,393.20	0.6250
1792.0420	3s	394.31	236.58	0.6000
1792.0426	6s	1,226.48	1,421.10	1.1587
1792.0414	Deferred 6s	1,600.00	1,000.00	0.6250
1792.0414	3s	940.63	564.37	0.6000
1792.0427	6s	3,000.00	3,225.00	1.0750
1792.0404	6s	1,000.00	1,000.00	1.0000
1792.0417	6s	25.21	25.00	0.9917
1792.0427	6s	3,446.60	3,618.93	1.0500
1792.0410	New York debt	21.33	21.33	1.0000
1792.0512	6s	16,663.50	21,800.00	1.3082
1792.0516	Deferred 6s	6,702.07	4,859.00	0.7250
1792.0516	3s	27,495.67	19,495.67	0.7090
1792.0516	Unfunded debt	109.39	100.00	0.9142
1792.0516	Deferred 6s	637.57	416.65	0.6535
1792.0516	6s	4,682.73	5,033.93	1.0750
1792.0516	New York debt	317.62	340.40	1.0717
1792.0526	6s	5,250.00	5,775.00	1.1000
1792.0526	Deferred 6s	397.50	288.00	0.7245
1792.0526	6s	128.00	140.80	1.1000
1792.0530	Deferred 6s	6,000.00	4,800.00	0.8000
1792.0531	3s	6,373.39	3,824.03	0.6000
1792.0521	Connecticut Debt	70.72	42.43	0.6000
1792.0531	Deferred 6s	5,883.53	3,987.08	0.6777
1792.0627	6s	1,200.00	1,800.00	1.5000
1792.0627	Deferred 6s	14,016.58	8,879.47	0.6335
1792.0726	6s	1,000.00	1,200.00	1.2000
1792.0726	Deferred 6s	1,000.00	700.00	0.7000
1792.0726	Deferred 6s	221.51	155.05	0.7000
1792.0726	3s	332.28	221.52	0.6667
1792.0726	6s	463.60	556.32	1.2000
1792.0807	Massachusetts debt	300.16	292.67	0.9750
1792.0807	Connecticut debt	460.76	460.06	0.9985

Source: Theodosius Fowler, Account Book, 1791–1792, New York Historical Society

TABLE 5: Theodosius Fowler's Equity Trades, 1792

Date	Equity	Number of Shares	Price Per Share ($)	Total ($)
1792.0128	BUS Half	20	428.00	8,560.00
1792.0113	SEUM	30	19.92	597.60
1792.0113	SEUM	10	19.92	199.20
1792.0120	BUS Half	30	420.00	12,600.00
1792.0120	BUS Half	5	416.00	2,080.00
1792.0121	BUS Half	10	420.00	4,200.00
1792.0203	BUS Half	20	400.00	8,000.00
1792.0210	BUS Half	27	403.68	10,899.42
1792.0210	BUS Half	26	400.00	10,400.00
1792.0213	BUS Half	10	410.00	4,100.00
1792.0211	BUS Half	5	400.00	2,000.00
1792.0228	BUS Half	40	358.25	14,330.00
1792.0203	BUS Half	5	416.00	2,080.00
1792.0210	BUS Half	10	412.5	4,125.00
1792.0210	BUS Half	10	391.00	3,910.00
1792.0211	BUS Half	11	401.00	4,411.00
1792.0211	BUS Half	5	398.50	1,992.50
1792.0211	BUS Half	42	400.1786	16,807.50
1792.0226	BUS Half	10	400.00	4,000.00
1792.0226	BUS Half	10	398.50	3,985.00
1792.0301	BUS Half	10	409.00	4,090.00
1792.0303	BUS Half	20	401.2775	8,025.55
1792.0305	BUS Half	24	401.5621	9,637.49
1792.0305	BUS Half	24	401.5621	9,637.49
1792.0307	BUS Half	20	440.00	8,800.00
1792.0307	BUS Half	43	400.00	17,200.00
1792.0307	BUS Half	5	402.00	2,010.00
1792.0307	BUS Half	7	398.6314	2,790.42
1792.0309	BUS Half	20	370.00	7,400.00
1792.0309	BUS Half	10	350.00	3,500.00
1792.0313	BUS Half	10	350.00	3,500.00
1792.0314	SEUM	10	19.92	199.20
1792.0316	BUS Half	20	380.00	7,600.00

(*Continued*)

Date	Equity	Number of Shares	Price Per Share ($)	Total ($)
1792.0319	BUS Half	19	300.00	5,700.00
1792.0319	BUS Half	5	400.00	2,000.00
1792.0328	BUS Half	20	440.00	8,800.00
1792.0310	BUS Half	30	428.00	12,840.00
1792.0317	BUS Half	10	336.00	3,360.00
1792.0301	BUS Half	10	402.00	4,020.00
1792.0301	BUS Half	10	401.00	4,010.00
1792.0301	BUS Half	20	402.00	8,040.00
1792.0302	BUS Half	20	406.00	8,120.00
1792.0305	BUS Half	10	404.00	4,040.00
1792.0307	BUS Half	10	404.00	4,040.00
1792.0307	BUS Half	7	398.63	2,790.42
1792.0312	BUS Half	10	350.00	3,500.00
1792.0312	BUS Half	20	425.75	8,515.00
1792.0319	BUS Half	10	293.00	2,930.00
1792.0323	BUS Half	10	311.00	3,110.00
1792.0323	BUS Half	10	304.00	3,040.00
1792.0411	BUS Half	35	300.00	10,500.00
1792.0412	BUS Half	20	380.00	7,600.00
1792.0427	BUS Half	20	280.00	5,600.00
1792.0427	BUS Half	25	365.00	9,125.00
1792.0430	BONY	1	680.00	680.00
1792.0521	BUS Half	10	525.00	5,250.00
1792.0531	BUS Half	35	320.00	11,200.00
1792.0517	BONY	2	640.00	1,280.00
1792.0525	BONY	2	640.00	1,280.00
1792.0525	BONY	1	640.00	640.00
1792.0728	SEUM	30	8.00	240.00
1792.1120	BUS Full	15	576.00	8,640.00

Source: Theodosius Fowler, Account Book, 1791–1792, New York Historical Society

TABLE 6: Volume of Public Securities Trading in Select U.S. Markets by Year, 1790–1834

Year	Total Volume of Trades ($)	Total No. of Trades
1790	447,857.92	246
1791	7,846,219.00	5,566
1792	7,171,626.47	7,077
1793	2,593,669.39	2,556
1794	1,936,077.64	2,074
1795	2,224,321.83	3,228
1796	1,585,086.93	2,108
1797	1,080,420.78	1,247
1798	1,061,315.79	950
1799	1,019,449.19	1,069
1800	2,970,559.22	2,186
1801	4,176,301.01	2,866
1802	4,353,652.96	3,052
1803	3,934,689.85	2,168
1804	4,194,508.92	2,190
1805	2,968,683.77	1,688
1806	4,381,071.57	2,303
1807	6,453,146.54	2,311
1808	8,933,783.61	1,904
1809	6,065,009.24	2,191
1810–19	49,503,929.71	9,915
1820–34	3,316,642.50	1,345
TOTALS	$128,218,023.84	60,240

Source: Record Group 53, Records of the Bureau of the Public Debt, National Archives and Records Administration

TABLE 7: Volume of Public Securities Trading in Select U.S. Markets by State Loan Office, 1790–1834

Loan Office	Total $	Total No.
Central Treasury	$18,805,539.67	2,302
Connecticut	$6,623,232.95	10,198
Georgia	$43,504.30	32
Maryland	$7,587,123.49	2,853
New Hampshire	$1,034,248.33	1,006
New Jersey	$410,037.39	812
New York	$14,374,509.31	9,454
North Carolina	$463,884.04	82
Pennsylvania	$61,628,734.62	17,486
Rhode Island	$5,235,983.90	6,443
South Carolina	$4,148,224.83	2,540
Virginia	$8,955,970.62	7,389
TOTALS	$129,310,993.45	60,597

Source: Record Group 53, Records of the Bureau of the Public Debt, National Archives and Records Administration

Note: The discrepancy in Tables 6 and 7 is due to data omissions (e.g., date) in some records.

TABLE 8: Residences of Federal Bond Owners, January 1, 1795

Residence	Number of Bondholders	Percent of Total
Accomack County, Va.	6	0.19
Albany, N.Y.	1	0.03
Albemarle County, Va.	8	0.25
Alexandria, Va.	5	0.16
Allegheny County, Pa.	2	0.06
Allegheny County, Md.	1	0.03
Allentown, Monmouth Co., N.J.	2	0.06
Amelia County, Va.	4	0.12
Amherst, N.H.	2	0.06
Amherst County, Va.	3	0.09
Amsterdam, Netherlands	3	0.09
Amwell, Hunterdon County, N.J.	2	0.06
Andover, N.H.	1	0.03
Ann Arundel County, Md.	16	0.50
Annapolis, Md.	41	1.27
Ashford, Conn.	3	0.09
Athirstone, Warwick Shire, Great Britain	1	0.03
Atkinson, N.H.	1	0.03
Attleborough, R.I.	11	0.34
Augusta, Ga.	1	0.03
Augusta County, Va.	22	0.68
Baltimore, Md.	32	0.99
Barrington, R.I.	8	0.25
Baskinridge, Somerset County, N.J.	2	0.06
Beaufort, S.C.	2	0.06
Bedford, N.H.	2	0.06
Bedford County, Pa.	3	0.09
Berkeley County, Va.	3	0.09
Berks County, Pa.	13	0.40
Berlin, Conn.	8	0.25
Bermuda, West Indies	18	0.56
Berwick, Mass.	1	0.03
Bethlehem, Pa.	3	0.09
Beverly, Pa.	1	0.03
Bladensburgh, Md.	1	0.03

(*Continued*)

Residence	Number of Bondholders	Percent of Total
Blockley, Pa.	1	0.03
Bolton, Conn.	16	0.50
Bordeaux, France	1	0.03
Bordentown, N.J.	2	0.06
Boston, Mass.	17	0.53
Botetourt County, Va.	4	0.12
Bozrah, Conn.	1	0.03
Bradford, Mass.	1	0.03
Branford, Conn.	2	0.06
Brintwood, N.H.	1	0.03
Bristol, Conn.	1	0.03
Bristol, R.I.	7	0.22
Brunswick, N.J.	1	0.03
Brunswick County, Va.	7	0.22
Bucks County, Pa.	24	0.75
Buckingham County, Va.	2	0.06
Burlington County, N.J.	19	0.59
Calvert County, Md.	4	0.12
Cambridge, Mass.	3	0.09
Camden, S.C.	5	0.16
Campbell County, Va.	3	0.09
Canaan, Conn.	6	0.19
Candia, N.H.	1	0.03
Canterbury, Conn.	4	0.12
Cape May, N.J.	1	0.03
Carlisle, Pa.	3	0.09
Caroline County, Va.	13	0.40
Carrollton, Md.	1	0.03
Cecil County, Md.	1	0.03
Charles City County, Va.	5	0.16
Charles County, Md.	4	0.12
Charleston, S.C.	211	6.55
Charlestown, R.I.	2	0.06
Charlotte County, Va.	4	0.12
Chatham, Conn.	5	0.16
Cheshire, Conn.	1	0.03

Residence	Number of Bondholders	Percent of Total
Chester County, Pa.	30	0.93
Chesterfield County, Va.	6	0.19
Chesterfield, Mass.	1	0.03
Cincinnati, Conn.	1	0.03
Clapton, Middlesex County, Great Britain	1	0.03
Claremont, N.H.	1	0.03
Colchester, Conn.	9	0.28
Columbia County, Ga.	1	0.03
Concord, N.H.	8	0.25
Cornwall, Conn.	3	0.09
Coventry, Conn.	16	0.50
Cranbury, N.J.	2	0.06
Cranston, R.I.	13	0.40
Culpepper County, Va.	8	0.25
Cumberland, R.I.	8	0.25
Cumberland County, Pa.	6	0.19
Danbury, Conn.	12	0.37
Dauphin County, Pa.	4	0.12
Deerfield, N.H.	1	0.03
Delaware County, Pa.	5	0.16
Delaware (state of)	3	0.09
Derby, Conn.	2	0.06
Dighton, R.I.	1	0.03
Dinwiddie County, Va.	8	0.25
Dobbs County, N.C.	1	0.03
Doden, Md.	1	0.03
Dorchester County	5	0.16
Dudley, R.I.	1	0.03
Dumfries, Va.	5	0.16
Durham, N.H.	5	0.16
East Greenwich, R.I.	10	0.31
East Guilford, Conn.	1	0.03
East Haddam, Conn.	7	0.22
East Hartford, Conn.	19	0.59
East Haven, Conn.	5	0.16
East Windsor, Conn.	16	0.50

(*Continued*)

Residence	Number of Bondholders	Percent of Total
Edinburgh, Scotland, Great Britain	1	0.03
Effingham County, Ga.	2	0.06
Elizabeth City County, Va.	3	0.09
Elizabeth Town, N.J.	3	0.09
Elkton, Md.	1	0.03
Ellington, Conn.	1	0.03
England, Great Britain	1	0.03
Essex County, N.J.	8	0.25
Essex County, Va.	4	0.12
Exeter, N.H.	16	0.50
Fairfax County, Va.	6	0.19
Fairfield, Conn.	14	0.43
Fairhaven, Vt.	1	0.03
Falmouth, Va.	2	0.06
Farmington, Conn.	18	0.56
Fauquier County, Va.	11	0.34
Fayette County, Pa.	2	0.06
Flemington, N.J.	1	0.03
Fluvanna County, Va.	1	0.03
Foster, R.I.	2	0.06
France	1	0.03
Frankford, Philadelphia County, Pa.	2	0.06
Franklin, Conn.	1	0.03
Franklin County, Pa.	1	0.03
Franklin County, Va.	6	0.19
Frederick County, Md.	18	0.56
Frederick Town, Md.	4	0.12
Fredericksburg, Va.	11	0.34
Freetown, R.I.	2	0.06
Gaandam, Md.	1	0.03
Geneva	1	0.03
Georgetown, Md.	5	0.16
Georgia (state of)	5	0.16
Germantown, Pa.	7	0.22
Gilmantown, N.H.	1	0.03
Glastonbury, Conn.	15	0.47

Residence	Number of Bondholders	Percent of Total
Gloster County, Va.	9	0.28
Gloucester, R.I.	5	0.16
Goochland County, Va.	6	0.19
Goose Creek, S.C.	1	0.03
Goshen, Conn.	3	0.09
Granby, Mass.	3	0.09
Great Britain	3	0.09
Greenbrier County, Va.	4	0.12
Greenfield, Mass.	1	0.03
Greenland, N.H.	2	0.06
Greenville County, Va.	1	0.03
Greenwich, Conn.	1	0.03
Groton, Conn.	9	0.28
Guilford, Conn.	8	0.25
Haddam, Conn.	2	0.06
Hadley, Mass.	1	0.03
Halifax County, Va.	3	0.09
Hampton, N.H.	4	0.12
Hampton, Va.	1	0.03
Hanover County	24	0.75
Hardy County, Va.	1	0.03
Harford County, Md.	9	0.28
Harrison County, Va.	1	0.03
Hartford, Conn.	84	2.61
Haverhill, N.H.	1	0.03
Hebron, Conn.	16	0.50
Henrico County, Va.	6	0.19
Henry County, Va.	1	0.03
Hoboken, N.J.	1	0.03
Hollis, N.H.	1	0.03
Hopewell, Hunterdon County, N.J.	3	0.09
Hudson, R.I.	2	0.06
Hunterdon County, N.J.	24	0.75
Huntington, Conn.	5	0.16
Ireland	1	0.03
Isle of Wight County, Va.	2	0.06

(Continued)

Residence	Number of Bondholders	Percent of Total
James City County, Va.	6	0.19
James Island	3	0.09
Jamestown, R.I.	1	0.03
Jefferson County, Va.	3	0.09
John's Island	1	0.03
Johnston, R.I.	5	0.16
Kendal, Great Britain	1	0.03
Kensington, N.H.	4	0.12
Kent County, Md.	1	0.03
Kentucky (district of)	2	0.06
Killingworth, Conn.	10	0.31
King and Queen County, Va.	10	0.31
King George County, Va.	3	0.09
King William County, Va.	6	0.19
Kingston, N.H.	2	0.06
Lancaster, Pa.	23	0.71
Lancaster County, Pa.	16	0.50
Lebanon, Conn.	12	0.37
Lebanon Valley, N.J.	1	0.03
Liecester, Mass.	1	0.03
Lisbon, Conn.	1	0.03
Litchfield, Conn.	3	0.09
Little Compton, R.I.	6	0.19
Liverpool, Great Britain	2	0.06
London, Great Britain	41	1.27
Londonderry, N.H.	3	0.09
Long Island, N.Y.	3	0.09
Long Meadow, Mass.	2	0.06
Loudon County, Va.	5	0.16
Louisa County, Va.	10	0.31
Lunenburg County, Va.	1	0.03
Lyme, Conn.	38	1.18
Lynches Creek, S.C.	1	0.03
Maidenhead, Hunterdon County, N.J.	6	0.19
Manchester, Great Britain	6	0.19
Mansfield, Conn.	6	0.19

Residence	Number of Bondholders	Percent of Total
Marlborough, Mass.	1	0.03
Marseilles, France	1	0.03
Maryland (state of)	4	0.12
Massachusetts (state of)	1	0.03
Matthews County, Va.	1	0.03
McCallisters Town, Pa.	1	0.03
Medfield, Mass.	1	0.03
Merrimac, N.H.	1	0.03
Middlesex County, N.J.	20	0.62
Middletown, Conn.	27	0.84
Milford, Conn.	8	0.25
Monmouth County, N.J.	17	0.53
Montgomery County, Md.	10	0.31
Montgomery County, Pa.	13	0.40
Montville, Conn.	8	0.25
Moreland Township, Philadelphia County, Pa.	1	0.03
Morris County, N.J.	4	0.12
Nansemond County, Va.	2	0.06
New Brunswick, N.J.	3	0.09
New Castle County, Dela.	2	0.06
New Fairfield, Conn.	1	0.03
New Hampshire (state of)	1	0.03
New Haven, Conn.	27	0.84
New Jersey (state of)	14	0.43
New Kent County, Va.	10	0.31
New London, Conn.	28	0.87
New Milford, Conn.	6	0.19
New River, S.C.	1	0.03
New York, N.Y.	67	2.08
New York (state of)	4	0.12
Newark, N.J.	1	0.03
Newburyport, Mass.	8	0.25
Newcastle, N.H.	1	0.03
Newington, Conn.	3	0.09
Newport, R.I.	60	1.86
Ninety Six District, S.C.	3	0.09

(Continued)

Residence	Number of Bondholders	Percent of Total
Norfolk, Va.	24	0.75
North Carolina (state of)	6	0.19
North Hampton, N.H.	3	0.09
North Haven, Conn.	1	0.03
North Kingston, R.I.	3	0.09
North Providence, R.I.	11	0.34
Northampton County, Pa.	6	0.19
Northampton County, Va.	5	0.16
Northumberland County, Pa.	6	0.19
Northumberland County, Va.	1	0.03
Norwalk, Conn.	2	0.06
Norwich, Conn.	27	0.84
Ohio County, Va.	2	0.06
Orange County, Va.	6	0.19
Patrick County, Va.	1	0.03
Peedee, S.C.	2	0.06
Pembroke, Mass.	1	0.03
Pendleton County, Va.	1	0.03
Petersburg, Va.	13	0.40
Philadelphia, Pa.	346	10.75
Philadelphia County, Pa.	21	0.65
Pittsburgh, Pa.	5	0.16
Pittsylvania County, Va.	2	0.06
Plainfield, Conn.	2	0.06
Pomfret, Conn.	7	0.22
Portland, Mass.	2	0.06
Portsmouth, N.H.	41	1.27
Powhatan County, Va.	5	0.16
Preston, Conn.	3	0.09
Prince Edward County, Va.	5	0.16
Prince George County, Md.	22	0.68
Princeton, N.J.	3	0.09
Providence, R.I.	133	4.13
Queen Anns County, Md.	4	0.12
Rahway, Essex County, N.J.	1	0.03
Raynham, Mass.	1	0.03

Residence	Number of Bondholders	Percent of Total
Reading, Berks County, Pa.	6	0.19
Readington, N.J.	1	0.03
Rehoboth, Mass.	14	0.43
Rhode Island (state of)	7	0.22
Richland County, Va.	1	0.03
Richmond, Va.	62	1.93
Ridgefield, Conn.	1	0.03
Rockbridge County, Va.	7	0.22
Rotterdam, Netherlands	2	0.06
Roxbury, Mass.	2	0.06
Rye, N.H.	2	0.06
Saint Marys County, Md.	4	0.12
Salem, Mass.	2	0.06
Salisbury, Mass.	2	0.06
Sandown, N.H.	1	0.03
Santee, S.D.	1	0.03
Savannah, Ga.	4	0.12
Saybrook, Conn.	8	0.25
Scituate, R.I.	13	0.40
Sharon, Conn.	1	0.03
Shenandoah County, Va.	1	0.03
Shrewsbury, Great Britain	1	0.03
Smithfield, R.I.	7	0.22
Smithfield, Va.	1	0.03
Somers, Conn.	3	0.09
Somerset County, Md.	6	0.19
Somerset County, N.J.	29	0.90
South Carolina (state of)	10	0.31
Southampton County, Va.	8	0.25
South Kingston, R.I.	4	0.12
Southampton, Mass.	2	0.06
Southington, Conn.	2	0.06
Spottsylvania County, Va.	2	0.06
Springfield, Mass.	8	0.25
Springfield, Burlington County, N.J.	2	0.06
St. Andrews	1	0.03

(Continued)

Residence	Number of Bondholders	Percent of Total
St. Bartholomew's Parish, S.C.	2	0.06
St. Croix	1	0.03
St. Eustatius	6	0.19
St. George's Parish, S.C.	2	0.06
St. Helena	2	0.06
St. James Santee	1	0.03
St. John's Parish	3	0.09
St. Marks, Clarendon County, S.C.	1	0.03
St. Thomas's Parish, S.C.	7	0.22
Stafford, Conn.	1	0.03
Stafford County, Va.	1	0.03
Stamford, Conn.	1	0.03
Stonington, Conn.	4	0.12
Stratford, Conn.	3	0.09
Stratham, N.H.	1	0.03
Suffield, Conn.	12	0.37
Suffolk, Va.	1	0.03
Sullivan County, Southwestern territory	1	0.03
Sunbury, Pa.	1	0.03
Surry County, Va.	6	0.19
Sussex County, N.J.	2	0.06
Sussex County, Va.	2	0.06
Swanzey, R.I.	5	0.16
Symsbury, Conn.	1	0.03
Talbot County, Md.	5	0.16
Thompson, Conn.	4	0.12
Tiverton, R.I.	14	0.43
Tolland, Conn.	2	0.06
Torrington, Conn.	5	0.16
Trenton, N.J.	34	1.06
Tulpehocken, Pa.	1	0.03
Tyringham, Mass.	2	0.06
Vermont (state of)	3	0.09
Virginia (state of)	23	0.71
Voluntown, Conn.	1	0.03
Wallingford, Conn.	3	0.09

Residence	Number of Bondholders	Percent of Total
Warren, R.I.	10	0.31
Warton, Great Britain	1	0.03
Warwick, R.I.	16	0.50
Warwick County, Va.	3	0.09
Warwick, Pa.	1	0.03
Washington County, Md.	1	0.03
Washington County, Va.	1	0.03
Waterbury, Conn.	1	0.03
West Chester, Pa.	1	0.03
West Greenwich, R.I.	4	0.12
West Hampton, Conn.	1	0.03
West Springfield, Mass.	1	0.03
Westerley, R.I.	1	0.03
Westmoreland County, Pa.	7	0.22
Westmoreland County, Va.	4	0.12
Weston, Conn.	2	0.06
Westport, R.I.	1	0.03
Wethersfield, Conn.	42	1.30
Wilkes County, Va.	1	0.03
Williamsburg, Va.	19	0.59
Willington, Conn.	4	0.12
Windham, Conn.	6	0.19
Windsor, Conn.	41	1.27
Woodbridge, Middlesex County, N.J.	1	0.03
Woodstock, Conn.	23	0.71
Worchester County, Md.	2	0.06
Wrentham, R.I.	1	0.03
York County, Pa.	18	0.56
York, Va.	12	0.37
	3,219	100

Source: Record Group 53, Records of the Bureau of the Public Debt, National Archives and Records Administration

TABLE 9: Occupations of Federal Bondholders, January 1, 1795

Occupation	Number	Percentage
Apothecary/Druggist	7	0.37
Attorney/Jurist	33	1.76
Baker	6	0.32
Blacksmith	12	0.64
Blockmaker	2	0.11
Book Trades	2	0.11
Brewer/Maltster	2	0.11
Cabinetmaker	2	0.11
Carpenter	4	0.21
Chaisemaker	1	0.05
Clerk	10	0.53
Cooper	2	0.11
Cordwainer	5	0.27
Corporate Officers	2	0.11
Distiller	1	0.05
Doctor	64	3.41
Educator	7	0.37
Esquire/Gentleman	280	14.91
Estate	168	8.95
Farmer/Yeoman	289	15.39
Financial Services	19	1.01
Glazier	1	0.05
Goldsmith/Silversmith	4	0.21
Guardian	14	0.75
Hatter	6	0.32
Housewright	3	0.16
Innkeeper	12	0.64
Joiner	7	0.37
Laborer	4	0.21
Leatherdresser	1	0.05
Locksmith	1	0.05
Mariner	36	1.92
Mason	3	0.16
Merchant/Factor/Trader	439	23.38

Occupation	Number	Percentage
Military	5	0.27
Municipality	18	0.96
Nonprofit	34	1.81
Planter	47	2.50
Politician	12	0.64
Printer	2	0.11
Reverend	50	2.66
Ropemaker	1	0.05
Saddler	2	0.11
Shipwright	4	0.21
Shoemaker	8	0.43
Shopkeeper	6	0.32
Spinster/Widow	161	8.57
Surveyor	2	0.11
Tailor/Clothier	16	0.85
Tanner	7	0.37
Trustee	47	2.50
Turner	1	0.05
Watchmaker	3	0.16
Weaver	1	0.05
Wheelwright	2	0.11
TOTALS	1,878	100

Source: Record Group 53, Records of the Bureau of the Public Debt, National Archives and Records Administration

TABLE 10: Concentration of Ownership of Federal Bonds, January 1, 1795

Total Holdings	Number	Dollars	No. % of total	$ % of Total
< $1	5	$2.40	0.14%	0.00%
> $1 < $10	63	$406.35	1.75%	0.00%
> $10 < $100	578	$28,894.92	16.05%	0.23%
> $100 < $1,000	1,589	$663,744.23	44.13%	5.36%
> $1,000 < $10,000	1,183	$3,676,526.69	32.85%	29.70%
> $10,000 < $100,000	174	$4,191,858.30	4.83%	33.86%
> $100,000 < $1 million	8	$2,370,747.88	0.22%	19.15%
> $ 1 million	1	$1,447,173.60	0.03%	11.69%
TOTALS	3,601	$12,379,354.37	100	100

Source: Record Group 53, Records of the Bureau of the Public Debt, National Archives and Records Administration

TABLE 11: Federal Bond Ownership by States, June 30, 1803

Loan Office	Sixes ($ millions)	Threes ($ millions)	Deferred ($ millions)
Treasury	11.524	7.639	4.564
New Hampshire	0.216	0.163	0.116
Massachusetts	5.146	2.432	2.005
Rhode Island	0.284	0.216	0.144
Connecticut	0.775	0.437	0.426
New York	4.363	3.243	2.405
New Jersey	0.196	0.117	0.110
Pennsylvania	3.419	3.430	2.810
Delaware	0.063	0.038	0.023
Maryland	0.346	0.412	0.162
Virginia	0.437	0.282	0.197
North Carolina	0.036	0.041	0.024
South Carolina	1.263	0.612	0.649
Georgia	0.087	0.011	0.013
TOTALS	28.155	19.073	13.648

Sources: Rafael A. Bayley, *The National Loans of the United States, from July 4, 1776 to June 30, 1880* 2nd ed. (Washington, D.C.: Government Printing Office, 1882), 34; Samuel Blodget, *Economica: A Statistical Manual for the United States of America* (Washington, D.C.: 1806), 199

TABLE 12: Federal Bond Ownership by Category, June 30, 1803

Bond	English	Dutch	Other foreign	States	Corpo- rations	Indivi- duals	TOTALS
Sixes ($ millions)	3.448	7.286	0.929	2.306	5.739	8.448	28.156
Threes ($ millions)	6.663	3.902	0.664	1.728	1.029	5.086	19.073
Deferred ($ millions)	4.207	1.904	0.546	1.558	1.564	3.869	13.648
TOTALS ($ millions)	14.318	13.092	2.139	5.592	8.332	17.403	60.877

Sources: Rafael A. Bayley, *The National Loans of the United States, from July 4, 1776 to June 30, 1880* 2nd ed. (Washington, D.C.: Government Printing Office, 1882), 34; Samuel Blodget, *Economica: A Statistical Manual for the United States of America* (Washington, D.C.: 1806), 198. See also Bernard Cohen, *Compendium of Finance* (London, 1822) in Robert E. Wright, ed., *The U.S. National Debt, 1787–1900* (London: Pickering & Chatto, 2005), 2:245

TABLE 13: Trading Volume of Different Types of U.S. Bonds, 1805–9

Year	1805	1806	1807	1808	1809
6s $	839,480.65	1,403,003.27	1,805,963.80	3,958,381.27	599,887.66
No. Sales	313	388	447	304	231
3s $	656,008.03	826,600.77	1,302,267.72	1,947,322.32	657,617.86
No. Sales	332	348	382	351	267
Deferred $	711,195.09	1,052,467.53	1,448,765.17	1,035,439.04	510,900.38
No. Sales	323	316	397	289	207
Sundry $			15,472.33	185,466.11	275,276.44
No. Sales			6	34	58
8s $	738,600.00	892,200.00	1,197,000.00	700,900.00	2,718,900.00
No. Sales	656	911	799	544	1,059
Navy 6s $	23,400.00	206,800.00	51,200.00	61,500.00	40,500.00
No. Sales	64	340	106	78	48
Louisiana 6s $				28,000.00	15,000.00
No. Sales				5	3
Converted 6s $			39,912.93	266,261.01	338,482.28
No. Sales			26	69	98
Exchanged 6s $			592,564.59	750,513.86	908,444.62
No. Sales			148	230	220

Source: Record Group 53, Records of the Bureau of the Public Debt, National Archives and Records Administration

TABLE 14: Sources of Federal Revenue during the War of 1812

Year	Customs ($ millions)	Excise ($ millions)	Other ($ millions)	Direct ($ millions)	Public Lands ($ millions)
1812	9	0	0.1	0	0.7
1813	13.2	0	0.3	0	0.8
1814	6	1.7	0.2	2.2	1.1
1815	7.3	4.7	0.3	2.2	1.3
	Customs (%)	Excise (%)	Other (%)	Direct (%)	Public Lands (%)
1812	91.83673	0	1.020408	0	7.142857
1813	92.30769	0	2.097902	0	5.594406
1814	53.57143	15.17857	1.785714	19.64286	9.821429
1815	46.20253	29.74684	1.898734	13.92405	8.227848

Source: Paul Studenski and Herman E. Krooss, *Financial History of the United States* (New York: McGraw-Hill, 1952), 54, 68, 77, 92, 100, 116, 125, 152, 162–63, 203, 215, 236, 264

TABLE 15: Payment of Principal and Interest on the U.S. National Debt, 1821–32

Year	Principal (millions $)	Interest (millions $)	Total (millions $)
1821	3.3	5.1	8.4
1822	2.7	5.2	7.9
1823	0.6	4.9	5.5
1824	11.6	5.0	16.6
1825	7.7	4.4	12.1
1826	7.7	4.0	11.7
1827	6.5	3.5	10.0
1828	9.1	3.1	12.2
1829	9.8	2.5	12.3
1830	9.4	1.9	11.3
1831	14.8	1.4	16.2
1832	17.1	0.8	17.9
Total from March 1789 to December 31, 1832	249.5	157.8	407.3

Sources: William Ouseley, *Remarks on the Statistical and Political Institutions of the United States* (Philadelphia: Carey & Lea, 1832), 222; George Watterson and N. B. Van Zandt, *Continuation of the Tabular Statistical Views of the United States* (Washington, D.C.: Way and Gideon, 1833), 176

TABLE 16: Residences of Federal Debt Holders Who Registered Their Bonds in Virginia, 1790–1834

Residence (Va. unless otherwise noted.)	Number of Debt Holders	Percent of Debt Holders
Accomack County	15	0.95
Albemarle County	22	1.39
Alexandria	24	1.52
Amelia County	9	0.57
Amherst County	10	0.63
Amsterdam, Netherlands	2	0.13
Annapolis, Md.	6	0.38
Augusta County	32	2.02
Baltimore, Md.	30	1.90
Bedford County	5	0.32
Berkeley County	11	0.70
Boston, Mass.	3	0.19
Botetourt County	7	0.44
Brandon	2	0.13
Brunswick County	6	0.38
Buckingham County	6	0.38
Camden County, S.C.	1	0.06
Campbell County	5	0.32
Caroline County	30	1.90
Charles City County	9	0.57
Charlotte County	6	0.38
Charlottesville	1	0.06
Chesterfield County	18	1.14
Culpeper County	15	0.95
Cumberland County	11	0.70
Dinwiddie County	11	0.70
Dobbs County, N.C.	1	0.06
Dumfries	13	0.82
Dunkirk	1	0.06
Elizabeth City County	5	0.32
Essex County	7	0.44
Fairfax County	11	0.70

(Continued)

Residence (Va. unless otherwise noted.)	Number of Debt Holders	Percent of Debt Holders
Falmouth	4	0.25
Fauquier County	21	1.33
Fayette County	2	0.13
Fluvanna County	1	0.06
Franklin County	3	0.19
Frederick County	11	0.70
Fredericksburg	35	2.21
Georgetown, Md.	2	0.13
Georgia (state of)	1	0.06
Glasgow, Scotland	1	0.06
Gloucester County	15	0.95
Goochland County	8	0.51
Greenbrier County	5	0.32
Greensville County	2	0.13
Halifax County	8	0.51
Hampshire County	1	0.06
Hampton County	8	0.51
Hanover County	43	2.72
Hardy County	3	0.19
Harrison County	1	0.06
Henrico County	20	1.27
Henry County	1	0.06
Isle of Wight County	12	0.76
James City County	13	0.82
Jefferson County	5	0.32
Kentucky (state of)	5	0.32
King and Queen County	21	1.33
King George County	8	0.51
King William County	18	1.14
Lancaster County	6	0.38
London, England	17	1.08
Loudon County	9	0.57
Louisa County	17	1.08
Lunenburg County	3	0.19
Manchester	26	1.64

Residence (Va. unless otherwise noted.)	Number of Debt Holders	Percent of Debt Holders
Maryland (state of)	2	0.13
Mathews County	2	0.13
Mecklenburg County	4	0.25
Middlesex	2	0.13
Monongalia County	1	0.06
Montgomery County	2	0.13
Nansemond County	3	0.19
New Jersey (state of)	1	0.06
New Kent County	20	1.27
Newport	1	0.06
New York City	28	1.77
New York State	3	0.19
Norfolk	122	7.72
Norfolk County	4	0.25
North Carolina (state of)	2	0.13
Northampton County	10	0.63
Northumberland County	2	0.13
Nottaway County	3	0.19
Ohio County	1	0.06
Orange County	9	0.57
Patrick County	1	0.06
Pennsylvania (state of)	5	0.32
Petersburg	70	4.43
Philadelphia, Pa.	37	2.34
Pittsylvania County	2	0.13
Port Royal	1	0.06
Portsmouth	5	0.32
Powhatan County	11	0.70
Prince Edward County	11	0.70
Prince George County	13	0.82
Prince William County	3	0.19
Princess Ann County	2	0.13
Providence, R.I.	1	0.06
Richmond	231	14.61
Richmond County	17	1.08

(Continued)

Residence (Va. unless otherwise noted.)	Number of Debt Holders	Percent of Debt Holders
Rockbridge County	22	1.39
Rocketts	1	0.06
Rockingham County	2	0.13
Shenandoah County	1	0.06
Shirley	1	0.06
Smithfield	2	0.13
Southampton County	13	0.82
Spottsylvania County	7	0.44
St. Petersburg	1	0.06
Stafford County	7	0.44
Staunton	3	0.19
Suffolk	1	0.06
Sullivan County, Southwest Territory	1	0.06
Surry County	12	0.76
Sussex County	2	0.13
Tappahannock	1	0.06
Virginia (state of)	74	4.68
Warwick County	5	0.32
Washington County	3	0.19
Western Territory	1	0.06
Westmoreland County	7	0.44
Wilkes County, Ga.	1	0.06
Wilkes County	1	0.06
Williamsburg	53	3.35
Wilton	1	0.06
Winchester	11	0.70
Woodford County	1	0.06
Wythe County	1	0.06
York County	7	0.44
Yorktown	14	0.89
TOTALS	1,580	100

Source: Record Group 53, Records of the Bureau of the Public Debt, National Archives and Records Administration

TABLE 17: Federal Bond Trading in South Carolina, November 1790–
January 1797

Month-Year	Amount Sold	Number of Sales	Average Sale Size
November 1790	$2,876.39	10	$287.64
December 1790	$4,667.92	4	$1,166.98
January 1791	$10,739.25	10	$1,073.93
February 1791	$15,704.86	3	$5,234.95
March 1791	$16,261.23	10	$1,626.12
April 1791	$17,260.66	29	$595.20
May 1791	$1,800.68	5	$360.14
June 1791	$1,686.01	6	$281.00
July 1791	$17,122.78	23	$744.47
August 1791	$7,759.47	21	$369.50
September 1791	$3,407.02	7	$486.72
October 1791	$26,841.11	26	$1,032.35
November 1791	$254,830.71	107	$2,381.60
December 1791	$104,626.72	75	$1,395.02
January 1792	$58,103.70	54	$1,075.99
February 1792	$113,527.63	64	$1,773.87
March 1792	$52,697.30	68	$774.96
April 1792	$98,032.16	91	$1,077.28
May 1792	$260,086.57	166	$1,566.79
June 1792	$74,815.37	65	$1,151.01
July 1792	$60,232.27	73	$825.10
August 1792	$46,229.91	54	$856.11
September 1792	$18,701.02	34	$550.03
October 1792	$44,650.38	60	$744.17
November 1792	$53,419.74	52	$1,027.30
December 1792	$11,337.71	21	$539.89
January 1793	$43,398.47	32	$1,356.20
February 1793	$40,686.19	51	$797.77
March 1793	$13,088.07	18	$727.12
April 1793	$124,353.24	63	$1,973.86
May 1793	$20,516.04	17	$1,206.83
June 1793	$6,228.97	12	$519.08
July 1793	$16,097.78	11	$1,463.43

(Continued)

Month-Year	Amount Sold	Number of Sales	Average Sale Size
August 1793	$66,272.57	36	$1,840.90
September 1793	$16,145.93	15	$1,076.40
October 1793	$85,467.64	29	$2,947.16
November 1793	$64,334.76	16	$4,020.92
December 1793	$11,047.36	18	$613.74
January 1794	$10,654.39	18	$591.91
February 1794	$34,178.08	28	$1,220.65
March 1794	$5,189.63	12	$432.47
April 1794	$17,706.84	21	$843.18
May 1794	$2,500.12	2	$1,250.06
June 1794	$4,414.35	9	$490.48
July 1794	$54,982.84	35	$1,570.94
August 1794	$7,619.83	9	$846.65
September 1794	$9,987.14	14	$713.37
October 1794	$3,029.57	10	$302.96
November 1794	$27,266.70	18	$1,514.82
December 1794	$1,526.72	4	$381.68
January 1795	$12,453.91	18	$691.88
February 1795	$27,711.80	30	$923.73
March 1795	$21,973.90	25	$878.96
April 1795	$35,455.43	39	$909.11
May 1795	$44,045.29	25	$1,761.81
June 1795	$17,679.84	7	$2,525.69
July 1795	$82,982.47	53	$1,565.71
August 1795	$78,518.71	40	$1,962.97
September 1795	$11,443.35	10	$1,144.34
October 1795	$43,156.04	26	$1,659.85
November 1795	$17,149.88	13	$1,319.22
December 1795	$12,437.45	7	$1,776.78
January 1796	$18,784.21	7	$2,683.46
February 1796	$15,331.31	19	$806.91
March 1796	$15,341.32	9	$1,704.59
April 1796	$20,574.70	20	$1,028.74
May 1796	$79,066.64	23	$3,437.68
June 1796	$15,875.23	9	$1,763.91

Month-Year	Amount Sold	Number of Sales	Average Sale Size
July 1796	$158,145.36	42	$3,765.37
August 1796	$37,559.98	22	$1,707.27
September 1796	$10,273.87	13	$790.30
October 1796	$28,426.54	12	$2,368.88
November 1796	$30,709.57	14	$2,193.54
December 1796	$14,503.65	15	$966.91
January 1797	$4,804.81	13	$369.60

Source: T719, Rolls 1 and 2, Record Group 53, Records of the Bureau of the Public Debt, National Archives and Records Administration

TABLE 18: Occupations, Locations, and Types of Federal Bondholders Registered in South Carolina

Group	Number of Accounts	Percentage of Accounts	Face Value of Bonds Purchased ($ millions)	Percentage of Bonds Purchased
Nonmerchants	253	29.54	1.033	13.09
Merchants	234	27.40	3.043	38.56
No Occupation Given	367	43.06	3.816	48.35
Occupation Totals	**854**	**100.00**	**7.892**	**100.00**
Non-Charleston U.S.	211	24.71	2.049	25.96
Charleston	375	43.91	2.991	37.90
Foreign	84	9.84	.728	9.23
No Location Listed	184	21.54	2.124	26.91
Location Totals	**854**	**100.00**	**7.892**	**100.00**
Estates	112	13.11	.349	4.42
Trusts	39	4.57	.223	2.83
Organizations	20	2.34	1.692	21.45
Partnerships	61	7.14	.957	12.12
Females	89	10.42	.208	2.64
Miscellaneous Accountholders	**321**	**37.58**	**3.429**	**43.46**

Source: T719, Rolls 1 and 2, Record Group 53, Records of the Bureau of the Public Debt, National Archives and Records Administration

TABLE 19: Financial Securities Listed in South Carolina Newspapers, 1810–45

Year	Number of Listed Securities
1810	14
1820	12
1830	15
1840	6
1845	15

Source: Richard E. Sylla, Jack W. Wilson, and Robert E. Wright, Price Quotations in Early United States Securities Markets, 1790–1860 [electronic file]. http://eh.net/databases/early-us-securities-prices

TABLE 20: Balance Sheets of 12 South Carolina Banks, January 1, 1850

Bank	ASSETS				LIABILITIES		
	Loans and discounts	Specie	Other Assets	Capital	Circulation	Deposits	Other Liabilities
Bank of Camden	$664,332	$23,445	$57,141	$400,000	$379,430	$76,490	$0
Bank of Charleston	$5,068,113	$554,039	$2,782,374	$3,160,800	$2,826,115	$536,343	$1,519,568
Bank of Georgetown	$395,543	$139,918	$5,500	$200,000	$280,407	$28,858	$3,122
Bank of Hamburg	$1,108,474	$70,695	$267,483	$403,500	$915,860	$73,534	$6,552
Bank of South Carolina	$1,243,220	$78,836	$200,709	$1,000,000	$154,092	$305,933	$23,244
Bank of the State of South Carolina	$4,635,561	$239,368	$857,910	$2,905,846	$1,169,541	$743,637	$818,586
Commercial Bank of Columbia	$1,738,570	$99,977	$214,321	$800,000	$930,475	$291,743	$743
Merchants' Bank of South Carolina at Cheraw	$748,812	$99,360	$88,519	$400,000	$426,875	$35,073	$321
Planters & Mechanics Bank of South Carolina	$1,403,184	$287,480	$517,619	$1,000,000	$528,795	$402,208	$182,205
South Western Rail Road Bank	$1,251,204	$122,367	$478,230	$869,425	$480,715	$274,369	$132,412
State Bank, South Carolina	$1,302,379	$159,583	$384,152	$1,000,000	$510,015	$299,982	$0
Union Bank of South Carolina	$1,041,745	$76,112	$287,641	$1,000,000	$139,445	$253,962	$3,255
TOTALS	$20,601,137	$1,951,180	$6,141,599	$13,139,571	$8,741,765	$3,322,132	$2,690,008

Source: Warren E. Weber, "Balance Sheets for U.S. Antebellum State Banks," Research Department, Federal Reserve Bank of Minneapolis, 2005. http://research.mpls.frb.fed.us/research/economists/wewproj.html

Note: Total assets ($28,693,916) exceed total liabilities ($27,893,476) for reasons unknown.

Table 21: New South Carolina Corporations and Their Authorized Capital, 1801–60

Year	Number of Corporations	Authorized Capital
1801	1	Unspecified
1802	1	$800,000
1803	0	
1804	0	
1805	2	$350,000+
1806	0	
1807	1	Unspecified
1808	2	Unspecified
1809	1	Unspecified
1810	5	$1,000,000+
1811	1	Unspecified
1812	1	Unspecified
1813	0	
1814	0	
1815	0	
1816	1	Unspecified
1817	1	Unspecified
1818	5	$1,700,000+
1819	2	$900,000
1820	1	$500,000
1821	2	$500,000+
1822	2	$500,000+
1823	1	Unspecified
1824	4	$230,000+
1825	4	$50,000+
1826	1	Unspecified
1827	7	$50,000+
1828	0	
1829	0	
1830	1	Unspecified
1831	1	$500,000
1832	2	$200,000
1833	5	$750,000+

Year	Number of Corporations	Authorized Capital
1834	7	$2,940,000+
1835	14	$8,810,000+
1836	13	$8,453,000+
1837	5	$230,000+
1838	5	$3,620,000+
1839	3	$50,000+
1840	1	Unspecified
1841	1	Unspecified
1842	1	Unspecified
1843	1	Not Applicable
1844	0	
1845	4	$1,550,000
1846	7	$4,750,000+
1847	8	$1,700,000+
1848	5	$795,000+
1849	7	$1,335,000+
1850	18	$1,940,000+
1851	11	$806,500+
1852	15	$8,550,000+
1853	8	$6,025,000+
1854	11	$447,100+
1855	6	$549,470+
1856	13	$3,775,000+
1857	13	$3,657,000+
1858	9	$2,360,000+
1859	9	$1,840,000+
1860	12	$3,750,000+
TOTALS	262	$75,963,070+

Source: South Carolina Statutes, Hein Collection, Williamsburgh, N.Y., 2006

Note: The plus sign (+) indicates that one or more corporations chartered that year were allowed to raise a range of equity capital rather than a specific sum. In some years, the capital is "unspecified" because many charters of joint-stock companies did not stipulate any maximum or minimum authorized capital. Capital was "not applicable" to mutuals, including most building and loans.

TABLE 22: Corporations in South Carolina by Type, 1800–60

Type	No.	Total Corps. (%)	Authorized Capitalization ($)	Total Capital (%)
Bank	24	9.16	$19,000,000	24.34
Bridge	16	6.11	$158,000	0.20
Building and Loan	16	6.11	$100,000	0.13
Canal	3	1.15	$100,000	0.13
Cemetery	3	1.15	$0	0.00
Construction	5	1.91	$25,000	0.03
Ferry	3	1.15	$60,000	0.08
Gas Lighting	5	1.91	$115,000	0.15
Hotel	3	1.15	$150,000	0.19
Ice	2	0.76	$10,000	0.01
Insurance	18	6.87	$4,700,000	6.02
Manufacturing	38	14.50	$3,260,000	4.18
Mining	7	2.67	$550,000	0.70
Plank Road	8	3.05	$160,000	0.20
Railroads	44	16.79	$40,465,000	51.85
Shipping	30	11.45	$5,556,000	7.12
Telegraph	3	1.15	$91,570	0.12
Theater	1	0.38	$0	0.00
Transportation	11	4.20	$1,630,000	2.09
Turnpike	14	5.34	$58,500	0.07
Water	3	1.15	$1,000,000	1.28
Wharf	2	0.76	$600,000	0.77
Unspecified	3	1.15	$260,000	0.33
TOTALS	262	100	$78,049,070	100

Source: South Carolina Statutes, Hein Collection, Buffalo, N.Y., 2006

TABLE 23: Estimated Sugar Crop of Louisiana, 1835–48

Year	Hogsheads of 1,000 pounds each
1835	30,000
1836	70,000
1837	65,000
1838	70,000
1839	115,000
1840	87,000
1841	91,000
1842	140,000
1843	100,000
1844	200,000
1845	187,000
1846	140,000
1847	230,000
1848	210,000

Source: Isaac Davis to William M. Meredith, Meredith Papers, November 8, 1849, 68:11, Historical Society of Pennsylvania. Davis's figures are in line with those of modern scholars like J. Carlyle Sitterson, *Sugar Country: The Cane Sugar Industry in the South, 1753–1950* (Lexington: University of Kentucky Press, 1952), Chart 2, 29.

TABLE 24: Estimated Sugar Crop of the World, 1843–47

Year	Total Pounds
1843	1,625,420,000
1844	1,929,620,000
1845	1,875,960,000
1846	1,964,280,000
1847	2,519,500,000

Source: Isaac Davis to William M. Meredith, Meredith Papers, November 8, 1849, 68:11, Historical Society of Pennsylvania

TABLE 25: Sources of U.S. Government Revenue, 1830–60 (Millions $)

Year	Tariff	Other	Bank Stock	Public Land Sales
1830	21.9	0.1	0.5	2.3
1831	24.2	0.6	0.5	3.2
1832	28.5	0.1	0.7	2.6
1833	29.0	0.3	0.6	4.0
1834	16.2	0.1	0.6	4.9
1835	19.4	0.7	0.6	14.8
1836	23.4	2.2	0.3	24.9
1837	11.2	5.6	1.4	6.8
1838	16.2	2.5	4.5	3.1
1839	23.1	1.3		7.1
1840	13.5	0.9	1.7	3.3
1841	14.5	0.3	0.7	1.4
1842	18.2	0.4		1.3
1843	7.0	0.3		0.9
1844	26.2	1.1		2.1
1845	27.5	0.3		2.1
1846	26.7	0.3		2.7
1847	23.7	0.3		2.5
1848	31.8	0.6		3.3
1849	28.3	0.3		1.7
1850	39.7	0.7		1.9
1851	49.0	1.2		2.4
1852	47.3	0.4		2.0
1853	58.9	1.2		1.7
1854	64.2	1.1		8.5
1855	53.0	0.8		11.5
1856	64.0	1.1		8.9
1857	63.9	1.3		3.8
1858	41.8	1.4		3.5
1859	49.6	2.2		1.8
1860	53.2	1.1		1.8

Source: Studenski and Krooss, 54, 68, 77, 92, 100, 116, 125, 152, 162–163, 203, 215, 236, 264

TABLE 26: Key U.S. Economic and Fiscal Indicators, 1830–50

Year	Output (Billions $)	Federal Revenue ($ Millions)	National Debt ($)	Debt/ Output (%)	Per Capita Debt ($)
1830	1.09	24.8	39,123,191.68	3.59	3.03
1831	1.16	28.5	24,322,235.18	2.10	1.83
1832	1.24	31.9	7,001,698.83	0.56	0.51
1833	1.34	33.9	4,760,082.08	0.36	0.34
1834	1.36	21.8	33,733.05	0.00	0.00
1835	1.60	35.5	37,513.05	0.00	0.00
1836	1.84	50.8	336,957.83	0.02	0.02
1837	1.80	25.0	3,308,124.07	0.18	0.21
1838	1.82	26.3	10,434,221.14	0.57	0.64
1839	1.95	31.5	3,573,343.82	0.18	0.21
1840	1.73	19.4	5,250,875.54	0.30	0.31
1841	1.76	16.9	13,594,480.73	0.77	0.77
1842	1.64	19.9	20,201,226.27	1.23	1.10
1843	1.61	8.2	32,742,922.00	2.03	1.73
1844	1.73	29.4	23,461,652.50	1.36	1.20
1845	1.89	29.9	15,925,303.01	0.84	0.79
1846	2.01	29.7	15,550,202.97	0.77	0.75
1847	2.31	26.5	38,826,534.77	1.68	1.81
1848	2.13	35.7	47,044,862.23	2.21	2.14
1849	2.25	30.3	63,061,858.69	2.80	2.79
1850	2.54	42.3	63,452,773.55	2.50	2.73

Sources: Studenski and Krooss, 54, 68, 77, 92, 100, 116, 125, 152, 162–63, 203, 215, 236, 264; Louis D. Johnston and Samuel H. Williamson, "The Annual Real and Nominal GDP for the United States, 1790–Present." Economic History Services, April 1, 2006. http://eh.net/hmit/gdp/

TABLE 27: Borrowing by U.S. States, 1820–38

Years	State Borrowing ($ Millions)
1820–25	12.791
1826–30	13.680
1831–35	41.513
1835–38	107.824

Source: Benjamin U. Ratchford, *American State Debts* (Durham, N.C.: Duke University Press, 1941), 79

TABLE 28: United States Stock Issues on Foreign Account

Country	Total $, October 2, 1848 to January 13, 1849
Belgium	3,000
Brazil	33,000
Canada	101,900
Cuba	7,000
England	2,787,550
France	515,550
Germany	801,200
Hayti	3,200
Ireland	23,000
Madeira	7,000
Portugal	7,000
Spain	62,000
Switzerland	84,300
TOTAL	4,435,700

Source: "Commercial Chronicle and Review," *Merchants' Magazine and Commercial Review* (February 1849), 192–93

FIGURES

FIGURE 1: Sums Borrowed Abroad by the U.S. National Government, 1776–94

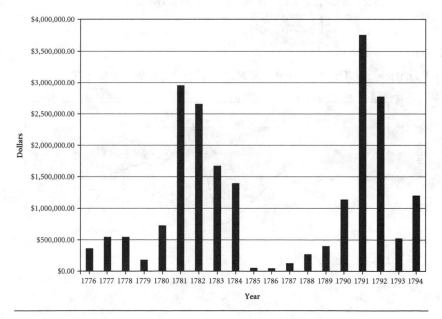

Sources: Jonathan Elliot, *The Funding System of the United States and of Great Britain* (1845); Rafael A. Bayley, *The National Loans of the United States, from July 4, 1776 to June 30, 1880* 2nd ed. (Washington, D.C.: Government Printing Office, 1882)

FIGURE 2: **Prices of U.S. Sixes in Three Markets During the Panic of 1792**

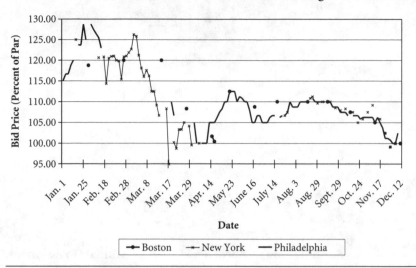

Source: Richard E. Sylla, Jack W. Wilson, and Robert E. Wright, Price Quotations in Early United States Securities Markets, 1790–1860 [Computer file]. eh.net/databases/early-us-securities-prices

FIGURE 3: **The Nominal U.S. National Debt, 1790–1836**

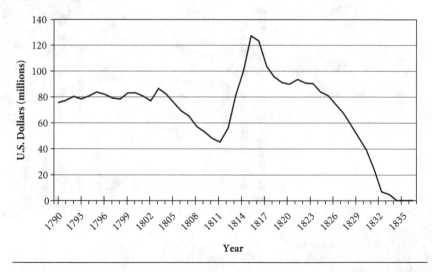

Source: Robert E. Wright, ed., *The US National Debt, 1787–1900* (London: Pickering and Chatto, 2005)

FIGURE 4: The U.S. National Debt Per Person, 1790–1836

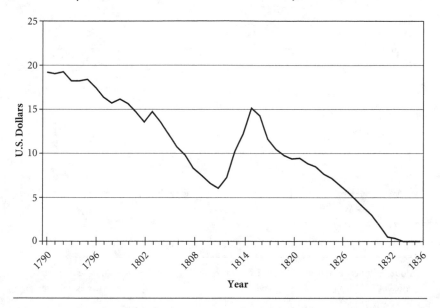

Source: Robert E. Wright, ed., *The U.S. National Debt, 1787–1900* (London: Pickering and Chatto, 2005)

FIGURE 5: The U.S. National Debt as a Percentage of Aggregate Output, 1790–1836

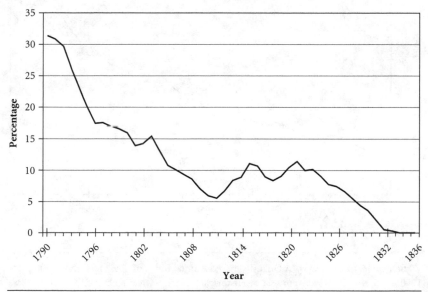

Source: Robert E. Wright, ed., *The U.S. National Debt, 1787–1900* (London: Pickering and Chatto, 2005)

FIGURE 6: U.S. Federal Revenue, 1790–1800

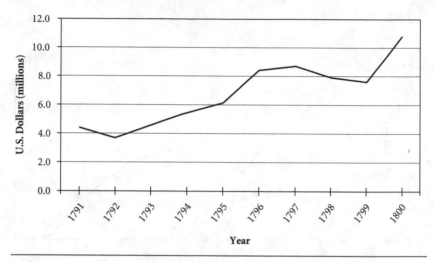

Source: Robert E. Wright, ed., *The U.S. National Debt, 1787–1900* (London: Pickering and Chatto, 2005)

FIGURE 7: Index of U.S. Industrial Production, 1790–1830

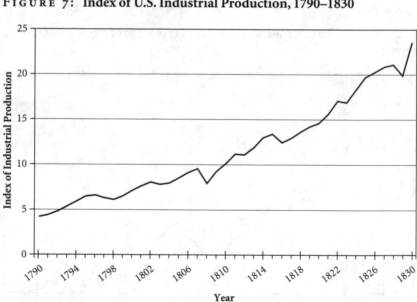

Source: Joseph H. Davis, "A Quantity-Based Annual Index of U.S. Industrial Production, 1790–1915: An Empirical Appraisal of Historical Business-Cycle Fluctuations" (Ph.D. diss., Duke University, 2002)

FIGURE 8: **Share Prices of Two South Carolina Insurance Companies, 1810–22**

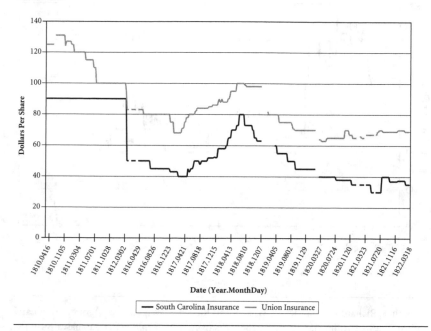

Source: Richard E. Sylla, Jack W. Wilson, and Robert E. Wright, Price Quotations in Early United States Securities Markets, 1790–1860 [electronic file]. http://eh.net/databases/early-us-securities-prices

FIGURE 9: Bank of South Carolina Stock Price, 1803–49

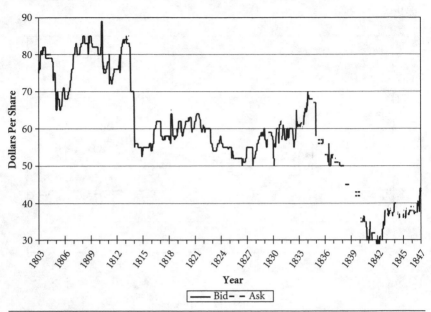

Source: Richard E. Sylla, Jack W. Wilson, and Robert E. Wright, Price Quotations in Early United States Securities Markets, 1790–1860 [electronic file]. http://eh.net/databases/early-us-securities-prices

FIGURE 10: Dividends Paid Investors in Four Charleston Banks, 1834–48

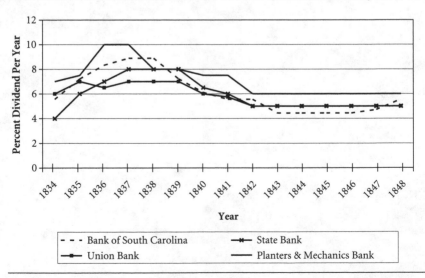

Source: Charleston (S.C.) City Council, *Census of the City of Charleston, South Carolina, for the Year 1848, Exhibiting the Condition and Prospects of the City* (Charleston, S.C., 1849), 160

NOTES

PREFACE

1. At the time of writing, autumn 2007, the comptroller general of the United States, David M. Walker, was a vocal critic of the U.S. government's fiscal policies, including its acceptance of the burgeoning national debt and the massive, and growing, off-balance-sheet obligations of health care and Social Security, among others. See the Government Accountability Office's Web site for more information on this subject: www.gao.gov/cghome/dwbiog.html.

2. I do not here delve into the nitty-gritty of the federal government's administration of the debt, which has an ugly history. For details, see Myers, "Retirement of the First Federal Debt"; Fridson, *Popular Delusions . . . And Confusion*, 147; Banner, *Anglo-American Securities Regulation*, vi.

3. Sobel, *Panic on Wall Street*, 5.

CHAPTER 1: A TWINKLE IN THE EYE: THE IMPORTANCE OF GOVERNMENT DEBT

1. All statistics in this paragraph were taken from NationMaster.com on August 12, 2006. The GDP figures are nominal, i.e., not adjusted for differences in purchasing power. Warsh, *Knowledge and the Wealth of Nations*, 247.

2. Recent studies of the causes of economic growth include Bernstein, *Birth of Plenty*; Baumol, Litan, and Schramm, *Good Capitalism, Bad Capitalism*; Bueno de Mesquita and Root, *Governing for Prosperity*; DeSoto, *Mystery of Capital*; Diamond, *Guns, Germs, and Steel*; Easterly, *Elusive Quest for Growth*; Easterly, *White Man's Burden*; Harford, *Undercover Economist*; Helpman, *Mystery of Economic Growth*; Kay, *Culture and Prosperity*; Landes, *Wealth and Poverty of Nations*; Lewis, *Power of Productivity*; McCraw, *Creating Modern Capitalism*; North, *Understanding the Process of Economic Change*; Sachs, *End of Poverty*; Vietor, *How Countries Compete*; Warsh, *Knowledge and the Wealth of Nations*; Wright, *Wealth of Nations Rediscovered*. For a biting critique of development agencies like the IMF, see Stiglitz, *Globalization and Its Discontents*. The quotation is from Warsh, *Knowledge and the Wealth of Nations*, 56.

3. The development diamond was initially formulated by George Smith and subsequently revised with help from Richard Sylla and myself. See Smith, Sylla, and Wright, "The Diamond of Sustainable Growth," 2007.

4. Koetter and Wedow, "Finance and Growth in a Bank-Based Economy"; Levine, "Financial Development and Economic Growth"; Levine, "More on Finance, More on Growth"; Levine, "Finance and Growth: Theory and Evidence"; Trew, "Finance and Growth."

5. Friedman, *Lexus and the Olive Tree*, 154; Log Raditlhokwa, "Molefhabangwe Deserves Presidential Award," *Mmegi/The Reporter* (Gaborone), August 16, 2004; Umar Bashir, "The Pull Him Down Syndrome," *This Day* (Nigeria), January 20, 2003; Franca Ogbeh, "Life As I See It: For a Better Life for Women, the 'Pull Her Down' Syndrome Should Stop—Mrs. Dayo Keshi," *Vanguard* (Nigeria), July, 18, 2004; Kofi Akosah-Sarpong, "Development and the 'Pull Him Down' Syndrome," *Expo Times*, July 7, 2004; Kufour Appiah-Danquah, "Rejoinder—Ghana Telecom—Pull Him Down Syndrome," *Home Page Ghana*, June 23, 2004.

6. Rubin, *Darwinian Politics*, 87–112.

7. Bernstein, *Birth of Plenty*.

8. J. D. Townes and Robert Bolling to Dolly Madison, July 5, 1836, Dolly Madison Papers, Virginia Historical Society (hereafter, VHS).

9. Ferguson, *Cash Nexus*, 14–16.

10. Anon. "Great Credit Is Claimed," *Connecticut Courant*, February 2, 1835.

11. Gordon, *Hamilton's Blessing*, 20; Thomas Jefferson to John Taylor, 1816, Andrew Lipscomb and Albert Bergh, eds., *The Writings of Thomas Jefferson* (Washington, D.C.: Thomas Jefferson Memorial Association, 1907), 15:23; Stabile and Cantor, *Public Debt*, 29.

12. Brown, *Redeeming the Republic*, xi, 38.

13. Walters, *Albert Gallatin*, 122.

14. Sloan, *Principle and Interest*.

15. Flaumenhaft, *Effective Republic*; Peterson, *Running on Empty*; Hormats, *Price of Liberty*; Kearny, *Sketch of American Finance*, iii–iv.

CHAPTER 2: PARENTAGE: EUROPEAN PRECEDENTS

1. Riley, *International Government Finance*, 3; Congleton, "America's (Neglected) Debt."

2. Adams, *For Good and Evil*.

3. Grellier, *History of the National Debt*, 1.

4. Grellier, *History of the National Debt*, 3, 4; Tracy, *Financial Revolution*, 8–9, 23–24.

5. Tracy, *Financial Revolution*, 108–222.

6. Adams, *Public Debts*, 9.

7. Riley, *International Government Finance*; Homer and Sylla, *History of Interest Rates*, 124–28.

8. Fridson, *Popular Delusions . . . And Confusion*, 124–214; Dickson, *Financial Revolution*, 5.

9. Homer and Sylla, *History of Interest Rates*, 146; Grellier, *History of the National Debt*, 10, 13–14; Bagehot, *Lombard Street*, 46; Anon., *The National Debt, As It Stood at Michaelmas 1730, Stated and Explained* (London: J. Peele, 1731), 6.

10. Grellier, *History of the National Debt*, 13, 15; Homer and Sylla, *History of Interest Rates*, 145–48; Stasavage, "Credible Commitment"; Stasavage, "Partisan Politics"; Bagehot, *Lombard Street*, 46.

11. Bagehot, *Lombard Street*, 46; Murray, *Inquiry*, 5; Grellier, *History of the National Debt*, 17–18, 23, 27–28, 37, 43–49, 365; Anon., *The Present State of the National Debt …* (London: T. Berwick, 1740), 5; A Country Gentleman, *Some Observations*, 6.

12. Grellier, *History of the National Debt*, 30, 50–53, 60–74.

13. Stasavage, "Credible Commitment"; Stasavage, "Partisan Politics"; Grellier, *History of the National Debt*, 77–82; Dickson, *Financial Revolution*, 24, 471; Sussman and Yafeh, "Institutional Reforms"; Wright, *Hamilton Unbound*, 26–34.

14. Grellier, *History of the National Debt*, 85–117; Fridson, *Popular Delusions … And Confusion*, 70; A Financier, *National Debt*, 143–44.

15. Anon., *Party Spirit in Time of Publick Danger …* (London: T. Waller, 1756), 18–19; Neal, *Rise of Financial Capitalism*, 141–65; Grellier, *History of the National Debt*, 143; Bagehot, *Lombard Street*, 29, 65.

16. Dickson, *Financial Revolution*, 5–6, 12, 407–14; A Financier, *National Debt*, 117–19, 122.

17. Anon., *Party Spirit in Time of Publick Danger …* (London: T. Waller, 1756), 13–14.

18. A Country Gentleman, *Some Observations*, 6–7; Anon., *The National Debt, As It Stood at Michaelmas 1730, Stated and Explained* (London: J. Peele, 1731), 7–8; Anon., *Reasons for the More Speedy Lessening the National Debt …* (London: J. Roberts, 1737), 23; Anon., *The Present State of the National Debt …* (London: T. Berwick, 1740), 18; Anon., *An Impartial Review of the Opposition …* (London: T. Cooper, 1742), 25; A Financier, *National Debt*, 135; *Party Spirit in Time of Publick Danger …* (London: T. Waller, 1756), 15–16.

19. Anon., *Party Spirit in Time of Publick Danger …* (London: T. Waller, 1756), 17–18; Dickson, *Financial Revolution*, 16.

20. Anon., *An Impartial Review of the Opposition …* (London: T. Cooper, 1742), 22; A Financier, *National Debt*, 6, 133; Anon., "Short View of the Present State of the Stocks or Public Funds in this Kingdom," *Gazetteer and New Daily Advertiser*, August 24, 1770.

21. A Financier, *National Debt*, 38, 44; Banning, *Sacred Fire of Liberty*, 36, 40–41; Murray, *Inquiry*, i, 21.

22. Dickson, *Financial Revolution*, 15–35; A Financier, *National Debt*, 3; Anon., *Rational Results Upon the Present State of the National Debt …* (London: J. White and T. Saint, 1768), 5.

23. Bird, *Proposal for Paying*, 11; Homer and Sylla, *History of Interest Rates*, 151; Anon., *Reflections on the National Debt …* (n.p., 1731), 14; Anon., *A Copy of a Letter Wrote to a Member of Parliament …* (London: W. Owen, 1750), 8.

24. Dickson, *Financial Revolution*, 24–32; Anon., *Reasons for the More Speedy Lessening the National Debt …* (London: J. Roberts, 1737), 12, 22; Anon., *A Proposal for Redressing the Grievances of the Nation …* (London: M. Cooper, 1745), 6-7; A Country Gentleman, *Some Observations*, 7; Murray, *Inquiry*, 12; Bird, *Proposal for Paying*, 5.

25. Price, *Appeal to the Public*, 44–46; Bird, *Proposal for Paying*, 6; Adams, *Public Debts*, 251–52; Anon., *Reasons for the More Speedy Lessening the National Debt …* (London: J. Roberts, 1737), 13–14; Anon., *A Proposal for Redressing the Grievances of the Nation …* (London: M. Cooper, 1745), 6; Anon., *An Attempt to Pay Off the National Debt …* (London: S. Bladon, 1767), 15–16; A Country Gentleman, *Some Observations*, 9; Murray, *Inquiry*, 2, 17–18.

26. Murray, *Inquiry*, 13; Fridson, *Popular Delusions ... And Confusion*, 172.

27. Fridson, *Popular Delusions ... And Confusion*, 162–63.

28. Ibid., 165, 192–97, 203.

29. Dickson, *Financial Revolution*, 32–34; Fridson, *Popular Delusions ... And Confusion*, 10.

30. Grellier, *History of the National Debt*, 118; Fridson, *Popular Delusions ... And Confusion*, 6–7, 75, 77–78; Neal, *Rise of Financial Capitalism*; Kindleberger, *Manias*.

31. Grellier, *History of the National Debt*, 119–25.

32. Grellier, *History of the National Debt*, 128–30, 132; Fridson, *Popular Delusions ... And Confusion*, 109–11.

33. Fridson, *Popular Delusions ... And Confusion*, 112; Bagehot, *Lombard Street*, 15, 88; Grellier, *History of the National Debt*, 118.

34. Murray, *Inquiry*, 9–14; Anon., "Short View of the Present State of the Stocks or Public Funds in this Kingdom," *Gazetteer and New Daily Advertiser*, August 24, 1770; Dickson, *Financial Revolution*, 34.

35. A Country Gentleman, *Some Observations*, 25, 39; Murray, *Inquiry*, 4; Anon., *An Attempt to Pay Off the National Debt ...* (London: S. Bladon, 1767), 25; Grellier, *History of the National Debt*, 314–16.

36. A Country Gentleman, *Some Observations*, 8; Cleeve, *Scheme for Preventing*, 10–14; Box, *Plans for Reducing*, 4; Grellier, *History of the National Debt*, 322. Smith; *Wealth of Nations*, Book 5, Chapter II, Part 2, "Of Taxes."

37. Murray, *Inquiry*, 24; Anon., *Reasons for the More Speedy Lessening the National Debt ...* (London: J. Roberts, 1737), 24; Anon., *A Proposal for Redressing the Grievances of the Nation ...* (London: M. Cooper, 1745), 7; Anon., *Considerations on the Propriety of Imposing Taxes in the British Colonies ...* (New York: John Holt, 1765); Bird, *Proposal for Paying*, 5–6.

38. Anon., *Reflections on the National Debt ...* (n.p., 1731), 12; Anon., *The Present State of the National Debt ...* (London: T. Berwick, 1740), 18–20; A Financier, *National Debt*, 38; Box, *Plans for Reducing*, 7; Anon., *A Copy of a Letter Wrote to a Member of Parliament ...* (London: W. Owen, 1750), 9–10; Murray, *Inquiry*, 16.

39. Anon., *A Method Is Hereby Humbly Proposed, That Will Enable the Government ...* (n.p., 1715); Anon., *Proposals Humbly Offered to the Parliament of Great Britain, For Easing the Nation of the Old Navy Debt ...* (London: R. Robinson, 1716); D—n S—t, *An Infallible Scheme to Pay the Publick Debt ...* (London: H. Whittbridge, 1732); Anon., *Machiavel's Letter to the Lords and Commons ...* (London: S. Garnsey, 1749), 21, 28–32; A Financier, *National Debt*, 158–61; Anon., *Reasons for the More Speedy Lessening the National Debt ...* (London: J. Roberts, 1737); Anon., *A Copy of a Letter Wrote to a Member of Parliament ...* (London: W. Owen, 1750), 19; M. D—Z, *The Public Welfare ...* (London: T. Hookham, 1778); Anon., *A Proposal for Redressing the Grievances of the Nation ...* (London: M. Cooper, 1745), 4; Murray, *Inquiry*, 25; Anon., *Rational Results Upon the Present State of the National Debt ...* (London: J. White and T. Saint, 1768), 8; Anon., *A Proposal for Redressing the Grievances of the Nation ...* (London: M. Cooper, 1745), 3; Anon., *An Attempt to Pay Off the National Debt ...* (London: S. Bladon, 1767), 9; Anon., *An Easy Method of Discharging the National Debt ...* (London: Henry Kent, 1763), 11; Price, *Appeal to the Public*, 2–7.

40. A Country Gentleman, *Some Observations*, 30; Cleeve, *Scheme for Preventing*, 8; Box, *Plans for Reducing*; Bird, *Proposal for Paying*, 8–10.

41. Cleeve, *Scheme for Preventing*, 7; Anon., *An Attempt to Pay Off the National Debt* … (London: S. Bladon, 1767).

42. Anon., *An Easy Method of Discharging the National Debt* … (London: Henry Kent, 1763).

43. Anon., "Short View of the Present State of the Stocks or Public Funds in this Kingdom," *Gazetteer and New Daily Advertiser*, August 24, 1770; Anon., *Considerations on the Propriety of Imposing Taxes in the British Colonies* … (New York: John Holt, 1765), 18, 23, 41; Grellier, *History of the National Debt*, 269–70.

44. Warsh, *Knowledge and the Wealth of Nations*, 29–30; Earl, *State of the National Debt*, 3; "A Catechism Relative to the English National Debt," in Jared Sparks, ed., *The Works of Benjamin Franklin* (Boston: Hilliard, Gray, and Co., 1837), 120–21.

45. Elkins and McKitrick, *Age of Federalism*, 112; Smith, *Wealth of Nations*, Book V, Chapter III, "Of Public Debts."

46. Anon., *The Present State of the National Debt* … (London: T. Berwick, 1740), 14–15; A Country Gentleman, *Some Observations*, 24; Price, *Appeal to the Public*, 10–12, 37; Grellier, *History of the National Debt*, 160–74, 284–85.

47. Dickson, *Financial Revolution*, 10.

48. Smith, *Adam Smith*, xiii; Fleischacker, "Adam Smith's Reception"; Anon., "Rivington's Literary Medley," *New York Independent Journal*, August 31, 1785; Anon., "Just Published, at Rice's Book-Store," *Pennsylvania Packet*, November 19, 1785; Anon., "Just Imported in the Last Vessels from London," *Middlesex Gazette*, July 10, 1786; Anon., "James Rivington Has Imported by the Ship Montgomery," *Pennsylvania Packet*, June 8, 1787; Hugh Gaine, *Hugh Gaine's Catalogue of Books Lately Imported from England, Ireland, and Scotland* (New York: Hugh Gaine, 1792), 6; Anon., "History of the English East-India Company," *Columbian Herald*, November 11, 1785; Anon., "Extract from Mr. Adam Smith's Enquiry," *Independent Gazetteer*, July 29, 1786; Anon., "Taxes Upon Consumable Commodities," *New-Haven Gazette*, November 2, 9, 1786; Anon., "On the Advantages of the Division of Labour," *New-Haven Gazette*, February 7, 1788; Anon., *Catalogue of the Books &c. Belonging to the Library Company of Baltimore* (Baltimore: John Hayes, 1797), 13; Anon., *Fourth Supplement to the Catalogue of Books Belonging to the Library Company of Philadelphia* (Philadelphia: Zachariah Poulson, 1798), 20; Anon., "Anecdotes of the Late Dr. Adam Smith," *Daily Advertiser*, October 6, 1790; George Logan, *Five Letters Addressed to the Yeomanry of the United States* (Philadelphia: Eleazar Oswald, 1792), 26; William Hunter, *An Oration Delivered in the Baptist Meeting House in Newport* (Newport: Henry Barber, 1795), 21–22; James McHenry, *A Petition and Brief Exposition of the Leading Principles of a Bank* (Baltimore: Edwards & Allen, 1795), 30; Thomas Cooper, *Political Arithmetic* (Philadelphia: 1798), 13; John Wood, *Mentor, or the American Teacher's Assistant* (New York: John Buel, 1795), 357; Anon., "It Is With Singular Pleasure," *The Federal Gazette, and Philadelphia Evening Post*, March 15, 1790; Bourne, "Alexander Hamilton"; McNamara, *Political Economy and Statesmanship*, 94, 114–24, 140, 171 n. 98.

Chapter 3: Conception: Financing Revolution

1. Ferguson, *Empire*.

2. Morgan, *Birth of the Republic*, 78; Sumner, *The Financier*, 1:306; Webster, *Plea for the Poor Soldiers*, 10; Anon., *Additions to Common Sense Addressed to the Inhabitants of America* (Philadelphia, 1776), 26.

3. Harlow, "Aspects of Revolutionary Finance," 48; Bird, *Proposal for Paying*, 6; A Friend in Time of Need, "Remarks on the Currency," *Pennsylvania Packet*, March 14, 1780.

4. Brock, *Currency of the American Colonies*; Ferguson, *Power of the Purse*; Michener and Wright, "State 'Currencies'"; Michener and Wright, "Development"; Perkins, *American Public Finance*; Wright, *Origins of Commercial Banking*.

5. Thomas Hutchinson, *The History of the Colony of Massachusetts-Bay* (Boston: Thomas and John Fleet, 1764), 402–3; Grellier, *History of the National Debt*, 33, 42. Nairne, *Letter from South Carolina*, 14–15.

6. Nairne, *Letter from South Carolina*, 34.

7. Brooks, *Financial History of Georgia*, 3.

8. Brock, *Currency of the American Colonies*, 272; Ferguson, *Power of the Purse*, 10.

9. Ratchford, *American State Debts*, 25; Wright, *Origins of Commercial Banking*, 24; Adams, *Public Debts*, 7.

10. Harlow, "Aspects of Revolutionary Finance"; Warsh, *Knowledge and the Wealth of Nations*, 43; Bagehot, *Lombard Street*, 46; Paine, *Common Sense*, 23; Stabile and Cantor, *Public Debt*, 12.

11. Morse, *American Geography*, 118; Higgins, "Financial History," 14–15; Cochran, *New York in the Confederation*, 44–45, 49; Molovinsky, "Tax Collection Problems," 255.

12. Becker, *Revolution*, 115–17; Studenski and Krooss, *Financial History*, 30; Merrill and Wilentz, *Key of Liberty*, 105–6; Cochran, *New York in the Confederation*, 44; Brooks, *Financial History of Georgia*, 4; Robinson, "Continental Treasury Administration," 87.

13. Higgins, "Financial History," 51.

14. Harlow, "Aspects of Revolutionary Finance," 48; Higgins, "Financial History," 17, 102–3, 186–220, 221–42; Morgan, *Birth of the Republic*, 125; Cochran, *New York in the Confederation*, 57–65.

15. Ferguson, *Power of the Purse*, 48, 67; Stabile and Cantor, *Public Debt*, 12; Studenski and Krooss, *Financial History*, 27 n5, 28; Higgins, "Financial History," 17–18; Robinson, "Continental Treasury Administration," 10–15, 120.

16. Morgan, *Birth of the Republic*, 106; Robinson, "Continental Treasury Administration," 97; Hazard, *Observations*, 5; Morse, *American Geography*, 118; Paine, *Decline and Fall*, 3; Harlow, "Aspects of Revolutionary Finance," 52–53; Higgins, "Financial History," 38.

17. Robinson, "Continental Treasury Administration," 24–25; Wright, *First Wall Street*, 131–46; Wright and Wolfe, "Michael Hillegas," 662–81; Stabile and Cantor, *Public Debt*, 13; Robinson, "Continental Treasury Administration," 48, 55, 63, 121–55.

18. Harlow, "Aspects of Revolutionary Finance," 58–59; Ferguson, *Power of the Purse*, 32; Hazard, *Observations*, 18; Morse, *American Geography*, 118; Callendar, *Sedgwick & Co.*, 16.

19. Brooks, *Financial History of Georgia*, 4–5; Robinson, "Continental Treasury Administration," 74, 75; Tiedemann, *Reluctant Revolutionaries*, 237; Anon., "Boston, October 9,"

Continental Journal, October 9, 1777; Anon., "By the Boston Post, Boston, Dec. 19," *The Massachusetts Spy*, December 31, 1778; Anon., "Continental Currency, in Answer to Hard Money," *Independent Chronicle and the Universal Advertiser*, April 15, 1779; Anon., "From the Pennsylvania Packet," *American Journal and General Advertiser*, April 22, 1779; Anon., "Boston, March 27," *Independent Ledger*, March 27, 1780; Anon., "From the New-York Gazette Advertisement," *The Massachusetts Spy*, December 6, 1781; Harlow, "Aspects of Revolutionary Finance," 56; Ratchford, *American State Debts*, 35–36; Anon., "Trenton, January 12," *New Jersey Gazette*, January 12, 1780; Anon., "Trenton, January 19," *New Jersey Gazette*, January 19, 1780; Kirshner, *Currency and Coercion*.

20. Harlow, "Aspects of Revolutionary Finance," 51; Higgins, "Financial History," 20–23, 47–49; Robinson, "Continental Treasury Administration," 73–75; Ratchford, *American State Debts*, 39, 40–41.

21. Stabile and Cantor, *Public Debt*, 13; Ferguson, *Power of the Purse*, 35–37; Studenski and Krooss, *Financial History*, 29; Robinson, "Continental Treasury Administration," 79–81, 163–69; Perkins, *American Public Finance*, 305–9; George Weedon, *Valley Forge Orderly Book of General George Weedon* (New York: Dodd, Mead and Co., 1902), 186; R. A. Brock, ed., *Proceedings of the Virginia Historical Society* (Richmond, 1892), 11:283; James Mercer to John Francis Mercer, June 26, 1783, Mercer Family Papers, VHS.

22. Table 1, in the Appendix, shows the number and par value of the bonds purchased in some of the Continental loan offices during the years 1776 through 1781, inclusive. Studenski and Krooss, *Financial History*, 28–29; Robinson, "Continental Treasury Administration," 147, 156, 327–28, 342; Perkins, *American Public Finance*, 97, 99; "Mr. Jefferson's Statement of Revolutionary Paper Emissions from June 23, 1775, to November 29, 1779," in Elliot, *Funding System*, 1:6–9; Grubb, "Continental Dollar"; Bullock, *Finances*.

23. Table 2 summarizes the experiences of the Continental loan office in each state for which data is available. M1008, Roll 1, M1006, Roll 1, M1005, Roll 2, Record Group 53, National Archives and Records Administration (hereafter NARA). Wright, *First Wall Street*; Webster, *Plea for the Poor Soldiers*, 10. Ferguson (*Power of the Purse*, 40, 53–55) argued that after 1778 most loan office certificates were not outright purchased but rather accepted by government creditors in lieu of Continental money. That distinction seems to me unimportant. The purchasers clearly preferred the bonds to the money and simply saved themselves the trouble and risk of receiving bills of credit. As Ferguson himself notes, the bonds, even when they did not pay specie in interest, held their value much better than bills of credit did.

24. Adams, *Public Debts*, 262; Robinson, "Continental Treasury Administration," 102–3; Swanson and Trout, "Alexander Hamilton's Hidden Sinking Fund," 108–109; Harlow, "Aspects of Revolutionary Finance," 61; Robinson, "Continental Treasury Administration," 103; Michener, "Backing Theories," 686.

25. Ferguson, *Power of the Purse*, 28, 70–105; Robinson, "Continental Treasury Administration," 99.

26. Ferguson, *Power of the Purse*, 45; Robinson, "Continental Treasury Administration," 105–8; Theodorick Bland, "Considerations on American Finance," 1779, "In Congress, 26th August 1779, Resolved," Bland Family Papers, VHS; A Friend in Time of Need, "Remarks on the Currency," *Pennsylvania Packet*, March 14, 1780.

27. Robinson, "Continental Treasury Administration," 109–10; Harlow, "Aspects of Revolutionary Finance," 55; Ford, *Present State*, 7; Ferguson, *Power of the Purse*, 110.

28. Theodorick Bland, "Notes," c. 1779, Bland Family Papers, VHS; Ford, *Present State*, 13; David Cobb to Henry Jackson, June 5, 1780, VHS.

29. Robinson, "Continental Treasury Administration," 115–20; Ferguson, *Power of the Purse*, 66; "Mr. Jefferson's Statement of Revolutionary Paper Emissions from June 23, 1775, to November 29, 1779," in Elliot, *Funding System*, 1:6–9.

30. Banning, *Sacred Fire of Liberty*, 16; Wright, "Banking and Politics," 684–96; Mintz, *Seeds of Empire*, 22, 138, 183.

31. Harlow, "Aspects of Revolutionary Finance," 47; Robinson, "Continental Treasury Administration," 15; Konigsberg, "Edward Carrington," 82, 92; John B. Dabney, "Sketches and Reminiscencies [*sic*] of the Dabney and Morris Families," 1850:21, VHS; Ford, *Present State*, 16.

32. Ferguson, *Power of the Purse*, 59–60, 64, 67; Robinson, "Continental Treasury Administration," 264–65; Banning, *Sacred Fire of Liberty*, 15; Konigsberg, "Edward Carrington," 112; Ford, *Present State*, 16; Higgins, "Financial History," 61–76; Sumner, *The Financier*, 2:22–23.

33. Nathaniel Irish to Samuel Hodgdon, November 3, 1780, VHS; Robinson, "Continental Treasury Administration," 114; Timothy Pickering to Col. Hughes, April 17, 1781, Timothy Pickering Revolutionary War Papers, 1778–1785, New York State Archives (hereafter NYSA); Ferguson, *Power of the Purse*, 48–52; Virginia, Commissioner of Specific Tax, 1781–1782, VHS; Sumner, *The Financier*, 1:258; Robinson, "Continental Treasury Administration," 258–63; Flannagan, "Trying Times," 214; Dabney, "Colonel Charles Dabney," 189; Robinson, "Continental Treasury Administration," 268; Banning, *Sacred Fire of Liberty*, 17.

34. Robinson, "Continental Treasury Administration," 200–14.

35. Ibid., 216–45.

36. Harry M. Ward, "Francis Hopkinson," *American National Biography Online* (hereafter *ANBO*); Robinson, "Continental Treasury Administration," 246–63.

37. Wright and Cowen, *Financial Founding Fathers*, 115–40; Wright, *Origins of Commercial Banking*; Ferguson, *Power of the Purse*, 109–24; Robinson, "Continental Treasury Administration," 269–71.

38. Sumner, *The Financier*, 1:261–70; Robinson, "Continental Treasury Administration," 269–81. A "Bank Company of Charlestown" operated in South Carolina by 1777 but little is known about its operations or purposes other than that it lent some bills of credit to the state government. As noted above, another "bank" also formed in Philadelphia but it was more a charitable organization than a financial institution. Higgins, "Financial History," 34; Banning, *Sacred Fire of Liberty*, 22.

39. Sumner, *The Financier*, 1:277, 2:33–35; Konigsberg, "Edward Carrington," 142–43; Ferguson, *Power of the Purse*, 136–38; Rappaport, *Stability and Social Change*; John Delafield Letterbook, 1783–1785, New York Public Library (hereafter NYPL); Wright, *Wealth of Nations Rediscovered*, 26–42, 47–50; Wright, *First Wall Street*, 36–38.

40. Morse, *American Geography*, 116; Sumner, *The Financier*, 1:302–9, 2:142, 278; Konigsberg, "Edward Carrington," 114; "Return of the Private Horse Teams Raised in the State of New Jersey for the Campaign, 1781," "Return of Public Property in the Waggon [*sic*] Department Commencing July 26th, 1781," Timothy Pickering Revolutionary War Papers, 1778–1785, NYSA.

41. Ferguson, *Power of the Purse*, 126; Higgins, "Financial History," 35–37; Buel, *In Irons*.

42. See Figure 1 in the Appendix. Bayley, *National Loans*, 5–12; Ferguson, *Power of the Purse*, 40–44, 126, 128; Kearny, *Sketch of American Finance*, 3–6; Riley, *International Government Finance*, 185–87; Perkins, *American Public Finance*, 110; Congleton, "America's (Neglected) Debt," 33.

43. Warsh, *Knowledge and the Wealth of Nations*, 38; Earl, *State of the National Debt*, 10; Grellier, *History of the National Debt*, 300, 308n., 311; Robert Lucas Nash, *Fenn's Compendium of the English and Foreign Funds*, 15th ed. (London: Effingham Wilson & Co., 1893) in Sylla and Wright, *History of Corporate Finance*, 2:10; Smith, *Wealth of Nations*, Book V, Chapter III, "Of Public Debts"; Bird, *Proposal for Paying*, 7; Riley, *International Government Finance*, 124–25.

44. Ferguson, *Papers of Robert Morris*; Morse, *American Geography*, 118; Sumner, *The Financier*, 1:151–55, 271–72, 305, 2:2–5, 274; Konigsberg, "Edward Carrington," 142; Ferguson, *Power of the Purse*, 129–30, 138–39; John Delafield Letterbook, 1783–1785, NYPL.

45. Timothy Pickering, "Conditions of the Sale of the Public Buildings at Mrs. Hasbroucks," October 18, 1783, Timothy Pickering Revolutionary War Papers, 1778–1785, NYSA; Ferguson, *Papers of Robert Morris*, 4:353; Ferguson, *Power of the Purse*, 129.

46. Sumner, *The Financier*, 2:135–48; Ratchford, *American State Debts*, 32; Perkins, *American Public Finance*, 85; Banning, *Sacred Fire of Liberty*, 29.

47. Sumner, *The Financier*, 1:283; "Kite, v," *Oxford English Dictionary Online*; Banning, *Sacred Fire of Liberty*, 28–29, 32–33, 40; Ferguson, *Power of the Purse*, 160.

48. Ferguson, *Power of the Purse*, 155–63; McDonald, *Alexander Hamilton*, 45–48.

49. Timothy Pickering to David Wolfe, May 13, 1783, Timothy Pickering Revolutionary War Papers, 1778–1785, NYSA; Edling, *Revolution in Favor of Government*, 153–55; Ferguson, *Power of the Purse*, 128–29, 139, 146–76; Bernard Cohen, *Compendium of Finance* (London, 1822) in Wright, *U.S. National Debt*, 2:232; Samuel Osgood and Walter Livingston to Nathaniel Appleton, August 29, 1785, Livingston Family Papers, NYPL; Hanson, *Remarks*, 29–35; Bowen, *Miracle at Philadelphia*, 11.

50. Borden, *Antifederalist Papers*, viii; Ferguson, *Colossus*; Mandelbaum, *Case for Goliath*; Mandelbaum, *Ideas That Conquered the World*; Nye, *Paradox of American Power*; Bowen, *Miracle at Philadelphia*, 5; Brutus, "Federalist Power Will Ultimately Subvert State Authority," 1788, in Borden, *Antifederalist Papers*, 42–45.

51. Einhorn, *American Taxation*; Brown, *Redeeming the Republic*, 11–31, 41, 48; William Lee to Nathaniel Burwell, April 12, 1789, Lee Family Papers, VHS.

52. Brown, *Redeeming the Republic*, 32, 122.

53. Citizen of New York, *Commercial Conduct*, 5–7; Morse, *American Geography*, 116, 119; Sumner, *The Financier*, 2:33–34, 158, 178–92; Goddard, *General History*, 48–50; Tench Coxe, *Thoughts Concerning the Bank of North America* (n.p.: December 6, 1786); Tench Coxe, *Further Thoughts Concerning the Bank* (n.p.: December 13, 1786); Merrill and Wilentz, *Key of Liberty*, 104–5, 114, 164.

54. Merrill and Wilentz, *Key of Liberty*, 104; Flannagan, "Trying Times," 215; Citizen of New York, *Commercial Conduct*, 11; Webster, *Plea for the Poor Soldiers*, 34; Bayley, *National Loans*, 31; Anon., *A Mournful Lamentation on the Untimely Death of Paper Money* (Boston: Samuel Adams, 1781); *Boston Gazette*, January 18, 1762; Thomas Jefferson to Thomas Cooper, January 16, 1814, Thomas Jefferson to James Madison, February 16, 1814, *Papers of Thomas Jefferson*;

William Newell, *Games and Songs of American Children* (New York: Harper & Brothers, 1883), 135–36; Perkins, *American Public Finance*, 137–72; Kaminski, *Paper Politics*; Hanson, *Remarks*, 16–43; Robert Gamble to James Breckinridge, June 5, 1809, Breckinridge Papers, VHS.

55. Merrill and Wilentz, *Key of Liberty*, 165; Brown, *Redeeming the Republic*, 3, 11–21, 33, 62, 108, 120, 122.

56. Cochran, *New York in the Confederation*, 160; Konigsberg, "Edward Carrington," 261–63; Flannagan, "Trying Times," 53, 186–244.

57. Flannagan, "Trying Times," 75–185.

58. Ibid., 245–98.

59. Flannagan, "Trying Times," 56, 298–355; Morse, *American Geography*, 121.

60. Downey, *Planting a Capitalist South*, 18, 35.

61. Higgins, "Financial History," 104–5, 114–15, 125–50, 243–61.

62. Cochran, *New York in the Confederation*, 151; Morgan, *Birth of the Republic*, 113; Rawleigh Colston to George Washington, November 19, 1786, Mercer Family Papers, VHS; Farmer, "Mr. Goddard, Please to Insert," *Maryland Journal*, July 7, 1786; Publicola, "Extract of a Letter from a Gentleman of Harford County," *Maryland Journal*, July 14, 1786; A Citizen, "For the Maryland Journal, &c.," *Maryland Journal*, July 21, 1786; An Old Soldier, "To the People of Maryland," *Maryland Journal*, July 11, 1786; A Marylander, "Mr. Goddard," *Maryland Journal*, June 27, 1786; Citizen of New York, *Commercial Conduct*, 4; Memoirs of Stephen Allen, 40, NYHS; Doerflinger, *Vigorous Spirit*, 261–80.

63. Bouton, "Road Closed"; Becker, *Revolution*, 219–25; Edling, *Revolution in Favor of Government*, 156–58.

CHAPTER 4: GESTATION: THE CONSTITUTION AND THE NATIONAL DEBT

1. Hislop, *Albany*, 209–10; Weise, *History of the City of Albany*, 393–94; Worth, *Random Recollections*, 20–21.

2. Memoirs of Stephen Allen, 39, NYHS; Weise, *History of the City of Albany*, 402; Worth, *Random Recollections*, 23.

3. Weise, *History of the City of Albany*, 412–13; Anon., "Extract of a Letter from Poughkeepsie, July 8," which was printed in several newspapers, including the *New York Packet*, July 11, 1788; Anon., "Extract of a Letter from Albany, July 6," *New York Journal*, July 14, 1788; Anon., "By a gentleman from Albany," *Vermont Gazete*, July 14, 1788; Anon., "Bloody News, Litchfield, July 7," which was also widely reprinted, as in the *Newport Mercury*, July 14, 1788; Anon., "Further Particulars of the Affray at Albany," *New York Packet*, July 15, 1788; Hammond, *History of Political Parties*, 1:20n.

4. Cornell, *Other Founders*; Anon., "A Federalist," *Boston Gazette*, November 26, 1787, in Borden, *Antifederalist Papers*, 1–2; Centinel, "The Hobgoblins of Anarchy and Dissensions Among the States," *Independent Gazetteer*, January 16, 1788, in Borden, *Antifederalist Papers*, 14–16.

5. Citizen of New York, *Commercial Conduct*, 15.

6. Chernow, *Alexander Hamilton*, 252; Worth, *Random Recollections*, 45–68.

7. Morgan, *Birth of the Republic*, 79.

8. Freeman, *Affairs of Honor*; Cornell, *Other Founders*, 110; Anon., "By a gentleman from Albany," *Vermont Gazette*, July 14, 1788.

9. Philanthropos, "Adoption of the Constitution Will Lead to Civil War," *Virginia Journal*, December 6, 1787, in Borden, *Antifederalist Papers*, 16–18.

10. Bowen, *Miracle at Philadelphia*, xi, 4, 37, 88; Beard, *Economic Interpretation*, 324–25; Brown, *Charles Beard*; McGuire, *To Form a More Perfect Union*, 4–8; Flannagan, "Trying Times," 352; Hoftstadter, *Progressive Historians*, 233; Wright, *Hamilton Unbound*.

11. Christopher Collier, "Roger Sherman," *ANBO*; Koch, *Notes of Debates*, 160; Brown, *Redeeming the Republic*, 184; Edling, *Revolution in Favor of Government*, 163–74.

12. Koch, *Notes of Debates*, 471; "Nemine contracidente," *Oxford English Dictionary Online*.

13. Account Book for New York State Loan of 1792, Albany County, Account Book of New York State Loan of 1808, NYSA; Morse, *American Geography*, 120–21; Michener and Wright, "State 'Currencies,'" 682 n.1; Ronald J. Lettieri, "Nathaniel Gorham," *ANBO*; Bowen, *Miracle at Philadelphia*, 118; McGuire, *To Form a More Perfect Union*, 72–74; Christopher Collier, "Roger Sherman," *ANBO*.

14. Koch, *Notes of Debates*, 470–71.

15. Bowen, *Miracle at Philadelphia*, 35; Koch, *Notes of Debates*, 292, 479–80.

16. Koch, *Notes of Debates*, 495; Stephen E. Siry, "Rufus King," *ANBO*.

17. Koch, *Notes of Debates*, 479.

18. Ibid., 511–12, 519, 528–29.

19. Koch, *Notes of Debates*, 529–30; John Kaminski, "New York: The Reluctant Pillar," in Schechter, *Reluctant Pillar*, 54.

20. Bowen, *Miracle at Philadelphia*, 34, 44, 86–87, 187.

21. Bowen, *Miracle at Philadelphia*, 3, 31; Chernow, *Alexander Hamilton*, 258.

22. Stahr, *John Jay*.

23. Fisher Ames to George Richards Minot, May 3, 1789, in Allen, *Fisher Ames*, 569; Bowen, *Miracle at Philadelphia*, 13.

24. McKay, *South Street*, 7–9, 125–26; Van Zandt, *Chronicles of the Hudson*, 127.

25. Van Zandt, *Chronicles of the Hudson*, 128.

26. Ibid., 131–47.

27. Chernow, *Alexander Hamilton*, 246; Donald M. Roper, "James Kent," *ANBO*.

28. Brookhiser, *Gentleman Revolutionary*.

29. Wright and Cowen, *Financial Founding Fathers*, 65–86.

30. Wright, Jacobson, and Smith, *Knowledge for Generations*.

31. Borden, *Antifederalist Papers*, viii.

32. Nicolson, *God's Secretaries*.

33. Starr, *Creation of the Media*, 48–77, 124.

34. Chernow, *Alexander Hamilton*, 251.

35. Centinel, "The Hobgoblins of Anarchy and Dissensions Among the States," *Independent Gazetteer*, January 16, 1788, in Borden, *Antifederalist Papers*, 14–16.

36. Brown, *Redeeming the Republic*, 4; Chernow, *Alexander Hamilton*, 252; Anon., "A Farmer," *Maryland Gazette*, March 7, 1788, in Borden, *Antifederalist Papers*, 6–8.

37. Lutz, "Relative Influence of European Writers," 189–97; Edwards, "'Righteousness Alone.'"

38. An Old Whig, "What Does History Teach?" *Massachusetts Gazette*, November 27, 1787, in Borden, *Antifederalist Papers*, 45–47; Brutus, "Federalist Power Will Ultimately Subvert State Authority," 1788, in Borden, *Antifederalist Papers*, 42–45; Anon., "A Farmer," *Maryland Gazette*, March 7, 1788, in Borden, *Antifederalist Papers*, 6–8.

39. Brown, *Redeeming the Republic*, 208–14.

40. Brent Tarter, "George Mason," *ANBO*.

41. Ethan S. Rafuse, "George Clinton," *ANBO*.

42. Patrick Henry, "Foreign Wars, Civil Wars, and Indian Wars—Three Bugbears," June 5, 7, 9, 1788, in Borden, *Antifederalist Papers*, 8–12.

43. Philanthropos, "Adoption of the Constitution Will Lead to Civil War," *Virginia Journal*, December 6, 1787, in Borden, *Antifederalist Papers*, 16–18; Alfred, "Europeans Admire and Federalists Decry the Present System," *New York Journal*, December 25, 1787, in Borden, *Antifederalist Papers*, 40–41.

44. Federal Republican, "The Power Vested in Congress . . . Will Always Enable Them to Stifle the First Struggles of Freedom," *Norfolk and Portsmouth Register*, March 5, 1788, in Borden, *Antifederalist Papers*, 18–20; Montezuma, "A Consolidated Government Is A Tyranny," *Independent Gazetter*, October 17, 1787, in Borden, *Antifederalist Papers*, 20–23; A Farmer, "The Expense of the New Government," *Freeman's Oracle*, January 11, 1788, in Borden, *Antifederalist Papers*, 33–34.

45. Anon., "A Federalist," *Boston Gazette*, November 26, 1787, in Borden, *Antifederalist Papers*, 1–2.

46. William Grayson, Speech of June 11, 1788, in Borden, *Antifederalist Papers*, 2–6.

47. Anon., "A Farmer," *Maryland Gazette*, March 7, 1788, in Borden, *Antifederalist Papers*, 6–8.

48. Patrick Henry, "Foreign Wars, Civil Wars, and Indian Wars—Three Bugbears," June 5, 7, 9, 1788, in Borden, *Antifederalist Papers*, 8–12; Agrippa, "Unrestricted Power Over Commerce Should Not Be Given the National Government," *Massachusetts Gazette*, various dates, November 23, 1787– February 5, 1788, in Borden, *Antifederalist Papers*, 27–30.

49. Montezuma, "A Consolidated Government Is A Tyranny," *Independent Gazetter*, October 17, 1787, in Borden, *Antifederalist Papers*, 20–23.

50. Brutus, "Federalist Power Will Ultimately Subvert State Authority," 1788, in Borden, *Antifederalist Papers*, 42–45.

51. Wright, *U.S. National Debt*; Brutus, "Certain Powers Necessary for the Common Defense, Can and Should Be Limited," 1788, in Borden, *Antifederalist Papers*, 57–62; Peterson, *Running on Empty*.

52. Arthur Campbell to Robert Gamble, July 28, 1789, Stuart Family Papers, VHS.

53. Anon., "A Farmer," *Maryland Gazette*, March 7, 1788, in Borden, *Antifederalist Papers*, 6–8.

54. Borden, *Antifederalist Papers*, viii; An Observer, "Scotland and England—A Case in Point," *Boston American Herald*, December 3, 1787, in Borden, *Antifederalist Papers*, 12–14.

55. Cato, "Extent of Territory Under Consolidated Government Too Large to Preserve Liberty or Protect Property," *New York Journal*, October 25, 1787, in Borden, *Antifederalist Papers*, 36–39; Prasad, *Politics of Free Markets*, 41.

56. Chernow, *Alexander Hamilton*, 259.

57. Ibid., 260.

58. Anon., "A Federalist," *Boston Gazette*, November 26, 1787, in Borden, *Antifederalist Papers*, 1–2.

59. Patrick Henry, "Foreign Wars, Civil Wars, and Indian Wars—Three Bugbears," June 5, 7, 9, 1788, in Borden, *Antifederalist Papers*, 8–12.

60. *New York Packet*, February 5, 1788; Anon., "A Federalist," *Boston Gazette*, November 26, 1787, in Borden, *Antifederalist Papers*, 1–2.

61. Berkin, *Brilliant Solution*, 187.

62. Ibid., 185–88.

63. Ibid., 188.

64. John Kaminski, "New York: The Reluctant Pillar," in Schechter, *Reluctant Pillar*, 60–65.

65. Ibid., 65–117; De Pauw, *Eleventh Pillar*.

66. De Pauw, *Eleventh Pillar*, 151; R. A. Brock, ed., *Proceedings of the Virginia Historical Society* (Richmond, 1892), 11:327.

67. De Pauw, *Eleventh Pillar*, 190.

68. Ibid., 195.

69. Ibid., 199–200.

70. Hislop, *Albany*, 215–16; Weise, *History of the City of Albany*, 397–401.

71. Bowen, *Miracle at Philadelphia*, 13.

72. De Pauw, *Eleventh Pillar*, 201.

73. Brown, *Redeeming the Republic*, 215–16.

74. Morris, *Witnesses at the Creation*, 149.

75. Edling, *Revolution in Favor of Government*, 161–62; Hazard, *Observations*, 27; Alexander, *Selling the Convention*, 30.

76. Alexander, *Selling the Convention*, 53, 102; Edling, *Revolution in Favor of Government*, 161.

77. Patrick Henry, "Foreign Wars, Civil Wars, and Indian Wars—Three Bugbears," June 5, 7, 9, 1788, in Borden, *Antifederalist Papers*, 8–12; Brutus, "Certain Powers Necessary for the Common Defense, Can and Should Be Limited," *New York Journal*, January 3, 10, 1788 in Borden, *Antifederalist Papers*, 57–62; Alexander, *Selling the Convention*, 30.

78. Ford, *Essays on the Constitution*, 60–61, 73–74, 77, 95, 97.

79. Brutus Junior, "Some Reactions to Federalist Arguments," *New York Journal*, November 8, 1787, in Borden, *Antifederalist Papers*, 101–3; Alexander, *Selling the Convention*, 134.

80. Anon., "Cincinnatus," *New York Journal*, November 29, December 6, 1787, in Borden, *Antifederalist Papers*, 30–33.

81. Brown, *Redeeming the Republic*, 235, 239; Konigsberg, "Edward Carrington," 397–98.

82. Hislop, *Albany*, 228.

83. Weise, *History of the City of Albany*, 402, 409–12; Hislop, *Albany*, 243–44; Worth, *Random Recollections*, 20; Brown, *Redeeming the Republic*, 235.

84. Downey, *Planting a Capitalist South*, 18.

85. Winterbotham, *Historical, Geographical, Commercial, and Philosophical View*, 3:295–96.

86. Ibid., 3:281.

CHAPTER 5: BIRTH: ALEXANDER HAMILTON'S GRAND PLAN

1. Anon., *Machiavel's Letter to the Lords and Commons* ... (London: S. Garnsey, 1749), 20; Grellier, *History of the National Debt*, 339–42; Gordon, *Hamilton's Blessing*, 1; Paine, *Decline and Fall*, 1, 33; Elkins and McKitrick, *Age of Federalism*, 120.

2. Pelatiah Webster gives a tighter range, from 2 to 2 shillings 6 pence on the pound, which is to say from 10 to 12.5 percent of par. Webster, *Plea for the Poor Soldiers*, 6. Elsewhere, though, he admits that "a few instances may be produced of sales at higher and lower prices" but 2/6 was most common, at least for final settlements. Webster, *Seventh Essay*, 4. Alexander Hanson notes that speculators mostly bought and sold from other speculators by 1787. Hanson, *Remarks*, 27. See also Bernard Cohen, *Compendium of Finance* (London, 1822) in Wright, *U.S. National Debt*, 2:232. Webster describes the markets as "*dull and low*" (italics his) and corroborating evidence abounds. Webster, *Plea for the Poor Soldiers*, 16.

3. Matthew McConnell, *An Essay on the Domestic Debts of the United States* (1787) in Wright, *U.S. National Debt*, 1:17–114; John Delafield to Alexander Robertson, February 1, 1784, John Delafield Letterbooks, 1783–1785, NYPL; Robert E. Wright, "John Delafield," *ANBO*; An Old Soldier, "To the People of Maryland," *Maryland Journal*, July 11, 1786.

4. Anon., "Miscellany ... The Speculator," *Boston Argus*, April 3, 1792; Ferguson, *Power of the Purse*, 251–86; Wright, *Wealth of Nations Rediscovered*, 62–67.

5. Elkins and McKitrick, *Age of Federalism*, 31–75; Samuel Osgood and Arthur Lee to Benjamin Walker, September 8, 1789, VHS.

6. Kenneth R. Bowling, "William Maclay," *ANBO*.

7. Elkins and McKitrick, *Age of Federalism*, 55.

8. Chernow, *Alexander Hamilton*, 81, 86, 245, 286–88; McDonald, *Alexander Hamilton*, 128.

9. McDonald, *Alexander Hamilton*, 128, 140; First Congress, Sess. I, Ch. 2, 1789, 24–27; Webster, *Plea for the Poor Soldiers*, 26; Elkins and McKitrick, *Age of Federalism*, 66–67.

10. First Congress, Sess. I, Ch. 5, 1789, 27–49; U.S. Treasury Department, Customs Bureau, Virginia, Bermuda Hundred and City Point, VHS.

11. First Congress, Sess. I, Ch. 12, 1789, 65–67; McDonald, *Alexander Hamilton*, 132–33; Bayley, *National Loans*, 28–30.

12. McDonald, *Alexander Hamilton*, 139–42; Elkins and McKitrick, *Age of Federalism*, 114–15; White, *Federalists*.

13. McDonald, *Alexander Hamilton*, 144–45, 171; Cochran, *New York in the Confederation*, 152–54; Samuel Wood affidavit, October 14, 1783, Timothy Pickering Revolutionary War Papers, 1778–1785, NYSA; Samuel Osgood and Walter Livingston to Nathaniel Appleton, August 29, 1785, Livingston Family Papers, NYPL; Elliot, *Funding System*, 1:23–66.

14. See Table 3 for details of U.S. government foreign loans to 1794. Kearny, *Sketch of American Finance*, 9–10.

15. Allen, *Fisher Ames*, 726, 736.

16. Perkins, *American Public Finance*, 241; Swanson and Trout, "Alexander Hamilton."

17. Allen, *Fisher Ames*, 787–800.

18. Allen, *Fisher Ames*, 727–28; John Beale Bordley, *National Credit and Character* (Philadelphia, 1790), in Wright, *U.S. National Debt*, 1:141–48; William Neilson to John Chaloner, February 17, 1790, Clements Library as cited in www.gwu.edu/~ffcp/exhibit/p13/p13_3.html.

19. Elliot, *Funding System*, 1:25; Ferguson, *Power of the Purse*, 257; Merrill and Wilentz, *Key of Liberty*, 99; Ratchford, *American State Debts*, 54; Webster, *Seventh Essay*, 12; McDonald, *Alexander Hamilton*, 173.

20. Banning, *Sacred Fire of Liberty*, 312; Chernow, *Alexander Hamilton*, 303; Ferguson, *Power of the Purse*, 272–86; Stabile and Cantor, *Public Debt*, 19; Elkins and McKitrick, *Age of Federalism*, 144; Banner, *Anglo-American Securities Regulation*, 122–60; Webster, *Seventh Essay*, 24.

21. Anon., "Worcester, March 8," *Columbian Centinel*, March 14, 1792; Webster, *Seventh Essay*, 16; Banner, *Anglo-American Securities Regulation*, 134; Konigsberg, "Edward Carrington," 437; A Friend to Justice, "Facts," *Salem Gazette*, April 10, 1792; Webster, *Plea for the Poor Soldiers*, 9.

22. Merrill and Wilentz, *Key of Liberty*, 101; Ferguson, *Power of the Purse*, 298–301; Thomas Jefferson to Duncan Rose, December 13, 1781, Haxall Family Papers, VHS; Farmer, "Mr. Goddard, Please to Insert," *Maryland Journal*, July 7, 1786; James Wilson and Thomas McKean, *Commentaries on the Constitution of the United States of America* (London: J. Debrett, 1792), 37; Farmer, "Mr. Goddard, Please to Insert," *Maryland Journal*, July 7, 1786; John Delafield to Deaves and Baker, May 29, 1784, John Delafield Letterbook, 1783–1785, NYPL; John H. Remsen to Henry Remsen, January 3, 1791, Henry Remsen Papers, NYPL; Speculator, "To the Editor of the General Advertiser," *General Advertiser*, March 23, 1792.

23. Webster, *Plea for the Poor Soldiers*, 8; Webster, *Seventh Essay*; Konigsberg, "Edward Carrington," 437.

24. Webster, *Seventh Essay*, 10; Higgins, "Financial History," 95; Perkins, *American Public Finance*, 222–30; An Old Soldier, "To the People of Maryland," *Maryland Journal*, July 11, 1786; William Lee to Nathaniel Burwell, April 12, 1789, Lee Family Papers, VHS; Ferguson, *Power of the Purse*, 285–86; Anon., "From a Correspondent," *New York Diary or Loudon's Register*, March 19, 1792.

25. Callendar, *Sedgwick & Co.*, 10; Beard, "Some Economic Origins"; Chernow, *Alexander Hamilton*, 303–4; Banning, *Sacred Fire of Liberty*, 322.

26. Bates, "Northern Speculators"; Adams, *Public Debts*, 48; Robert Gamble to Thomas Massie, October 31, 1808, Massie Family Papers, VHS.

27. Merrill and Wilentz, *Key of Liberty*, 102–9, 147; Hanson, *Remarks*, 27–29.

28. Ferguson, *Power of the Purse*, 302–4; McDonald, *Alexander Hamilton*, 172–77.

29. Ellis, *Founding Brothers*, 53–60; Elkins and McKitrick, *Age of Federalism*, 136–61; Chernow, *Alexander Hamilton*, 305; Banning, *Sacred Fire of Liberty*, 313.

30. Banning, *Sacred Fire of Liberty*, 294–95; Elkins and McKitrick, *Age of Federalism*, 114; Allen, *Fisher Ames*, 729.

31. Chernow, *Alexander Hamilton*, 305–6; Allen, *Fisher Ames*, 729; McDonald, *Alexander Hamilton*, 178.

32. Allen, *Fisher Ames*, 737–836; McNamara, *Political Economy and Statesmanship*, 114–24, 140, 171 n. 98; Elliot, *Funding System*, 1:25–26.

33. McDonald, *Alexander Hamilton*, 181; Robert Livingston, *Considerations on the Nature of a Funded Debt* (New York, 1790), in Wright, *U.S. National Debt*, 1:147–61; Arbuckle, *Pennsylvania Speculator*, 61–67; Ratchford, *American State Debts*, 56.

34. Ellis, *Founding Brothers*, 48–80; Allen, *Fisher Ames*, 736–37; McDonald, *Alexander Hamilton*, 181–87; Chernow, *Alexander Hamilton*, 326–31; Elkins and McKitrick, *Age of Federalism*, 146–61.

35. Elliot, *Funding System*, 1:83–90; First Congress, Sess. II, Ch. 34, 1790, 138–44; James and Sylla, "Changing Nature of American Public Debt," 255–56.

36. McDonald, *Alexander Hamilton*, 191.

37. Ferguson, *Power of the Purse*, 302; Allen, *Fisher Ames*, 728; Pickering Note, number 742, issued February 8, 1781, Timothy Pickering Revolutionary War Papers, 1778–1785, NYSA; Ratchford, *American State Debts*, 61–78; Sylla, Legler, and Wallis, "Banks and State Public Finance," 392; Studenski and Krooss, *Financial History*, 56–59.

38. First Congress, Sess. II, Ch. 47, 1790, 186–87.

39. McDonald, *Alexander Hamilton*, 195–97; Blodget, *Thoughts*, 16–17; Columbus, *Cautionary Hints to Congress Respecting the Sale of the Western Lands Belonging to the United States* 2nd ed. (Philadelphia: Mathew Carey, 1796), 5–6.

40. McDonald, *Alexander Hamilton*, 192–95; Elliot, *Funding System*, 1:91–95; First Congress, Sess. III, Ch. 10, 1791, 191–96.

41. Second Congress, Sess. I, Ch. 16, 1792, 246–51; Second Congress, Sess. II, Ch. 5, 1793, 300–301; Wright, *First Wall Street*, 54–65; Perkins, *American Public Finance*, 247; Bradford, *History of the Federal Government*, 125.

42. McDonald, *Alexander Hamilton*, 198–210; Banning, *Sacred Fire of Liberty*, 310–11, 326; Killenbeck, *M'Culloch v. Maryland*, 9–30.

43. Banner, *Anglo-American Securities Regulation*, 141; Cowen, *Origins and Economic Impact*; Elliot, *Funding System*, 1: 219–20, 440, 515; Perkins, *American Public Finance*, 235–65; William Constable to [?] Copper, April 15, 1794, Wettereau Papers, Columbia University Library; Kearny, *Sketch of American Finance*, 46–47; Goddard, *General History*, 97.

44. First Congress, Sess. 3, Chap. 15, 199–214; Elliot, *Funding System*, 1:347; McNamara, *Political Economy and Statesmanship*, 118–20; Brownlee, *Federal Taxation*, 17–18.

45. McDonald, *Alexander Hamilton*, 231–36, 241, 246, 249; Davis, *Essays*.

46. Henry Knox to Edward Carrington, July 24, 1792, Edward Carrington Papers, VHS; Grellier, *History of the National Debt*, 366; Riley, *International Government Finance*, 187–94.

47. William Findley, *A Review of the Revenue System* (Philadelphia, 1794), in Wright, *U.S. National Debt*, 1:163–296.

48. Callendar, *Sedgwick & Co.*, 30.

49. Elliot, *Funding System*, 1:382.

50. John H. Remsen to Henry Remsen, July 20, 1791, Henry Remsen Papers, NYPL; Gordon, *Hamilton's Blessing*, 39–41; Winterbotham, *Historical, Geographical, Commercial, and Philosophical View*, 3:285.

51. Except where otherwise noted, this section is based on Swanson, *Origins*, as well as discussions with financial historian and Hamilton expert Richard Sylla. Anon., *A Definition of Parties*, 7; Cornell, *Other Founders*, 177.

52. Bruchey, "Alexander Hamilton"; Perkins, *American Public Finance*, 235–36; McDonald, *Alexander Hamilton*, 195.

53. Albert Gallatin, *Views of the Public Debt, Receipts and Expenditures of the United States* (Philadelphia, 1801), in Wright, *U.S. National Debt*, 1:317–95; Walters, *Albert Gallatin*, 40–41.

54. Elliot, *Funding System*, 1:149–56, 1:345, 348–49.

55. Elliot, *Funding System*, 1:360–61, 389; Anon., *A Plan for the Repayment of the National Debt, By Means of a National Bank* (New York, 1785) in Wright, *U.S. National Debt*, 1:1–15;

Adams, *Public Debts*, 252–54, 261–65; Swanson and Trout, "Alexander Hamilton's Hidden Sinking Fund," 108–16; *A Correct Table Shewing the Net Amount of Funded 6 Per Cent. Stock* (Boston, 1798) in Wright, *U.S. National Debt*, 1:303–15; Fourth Congress, Sess. I, Ch. 16, 1796, 458–59.

56. Wright and Cowen, *Financial Founding Fathers*; Davis, *Essays*; Banner, *Anglo-American Securities Regulation*, 144; Anon., "Extract of a Letter from New York, dated March 20, 1792," *American Mercury*, April 9, 1792; Anon., "A Correspondent Observes," *Argus*, April 6, 1792; Citizen of New York, *Commercial Conduct*, 12; Webster, *Plea for the Poor Soldiers*.

57. Figure 2 shows the prices of U.S. 6 percent bonds in three markets during the Panic. For details of one broker's trading activity before, during, and after the Panic, see Tables 4 and 5 in the Appendix. Anon., "Is Anything More Absurd," *Gazette of the United States*, April 21, 1792; Bagehot, *Lombard Street*, 28; Cowen, Sylla, and Wright, "The U.S. Panic of 1792"; Cowen, "The First Bank of the United States"; Riley, *International Government Finance*, 187–94; Elliot, *Funding System*, 1:171, 173, 217–18; A Stockholder in the Bank, "Observations on the Late Failures," *Federal Gazette*, May 8, 1792; Anon., "Extract of a Letter from One of the Directors of the Bank ... Dated April 29," Boston *Independent Chronicle*, May 10, 1792.

58. Sobel, *Panic on Wall Street*, 28; Anon., "Stock Marine List," *Federal Gazette*, March 29, 1792; Anon., "Stock Marine List," *New York Gazette*, April 2, 1792.

59. Anon., *An Inquiry into the Causes of the Present Derangement of Public Credit in Great Britain* (London: G. G. J. and J. Robinson, 1793), 1–4; Anon., *Reflections on the Causes Which Have Produced the Present Distress in Commercial Credit ...* (London: J. Sewell, 1793), 1; Travers Twiss, *View of the Progress of Political Economy in Europe* (London: Longman, Brown, Green, and Longmans, 1847), 256–58; Evans, *History of the Commercial Crisis*, 12–13; Bagehot, *Lombard Street*, 25, 31, 97–99.

60. A Republican, "To the South Carolina Federalist," *Carolina Gazette*, September 18, 1800.

CHAPTER 6: YOUTH AND MATURITY: THE PUBLIC DEBT GROWS UP, THEN SLIMS DOWN

1. Adams, *Public Debts*, 44–48; Robert Livingston, *Considerations on the Nature of a Funded Debt* (New York, 1790), in Wright, *U.S. National Debt*, 1:147–61.

2. Just how liquid the markets were is shown in Table 6, which represents only a fraction of total trading in the first national debt. Unfortunately, what fraction is unknown, but I suspect about a half because the register books of two important markets, Boston and New York, were not examined. Elliot, *Funding System*, 1:351, 357, 366; Banner, *Anglo-American Securities Regulation*, 194–96; Evans, *History of the Commercial Crisis*, 34; John H. Remsen to Henry Remsen, June 30, 1794, Henry Remsen Papers, NYPL.

3. Banner, *Anglo-American Securities Regulation*, 142–43; Arbuckle, *Pennsylvania Speculator*, 67–68.

4. Table 7.

5. John H. Remsen to Henry Remsen, August 7, 1794, Henry Remsen Papers, NYPL.

6. Tables 8 and 9 contain the details. Ferguson, *Power of the Purse*, 285. My sample included $4,998,606.52; $2,248,481.21; and $3,210,493.99 par value worth of Sixes, Deferred

Sixes, and Threes, respectively. On December 31, 1794, the outstanding par value of those three types of bonds were, again respectively, $29,345,596.45; $14,523,365.45; and $19,538,086.21. Assuming that my sample is representative, my 3,607 different accountholders should be multiplied by 6, which provides the estimate given in the text. Elliot, *Funding System*, 1:391–92. The percentage is 21,500 divided by 4,555,946, the U.S. population in 1795 given by Blodget, *Thoughts*, 41. The one out of 212 is the reciprocal.

    7. Table 10.

    8. Tables 11 and 12. Blodget, *Economica*, 199.

    9. Ferguson, *Cash Nexus*, 198; Blodget, *Thoughts*, 17–18, 41; Anon., "Price of American Stocks At Philadelphia, April 12, At London, Jan. 30," *Herald of the United States*, April 21, 1792; Anon., "The American Stocks," *London Times*, March 13, 1795; Anon., "American Stock," *London Times*, March 3, 1797; Callendar, *Sedgwick & Co.*, 9; Henry Remsen to Daniel Dulany, May 12, 1815, Henry Remsen Papers, NYPL.

    10. Grellier, *History of the National Debt*, 202, 406–8, 420; Anon., "American Stock," *London Times*, March 3, 1797; Rufus King to Alexander Hamilton, March 8, 1797, in Syrett and Cooke, *Papers of Alexander Hamilton*, 20:533; Paine, *Decline and Fall*, 2.

    11. Figures 3, 4, and 5 show the course of the first national debt in nominal, per capita, and GDP terms, respectively.

    12. Adams, *Public Debts*, 4.

    13. Blodget, *Thoughts*, 9–15; Blodget, *Economica*, 187; Callendar, *Sedgwick & Co.*, 6, 25; Walters, *Albert Gallatin*, 92; Elliot, *Funding System*, 1:220.

    14. In 1796, in order to pay off its bank debt, the Treasury tried to sell $5 million worth of 6 percent bonds (the Six Per Cent. Stock of 1796) but could dispose of only $80,000, and at a 12.5 percent discount at that, because market interest rates were in the neighborhood of 9 percent. Rather than continue the bank loan, the government sold some of its stock in the Bank of the United States at a premium of 25 percent. In 1798, the government issued $711,700 worth of 6 percent bonds (Navy Sixes or Navy Six Per Cent. Stock) in partial payment for new naval ships. That was a great deal, for the government that is, because later that same year it had to issue 8 percent bonds (Eight Per Cent. Stock of 1798), at which rate all $5 million worth of the bonds, which were redeemable at the government's pleasure anytime after December 31, 1808, were quickly subscribed. In 1800, another $1.565 million worth of Eights were issued via the Bank of the United States, at an average premium of over 5.5 percent. Investors were again quite eager to obtain that 8 percent coupon. Bayley, *National Loans*, 35–40, 42–45; Kearny, *Sketch of American Finance*, 47–48, 51–52; Lane, "'For a Positive Profit'"; Kearny, *Sketch of American Finance*, 51–52; Thomas Willing to Mary Byrd, May 30, 1800, Byrd Family Papers, VHS; Callendar, *Sedgwick & Co.*, 6.

    15. See Figure 6 for details. Chew, "Certain Victims"; Blodget, *Thoughts*, 25; Alberts, *Golden Voyage*, 318–19.

    16. Brownlee, *Federal Taxation*, 18; Kearny, *Sketch of American Finance*, 51, 57, 74; Gordon, *Hamilton's Blessing*, 43; Studenski and Krooss, *Financial History*, 67.

    17. John Stratton to John Cropper, John Cropper Papers, VHS; Wright, *Hamilton Unbound*, 127–52; Gordon, *Hamilton's Blessing*, 43; Walters, *Albert Gallatin*, 120, 124–26, 230.

    18. Gallatin, *Report*, 30; Bayley, *National Loans*, 45–46.

19. Harrison G. Otis, *Eulogy on Gen. Alexander Hamilton, Pronounced at the Request of the Citizens of Boston, July 26, 1804* (Boston: Manning & Loring, 1840), 5, 7, 11–12.

20. The official title of the law was actually "An Act Making Provision for the Redemption of the Whole of the Public Debt of the United States," Seventh Congress, Sess. I, Ch. 32, (1802), 167–70; Hume, "Review of Jefferson's Administration," *Massachusetts Spy*, October 3, 1804; Bernard Cohen, *Compendium of Finance* (London, 1822) in Wright, *U.S. National Debt*, 2:256; Kearny, *Sketch of American Finance*, 56–61.

21. Walters, *Albert Gallatin*, 90, 122, 145–47.

22. Gallatin, *Report*, 25–28, 53–54; Elliot, *Funding System*, 1:458, 468, 471, 472–74; Kearny, *Sketch of American Finance*, 45–46; Bayley, *National Loans*, 40–41; Studenski and Krooss, *Financial History*, 70–71.

23. Kearny, *Sketch of American Finance*, 62–64, 143; Adams, *Public Debts*, 225–26; Stabile and Cantor, *Public Debt*, 36; Studenski and Krooss, *Financial History*, 95; Elliot, *Funding System*, 2:822–23; Anon., "Abstract of the Annual Report of the Secretary of the Treasury," *Connecticut Courant*, January 18, 1825.

24. Table 13 presents the details. Elliot, *Funding System*, 1:490, 492–96; Adams, *Public Debts*, 167; Bayley, *National Loans*, 46–49; Bernard Cohen, *Compendium of Finance* (London, 1822) in Wright, *U.S. National Debt*, 2:246; Kearny, *Sketch of American Finance*, 64–67.

25. Gordon, *Hamilton's Blessing*, 44, 49; Robert Gamble to Thomas Massie, December 21, 1807, Massie Family Papers, VHS; Bayley, *National Loans*, 47–48.

26. Hare, *Brief View*, iii, 48, 75; Walters, *Albert Gallatin*, 237–50.

27. Murat, *Moral and Political Sketch*, 328.

28. Table 14 provides details on the federal tax haul during the war. Brownlee, *Federal Taxation*, 21; Adams, *Public Debts*, 119, 124–25; Dewey, *Early Financial History*, 138–39; Perkins, *American Public Finance*, 324; Studenski and Krooss, *Financial History*, 77; Kearny, *Sketch of American Finance*, 68–69; Robert Gamble to James Breckinridge, January, 1815, Breckinridge Papers, VHS.

29. Adams, *Public Debts*, 116–26; Memoirs of Stephen Allen, 57, NYHS; John Eppes to Albert Gallatin, June 18, 1811, VHS; Bernard Cohen, *Compendium of Finance* (London, 1822) in Wright, *U.S. National Debt*, 2:252; Timberlake, *Monetary Policy*, 15; Dewey, *Early Financial History*, 136; Studenski and Krooss, *Financial History*, 79; Bayley, *National Loans*, 48–49; Warren E. Weber, Balance sheets for U.S. Antebellum State Banks, Research Department, Federal Reserve Bank of Minneapolis. http://research.mpls.frb.fed.us/research/economists/wewproj.html; Elliot, *Funding System*, 1:549–51.

30. Elliot, *Funding System*, 1:385–90, 547; Perkins, *American Public Finance*, 325–26, 334–35; Sylla, Wilson, and Wright, "Integration," 626; Kearny, *Sketch of American Finance*, 82–83, 97.

31. Adams, "Beginning of Investment Banking," 102; Bayley, *National Loans*, 48; Kearny, *Sketch of American Finance*, 78–79; Elliot, *Funding System*, 1:539–45.

32. Adams, *Public Debts*, 118; Adams, "Beginning of Investment Banking," 100, 102; Perkins, *American Public Finance*, 332. But see Elliot, *Funding System*, 1:548, which shows that in 1812 Boston-area investors lagged only those of New York and Philadelphia in terms of total subscriptions to government loans. Davis Dewey has it right, I think, when he notes that New England's resistance was obvious only beginning in 1813, when the "states east of New York" contributed less than half a million dollars to the loan of $16 million. Dewey,

Early Financial History, 133. Kearny lists only 10 cities, having missed Portsmouth: "Salem, Boston, Providence, Albany, New York, Philadelphia, Baltimore, Washington, Richmond, and Charleston." Kearny, *Sketch of American Finance*, 84; Elliot, *Funding System*, 1:560; Gordon, *Hamilton's Blessing*, 50–52; Adams, "Beginning of Investment Banking," 99–116; Kearny, *Sketch of American Finance*, 86, 91; Bayley, *National Loans*, 50–51.

33. Perkins, *American Public Finance*, 333–34; Memoirs of Stephen Allen, NYHS, 58; Bayley, *National Loans*, 52–56; Kearny, *Sketch of American Finance*, 94–96.

34. Kearny, *Sketch of American Finance*, 99–101, 111–17; Perkins, *American Public Finance*, 335–36; Elliot, *Funding System*, 1:588–89, 602, 663; Timberlake, *Monetary Policy*, 17–18; Robert Gamble to James Breckinridge, June 2, 1815, Breckinridge Papers, VHS; Bayley, *National Loans*, 56–60; Henry Remsen to John P. Van Ness, June 16, 1815, Van Ness—Philip Papers, Box 2, NYHS.

35. Schur, "Second Bank," 119 n7; Killenbeck, *M'Culloch v. Maryland*, 55; Elliot, *Funding System*, 1:602–3, 688–89, 2:699; Kearny, *Sketch of American Finance*, 106–8; Adams, *Public Debts*, 123; Perkins, *American Public Finance*, 337; Dewey, *Early Financial History*, 137.

36. Bayley, *National Loans*, 60; John Preston to James Breckinridge, January 20, 1817, Breckinridge Papers, VHS; Kearny, *Sketch of American Finance*, 135.

37. Allen, *Fisher Ames*, 733; Perkins, *American Public Finance*, 324–48; Elliot, *Funding System*, 1:614, 2:702–11; Bayley, *National Loans*, 58; Bradford, *History of the Federal Government*, 230, 253 n, 263, 350; Dewey, *Early Financial History*, 141; Studenski and Krooss, *Financial History*, 93; Bernard Cohen, *Compendium of Finance* (London, 1822) in Wright, *U.S. National Debt*, 2:258; Anon., "Great Credit Is Claimed," *Connecticut Courant*, February 2, 1835; Kearny, *Sketch of American Finance*, 121–29; Hodgson, *Letters from North America*, 1:271; Timberlake, *Monetary Policy*, 23–26.

38. In 1822, the government tried to take advantage of low market interest rates by exchanging Fives for Sixes and Sevens due to become redeemable in 1825 and 1826. The inducement for investors was that the principal of the new bonds would not become redeemable until various dates in the 1830s. Investors didn't bite; only $56,704.77 was exchanged. Bradford, *History of the Federal Government*, 263; Kearny, *Sketch of American Finance*, 138–44; Bayley, *National Loans*, 61–64.

39. Bayley, *National Loans*, 64–66; Kearny, *Sketch of American Finance*, 146–50; Elliot, *Funding System*, 2:702–804.

40. Murat, *Moral and Political Sketch*, 336.

41. Elliot, *Funding System*, 2:825; Murat, *Moral and Political Sketch*, 316, 329; Studenski and Krooss, *Financial History*, 98–99; Brownlee, *Federal Taxation*, 22.

42. Francis Corbin to Robert Beverely, January 12, 1820, Beverley Family Papers, VHS.

43. Table 15 shows how quickly the debt was paid off. Elliot, *Funding System*, 2:823; Oliver Wolcott, *Remarks on the Present State of Currency, Credit, Commerce, and National Industry* (New York, 1820) in Wright, *U.S. National Debt*, 2:1–45; Bradford, *History of the Federal Government*, 373.

44. See, for example, Volume 1 of the Six Per Cent. Loan of 1813, Record Group 53, NARA; Adams, "Beginning of Investment Banking," 114; Anon., *The Speeches of Henry Clay* (Philadelphia: H.C. Carey & Lea, 1827), 289–90; Bernard Cohen, *Compendium of Finance* (London, 1822) in Wright, *U.S. National Debt*, 2:232–64; Anon., "Public Debt," *Eastern Argus*, January 24, 1825; Tibbits, *Memoir*, 19; Elliot, *Funding System*, 2:1026.

CHAPTER 7: THE LIFE AND TIMES OF
FEDERAL BONDHOLDERS IN VIRGINIA

1. See Table 16 for additional details. Charles Lee to Richard B. Lee, June 6, 1790, Pollock-Lee Papers, VHS.

2. John B. Dabney, "Sketches and Reminiscencies [sic] of the Dabney and Morris Families," 1850:20, VHS; Royster Lyle Jr., "John Bowyer," *Dictionary of Viriginia Biography* (hereafter *DVB*), 2:163–64.

3. Daphne Gentry, "William Cabell," *DVB*, 2:497–98; Randolph Campbell and L. Moody Simms, "Revolutionary Virginian: The Life and Times of Colonel William Cabell," *Virginia Phoenix* (1974), 53–61.

4. William Anderson & Co. to John Cropper, March 15, 1786, George Corbin to John Cropper, October 28, 1777, July 21, 1778, John Cropper Papers, VHS; R. A. Brock, ed., *Proceedings of the Virginia Historical Society* (Richmond, 1892), 11:273–315.

5. John G. Kolp, "John Cropper," *DVB*, 3:568–70; Richard C. Anderson to William Steele, November 1, 1797, Robert Gamble to John Cropper, December 11, 1798, January 24, 1799, January 9, 1800, April 4, 1801, John Cropper Papers, VHS.

6. William Austin to John Cropper, various dates, John Patterson to John Cropper, December 15, 1819, Linah Mims to John Cropper, April 4, 1817, John Cropper Papers, VHS.

7. Thomas E. Buckley and Brent Tarter, "Burwell Bassett," *DVB*, 1:384–85; Warren Ashley receipt, February 15, 1804, James Sampson receipt, September 19, 1806, Bassett Family Papers, VHS; Burwell Bassett to Robert Lee Traylor, May 22, 1810, VHS; Burwell Bassett circular, April 1810, John Cropper Papers, VHS; U.S. Thirteenth Congress, Sess. II, 1813–1814, House of Representatives, Committee of Elections, VHS.

8. See the sundry loans and guarantees, large and small, mentioned in the Bassett Family Papers, VHS.

9. Brooks Miles Barnes, "Thomas Monteagle Bayly," *DVB*, 1:408–9.

10. Mark Fernandez, "John Blair," *DVB*, 1:544–46; M. E. Bradford, *Founding Fathers* 2nd ed. (Kansas: University of Kansas Press, 1994), 163–65; Jack Lynch, "A Man of Firmness: Justice John Blair and the Letter of the Law," *Colonial Williamsburg* (Spring 2006), 52–57.

11. Brent Tarter, "Cornelius Calvert," *DVB*, 2:525–26.

12. Timothy Alden, *A Collection of American Epitaphs* (New York: 1814), 13–14; Return of Men of Captain Gamble's Company When Stoney Point Was Taken from the Enemy," July 15, 1779, Claiborne Family Papers, VHS; Robert Gamble to John Cropper, July 11, 1798, Banks Family Papers, VHS.

13. Robert Gamble to John Cropper, July 3, 1799, January 9, 1800, Cropper Papers, VHS; Robert Gamble to Thomas Massie, March 24, 1806, November 3, 10, 17, December 21, 1807, Massie Family Papers, VHS; Robert Gamble to Henry Banks, July 27, 1797, Banks Family Papers, VHS.

14. Robert Gamble to James Breckinridge, September 26, 1792, May 12, 1797, August 9, 1800, February 26, 1802, October 26, 1803, April 19, 1804, Breckinridge Papers, VHS; Robert Gamble to Henry Banks, June 28, 1797, Banks Family Papers, VHS; Robert Gamble to Robert Preston, March 4, 1803, Preston Family Papers, VHS; Robert Gamble to Thomas Massie, January 5, 1808, Massie Family Papers, VHS.

15. Throughout this chapter, Virginia pounds are converted to U.S. dollars using the standard conversion of $3.3333 per pound, which reflects Virginia's rating of the dollar as six shillings Virginia money of account. For details, see Michener and Wright, "Development of the U.S. Monetary Union."

16. Robert Gamble to Henry Banks, June 12, 1797, Banks Family Papers, VHS; Robert Gamble to James P. Preston, May 6, 1796, Preston Family Papers, VHS; Amicable Society of Richmond Papers, VHS.

17. Thomas Massie to Robert Gamble, August 20, 1806, January 7, February 4, May 20, June 18, October 1, November 12, December 17, 23, 1805, February 18, 24, March 3, 24, June 10, August 18, 20, September 9, October 14, December 22, 1806, January 16, November 3, December 21, 1807, January 5, 19, 1808, January 17, 1809, Massie Family Papers, VHS.

18. Robert Gamble to Thomas Massie, December 21, 1807, April 5, 1810, Massie Family Papers, VHS; Robert Gamble to James Breckinridge, February 8, April 18, 1810, Robert Gamble to Andrew Hamilton, April 17, 1810, Breckinridge Papers, VHS; J. Stanton Moore, ed., *Annals of Henrico Parish* (1904), 449–50; R. A. Brock, ed., *Proceedings of the Virginia Historical Society* (Richmond, 1892), 11:230; Fillmore Norfleet, *Saint-Memin in Virginia: Portraits and Biographies* (Richmond: Dietz Press, 1942), 164.

19. James Breckinridge to John Preston, July 28, 1790, Preston Family Papers, VHS; Robert Gamble to James Breckinridge, September 26, 1792, Breckinridge Papers, VHS; Thomas Rust to James Breckinridge, September 30, 1822, Allison, Smyth & Co. to James Breckinridge, November 7, 1822, William Neal & Co. to James Breckinridge, November 11, 1822, September 11, 1826, Robert Pollard et al to James Breckinridge, August 9, 1824, April 12, October 3, 1825, April 6, 1827, James Breckinridge Papers, VHS.

20. John H. Cocke to James Breckinridge, October 13, 1826, Breckinridge Papers, VHS.

21. Joseph Lewis to James Breckinridge, May 6, 1809, Edward Graham to James Breckinridge, June 10, 1809, Breckinridge Family Papers, VHS; Robert Gamble to James Breckinridge, March 7, 1809, Breckinridge Papers, VHS.

22. James Breckinridge Circular, February 27, 1811, John Floyd to James Breckinridge, May 18, 1824, Breckinridge Papers, VHS; McNulty, "James Breckinridge"; Donald Gunter, "James Breckinridge," *DVB*, 2:208–10.

23. Robert Gamble to James Breckinridge, March 22, May 25, December 5, 30, 1809, January 20, 1810, February 6, April 20, 1812, John Gamble to James Breckinridge, February 24, 1812, VHS.

24. Robert Gamble to James Breckinridge, February 6, 1812, Robert Gamble and James McCaoulling, Receipt, February 12, 1812, James Breckinridge to Henry Lee, ?, Breckinridge Family Papers, VHS; Robert Gamble to James Breckinridge, March 22, 1809, Breckinridge Papers, VHS; James Breckinridge deed to John Taylor, May 24, 1810, Taylor Family Papers, VHS; McNulty, "James Breckinridge," 89.

25. Robert Gamble to James Breckinridge, April 19, May 15, 1804, March 28, 1809, January 5, 17, 1812, Breckinridge Papers, VHS; Wermeil, *Fireproof Building*.

26. James Breckinridge to Fleming Saunders, November 16, 1815, June 2, 1816, Saunders Family Papers, VHS; Robert Gamble to James Breckinridge, December 2, 1815, January 2, 1816, Breckinridge Papers, VHS.

27. John Gamble to James Breckinridge, June 25, 1815, April 6, 1816, Breckinridge Papers, VHS.

28. Robert Gamble to James Breckinridge, January 5, December 8, 1812, January 22, February 5, June 17, November 2, 27, December 23, 1816, November 10, 1824, August 25, 1823, November 10, 1824, December 27, 1826, Breckinridge Papers, VHS.

29. Robert Gamble to James Breckinridge, January 23, December 24, 1817, August 16, 1819, July 22, 1822, August 4, 1823, James Breckinridge to Robert Gamble, June 26, July 18, 1819, Breckinridge Papers, VHS.

30. Robert Gamble to James Breckinridge, May 25, July 5, 8, 15, 1809, November 10, 1826, January 19, July 24, 1827, August 16, 1827, Robert Gamble to Cary Breckinridge, March 7, 1845, Breckinridge Papers, VHS; R. A. Brock, ed., *Proceedings of the Virginia Historical Society* (Richmond, 1892), 11:229.

31. Alexander McRae to Joseph Jones, June 16, 1798, Joseph Jones to Alexander McRae, June 22, 1798, Jones Family Papers, VHS; Reuben Norvell to Daniel Call, February 18, 1804, VHS; E. Lee Shepard, "Daniel Call," *DVB*, 2:513–15.

32. William Austin to John Bassett, December 9, 1800, February 13, 1801, Bassett Family Papers, VHS; William Austin broadside, Richmond, February 11, 1800, VHS; William Austin broadside, Richmond, May 26, August 19, September 22, 1800, VHS.

33. Henry Banks promissory notes to William Austin, December 27, 1796, William Austin to Henry Banks, June 16, August 21, 1797, January 14, June 8, 1798, Henry Banks promissory notes to William Austin, April 25, June 13, 1796, Henry Banks Papers, VHS.

34. Blanton, *Medicine in Virginia*, 12–25; William Baynton to Mrs. Garlick, April 12, 1805, Thomas Chrystie Papers, VHS; E. Randolph Trice, "William Baynham," *DVB*, 1:411–12; George Johnston, "Some Medical Men of Mark from Virginia," *Old Dominion Journal of Medicine and Surgery* (June 1905), 7–8; L. B. Anderson, *Brief Biographies of Virginia Physicians of Olden Times* (Richmond: Southern Clinic Print, 1889), 35–36.

35. Malcolm Hart Harris, "Chrystie of Hanover Co., Va., and New York," *Virginia Genealogist* (January–March, 1972), 134; Blanton, *Medicine in Virginia*, 4–177, 408; William Baynham to Mrs. Garlick, April 12, 1805, Thomas Chrystie Papers, VHS.

36. Thomas Chrystie Accounts, VHS.

37. Dephne Gentry, "Chrystie of Hanover Co., Va. and New York," *Virginia Genealogist* (October–December 1971), 277–78; Thomas Chrystie Accounts, VHS.

38. Bob Piazza, "Historic Grave Restored: Hanover Surgeon Served During Revolutionary War," *Richmond Times-Dispatch*, June 11, 2003; Spencer Roane to Benjamin Oliver, May 21, 1814, Thomas Chrystie Inventories, VHS.

39. J. Stanton Moore, ed., *Annals of Henrico Parish* (1904), 159, 426; Blanton, *Medicine in Virginia*, 27, 38, 335; David Leitch Dr. to James Currie, Joseph Lyon Miller Accounts, VHS.

40. Brent Tarter, "Archibald Cary," *DVB*, 3:101–3; Archibald Cary to James Currie, July 10, 1785, Archibald Cary Papers, VHS.

41. Blanton, *Medicine in Virginia*, 11, 23, 28, 36, 39, 75, 79, 86, 243, 251, 282, 316, 389, 404; Pulliam, *Constitutional Conventions*, 22; Courtlandt Canby, "The Commonplace Book of Doctor George Gilmer," *Virginia Magazine of History and Biography* (hereafter *VMHB*) (1948): 379–407; George Gilmer to Col. Bland, June 16, 1779, Bland Family Papers, VHS.

42. George Gilmer's Bond, August 8, 1793, Barbour Family Papers, VHS; R. A. Brock, ed., *Proceedings of the Virginia Historical Society* (Richmond, 1892), 11:229; Robert Gamble to Thomas Massie, October 1, 1805, Massie Family Papers, VHS.

43. George H. S. King, "Further Notes on Captain George Buckner (1760–1828) and the Caroline County Buckners," *VMHB* (1956), 358–72.

44. Konigsberg, "Edward Carrington," 3, 336; Paul Carrington Promissory Note to Anthony Hundley, November 9, 1792, "Paul Carrington now holds lands," January 1, 1793, "Land Held by P. Carrington Senr. at his death," n.d., Carrington Family Papers, VHS; John Deal, "Paul Carrington," *DVB*, 3:41–43.

45. James River Company Account Book, 1785–1789, VHS; Robert Munford to William Byrd, April 20, 1775, Carrington Family Papers, VHS.

46. "Negroe Accot.," May 1772, Carrington Family Papers, VHS.

47. F. Claiborne Johnston, "George Carrington," *DVB*, 3:38–39.

48. George Corbin to John Cropper, April 30, June 8, October 28, 29, 1777, July 21, 28, 1778, William Davies to George Corbin, May 21, 1782, John Cropper Papers, VHS; Wesley Frank Craven, "George Corbin," in McLaughlin, *Princetonians*, 488–89.

49. Isaac Hite Papers, VHS.

50. Joseph Eggleston Accounts, Extract from General Porterfield's Letter, n.d., Eggleston Family Papers, VHS; John Holcombe to William Branch Giles, December 3, 1791, VHS; "Eggleston, Joseph," *Biographical Directory of the United States Congress, 1774–1989*, 955; "Eggleston, Joseph," *The National Cyclopedia of American Biography* (New York: James T. White and Company, 1892) 2:397; Carter, *Virginia Journals*, 539.

51. William Woolfolk to John G. Woolfolk, June 7, 1816, Woolfolk Family Papers, VHS; Anon., "Thomas Willock of Norfolk County, Virginia, 1784," *National Genealogical Society Quarterly* (March 1974), 35; Anon., "Diary of Powhatan Robertson During His Student Days at William and Mary, 1816," *William and Mary Quarterly* (January 1931), 61–68; Abigail DeHart Mayo to Margaret Lowther Page, July 8, 1818, Abigail Mayo Papers, VHS.

52. Thomas Chilton, Fauquier County, Virginia, Court Records, VHS; Thomas Hooper to John Ambler, February 24, 1802, Ambler Family Papers, VHS.

53. Daphne Gentry, "James Anderson," *DVB*, 1:139–41.

54. George B. Cutten, *The Silversmiths of Virginia* (Richmond: Dietz Press, 1952), 130–31; Whisker, *Virginia Clockmakers*, 10–11.

55. Harold B. Gill Jr., "Benjamin Bucktrout," *DVB*, 2:381–82.

56. Whisker, *Virginia Clockmakers*, 28–29; Agnes Gish, *Virginia Taverns, Ordinaries, and Coffee Houses* (Westminster, Md.: Willow Bend Books, 2005), 121–22.

57. Frederick Johnston, *Memorials of Old Virginia Clerks* (Lynchburg, Va.: J. P. Bell Company, 1888), 62–63; J. T. McAllister, *Virginia Militia in the Revolutionary War* (Hot Springs, Va.: McAllister Publishing Co., 1913), 62–63.

58. Pulliam, *Constitutional Conventions*, 50; Susan Gibson, "Revolutionary Officers of West Virginia," *Southern Magazine* (January–February 1936), 11.

59. Unfortunately, very little has been written about early female investors. See Wright, *Hamilton Unbound*, 173–94; Wright, "Women and Finance"; Sparks, *Capital Intentions*; J. Stanton Moore, ed., *Annals of Henrico Parish* (1904), 443; C. Grinnan to Mary J. Lee, July 18, 1828, Grinnan Family Papers, VHS; Griffin, et al. v. Birkhead, et al, Virginia Supreme

Court of Appeals, VHS; Martha Miller to Thomas Adams, November 13, 1787, Adams Family Papers, VHS.

60. Henry Edmundson to Charles Johnston, April 20, 1821, Charles Johnston to Henry Edmundson, February 26, July 20, 1821, VHS.

61. John Baylor to John Baylor, February 16, 1770, Frances Baylor to John Baylor, May 25, 1770, James Clay to John Baylor, July 25, 1779, Baylor Family Papers, VHS; Anon., "Grandeur in Caroline," *The Virginia Historical Society: An Occasional Bulletin* (October 1964), 3–4; Ellen Carter Bruce Baylor Commonplace Book, 1752–1906, 31, 50–51, 58–59, 184, VHS.

62. Caroline County Court, Judgment, May 15, 1790, in favor of Robert Gilchrist, administrator of William Dickson, against John Baylor and Mann Page, executors of George Baylor, Baylor Family Papers, VHS; Robert Wellford to John Spotswood, August 28, 1800, Robert Wellford Papers, VHS; Account of John Baylor with John Taliaferro, John Taliaferro Papers, VHS.

63. Daphne Gentry, "Robert Andrews," *DVB*, 1:167–68; Carter, *Virginia Journals*, 533.

64. U.S. Treasury Department, Customs Bureau, Virginia, Bermuda Hundred and City Point, VHS; R. A. Brock, ed., *Proceedings of the Virginia Historical Society* (Richmond, 1892), 11:317–76.

65. At a Meeting of the Society of Cincinnati, in the State of Virginia, January 27, December 13, 1802, VHS.

66. James River Company Account Book, 1785–1789, VHS.

67. Charles F. Hobson, "Jacquelin Ambler," *DVB*, 1:115–16.

68. Alexander Tarte to William Grayson, September 1, ?, Alexander Dunscomb to John Cropper, December 20, 1788, VHS; Carter, *Virginia Journals*, 540.

69. *Valley Forge Orderly Book of General George Weedon* (New York: Dodd, Mead and Co., 1902); Harry M. Ward, "George Weedon," *ANBO*; George King, "General George Weedon," *William and Mary Quarterly* (1940), 237–52.

70. John Chilton to Joseph Blackwell, September 13, 1776, John Chilton Papers, VHS; Payroll for Captain John Blackwell Company, March 1778, VHS; Deed, John Blackwell to Thomas Keith, October 1, 1796, Keith Family Papers, VHS.

71. Townsend Stith to Robert Bolling, April 1, 1808, Nottoway County, Virginia, Records, VHS; Orders, Petersburg Common Council, Robert Bolling to Lewis Mabry, June 6, 1825, At the Supreme Court of Chancery, April 8, 1830, J. F. Macy Report, September 24, 1831, Mayor of Petersburg vs. Bolling, July 28, 1831, Bolling Family Papers, VHS; Joseph Jones to Abraham Buford, July 14, 1822, Jones Family Papers, VHS; Robert Bolling to Dolly Madison, July 12, 1836, Dolly Madison Papers, VHS.

72. Richard H. Venable to Robert Bolling, July 25, 1817, "Notes on Mileage and Elevations," January 25, 1818, Bernard Fox to the Mayor of Petersburg, March 24, 1818, L. Baldwin to the President and Directors of the Board of Public Works of Virginia, March 2, 1818, C. Mackenzie and Robert Bolling, "Roanoke Report," June 1818, Bolling Family Papers, VHS; Peter Randolph Beverely to Robert Beverely, April 21, 1816, Beverley Family Papers, VHS.

73. Dabney, "Colonel Charles Dabney," 186–99; John B. Dabney, "Sketches and Reminiscencies [*sic*] of the Dabney and Morris Families," 1850:9–36, VHS; Account Book of Charles Dabney, 1773–1775, VHS.

74. Return of Officers of the State Legion, Nash Papers, VHS.

75. Charles Dabney to Patrick Henry, April 29, 1785, Dabney Family Papers, VHS; Charles Dabney Commonplace Book, 1791–1805, Charles Dabney Ledger, 1793–1829, VHS.

76. Charles Dabney Commonplace Book, 1791–1805, VHS.

77. Charles Dabney Commonplace Book, 1791–1805, 1811–1825, Charles Dabney Ledger, 1793–1829, VHS.

78. Charles Dabney Accounts, Charles Dabney Commonplace Book, 1811–1825, VHS.

79. Charles Johnston to ?, 1792?, VHS; Nathaniel Anderson to Thomas Massie, February 29, 1795, November 1, 1797, June 11, 1799, January 20, 1801, Massie Family Papers, VHS.

80. Charles Johnston to ?, 1792?, VHS; Anon., "Notes on Hollins College," *William and Mary Quarterly* (October 1929), 330–31; Johnston, *Narrative of the Incidents.*

81. Henry Edmundson to Charles Johnston, April 20, 1821, Charles Johnston to Henry Edmundson, February 26, July 20, 1821, Charles Johnston to James Breckenridge, July 11, 1821, VHS; Anon., "Notes on Hollins College," *William and Mary Quarterly* (October 1929), 330–31; Johnston, *Narrative of the Incidents*, 98.

82. Frank Corum, "Will of Mace Clements, 1806," *Tidewater Virginia Families: A Magazine of History and Genealogy* (November–December 1993), 169–70.

83. Samuel Beall to Thomas Massie, May 19, 1780, June 11, July 20, 1783, Massie Family Papers, VHS; Memorial of Duncan Ross, December 1781, Thomas Jefferson to Duncan Rose, December 13, 1781, Haxall Family Papers, VHS; William Lee to Samuel Beale, December 29, 1783, Letterbook of William Lee, 1783–1787, VHS; Agreement between Samuel Beall and Herbert Clairborne, March 25, 1784, A. Clairborne to Samuel Beall, December 29, 1784, Samuel Beall to Herbert Clairborne, January 14, 1785, Bassett Family Papers, VHS; Samuel Beall to Fielding Lewis, November 27, 1781, VHS.

84. William Booker and Jess Smith bond to Alexander Buchanan and William Mitchell, May 1797, Smith Family Papers, VHS; Alexander Buchanan sale to John Cringan, April 9, 1798, Robinson Family Papers, VHS; James River Company Account Book, 1785–1789, VHS; Amicable Society of Richmond Papers, VHS.

85. Daphne Gentry, "Archibald Blair," *DVB*, 1:536–37.

86. William Galt to Robert Preston, May 22, 1804, Preston Family Papers, VHS; G. Melvin Herndon, "From Scottish Orphan to Virginia Planter: William Galt, Jr., 1801–1851," *VMHB* (1979): 326–43.

87. Peter Randolph Beverely to Robert Beverely, June 1, 1819, Beverely Family Papers, VHS.

88. Francis Corbin to Robert Beverely, August 5, 1810, Peter Randolph Beverely to Robert Beverely, June 1, 1819, Beverely Family Papers, VHS; William Haxall to Petersburg Marine Insurance Company, April 18, 1850, VHS; Wright, *Old South, New South*, 87; Gudmestad, *Troublesome Commerce*, 35–61, 98–115, 141–42, 185–86; William Booker and Jess Smith bond to Alexander Buchanan and William Mitchell, May 1797, Smith Family Papers, VHS; Robert Gamble to James Breckinridge, June 17, 1816, Breckinridge Papers, VHS.

89. Richard Blow to Hicks, Jenkins, & Co., August 10, 1807, to John M. St. George, August 19, 1807, to James Strange, August 29, 1807, to William Barksdale, August 14, 1807, Richard Blow Account Book, 1807–1809, VHS.

90. Joseph Jones to William Barksdale, June 13, 1794, Joseph Jones Papers, VHS; Richard Blow to William Barksdale, February 19, March 21, May 18, 23, 24, 1807, Richard Blow

Account Book, 1807–1809, VHS; Robert Gamble to James Breckinridge, August 7, 1812, Breckinridge Papers, VHS.

91. Archibald Campbell to William and Henry Haxall, February 20, 1802, Andrew Blackwood to William and Henry Haxall, June 11, 1815, Henry Haxall to William Haxall, September 28, 1797, Josiah Cowper to William and Henry Haxall, February 12, 1810, Conway F. Whittle to William and Henry Haxall, July 19, 1815, *Ming's New York Price Current*, February 17, 1810, with subscription tag attached, Haxall Family Papers, VHS.

92. Conway Whittle to Henry Haxall, August 18, September 12, 1798, Conway Whittle to William and Henry Haxall, February 26, October 18, December 29, 1801, Conway Whittle to William Haxall, October 17, 1797, March 11, June 26, July 19, November 25, 1798, Haxall Family Papers, VHS.

93. Joseph C. Cabell to Carter Braxton Page, December 29, 1819, VHS; Warren Ashley to Robert Beverley, November 29, 1819, Beverley Family Papers, VHS; Henry Allmand to Reed Irving and Co., July 27, 1804, Henry Allmand to Stephen Harris, December 15, 1804, "Lists of Assets and Liabilities of Harrison Allmand," "Accounts of Harrison Allmand," Deed of William Dangerfield to Harrison Allmand, Allmand Family Papers, VHS.

94. Henry Allmand to the President and Directors of the Bank of the United States, December 23, 1820, Henry Allmand to the President and Directors of the Virginia Bank, December 26, 1820, Obituary Notice of Harrison Allmand, Allmand Family Papers, VHS.

95. Warren Ashley to John Basset, March 24, 1803, Bassett Family Papers, VHS; Martin Fisk affidavit, August 22, 1809, Warren Ashley to Benjamin Oliver, January 18, February 8, March 22, April 19, 1807, January 30, September 12, October 22, 26, 1808, August 2, 1809, January 7, March 11, 18, June 18, 23, July 30, August 6, 1810, April 15, May 27, December 2, 1811, Benjamin Brand Papers, VHS; Warren Ashley to Robert Beverley, September 10, 1817, March 24, 1819, October 16, 1819, November 29, 1819, Beverley Family Papers, VHS; Bill of Complaint, Grinnan Family Papers, VHS.

96. Autobiography of Rawleigh Colston, Colston Family Bible, VHS.

97. "Rawleigh Colston," in F. Vernon Aler, *Aler's History of Martinsburg and Berkeley County, West Virginia* (Hagerstown, Md.: Mail Publishing Company, 1888), 90–91; Rawleigh Colston to John Mercer, June 14, 1784, Mercer Family Papers, VHS; Rawleigh Colston to John Ambler, August 12, 1807, Ambler Family Papers, VHS.

98. Robert Gamble to Thomas Massie, March 24, 1806, Massie Family Papers, VHS; John Cowper to William & H. Haxall, June 24, 1819, Haxall Family Papers, VHS; John Cowper to Don Pablo Chacon, April 17, 1823, Spain, Consulado, Norfolk, VHS.

99. Ellen Carter Bruce Baylor Commonplace Book, 1752–1906, p. 181, VHS; James Bruce to ?, August 5, 1793, Spragins Family Papers, VHS; List of Subscribers, n.d., Bailey Family Papers, VHS; James Bruce to James C. Bruce, December 5, 1831, December 18, 1832, Last Will and Testament of James Bruce, October 3, 1836, James C. Bruce to Col. James Madison, September 18, 1838, James C. Bruce to Edward C. Carrington, July 10, 1840, Bruce Family Papers, VHS; James Bruce to ?, July 26, 1819, Spragins Family Papers, VHS; Robert Gamble to James Breckinridge, May 5, 1823, Breckinridge Papers, VHS.

100. Indenture of Lease, October 18, 1792, James Young Papers, VHS; Alexander Macauley to James Boyce, June 19, 1798, Anderson Family Papers, VHS.

CHAPTER 8: BLESSINGS: AMERICAN ECONOMIC GROWTH

1. Kenneth Hafertepe, "Samuel Blodget," *ANBO*; Blodget, *Thoughts*, iii, v.

2. Bagehot, *Lombard Street*, 8; Carey Roberts, "Alexander Hamilton and the 1790s: A Reappraisal," in Ambrose and Martin, *Many Faces*, 211–30.

3. Johnson, *Inquiry*, 62–64, 70, 82; Winterbotham, *Historical, Geographical, Commercial, and Philosophical View*, 3:285; Elliot, *Funding System*, 2:827.

4. Anon., "Of the Causes of the Wealth of States," *An Essay on the Principles of Political Economy* (March 1805), 7, 16; Blodget, *Thoughts*, iii–iv; Albany and Schenectady Turnpike Stockholder List, NYSA; Wright, *Wealth of Nations Rediscovered*; Majewski, *House Dividing*.

5. See Figure 7. Murat, *Moral and Political Sketch*, 323, 332; Paul Carrington to Henry Carrington, May 1, 1813, Carrington Family Papers, VHS; Gordon, *Hamilton's Blessing*, 55.

6. Stasavage, *Public Debt*; Ferguson, *Cash Nexus*; Macdonald, *Free Nation*; Elliot, *Funding System*, 1:389; Bayley, *National Loans*, 30.

7. Ouseley, *Remarks*, 74.

8. Young, "Comparative Economic Development," 80–81; Gourlay, *Statistical Account*, 243; Wright, "Banking and Politics," 992, 1019; Hincks, *Canada*, 29; Talbot, *Five Years' Residence*, 1:223–24; Lucas, *Lord Durham's Report*, 2:158, 215–16.

9. Lanctot, *Documents Relating to Currency*; Altman, "Economic Growth in Canada"; Hall, *Travels in North America*, 1:237; Stuart, *Three Years*, 1:109.

10. John M. Duncan, *Travels Through Part of the United States and Canada in 1818 and 1819* (Glasgow, 1823) in Craig, *Early Travellers*, 51–52; Talbot, *Five Years' Residence*, 1:76–77; Anon., *Financial Difficulties of Lower Canada* (n.p.: *Quebec Gazette*, 1824), 14–25.

11. Canadians in the early nineteenth century used three different ratings of the dollar, "Halifax currency" ($1 = £.25 or 5s to $1), "Quebec currency" ($1 = £.3), and "York currency" ($1 = £.4 or 8s to $1), the rating of colonial New York. In most official documents, Canadians used Halifax currency, rating the dollar at 5 shillings. Gourlay, *Statistical Account*, 215–17; McIvor, *Canadian Monetary, Banking and Fiscal Development*, 42; Shortt, *Adam Shortt's History*, 211, 213, 217, 226, 238; White, *Lord Selkirk's Diary*, 224; Pickering, *Emigration*, 78. So one unit of Canadian currency equaled $4. Canadian banking histories are rife with references like the following: "The stock . . . was limited to £250,000, or $1,000,000 in shares of £25, or $100 each." Shortt, *Adam Shortt's History*, 17.

12. Based on Upper Canada's population of 151,097 in 1824. Hincks, *Canada*, 27; Preston, *Three Years' Residence*, 196–211; Gourlay, *Statistical Account*, 139.

13. McIvor, *Canadian Monetary, Banking and Fiscal Development*, 36; Talbot, *Five Years' Residence*, 1:72, 222; Preston, *Three Years' Residence*, 192–93; Breckenridge, *Canadian Banking System*, 84; Shortt, *Adam Shortt's History*, 274; Hubbard, *For Each*, 71–72; Pickering, *Emigration*, 77–78; Hebert, *Present State*, 152–53.

14. William Thomson, *A Tradesman's Travels in the United States and Canada, in the Years 1840, 41 & 42* (Edinburgh, 1842) in Craig, *Early Travellers*, 135; John Robert Godley, *Letters from America* (London, 1844) in Craig, *Early Travellers*, 148–50.

15. Ryerson, *Affairs of the Canadas*, 21–27; White, *Lord Selkirk's Diary*, 217–18; Lucas, *Lord Durham's Report*, 2:48–50; Ouellet, *Lower Canada*, 244; Shortt, *Adam Shortt's History*, 269; Neufeld, *Financial System of Canada*, 35; Rudin, "Banking on Quebec," 47.

16. Lucas, *Lord Durham's Report*, 1:264; 2:99–100, 141, 148, 170, 299–303.

17. Hammond, *Banks and Politics*, 631–70; Shortt, *Adam Shortt's History*; McIvor, *Canadian Monetary, Banking and Fiscal Development*, 15–26, 59; Preston, *Three Years' Residence*, 169–87.

18. Hincks, *Canada*, 29; McLean, *Essays*; Hall, *Travels in North America*, 1:227–30; Evans, *Fortune's Epitome of the Stocks*, 97; Tucker, *Canadian Commercial Revolution*.

19. Preston, *Three Years' Residence*, 185; James Dixon, *Personal Narrative of a Tour Through a Part of the United States and Canada* (New York, 1849) in Craig, *Early Travellers*, 167–69; Neufeld, *Financial System of Canada*, 45–46; Michie, "Canadian Securities Market," 35; Whiteside, "Toronto Stock Exchange"; Werner and Smith, *Wall Street*, 158; Firestone, "Development," 222; Richard E. Sylla, Jack Wilson, and Robert E. Wright, "America's First Securities Markets, 1787–1836: Emergence, Development, Integration," (National Science Foundation, grant no. SES–9730692, 2003). Data housed by ICPSR and EH.net.

20. Ashworth, *Slavery*; Bateman and Weiss, *Deplorable Scarcity*; Carlton and Coclanis, *The South*; Coclanis, *Shadow of a Dream*; David et al., *Reckoning With Slavery*; Elkins, *Slavery*; Fogel, *Without Consent*; Genovese, *Roll, Jordan, Roll*; Huston, *Calculating the Value of the Union*; Kilbourne, *Debt, Investment, Slaves*; Wright, *African Americans*; Wright, *Political Economy of the Cotton South*; Delfino and Gillespie, *Global Perspectives*; Dupre, *Transforming the Cotton Frontier*; Chaplin, *Anxious Pursuit*; Ford, *Origins of Southern Radicalism*; Greb, "Charleston, South Carolina, Merchants"; Pease and Pease, *Web of Progress*; Goloboy, "Success to Trade"; Majewski, *House Dividing*, 3; Downey, *Planting a Capitalist South*.

21. "Capitalist," *Oxford English Dictionary Online*, 1792 example; "Capital" and "Capitalist," in George Mason, *A Supplement to Johnson's English Dictionary of Which the Palpable Errors Are Attempted to Be Rectified, and Its Material Omissions Supplied* (New York: H. Caritat, 1803); Prindle, *Paradox of Democratic Capitalism*, 17. Even mortgages on land and slaves were short-term. Most ran a year, or at most a few years, before becoming callable at the will of the lender. Corporate bonds, by contrast, enjoyed maturities that ran into decades and equities were callable by stockholders only upon dissolution of the company.

22. Bodenhorn, *History of Banking*; Bodenhorn, *State Banking*; Kilbourne, *Slave Agriculture and Financial Markets*; Perkins, *American Public Finance*; Wright, *Origins of Commercial Banking*; Wright, *Hamilton Unbound*; Wright, *Wealth of Nations Rediscovered*; Wright, *First Wall Street*; Wright and Cowen, *Financial Founding Fathers*. According to U.S. Census data, South Carolina was home to about 250,000 people in 1790 and approximately 704,000 in 1860. Some scholars believe that "Charlestonians on a per capita basis had about as much capital as Bostonians to invest in their city. Indeed, if one excludes slaves from the per capita count, they probably had more." That makes sense given that per capita incomes in the South equaled or bettered those of the North. Pease and Pease, *Web of Progress*, 185; Huston, *Calculating the Value of the Union*, 30–31.

23. This is not to say, however, that they were the most important class of investors in South Carolina or that they invested as much in financial securities as people of similar wealth in the North. After all, southerners could earn returns of 7 to 9 percent from planting but would seldom receive more than 6 percent from safe financial investments. Ford, "Tale of Two

Entrepreneurs"; Greb, "Charleston, South Carolina, Merchants, 1815–1860," 79–147; Pease and Pease, *Web of Progress*, 19, 47, 58, 174–77, 182–83, 269 n.13. Careful work in probate records like that conducted by Jones and Rothenberg could improve our understanding but financial securities, particularly bearer instruments like cash and certain bonds, are notoriously difficult to capture through estate records. Lindert, "Algorithm"; Jones, *Wealth of a Nation to Be*; Rothenberg, *Market-Places*.

24. See Tables 17 and 18 for details.

25. By way of illustration, Figure 8 shows the bid prices of the shares of two South Carolina insurance companies between 1810 and 1822. For the number of financial securities listed in South Carolina newspapers, refer to Table 19. Pease and Pease, *Web of Progress*; Greb, "Charleston, South Carolina, Merchants, 1815–1860," 107.

26. Figure 9 plots the bid and ask prices for shares of the Bank of South Carolina from 1803 until 1849. See also Table 20.

27. Mason, *From Buildings and Loans*, 12–39; Charleston (S.C.) City Council, *Census of the City of Charleston, South Carolina, for the Year 1848, Exhibiting the Condition and Prospects of the City* (Charleston, S.C., 1849), 158–59; Schweikart, *Banking in the American South*, 67, 99–108, 199–202, 209–10, 242–43; Pease and Pease, *Web of Progress*, 178; Ford, *Origins of Southern Radicalism*, 320–35.

28. Figure 10 illustrates dividends. The annual count of corporations is in Table 21. Pease and Pease, *Web of Progress*, 17, 172; Ford, *Origins of Southern Radicalism*, 314–18.

29. See Table 22 for details.

30. Levine, "Finance and Growth: Theory and Evidence," 887.

31. Ben-Atar, *Trade Secrets*; Khan, *Democratization of Invention*.

32. Pickering, *Emigration*, 78.

33. Anon., "Travels," *The Port-Folio* (January 3, 1801), 1; Richard Bright, *Travels from Vienna Through Lower Hungary* (Edinburgh: Archibald Constable and Co., 1818), 231; Surface, *Story of Sugar*, map facing the title page, 110; Anon., *Beet Sugar Story*, 9; John Quincy Adams, *Letters on Silesia, Written During a Tour Through That Country in the Years 1800, 1801* (London: J. Budd, 1804), 4, 5; Anon.,*The Agricultural Magazine* (London, 1804), 315.

34. Cambreleng, *Examination*, 103; Surface, *Story of Sugar*, 111; Anon.,*The Technical Repository: Containing Practical Information on Subjects Connected with Discoveries and Improvements in the Useful Arts* 11 vols. (London: T. Cadell, 1822–27), 4:60–62.

35. Anon., *The Repertory of the Arts, Manufactured and Agriculture* (London: J. Wyatt, 1819), 61–62.

36. John Perkins and Roger Munting, "Science Versus Nature: The Cane-Beet Sugar Rivalry," in Ahluwalia, Ashcroft, and Knight, *White and Deadly*, 159–60; Amphicon, "Beet Sugar," in John S. Skinner, ed., *American Farmer: Containing Original Essays and Selections on Agriculture, Horticulture, Rural and Domestic Economy, and Internal Improvements* (Baltimore: John D. Toy, 1829), 11:149; Geerligs, *World's Cane Sugar Industry*, 16–22; Thomas P. Thompson, *A Free Trader's Defense of the Mercantile System* (London: Robert Heward, 1833), 13; Richard Broun, *Appeal to Our Rulers and Ruled, In Behalf of a Consolidation of the Post Office, Roads, and Mechanical Conveyance, for the Service of the State* (London: John Mortimer, 1834), 22; Michael Donovan, *Domestic Economy* (London: Longman, Rees, Orme, Brown and Green, 1830–37), 2:321.

37. B. Henderson to John Beale Bordley, January 14, 1788, Library Company of Philadelphia (hereafter LCP); "Winter Food for Stock: Mangel Wurtzel and Sugar Beet," n.d., VHS; Anon., *The Western Agriculturist and Practical Farmer's Guide* (Cincinnati: Robinson and Fairbank, 1830), 219; William Johnson, "On Making Sugar from Beets," *Southern Agriculturist and Register of Rural Affairs* (October 1830), 505; Anon., "Sign of the Times: Beet Sugar," *Philanthropist*, July 8, 1836; Anon., "Beet Sugar" *The Liberator*, April 3, 1840; Pease and Pease, *Bound With Them in Chains*, 4; Anon., *Third Annual Report of the Board of Managers of the New England Anti-Slavery Society* (Boston: Garrison and Knapp, 1835), 4, 309–10; Charles W. Carey, Jr., "David Lee Child," *ANBO*.

38. Horace Greeley, "Protection vs. Free Trade," *Hunt's Merchants' Magazine* (1841), 166; Anon., *The Banner of the Constitution: Devoted to General Politics, Political Economy, State Papers, Foreign and Domestic News &c.*, April 6, 1831; Carey, *Principles*, 2:89.

39. Raguet, *Principles of Free Trade*, 42–44; Anon., "Note, by the Editor," *Southern Agriculturist and Register of Rural Affairs* (November 1828), 485; Sitterson, *Sugar Country*, 175–77; Anon., "Speech of Mr. Bullard, of Louisiana," *Niles' Weekly Register*, August 25, 1832.

40. Anon., "Editor's Budget: The Beet-Sugar Manufacture," *The Western Literary Journal and Monthly Review* (July 1836), 138; Anon., "Beet Sugar: From the Alton Observer," *The Farmer and Gardener, and Live-Stock Breeder and Manager*, May 23, 1837; "James Ronaldson: Brief Sketch of His Life," Society Collection, Historical Society of Pennsylvania (hereafter HSP). A similar narrative with a somewhat different timeline can be found in Browne, "Centenary of the Beet Sugar Industry," 46–51. Jackson's experience is well-known. For Ronaldson's run-ins with banks, see Farmers and Mechanics Bank to James Ronaldson, February 7, May 18, 1820, McAllister Manuscripts, LCP; James Ronaldson to Mathew Carey, April 11, 1819?, Edward Carey Gardiner Collection, Mathew Carey Papers, HSP; Peter Randolph Beverely to Robert Beverely, February 16, 1819, Beverely Family Papers, VHS; James Ronaldson to Richard Ronaldson, November 18, 1820, "James Ronaldson," Society Collection, HSP.

41. Anon., "Obituary," *The Historical Magazine, and Notes and Queries Concerning the Antiquities* (October 1859), 319; Browne, "Centenary of the Beet Sugar Industry," 46–51. Pirating foreign books was common practice in American publishing in the nineteenth century. Wright, Jacobson, and Smith, *Knowledge for Generations*. Anon., "Beet Sugar," *Fessenden's Silk Manual and Practical Farmer* (June 1836), 28; Anon., "The Beet," *Western Literary Journal and Monthly Review* (June 1836), 67; J.M., "Beet Sugar," *Maine Farmer and Journal of the Useful Arts*, June 10, 1836; Anon., "Beet Sugar," *The Genesee Farmer and Gardener's Journal*, June 11, 1836; Anon., "Beet Sugar," *New York Evangelist*, June 18, 1836; Anon., "The Silesian, or Sugar Beet," *The Farmer & Gardener, and Live-Stock Breeder and Manager*, June 21, 1836; M. Pelletan, "On the Purification of Beet Juice, and a Method of Preparing It in the Best Manner," *American Journal of Pharmacy* (July 1836), 151; Anon., "Beet Sugar," *The Cultivator* (July 1836), 63; Le Ray De Chaumont, "On the Manufacture of Beet Sugar in the U.S.," *The Cultivator* (July 1836), 65; Anon., "Epitome of the Times," *Atkinson's Saturday Evening Post*, April 2, 1836; Anon., "Beet Sugar," *Fessenden's Silk Manual and Practical Farmer* (May 1836), 9.

42. Anon., "Beet Culture: Interesting Correspondence," *The Farmer and Gardener, and Live-Stock Breeder and Manager*, February 21, 1837; Anon., *Illinois in 1837: A Sketch Descriptive of the Situation, Boundaries, Face of the Country, … of the State of Illinois* (Philadelphia: S. Augustus Mitchell and Grigg and Elliot, 1837), 26, 45–46, 132; Ellsworth, *Valley of the*

Upper Wabash, 43; Abner Jones Dumant, *Illinois and the West: With a Township Map, Containing the Latest Surveys and Improvements* (Boston: Weeks, Jordan and Co., 1838), 190; Anon., "Beet Culture and Beet Root Sugar," *The Farmer and Gardener, and Live-Stock Breeder and Manager*, December 6, 1836; Anon., "Estimated Expense of an Acre of Sugar Beets," *American Silk-Grower and Farmer's Manual* (Philadelphia, 1838–39), 2:68; Anon., "Beet Sugar in Massachusetts," *London Times*, January 28, 1837; Anon., "Editor's Budget: The Beet-Sugar Manufacture," *The Western Literary Journal and Monthly Review* (July 1836), 138; Anon., "Anticipated Change in the Agriculture of the United States—Silk, and Beet Sugar," *Farmer's Register: A Monthly Publication* (August 1836), 251; Anon., "Beet Sugar Culture," *The Delaware Register and Farmers' Magazine* (May 1838), 290.

43. Ellsworth, *Valley of the Upper Wabash*, 97; Anon., "Beet Sugar," *The Farmer and Gardener, and Live-Stock Breeder and Manager*, March 21, 1837, 370–71; Anon., "Manufacture of Beet Sugar," *The Colored American*, November 17, 1838. But David Child probably had it right when he argued that "the larger the scale, provided it do not exceed the limits of good management, the greater will be the profit." Child, *Culture of the Beet*, 117; Dr. F. Wurdemann, "Preparation of Beet Sugar," *New York Farmer* (1834), 41; Pedder, *Report Made to the Beet Sugar Society*; Banner, *Anglo-American Securities Regulation*, 190–92; Davis, *Essays*; Blandi, *Maryland Business Corporations*; Evans, *Business Incorporations*; Cadman, *Corporation in New Jersey*; Seavoy, *Origins of the American Business Corporation*; Majewski, *House Dividing*; Wright, *Hamilton Unbound*; Wright, *Wealth of Nations Rediscovered*; Wright et al., *History of Corporate Governance*.

44. Anon., "Beet Sugar Company," *The Farmer and Gardener, and Live-Stock Breeder and Manager*, December 6, 1836. Not enough is known of the organizers to characterize them here. They were: H. O. Apthorp, Benjamin Barrett, Isaac C. Bates, Henry G. Bowers, Edward Church, Munroe Clapp, Theodore Clapp, Chauncey Clark, Luther C. Clark, William Clark Jr., Christopher Clarke, John Clarke, Azariah Clapp, Chester Clark, George Cook, C. Delano, Cecil Dwight, Hiram Ferry, John Frink, Elisha Graves, Samuel L. Hinckley, Roswell Hubbard, David Hunt, C. P. Huntington, Sylvester Judd, Asahael Lyman, Leander Moody, Samuel Parsons, John Philips, Thomas Pomeroy, John Rogers, Theodore Sheldon, Geo. Shepherd, Henry Shepherd, Thomas Shepherd, Hervey Smith, H. K. Starkweather, Daniel Stebbins, Elisha Strong, J. A. Strong, Jonathan Strong, Nathan Storrs, W. W. Thompson, Joseph Warner, Oliver Warner, Solomon Warner, Samuel Wells Jr., Samuel Whitemarsh, Samuel Williams, Christopher Wright, John Wright. Apparently, many were related. Sylvester Judd may have been the novelist and Unitarian minister (1813–53). Born in Westhampton, Judd ran a newspaper in Northampton before stints at Yale College (1832–36) and Harvard Divinity School (1837–40). Richard D. Hathaway, "Sylvester Judd," *ANBO*. Apthorp was apparently a farmer. The *London Times* (Anon., "Beet Sugar in Massachusetts," January 28, 1837) reported that he grew 40 tons of beets per acre. Anon., "Beet Culture and Beet Root Sugar," *The Farmer and Gardener, and Live-Stock Breeder and Manager*, December 6, 1836; Browne, "Centenary of the Beet Sugar Industry," 46–51; Anon., "Beet Sugar Company," *Fessenden's Silk Manual and Practical Farmer* (December 1836), 122.

45. Anon., "An Example," *The National Atlas and Tuesday Morning Mail* (April 1837), 175; Surface, *Story of Sugar*, 115; Anon., "Beet Sugar—Again," *The Liberator*, March 13, 1840; Anon., "Beet Sugar Manufactory," *The Farmer and Gardener, and Live-Stock Breeder*

and Manager, October 16, 1838; Anon., "Manufacture of Beet Sugar," *The Colored American*, November 17, 1838; Anon., "Beet Sugar" *The Liberator*, April 3, 1840; *The American Farmer* (Baltimore: 1839–40), 118; Anon., "Communication," *The Liberator*, April 21, 1837; Anon., "Beet Sugar Culture," *The Delaware Register and Farmers' Magazine* (May 1838), 290; Massachusetts Society for Promoting Agriculture, *Massachusetts Society for Promoting Agriculture: Premium List, 1838* (1838); John Welles, "Report on Beet Sugar Premiums," *Maine Farmer and Journal of the Useful Arts*, July 25, 1840; *The American Farmer* (Baltimore, 1839–40), 290, 297; Anon., "Miscellany," *The Liberator*, February 28, 1840; Child, *Culture of the Beet*, 99. Again, this section accords in spirit but not always in detail with the narrative of Browne, "Centenary of the Beet Sugar Industry," 46–51. No evidence of any formal patent by Child appears in United States Patent Office, *List of Patents for Inventions and Designs Issued by the United States from 1790 to 1847* (Washington: Government Printing Office, 1847), 4, 27, 117–18, 401, 470. Pages 117, 312, and 470 indicate, however, that one Joseph Hurd/Herd Jr. of Boston received a patent for "sugar, manufacturing from beets" on July 26, 1838. Apparently a contraption for cutting beet roots, Hurd's was the only beet-related patent issued before 1847. Anon., "Beet Sugar," *The Liberator*, April 10, 1840; Blakey, *United States Beet-Sugar*, 33; Guilfoyle, "Beet Sugar," 19; Charles W. Carey, Jr., "David Lee Child," *ANBO*; Anon., *Beet Sugar Story*, 15; Anon., "Selections from 1 Douglass' Michigan Reports," *The Western Law Journal* (April 1847), 328; Sylla and Wright, *History of Corporate Finance*; Browne, "Centenary of the Beet Sugar Industry," 50.

46. *Journal of the Senate of the Commonwealth of Pennsylvania*, Vol. 47, 102, 805; Anon., "Beets and Banking in New Jersey," *The National Atlas and Sunday Morning Mail* (September 1836), 142; Henry O'Reilly, *Settlement in the West: Sketches of Rochester* (Rochester: W. Alling, 1838), 44; Ezekiel Holmes, *Report of an Exploration and Survey of the Territory on the Aroostook River* (Augusta: Smith & Robertson, 1839), 66; James Gray Smith, *A Brief Historical, Statistical, and Descriptive Review of East Tennessee* (London: J. Leath, 1842), 14.

47. Anon., "Beet Sugar: From the Alton Observer," *The Farmer and Gardener, and Live-Stock Breeder and Manager*, May 23, 1837.

48. William A. Jones, "Beet Sugar &c.," *The Cultivator* (August 1835), 80; Anon., "Beet Sugar in Michigan," *American Silk-Grower and Farmer's Manual* (Philadelphia: 1838–1839), 2:16; John T. Blois, *Gazetteer of the State of Michigan* (Detroit: S. L. Rood and Co., 1838), 110; Ronald Henley, "Sweet Success … The Story of Michigan's Beet Sugar Industry, 1898–1974," accessed at: www.michigan.gov/hal/0,1607,7–160–17451_18670_18793–53367--,00.html on August 28, 2007; Anon., "Beet Sugar Manufactory," *The Genesee Farmer and Gardener's Journal*, February 23, 1839; Anon., "Items," *United States Commercial and Statistical Register* (September 1839), 176; David Dale Owen, *Report of a Geological Exploration of Iowa, Wisconsin, and Illinois, Made Under Instructions from the Secretary of the Treasury of the United States* (Washington: Government Printing Office, 1844), 62; Anon., *Beet Sugar Story*, 15.

49. *The American Farmer*, Baltimore, 1840–41, 49, 218; Anon., "Important Improvements in Making Beet Sugar," *Daily Courant*, January 16, 1839; Anon., "Beet Sugar," *The Cultivator* (January 1842), 10; Anon., "List of Books Published by Marsh, Capen, Lyon, and Webb" (Boston, June 1839); Anon., "Beet Sugar," *Hartford Daily Courant*, May 21, 1840; Anon., "Beet Sugar," *Prairie Farmer* (August 1844), 194; Anon., "Beet Sugar," *Southern Agriculturist, Horticulturist, and Register of Rural Affairs* (November 1844), 433.

50. Surface, *Story of Sugar*, map facing the title page, 98–99.

51. Louis D. Johnston and Samuel H. Williamson, "The Annual Real and Nominal GDP for the United States, 1790–Present," Economic History Services, October 2005, URL: www. eh.net/hmit/gdp/; Sitterson, *Sugar Country*, Chart 4, 171, 177; *The American Farmer* (Baltimore, 1840–41), 35; Lawrence H. Officer, "What Was the Interest Rate Then?" Economic History Services, EH.Net, 2003, http://eh.net/hmit/interest_rate/; Anon., "Money Matters in Cincinnati," *Portsmouth Journal of Literature and Politics*, September 14, 1839, 3; Anon., "Banks and Banking," *Essex Gazette*, December 27, 1839; Anon., "Business and Currency," *Portsmouth Journal of Literature and Politics*, August 22, 1840; *New Orleans Daily Delta*, January 6, 1855.

52. Forsyth, *Principles and Practice*, 2:335–36; Anon., "Beet Sugar: From the Alton Observer," *The Farmer and Gardener, and Live-Stock Breeder and Manager*, May 23, 1837; Anon., *Beet Sugar Story*, 2–4; John Perkins and Roger Munting, "Science Versus Nature: The Cane-Beet Sugar Rivalry," in Ahluwalia, Ashcroft, Knight, *White and Deadly*, 157; Baumol, "Entrepreneurship and Innovation"; *Philanthropist*, March 10, 1840; William Webb, "Agricultural," *Philanthropist*, October 20, 1841; "Speech of Wendell Phillips," *The Liberator*, September 4, 1840; Fogel, *Without Consent*, 29, 274; Anon., "On Abstinence from the Products of Slave Labor," *The Quarterly Anti-Slavery Magazine* (July 1836), 398–99; Pease and Pease, *Bound With Them in Chains*, 38, 100–4, 181–84.

53. "Beet Sugar," *American Silk-Grower and Farmer's Manual* (Philadelphia: 1838–39), 2:35.

54. Browne, "Centenary of the Beet Sugar Industry," 49. The Northampton factory, for example, paid "$5 a ton for beets, and some of the farmers have raised 20 tons to the acre," which of course is only $100 per acre. Anon., "Beet Sugar Manufactory," *The Farmer and Gardener, and Live-Stock Breeder and Manager*, October 16, 1838; Anon., "Beet Sugar: From the Alton Observer," *The Farmer and Gardener, and Live-Stock Breeder and Manager*, May 23, 1837; Anon., "Beet Culture: Interesting Correspondence," *The Farmer and Gardener, and Live-Stock Breeder and Manager*, February 21, 1837; Blakey, *United States Beet-Sugar*, 32–33, found the early estimates optimistic even by the standards of the early twentieth century. Anon., "On the Manufacture of Sugar from the Beet," *American Farmer* (Baltimore, 1839–40), 221; Henry Lee, *Considerations on the Cultivation, Production and Consumption of Cotton* (Boston: Dutton and Wentworth, 1845), 182; Anon., "Beet and Maple Sugar," *The Virginia Literary Museum and Journal of Belles Lettres, Arts, Sciences, &c.*, October 14, 1829; Surface, *Story of Sugar*, 106, 115; Anon., "Beet Culture: Interesting Correspondence," *The Farmer and Gardener, and Live-Stock Breeder and Manager*, February 21, 1837.

55. Ibid.

56. Details are provided in Tables 23 and 24. Isaac Davis to William M. Meredith, Meredith Papers, November 8, 1849, 68:11, HSP.

57. Benjamin P. Johnson, *Report of Benj. P. Johnson: Agent of the State of New York Appointed to Attend the Exhibition of the Industry of All Nations, Held in London, 1851* (Albany, 1852), 43. "This [1890s] may be reckoned as the first period of any considerable and successful interest in the beet-sugar industry in the United States," Blakey, *United States Beet-Sugar*, 36; "When beet sugar first came into production at the end of the 1890s ...," Chandler, *Visible Hand*, 256, 328; United States Patent Office, *List of Patents for Inventions and Designs Issued by the United States from 1790 to 1847* (Washington: Government Printing Office, 1847); Anon., "More Fallacy and Fiction," *New York Daily Times*, March 20, 1857; Anon., "The French Sugar Duties," *New York Daily Times*, March 27, 1857.

58. Anon., "A Peculiarity of Country," *Hartford Daily Courant*, April 18, 1854; Anon., "New England Sugar," *New York Daily Times*, May 18, 1857; W. S. Clark, "Beet Sugar: Abstract of an Address" (Amherst, Mass.: January 12, 1872); Anon., "Beet Sugar in California," *London Times*, August 27, 1872; Blakey, *United States Beet-Sugar*, 33–35; Guilfoyle, "Beet Sugar," 19; Anon., *Beet Sugar Story*, 15–16.

59. Surface, *Story of Sugar*, 116; Blakey, *United States Beet-Sugar*, 34–41, 205–19, 235–43; Blakey, "Beet Sugar and the Tariff"; Taussig, "Beet Sugar and the Tariff"; Cherington, "State Bounties"; Phillips, "Encouragement to Industry"; Markoff, "Beet Sugar Industry," 6–7, 18. But see also Hutchinson, "Import Substitution," who claims that effective tariffs were low. For the development of the Sugar Trust, see Chandler, *Visible Hand*, 328–29; Markoff, "Beet Sugar Industry," 9–12, 371–79; Guilfoyle, "Beet Sugar," 19; *Beet Sugar Story*, 16–19; "Beet Sugar Mfg.," NAICS 311313, Table 1: Selected Industry Statistics for the U.S. and States, U.S. Census Bureau, 2002.

60. Cole, "Agricultural Crazes"; Acs et al., "Growth and Entrepreneurship"; Djankov, McLiesh, and Ramalho, "Regulation and Growth"; Manuel, "Entrepreneurship and Economics."

CHAPTER 9: DEATH AND REINCARNATION: JACKSON'S TRIUMPH AND FAILURE

1. The Treasury could have and would have paid off on small outstanding sums had the owners presented their bonds for repayment. Sobel, *Panic on Wall Street*, 46; Elliot, *Funding System*, 2:890; Anon., "The Heroites," *Salem Gazette*, January 13, 1835; Anon., "Eighth of January at Brunswick," *Eastern Argus*, January 23, 1835; Anon., "Rev. John Leland," *The Pittsfield Sun*, February 5, 1835; Anon., "From the Globe: Celebration of the Eighth of January at Washington," *Eastern Argus*, January 27, 1835; Anon., "Celebration of the Extinguishments of the Public Debt and The Victory of New-Orleans at Washington," *Eastern Argus*, January 23, 1835; Anon., "Celebration of the Extinguishments of the Public Debt and The Victory of New-Orleans at Washington," *New Hampshire Patriot*, January 26, 1835; Anon., "Proceedings at the Republican Celebration," *Nashville Banner and Nashville Whig*, January 30, 1835.

2. Stabile and Cantor, *Public Debt*, 37; Gordon, *Hamilton's Blessing*, 59; Anon., "Eighth of January at Brunswick," *Eastern Argus*, January 23, 1835; Brands, *Andrew Jackson*.

3. Brands, *Money Men*, 107; Anon., "The Heroites," *Salem Gazette*, January 13, 1835; Anon., "The National Debt Paid Out of General Jackson's Own Pocket," *Portsmouth Journal of Literature and Politics*, January 31, 1835; Anon., "Great Credit Is Claimed," *Connecticut Courant*, February 2, 1835; Sobel, *Panic on Wall Street*, 75.

4. Adams, *Public Debts*, 4–5, 16–17, 23–24.

5. E. Cary Brown, "Episodes in the Public Debt History of the United States," in Dornbusch and Draghi, *Public Debt Management*, 231; Myers, "Retirement of the First Federal Debt."

6. Table 25. Peskin, *Manufacturing Revolution; The Speeches of Henry Clay* (Philadelphia: H. C. Carey & Lea, 1827), 290; Einhorn, *American Taxation*; Elliot, *Funding System*, 2:802.

7. E. Cary Brown, "Episodes in the Public Debt History of the United States," in Dornbusch and Draghi, *Public Debt Management*, 229–62; Myers, "Retirement of the First Federal Debt." I follow here the research of economic historians like John Wallis rather than the interpretations of historians like John Larson. Larson, *Internal Improvement*;

Wallis, "State Constitution Reforms"; Banner, *Anglo-American Securities Regulation*, 191–92; Anon., "National Debt," *Eastern Argus*, January 9, 1835; Archibald Stuart, "An Address to the Voters of the Congressional District Composed of the Counties of Bedford, Franklin, Patrick, and Henry," *Richmond Enquirer*, March 24, 1835; Richard E. Ellis, *Union at Risk*; Studenski and Krooss, *Financial History*, 101; Anon., "Eighth of January at Brunswick," *Eastern Argus*, January 23, 1835.

8. "Mr. Wickliffe's Letter Relative to the Expenditures of the Government … in Reply to a Communication Previously Published on the Same Subject," and "Letter From the Secretary of the Treasury to the Chairman of the Committee on Retrenchment," in *Reports of 1830–31*, VHS; Webber and Wildavsky, *History of Taxation*, 373; Simpson, *Working Man's Manual*, 161–69; Walters, *Albert Gallatin*, 92.

9. Hare, *Proofs*, 11–12.

10. Anon., *Webster and Hayne's Celebrated Speeches in the United States Senate on Mr. Foote's Resolution* (Philadelphia: T. B. Peterson and Brothers, 1830), 8, 58.

11. Table 26. Anon., "We Rejoice," *New Hampshire Sentinel*, February 12, 1835; Dewey, *Early Financial History*, 217–22; Studenski and Krooss, *Financial History*, 102, 116–17; Elliot, *Funding System*, 2:927–35; Adams, *Public Debts*, 246–47; Gordon, *Hamilton's Blessing*, 64; Timberlake, *Monetary Policy*, 51–64.

12. William C. Rives to Waddy Thompson, December 18, 1840, VHS; Anon., *Harrison's National Debt* (1840) in Wright, *U.S. National Debt*, 3:287–92; Anon., *The National Debt As It Was, and As It Is* (Washington, 1843), in Wright, *U.S. National Debt*, 3:293–302.

13. Table 27 summarizes the state debt situation. Sylla, Legler, and Wallis, "Banks and State Public Finance"; E. Cary Brown, "Episodes in the Public Debt History of the United States," in Dornbusch and Draghi, *Public Debt Management*, 231; Adams, *Public Debts*, 318; Ratchford, *American State Debts*, 79–80, 88; Adams, *Public Debts*, 343; Memoirs of Stephen Allen, 83, NYHS; Elliot, *Funding System*, 2:1037; "An Ordinance to Provide for the Payment of the Balance," December 16, 1826, Bolling Family Papers, VHS.

14. Ratchford, *American State Debts*, 81–84; Studenski and Krooss, *Financial History*, 103; William Spackman, *Statistical Tables of the … United Kingdom of Great Britain* (London: Longman and Co., 1842), 70–72.

15. Heins, *Constitutional Restrictions*, 7–8.

16. *Harrison's National Debt: Assumption of the State Debts* (London, 1844) in Wright, *U.S. National Debt*, 3:287–92; Thomas Cary, *The Americans Defended by an American* (London, 1844) in Wright, *U.S. National Debt*, 3:303–41; Ratchford, *American State Debts*, 100–104.

17. Table 28. Thomas Cary, *The Americans Defended by an American* (London, 1844) in Wright, *U.S. National Debt*, 3:303–41; Mercator, "American Stocks," *London Times*, December 19, 1846; Anon., "Commercial Chronicle and Review," *Merchants' Magazine and Commercial Review* (February 1849), 193–94, 196.

18. Heins, *Constitutional Restrictions*, 8–12.

19. E. Cary Brown, "Episodes in the Public Debt History of the United States," in Dornbusch and Draghi, *Public Debt Management*, 233; Heins, *Constitutional Restrictions*, vi, 36–68; Ratchford, *American State Debts*, 1–8, 288–91, 328–32, 369–81, 429–45, 567–68.

20. E. Cary Brown, "Episodes in the Public Debt History of the United States," in Dornbusch and Draghi, *Public Debt Management*, 236; Anon., "Proceedings at the Republican Celebration," *Nashville Banner and Nashville Whig*, January 30, 1835; Adams, *Public Debts*, 176.

21. Hormats, *Price of Liberty*; Webber and Wildavsky, *History of Taxation*, 370–71. Unless otherwise noted, this section draws on discussions with colleagues, David M. Walker's speech at the Museum of American Finance on June 28, 2006, the Money Marketeers dinner of March 8, 2007, and the "Is the Sky Falling? Challenging the Conventional Economic Wisdom" symposium at the New School, March 9, 2007.

22. For an excellent overview of this transformation, see Fishback et al, *Government*.

23. For similar analyses, see Hormats, *Price of Liberty* and Vietor, *How Countries Compete*, 275–76, 281.

24. Baumol, Litan, and Schramm, *Good Capitalism, Bad Capitalism*, 30; Bladen, *How to Cope*; King, *Chaos in America*; Bonner and Wiggin, *Empire of Debt*; Paine, *Decline and Fall*, 21.

25. Hormats, *Price of Liberty*.

26. Lindert, *Growing Public*; Shaviro, *Taxes*.

27. Anon., "Are Deficits Unfair to Future Generations?" *Wall Street Journal*, May 10, 2007.

28. Adams, *Public Debts*, 248; Elliot, *Funding System*, 2:892.

29. A good introduction to the federal bureaucracy is Gary Libecap, "The Federal Bureaucracy: From Patronage to Civil Service," in Price Fishback et al., *Government*, 364–83; Bullock, *Finances*.

30. LePatner, Jacobson, and Wright, *Broken Buildings, Busted Budgets*; Wright, "On the Economic Efficiency of Organizations"; Henry Knox to Edward Carrington, July 24, 1792, Edward Carrington Papers, VHS; Adams, *For Good and Evil*, 163–64, 167, 183–90.

BIBLIOGRAPHY

A Country Gentleman. *Some Observations on the National Debt* ... (London: Bizett, Barnes, and Gibson, 1753?).

Acs, Zolton J., David B. Audretsch, Pontus Braunerhjelm, and Bo Carlsson. "Growth and Entrepreneurship: An Empirical Assessment," CEPR Discussion Paper No. 5409, January 2006.

Adams, Charles. *For Good and Evil: The Impact of Taxes and the Course of Civilization* 2nd ed. (New York: Madison Books, 1999).

Adams, Donald R. "The Beginning of Investment Banking in the United States," *Pennsylvania History* 45 (April 1978), 99–116.

Adams, Henry C. *Public Debts: An Essay in the Science of Finance* (New York: D. Appleton and Company, 1898).

A Financier. *The National Debt No National Grievance* ... (London: J. Wilkie, 1768).

Ahluwalia, Paul, Bill Ashcroft, and Roger Knight, eds. *White and Deadly: Sugar and Colonialism* (Commack, N.Y.: Nova Science Publishers, 1999).

Alberts, Robert C. *The Golden Voyage: The Life and Times of William Bingham, 1752–1804* (Boston: Houghton Mifflin Co., 1969).

Alexander, John K. *The Selling of the Constitutional Convention: A History of News Coverage* (Madison, Wisc.: Madison House, 1990).

Allen, W. B., ed. *Works of Fisher Ames: As Published by Seth Ames* (Indianapolis: Liberty Classics, 1983).

Altman, Morris. "Economic Growth in Canada, 1695–1739," *William and Mary Quarterly* 45 (1988), 684–711.

Ambrose, Douglas and Robert W. T. Martin, eds. *The Many Faces of Alexander Hamilton: The Life and Legacy of America's Most Elusive Founding Father* (New York: New York University Press, 2006).

Anon. *The Beet Sugar Story* (Washington, D.C.: United States Beet Sugar Association, 1959).

Arbuckle, Robert D. *Pennsylvania Speculator and Patriot: The Entrepreneurial John Nicholson, 1757–1800* (University Park: Pennsylvania State University Press, 1975).

Ashworth, John. *Slavery, Capitalism, and Politics in the Antebellum Republic* (New York: Cambridge University Press, 1995).

Bagehot, Walter. *Lombard Street: A Description of the Money Market* (Homewood, Ill.: Richard D. Irwin, 1962).

Banner, Stuart. *Anglo-American Securities Regulation: Cultural and Political Roots, 1690–1860* (New York: Cambridge University Press, 1998).

Banning, Lance. *The Sacred Fire of Liberty: James Madison and the Founding of the Federal Republic* (Ithaca, N.Y.: Cornell University Press, 1995).

Bateman, Fred and Thomas Weiss. *A Deplorable Scarcity: The Failure of Industrialization in the Slave Economy* (Chapel Hill: University of North Carolina Press, 1981).

Bates, Whitney K. "Northern Speculators and Southern State Debts: 1790," *William and Mary Quarterly* 19 (January 1962), 30–48.

Baumol, William. "Entrepreneurship and Innovation: (Micro)Theory of Price and Profit," Working Paper, July 6, 2006.

Baumol, William, Robert Litan, and Carl Schramm. *Good Capitalism, Bad Capitalism and the Economics of Growth and Prosperity* (New Haven, Conn.: Yale University Press, 2007).

Bayley, Rafael A. *The National Loans of the United States, from July 4, 1776 to June 30, 1880* 2nd ed. (Washington, D.C.: Government Printing Office, 1882).

Beard, Charles A. *An Economic Interpretation of the Constitution of the United States* (New York: Free Press, 1913).

———. "Some Economic Origins of Jeffersonian Democracy," *American Historical Review* 19 (January 1914), 282–98.

Becker, Robert A. *Revolution, Reform, and the Politics of American Taxation, 1763–1783* (Baton Rouge: Louisiana State University Press, 1980).

Ben-Atar, Doron. *Trade Secrets: Intellectual Piracy and the Origins of American Industrial Power* (New Haven, Conn.: Yale University Press, 2004).

Berkin, Carol. *A Brilliant Solution: Inventing the American Constitution* (New York: Harcourt, 2002).

Bernstein, William. *The Birth of Plenty: How the Prosperity of the Modern World Was Created* (New York: McGraw-Hill, 2004).

Bird, Robert. *Proposals for Paying Great Part of the National Debt* ... (London: J. Dodsley, 1780).

Bladen, Ashby. *How to Cope with the Developing Financial Crisis* (New York: McGraw-Hill Book Company, 1980).

Blakey, Roy. *The United States Beet-Sugar Industry and the Tariff* (New York: Columbia University, 1912).

———. "Beet Sugar and the Tariff," *Journal of Political Economy* 21 (June 1913), 540–54.

Blandi, Joseph. *Maryland Business Corporations, 1783–1852* (Baltimore: The Johns Hopkins Press, 1934).

Blanton, Wyndham. *Medicine in Virginia in the Eighteenth Century* (Richmond: Garrett & Massie, 1931).

Blodget, Samuel. *Thoughts on the Increasing Wealth and National Economy of the United States of America* (Washington, D.C.: Way and Groff, 1801).

———. *Economica: A Statistical Manual for the United States of America* (Washington, D.C.: 1806).

Bodenhorn, Howard. *A History of Banking in Antebellum America: Financial Markets and Economic Development in an Age of Nation Building* (New York: Cambridge University Press, 2000).

——. *State Banking in Early America: A New Economic History* (New York: Oxford University Press, 2003).

Bonner, William and Addison Wiggin. *Empire of Debt: The Rise of an Epic Financial Crisis* (Hoboken, N.J.: John Wiley and Sons, 2005).

Borden, Morton, ed. *The Antifederalist Papers* (East Lansing: Michigan State University Press, 1965).

Bourne, Edward. "Alexander Hamilton and Adam Smith," *Quarterly Journal of Economics* 8 (April 1894), 328–44.

Bouton, Terry. "A Road Closed: Rural Insurgency in Post-Independence Pennsylvania," *Journal of American History* 87 (December 2000), 855–87.

Bowen, Catherine Drinker. *Miracle at Philadelphia: The Story of the Constitutional Convention May to September 1787* (Boston: Little, Brown, 1966).

Box, George. *Plans for Reducing the Extraordinary Expences of the Nation* ... (London: J. Stockdale, 1783).

Bradford, Alden. *History of the Federal Government for Fifty Years* (Boston: Samuel G. Simpkins, 1840).

Brands, H. W. *Andrew Jackson: His Life and Times* (New York: Doubleday, 2005).

——. *The Money Men: Capitalism, Democracy, and the Hundred Years' War Over the American Dollar* (New York: W. W. Norton and Co., 2006).

Breckenridge, Roeliff. *The Canadian Banking System, 1817–1890* (New York: Macmillan, 1895).

Brock, Leslie. *The Currency of the American Colonies, 1700–1764: A Study in Colonial Finance and Imperial Relations* (New York: Arno Press, 1975).

Brookhiser, Richard. *Gentleman Revolutionary: Gouverneur Morris, the Rake Who Wrote the Constitution* (New York: Free Press, 2003).

Brooks, Robert Preston. *The Financial History of Georgia, 1732–1950* (Athens: University of Georgia, 1952).

Brown, Robert E. *Charles Beard and the Constitution: A Critical Analysis of "An Economic Interpretation of the Constitution"* (Princeton, N.J.: Princeton University Press, 1956).

Brown, Roger H. *Redeeming the Republic: Federalists, Taxation, and the Origins of the Constitution* (Baltimore: Johns Hopkins University Press, 1993).

Browne, Charles A. "Centenary of the Beet Sugar Industry in the United States," in *Sugar Reference Book and Directory* (1937).

Brownlee, W. Elliot. *Federal Taxation in America: A Short History* (New York: Cambridge University Press, 1996).

Bruchey, Stuart. "Alexander Hamilton and the State Banks, 1789 to 1795," *William and Mary Quarterly* 27 (July 1970), 347–78.

Buel, Richard. *In Irons: Britain's Naval Supremacy and the American Revolutionary Economy* (New Haven, Conn.: Yale University Press, 1998).

Bueno de Mesquita, Bruce and Hilton Root, eds. *Governing for Prosperity* (New Haven, Conn.: Yale University Press, 2000).

Bullock, Charles. *The Finances of the United States from 1775 to 1789, with Especial Reference to the Budget* (Madison: University of Wisconsin, 1895).

Cadman, John W. *The Corporation in New Jersey: Business and Politics, 1791–1875* (Cambridge, Mass.: Harvard University Press, 1949).

Callendar, James. *Sedgwick & Co. or a Key to the Six Per Cent Cabinet* (Philadelphia: James Callendar, 1798).

Cambreleng, Churchill. *An Examination of the New Tariff Proposed by the Hon. Henry Baldwin* (New York: Gould and Banks, 1821).

Carey, Henry C. *Principles of Political Economy* (Philadelphia: Carey, Lea, and Blanchard, 1838).

Carlton, David and Peter Coclanis. *The South, the Nation, and the World: Perspectives on Southern Economic Development* (Charlottesville: University Press of Virginia, 2003).

Carter, Edward, ed. *The Virginia Journals of Benjamin Henry Latrobe, 1795–1798* (New Haven, Conn.: Yale University Press, 1977).

Chandler, Alfred D., Jr. *The Visible Hand: The Managerial Revolution in American Business* (Cambridge, Mass.: Harvard University Press, 1977).

Chaplin, Joyce. *An Anxious Pursuit: Agricultural Innovation and Modernity in the Lower South, 1730–1815* (Chapel Hill: University of North Carolina Press, 1993).

Cherington, P. T. "State Bounties and the Beet-Sugar Industry," *Quarterly Journal of Economics* 26 (February 1912), 381–86.

Chernow, Ron. *Alexander Hamilton: A Biography* (New York: Penguin Press, 2004).

Chew, Richard S. "Certain Victims of an International Contagion: The Panic of 1797 and the Hard Times of the Late 1790s Baltimore," *Journal of the Early Republic* 25 (Winter 2005), 565–613.

Child, David Lee. *The Culture of the Beet, and Manufacture of Beet Sugar* (Boston: Weeks, Jordan & Co., 1840).

Citizen of New York. *The Commercial Conduct of the United States of America Considered* (New York: S. and J. Loudon, 1786).

Cleeve, Bourchier. *A Scheme for Preventing a Further Increase of the National Debt …* (London: R. and J. Dodsley, 1756).

Cochran, Thomas. *New York in the Confederation: An Economic Study* (Philadelphia: University of Pennsylvania Press, 1932).

Coclanis, Peter. *The Shadow of a Dream: Economic Life and Death in the South Carolina Low Country, 1670–1920* (New York: Oxford University Press, 1991).

Cole, Arthur H. "Agricultural Crazes: A Neglected Chapter in American Economic History," *American Economic Review* 16 (December 1926), 622–39.

Congleton, Roger D. "America's (Neglected) Debt to the Dutch, An Institutional Perspective," Working Paper, January 19, 2006.

Cornell, Saul. *The Other Founders: Anti-Federalism and the Dissenting Tradition in America, 1788–1828* (Chapel Hill: University of North Carolina Press, 1999).

Cowen, David. *The Origins and Economic Impact of the First Bank of the United States, 1791–1797* (New York: Garland, 2000).

——. "The First Bank of the United States and the Securities Market Crash of 1792," *Journal of Economic History* 60 (December 2000), 1040–60.

Cowen, David, Richard Sylla, and Robert E. Wright. "The U.S. Panic of 1792: Financial Crisis Management and the Lender of Last Resort," NBER DAE Summer Institute, July 2006, and XIV International Economic History Congress, Session 20, "Capital Market Anomalies in Economic History," Helsinki, August 2006.

Craig, Gerald, ed. *Early Travellers in the Canadas, 1791–1867* (Toronto: The MacMillan Company of Canada, 1955).

Dabney, Charles William. "Colonel Charles Dabney of the Revolution: His Service as Soldier and Citizen," *Virginia Magazine of History and Biography, 51* (April 1943), 186–99.

David, Paul, Herbert Gutman, Richard Sutch, Peter Temin, and Gavin Wright. *Reckoning With Slavery: A Critical Study in the Quantitative History of American Negro Slavery* (New York: Oxford University Press, 1976).

Davis, Joseph S. *Essays in the Earlier History of American Corporations* 2 vols. (Cambridge, Mass.: Harvard University Press, 1917).

Delfino, Susanna and Michele Gillespie, eds. *Global Perspectives on Industrial Transformation in the American South* (Columbia: University of Missouri Press, 2005).

De Pauw, Linda Grant. *The Eleventh Pillar: New York State and the Federal Constitution* (Ithaca, N.Y.: Cornell University Press, 1966).

DeSoto, Hernando. *The Mystery of Capital: Why Capitalism Triumphs in the West and Fails Everywhere Else* (New York: Basic Books, 2000).

Dewey, Davis. *Early Financial History of the United States* 12th ed. (New York: Longmans Green, 1934).

Diamond, Jared. *Guns, Germs, and Steel: The Fates of Human Societies* (New York: W. W. Norton, 1997).

Dickson, P. G. M. *The Financial Revolution in England: A Study in the Development of Public Credit, 1688–1756* (London: Macmillan, 1967).

Djankov, Simeon, Caralee McLiesh, and Rita Ramalho. "Regulation and Growth," World Bank Working Paper, March 17, 2006.

Doerflinger, Thomas. *A Vigorous Spirit of Enterprise: Merchants and Economic Development in Revolutionary Philadelphia* (Chapel Hill: University of North Carolina Press, 1986).

Dornbusch, Rudiger and Mario Draghi, eds. *Public Debt Management: Theory and History* (New York: Cambridge University Press, 1990).

Downey, Tom. *Planting a Capitalist South: Masters, Merchants, and Manufacturers in the Southern Interior, 1790–1860* (Baton Rouge: Louisiana State University Press, 2006).

Dupre, Daniel S. *Transforming the Cotton Frontier: Madison County, Alabama, 1800–1840* (Baton Rouge: Louisiana State University Press, 1997).

Earl, John. *The State of the National Debt ...* (London: J. Almon, 1776).

Easterly, William. *The Elusive Quest for Growth: Economists' Adventures and Misadventures in the Tropics* (Cambridge, Mass.: MIT Press, 2001).

———. *The White Man's Burden: Why the West's Efforts to Aid the Rest Have Done So Much Ill and So Little Good* (New York: Penguin Press, 2006).

Edling, Max. *A Revolution in Favor of Government: Origins of the U.S. Constitution and the Making of the American State* (New York: Oxford University Press, 2003).

Edwards, Gregory. "'Righteousness Alone Exalts a Nation': Protestantism and the Spirit of the American Revolution," (Ph.D. diss., SUNY Buffalo, 2002).

Einhorn, Robin. *American Taxation, American Slavery* (Chicago: University of Chicago Press, 2006).

Elkins, Stanley. *Slavery: A Problem in American Institutional and Intellectual Life* 3rd ed. (Chicago: University of Chicago Press, 1976).

Elkins, Stanley and Eric McKitrick. *The Age of Federalism* (New York: Oxford University Press, 1993).

Elliot, Jonathan. *The Funding System of the United States and of Great Britain* (1845).

Ellis, Joseph J. *Founding Brothers: The Revolutionary Generation* (New York: Alfred Knopf, 2001).

Ellis, Richard E. *The Union At Risk: Jacksonian Democracy, States' Rights, and the Nullification Crisis* (New York: Oxford University Press, 1989).

Ellsworth, Henry William. *Valley of the Upper Wabash, Indiana, With Hints on Its Agricultural Advantages* (New York: Pratt, Robinson, and Co., 1838).

Evans, David Morier. *Fortune's Epitome of the Stocks & Public Funds, English, Foreign and American* 15th ed. (London: Letts, Son, and Steer, 1850).

———. *The History of the Commercial Crisis, 1857–58 and the Stock Exchange Panic of 1859* (London, 1859).

Evans, George, Jr. *Business Incorporations in the United States, 1800–1943* (New York: National Bureau of Economic Research, No. 49, 1948).

Ferguson, E. James. *The Power of the Purse: A History of American Public Finance, 1776–1790* (Chapel Hill: University of North Carolina Press, 1961).

Ferguson, E. James, et al., eds. *The Papers of Robert Morris* 9 vols. (Pittsburgh: University of Pittsburgh Press, 1973–99).

Ferguson, Niall. *The Cash Nexus: Money and Power in the Modern World, 1700–2000* (New York: Basic Books, 2001).

———. *Empire: The Rise and Demise of the British World Order and the Lessons for Global Power* (New York: Basic Books, 2002).

———. *Colossus: The Rise and Fall of the American Empire* (New York: Penguin, 2005).

Fishback, Price, et al. *Government and the American Economy: A New History* (Chicago: University of Chicago Press, 2007).

Flannagan, John, Jr. "Trying Times: Economic Depression in New Hampshire, 1781–1789," (Ph.D. diss., Georgetown University, 1972).

Flaumenhaft, Harvey. *The Effective Republic: Administration and Constitution in the Thought of Alexander Hamilton* (Durham, N.C.: Duke University Press, 1992).

Fleischacker, Samuel. "Adam Smith's Reception Among the American Founders, 1776–1790," *William and Mary Quarterly, 59* (October 2002), 897–924.

Firestone, O. J. "Development of Canada's Economy, 1850–1900," in *Trends in the American Economy in the Nineteenth Century: Studies in Income and Wealth* (Princeton, N.J.: Princeton University Press, 1960).

Fogel, Robert. *Without Consent or Contract: The Rise and Fall of American Slavery* (New York: W. W. Norton and Company, 1989).

Ford, Lacy K., Jr. *Origins of Southern Radicalism: The South Carolina Upcountry, 1800–1860* (New York: Oxford University Press, 1988).

———. "The Tale of Two Entrepreneurs in the Old South: John Springs III and Hiram Hutchison of the South Carolina Upcountry," *South Carolina Historical Magazine* (July 1994), 198–224.

Ford, Paul Leicester, ed. *The Present State of the American Rebel Army, Navy, and Finances Transmitted to the British Government in October, 1780* (Brooklyn, N.Y.: Historical Printing Club, 1891).

——. *Essays on the Constitution of the United States, Published During Its Discussion by the People, 1787–1788* (Brooklyn, N.Y.: Historical Printing Club, 1892).

Forsyth, Robert. *The Principles and Practice of Agriculture, Systematically Explained* (Edinburgh: The Proprietor, 1804).

Freeman, Joanne. *Affairs of Honor: National Politics in the New Republic* (New Haven, Conn.: Yale University Press, 2002).

Fridson, Martin, ed. *Extraordinary Popular Delusions ... And Confusion de Confusiones* (New York: John Wiley & Sons, 1996).

Friedman, Thomas. *The Lexus and the Olive Tree: Understanding Globalization* (New York, 1999).

Gallatin, Albert. *Report of Mr. Gallatin on the Finances* (Bennington, Vt.: A. Haswell, 1802).

Geerligs, H. C. Prinsen. *The World's Cane Sugar Industry, Past and Present* (Manchester, England: Norman Rodger, 1912).

Genovese, Eugene. *Roll, Jordan, Roll: The World the Slaves Made* (New York: Vintage, 1976).

Goddard, Thomas. *A General History of the Most Prominent Banks in Europe ...* (New York: H. C. Sleight and G. & C. & H. Carvill, 1831).

Goloboy, Jennifer. "'Success to Trade': Charleston's Merchants in the Revolutionary Era," (Ph. D. diss., Harvard University, 2003).

Gordon, John Steele. *Hamilton's Blessing: The Extraordinary Life and Times of Our National Debt* (New York: Penguin Books, 1997).

Gourlay, Robert. *Statistical Account of Upper Canada* (London: Simpkin & Marshall, 1822).

Greb, Gregory. "Charleston, South Carolina, Merchants, 1815–1860: Urban Leadership in the Antebellum South" (Ph.D. diss., University of California, San Diego, 1978).

Grellier, J. J. *The History of the National Debt ...* (London: John Richardson and J. Johnson, 1810).

Grubb, Farley. "The Continental Dollar: How Much Was Issued and What Happened to It?" NBER Working Paper Series, Working Paper No. 13047, April 2007.

Gudmestad, Robert. *A Troublesome Commerce: The Transformation of the Interstate Slave Trade* (Baton Rouge: Louisiana State University Press, 2003).

Guilfoyle, Joseph M. "Beet Sugar, A Bright Spot in Agriculture," *Barron's*, March 13, 1933.

Hall, Basil. *Travels in North America in the Years 1827 and 1828* 3 vols. (Edinburgh: Cadell and Co., 1829).

Hammond, Bray. *Banks and Politics in America From the Revolution to the Civil War* (Princeton, N.J.: Princeton University Press, 1957).

Hammond, Jabez D. *The History of Political Parties in the State of New York: From the Ratification of the Federal Constitution to December, 1840* (Albany: C. Van Benthuysen, 1842).

Hanson, Alexander. *Remarks on the Proposed Plan of an Emission of Paper* (Annapolis, Md.: Frederick Green, 1787).

Hare, Robert. *A Brief View of the Policy and Resources of the United States* (London: J. Ridgway, 1810).

——. *Proofs That Credit as Money in a Truly Free Country is to a Great Extent Preferable to Coin* (Philadelphia: John C. Clark, 1834).

Harford, Tim. *The Undercover Economist: Exposing Why the Rich Are Rich, the Poor Are Poor, and Why You Can Never Buy a Decent Used Car!* (New York: Oxford University Press, 2006).

Harlow, Ralph. "Aspects of Revolutionary Finance, 1775–1783," *American Historical Review* 35 (October 1929), 46–68.

Hazard, Nathaniel. *Observations on the Peculiar Case of the Whig Merchants Indebted to Great Britain at the Commencement of the Late War* (New York, 1785).

Hebert, George. *Present State of the Canadas; Containing Practical and Statistical Information* (London, 1833).

Heins, A. James. *Constitutional Restrictions Against State Debt* (Madison: University of Wisconsin Press, 1963).

Helpman, Elhanan. *The Mystery of Economic Growth* (Cambridge, Mass.: Harvard University Press, 2004).

Higgins, W. Robert. "A Financial History of the American Revolution in South Carolina," (Ph. D. diss., Duke University, 1970).

Hincks, Francis. *Canada: Its Financial Position and Resources* (London: Richard Kinter, 1849).

Hislop, Codman. *Albany: Dutch, English, and America* (Albany: Argus Press, 1936).

Hodgson, Adam. *Letters from North America* (London: Hurst, Robinson, & Co., 1824).

Hofstadter, Richard. *The Progressive Historians: Turner, Beard, Parrington* (New York: Alfred A. Knopf, 1968).

Homer, Sidney and Richard Sylla. *A History of Interest Rates* 4th ed. (Hoboken, N.J.: John Wiley & Sons, 2005).

Hormats, Robert D. *The Price of Liberty: Paying for America's Wars* (New York: Henry Holt, 2007).

Hubbard, J. T. W. *For Each the Strength of All: A History of Banking in the State of New York* (New York: New York University Press, 1995).

Huston, James. *Calculating the Value of the Union: Slavery, Property Rights, and the Economic Origins of the Civil War* (Chapel Hill: University of North Carolina Press, 2003).

Hutchinson, William K. "Import Substitution, Structural Change, and Regional Economic Growth in the United States: The Northeast, 1870–1910," *Journal of Economic History* 45 (June 1985), 319–25.

James, John and Richard Sylla. "The Changing Nature of American Public Debt, 1690–1835," in *La Dette Publique* (Brussels: Credit Communal de Belgique, 1980).

Johnson, Alexander Bryan. *An Inquiry Into the Nature and Value of Capital* (New York: John Forbes, 1813).

Johnston, Charles. *A Narrative of the Incidents Attending the Capture, Detention, and Ransom of Charles Johnston, of Botetout County Virginia* (New York: J. & J. Harper, 1827).

Jones, Alice Hanson. *Wealth of a Nation to Be: The American Colonies on the Eve of the Revolution* (New York: Columbia University Press, 1980).

Kaminski, John. *Paper Politics: The Northern State Loan Offices During the Confederation, 1783–1790* (New York: Garland, 1990).

Kay, John. *Culture and Prosperity: The Truth About Markets; Why Some Nations Are Rich but Most Remain Poor* (New York: HarperBusiness, 2004).

Kearny, John Watts. *Sketch of American Finance, 1789–1835* (New York: G. P. Putnam's Sons, 1887).

Khan, B. Zorina. *The Democratization of Invention: Patents and Copyrights in American Economic Development, 1790–1920* (New York: Cambridge University Press, 2005).

Kilbourne, Richard H., Jr. *Debt, Investment, Slaves: Credit Relations in East Feliciana Parish, Louisiana, 1825–1885* (Tuscaloosa: University of Alabama Press, 1995).

———. *Slave Agriculture and Financial Markets in Antebellum America: The Bank of the United States in Mississippi, 1831–1852* (London: Pickering & Chatto, 2006).

Killenbeck, Mark. *M'Culloch v. Maryland: Securing a Nation* (Lawrence: University Press of Kansas, 2006).

Kindleberger, Charles P. *Manias, Panics, and Crashes: A History of Financial Crises* 4th ed. (New York: John Wiley & Sons, 2000).

King, John L. *Chaos in America* (Tehachapi, Calif.: America West Publishers, 1990).

Kirshner, Jonathan. *Currency and Coercion: The Political Economy of International Monetary Power* (Princeton, N.J.: Princeton University Press, 1995).

Koch, Adrienne, ed. *Notes of Debates in the Federal Convention of 1787, Reported by James Madison* (Athens: Ohio University Press, 1984).

Koetter, Michael and Michael Wedow. "Finance and Growth in a Bank-Based Economy: Is It Quantity or Quality That Matters?" Working Paper, June 10, 2006.

Konigsberg, Charles. "Edward Carrington, 1748–1810: 'Child of the Revolution': A Study of the Public Man in Young America," (Ph.D. diss., Princeton University, 1966).

Lanctot, Gustave, ed. *Documents Relating to Currency, Exchange and Finance in Nova Scotia, With Prefatory Documents, 1675–1758* (Ottawa: J. O. Patenaude, 1933).

Landes, David. *The Wealth and Poverty of Nations: Why Some Are So Rich and Some So Poor* (New York: W. W. Norton, 1998).

Lane, Carl. "'For a Positive Profit': The Federal Investment in the First Bank of the United States, 1792–1802," *William and Mary Quarterly* 54 (July 1997), 601–12.

Larson, John L. *Internal Improvement: National Public Works and the Promise of Popular Government in the Early United States* (Chapel Hill: University of North Carolina Press, 2001).

LePatner, Barry, Timothy Jacobson, and Robert E. Wright. *Broken Buildings, Busted Budgets: How to Fix America's Trillion-Dollar Construction Industry* (Chicago: University of Chicago Press, 2007).

Levine, Ross. "Financial Development and Economic Growth," *Journal of Economic Literature* 35 (June 1997), 688–726

———. "More on Finance, More on Growth: More Finance, More Growth?" *Federal Reserve Bank of St. Louis Review* (July/August 2003), 31–46.

———. "Finance and Growth: Theory and Evidence," in Philippe Aghion and Steven Durlauf, eds., *Handbook of Economic Growth* (New York: Elsevier North-Holland, 2005).

Lewis, William. *The Power of Productivity: Wealth, Poverty, and the Threat to Global Stability* (Chicago: University of Chicago Press, 2004).

Lindert, Peter. "An Algorithm for Probate Sampling," *Journal of Interdisciplinary History* 11 (Spring 1981), 649–68.

———. *Growing Public: Social Spending and Economic Growth Since the Eighteenth Century* (New York: Cambridge University Press, 2004).

Lucas, Charles, ed. *Lord Durham's Report on the Affairs of British North America* 3 vols. (New York: Augustus M. Kelley, 1970).

Lutz, Donald. "The Relative Influence of European Writers on Late Eighteenth Century American Political Thought," *American Political Science Review* 78 (March 1984), 189–97.

Macdonald, James. *A Free Nation Deep in Debt: The Financial Roots of Democracy* (New York: Farrar, Straus and Giroux, 2003).

Majewski, John. *A House Dividing: Economic Development in Pennsylvania and Virginia Before the Civil War* (New York: Cambridge University Press, 2000).

Mandelbaum, Michael. *The Ideas That Conquered the World: Peace, Democracy, and Free Markets in the Twenty-First Century* (Washington, D.C.: Public Affairs, 2003).

———. *The Case for Goliath: How America Acts as the World's Government in the Twenty-First Century* (Washington, D.C.: Public Affairs, 2005).

Manuel, Eduardo. "Entrepreneurship and Economics," SSRN Working Paper Series, August 2006.

Markoff, Dena. "The Beet Sugar Industry in Microcosm: The National Sugar Manufacturing Company, 1899 to 1967," (Ph.D. diss., University of Colorado, Boulder, 1980).

Mason, David L. *From Buildings and Loans to Bailouts: A History of the American Savings and Loan Industry, 1831–1995* (New York: Cambridge University Press, 2004).

McCraw, Thomas, ed. *Creating Modern Capitalism: How Entrepreneurs, Companies, and Countries Triumphed in Three Industrial Revolutions* (Cambridge, Mass.: Harvard University Press, 1997).

McDonald, Forrest. *Alexander Hamilton: A Biography* (New York: W. W. Norton and Co., 1979).

McGuire, Robert A. *To Form a More Perfect Union: A New Economic Interpretation of the United States Constitution* (New York: Oxford University Press, 2003).

McIvor, R. Craig. *Canadian Monetary, Banking and Fiscal Development* (Toronto: Macmillan, 1958).

McKay, Richard. *South Street: A Maritime History of New York* (New York: G. P. Putnam's Sons, 1934).

McLaughlin, James, ed. *Princetonians, 1748–1768: A Biographical Dictionary* (Princeton, N.J.: Princeton University Press, 1976).

McLean, James A. *Essays in the Financial History of Canada* (New York: Columbia College, 1894).

McNamara, Peter. *Political Economy and Statesmanship: Smith, Hamilton, and the Foundation of the Commercial Republic* (DeKalb: North Illinois University Press, 1998).

McNulty, Katherine. "James Breckinridge," (MA thesis, Virginia Polytechnic Institute, 1970).

Merrill, Michael and Sean Wilentz, eds. *The Key of Liberty: The Life and Democratic Writings of William Manning, "A Laborer," 1747–1814* (Cambridge, Mass.: Harvard University Press, 1993).

Michener, Ron. "Backing Theories and the Currencies of Eighteenth-Century America: A Comment," *Journal of Economic History* 48 (September 1988), 682–92.

Michener, Ron and Robert E. Wright. "State 'Currencies' and the Transition to the U.S. Dollar: Clarifying Some Confusions," *American Economic Review* 95 (June 2005), 682–703.

———. "Development of the U.S. Monetary Union," *Financial History Review,* 13 (April 2006), 19–41.

Michie, Ranald. "The Canadian Securities Market, 1850–1914," *Business History Review* 62 (Spring 1988), 35–73.

Mintz, Max. *Seeds of Empire: The American Revolutionary Conquest of the Iroquois* (New York: New York University Press, 1999).

Molovinsky, Lemuel. "Tax Collection Problems in Revolutionary Pennsylvania," *Pennsylvania History* 47 (July 1980), 253–59.

Morgan, Edmund S. *The Birth of the Republic, 1763–89* 3rd ed. (Chicago: University of Chicago Press, 1992).

Morris, Richard B. *Witnesses at the Creaton: Hamilton, Madison, Jay, and the Constitution* (New York: Holt, Rinehart and Winston, 1985).

Morse, Jedidiah. *The American Geography* 2nd ed. (London: John Stockdale, 1792).

Murat, Achille. *A Moral and Political Sketch of the United States of North America* (London: Effingham Wilson, 1833).

Murray, Patrick. *An Inquiry Into the Original and Consequences of the Public Debt* (Edinburgh: Sands, Murray, and Cochran, 1753).

Myers, Charles. "Retirement of the First Federal Debt: A Test of Vincent Ostrom's Theory of Democratic Administration," (Ph.D. diss., Golden Gate University, 1994).

Nairne, Thomas. *A Letter from South Carolina, Giving an Account of the Soil, Air, Product …* 2nd ed. (London: R. Smith, 1718).

Neal, Larry. *The Rise of Financial Capitalism: International Capital Markets in the Age of Reason* (New York: Cambridge University Press, 1990).

Neufeld, E. P. *The Financial System of Canada: Its Growth and Development* (Toronto: Macmillan Company, 1972).

Nicolson, Adam. *God's Secretaries: The Making of the King James Bible* (New York: Perennial, 2003).

North, Douglass. *Understanding the Process of Economic Change* (Princeton, N.J.: Princeton University Press, 2005).

Nye, Joseph. *The Paradox of American Power: Why the World's Only Superpower Can't Go It Alone* (New York: Oxford University Press, 2002).

Ouellet, Fernand. *Lower Canada, 1791–1840: Social Change and Nationalism* (Toronto: McClelland and Stewart, 1980).

Ouseley, William. *Remarks on the Statistical and Political Institutions of the United States* (Philadelphia: Carey & Lea, 1832).

Paine, Thomas. *Common Sense: Addressed to the Inhabitants of America* (Philadelphia: W. and T. Bradford, 1776).

——. *The Decline and Fall of the English System of Finance* (Philadelphia: Benjamin Franklin Bache, 1796).

Pease, William H. and Jane H. Pease. *Bound With Them in Chains: A Biographical History of the Antislavery Movement* (Westport, Conn.: Greenwood Press, 1972).

——. *The Web of Progress: Private Values and Public Styles in Boston and Charleston, 1828–1843* (New York: Oxford University Press, 1985).

Pedder, James. *Report Made to the Beet Sugar Society of Philadelphia, on the Culture in France of the Beet Root, and Manufacture of Sugar Therefrom* (Philadelphia: Beet Sugar Society, 1836).

Perkins, Edwin. *American Public Finance and Financial Services, 1700–1815* (Columbus: Ohio State University Press, 1994).

Peskin, Lawrence. *Manufacturing Revolution: The Intellectual Origins of Early American Industry* (Baltimore: Johns Hopkins University Press, 2003).

Peterson, Peter G. *Running on Empty: How the Democratic and Republican Parties Are Bankrupting Our Future and What Americans Can Do About It* (New York: Farrar, Straus, and Giroux, 2004).

Phillips, John Burton. "Encouragement to Industry by Exemption from Taxation," *Quarterly Journal of Economics* 19 (May 1905), 498–500.

Pickering, Joseph. *Emigration or No Emigration* (London: Longman, Rees, Orme, Brown, and Green, 1830).

Prasad, Monica. *The Politics of Free Markets: The Rise of Neoliberal Economic Policies in Britain, France, Germany, and the United States* (Chicago: University of Chicago Press, 2006).

Preston, T. R. *Three Years' Residence in Canada, from 1837 to 1839* 2 vols. (London: Richard Bentley, 1840).

Price, Richard. *An Appeal to the Public, on the Subject of the National Debt* ... (London: T. Cadell, 1772).

Prindle, David. *The Paradox of Democratic Capitalism: Politics and Economics in American Thought* (Baltimore: Johns Hopkins University Press, 2006).

Pulliam, David. *The Constitutional Conventions of Virginia* (Richmond: John T. West, 1901).

Raguet, Condy. *The Principles of Free Trade Illustrated in a Series of Short and Familiar Essays* (Philadelphia, 1835).

Rappaport, George. *Stability and Social Change in Revolutionary Pennsylvania* (College Park: Penn State University Press, 1996).

Ratchford, Benjamin U. *American State Debts* (Durham, N.C.: Duke University Press, 1941).

Riley, James C. *International Government Finance and the Amsterdam Capital Market, 1740–1815* (New York: Cambridge University Press, 1980).

Robinson, Edward Forbes. "Continental Treasury Administration, 1775–1781: A Study in the Financial History of the American Revolution," (Ph.D. diss., University of Wisconsin, 1969).

Rothenberg, Winifred. *From Market-places to a Market Economy: The Transformation of Rural Massachusetts, 1750–1850* (Chicago: University of Chicago Press, 1992).

Rubin, Paul H. *Darwinian Politics: The Evolutionary Origin of Freedom* (New Brunswick, N.J., 2002).

Rudin, Ronald. "Banking on Quebec: The French Banks and the Mobilization of French Funds, 1835–1925," *Journal of Canadian Studies* 20 (1985), 47–63.

Ryerson, Egerton. *The Affairs of the Canadas: In a Series of Letters by a Canadian* (London: J. King, 1837).

Sachs, Jeffrey. *The End of Poverty: Economic Possibilities for Our Time* (New York: Penguin Press, 2005).

Schechter, Stephen, ed. *The Reluctant Pillar: New York and the Adoption of the Federal Constitution* (Troy, N.Y.: Russell Sage College, 1985).

Schur, Leon. "The Second Bank of the United States and the Inflation After the War of 1812," *Journal of Political Economy* 68 (April 1960), 118–34.

Schweikart, Larry. *Banking in the American South from the Age of Jackson to Reconstruction* (Baton Rouge: Louisiana State University Press, 1987).

Seavoy, Ronald. *The Origins of the American Business Corporation, 1784–1885: Broadening the Concept of Public Service During Industrialization* (Westport, Conn.: Greenwood, 1982).

Shaviro, Daniel N. *Taxes, Spending, and the U.S. Government's March Toward Bankruptcy* (New York: Cambridge University Press, 2006).

Shortt, Adam. *Adam Shortt's History of Canadian Currency and Banking, 1600–1880* (Toronto: Canadian Bankers' Association, 1986).

Simpson, Stephen. *Working Man's Manual: A New Theory of Political Economy* (Philadelphia: Thomas L. Bonsal, 1831).

Sitterson, J. Carlyle. *Sugar Country: The Cane Sugar Industry in the South, 1753–1950* (Lexington: University of Kentucky Press, 1952).

Sloan, Herbert. *Principle and Interest: Thomas Jefferson and the Problem of Debt* (New York: Oxford University Press, 1995).

Smith, Adam. *An Inquiry into the Nature and Causes of the Wealth of Nations* (1776).

Smith, George D., Richard E. Sylla, and Robert E. Wright. "The Diamond of Sustainable Growth: A Historical Framework for the Study of Political Economy and Economic Development," *Business History Review*, forthcoming.

———. "The Diamond of Sustainable Growth," *Sternbusiness* (Spring/Summer 2007), 26–29.

Smith, Roy. *Adam Smith and the Origins of American Enterprise: How the Founding Fathers Turned to a Great Economist's Writings and Created the American Economy* (New York: St. Martin's, 2002).

Sobel, Robert. *Panic on Wall Street: A History of America's Financial Disasters* (New York: Macmillan, 1968).

Sparks, Edith. *Capital Intentions: Female Proprietors in San Francisco, 1850–1920* (Chapel Hill: University of North Carolina Press, 2006).

Stabile, Donald and Jeffrey Cantor. *The Public Debt of the United States: An Historical Perspective, 1775–1990* (New York: Praeger, 1991).

Stahr, Walter. *John Jay* (New York: Hambledon and London, 2005).

Starr, Paul. *The Creation of the Media: Political Origins of Modern Communications* (New York: Basic Books, 2004).

Stasavage, David. "Credible Commitment in Early Modern Europe: North and Weingast Revisited," *Journal of Law, Economics & Organization* 18 (2002), 155–86.

———. *Public Debt and the Birth of the Democratic State: France and Great Britain, 1688–1789* (New York: Cambridge University Press, 2003).

———. "Partisan Politics and Public Debt: The Importance of the Whig Supremacy for Britain's Financial Revolution," Working Paper, December 2005.

Stiglitz, Joseph. *Globalization and Its Discontents* (New York: W. W. Norton and Company, 2002).

Stuart, James. *Three Years in North America* (New York: J & J Harper, 1833).

Studenski, Paul and Herman E. Krooss. *Financial History of the United States* (New York: McGraw-Hill, 1952).

Sumner, William Graham. *The Financier and the Finances of the American Revolution* 2 vols. (New York: Dodd, Mead & Co., 1891).

Surface, George. *The Story of Sugar* (New York: D. Appleton and Co., 1910).

Sussman, Nathan and Yishay Yafeh. "Institutional Reforms, Financial Development and Sovereign Debt: Britain, 1690–1790," *Journal of Economic History* 66 (December 2006), 906–35.

Swanson, Donald. *The Origins of Hamilton's Fiscal Policies* (Gainesville: University of Florida Press, 1963).

Swanson, Donald and Andrew Trout. "Alexander Hamilton, Conversion, and Debt Reduction," *Explorations in Economic History* 29 (1992), 417–29.

——. "Alexander Hamilton's Hidden Sinking Fund," *William and Mary Quarterly* 49 (January 1992), 108–16.

Sylla, Richard, John B. Legler, and John J. Wallis. "Banks and State Public Finance in the New Republic: The United States, 1790–1860," *Journal of Economic History* 47 (June 1987), 391–403.

Sylla, Richard, Jack Wilson, and Robert E. Wright. "Integration of Trans-Atlantic Capital Markets, 1790–1845," *Review of Finance* 10 (2006), 613–44.

Sylla, Richard E. and Robert E. Wright, eds. *The History of Corporate Finance: Development of Anglo-American Securities Markets, Financial Practices, Theories and Laws* (London: Pickering & Chatto, 2003).

Syrett, Harold and Jacob E. Cooke, eds. *The Papers of Alexander Hamilton* 27 vols. (New York: Columbia University Press, 1961–87).

Talbot, Edward. *Five Years' Residence in the Canadas* (London: Longman, Hurst, Rees, Orme, Brown and Green, 1824).

Taussig, F. W. "Beet Sugar and the Tariff," *Quarterly Journal of Economics* 26 (February 1912), 189–214.

Tibbits, George. *A Memoir on the Expediency and Practicability of Improving or Creating Home Markets* (Albany: Packard & Van Benthuysen, 1825).

Tiedemann, Joseph S. *Reluctant Revolutionaries: New York City and the Road to Independence, 1763–1776* (Ithaca, N.Y.: Cornell University Press, 1997).

Timberlake, Richard. *Monetary Policy in the United States: An Intellectual and Institutional History* (Chicago: University of Chicago Press, 1993).

Tracy, James D. *A Financial Revolution in the Hapsburg Netherlands: Renten and Renteniers in the County of Holland, 1515–1565* (Los Angeles: University of California Press, 1985).

Trew, Alex. "Finance and Growth: A Critical Survey," *Economic Record* 82 (December 2006), 481–90.

Tucker, Gilbert. *The Canadian Commercial Revolution, 1845–1851* (New Haven, Conn.: Yale University Press, 1936).

Van Zandt, Roland. *Chronicles of the Hudson: Three Centuries of Travelers' Accounts* (New Brunswick, N.J.: Rutgers University Press, 1971).

Vietor, Richard H. K. *How Countries Compete: Strategy, Structure, and Government in the Global Economy* (Boston: Harvard Business School Press, 2007).

Wallis, John. "State Constitution Reforms in the 1840s and 1850s and the Relationship of American Government and the Economy," DAE Summer Institute Working Paper, July 2001.

Walters, Raymond, Jr. *Albert Gallatin: Jeffersonian Financier and Diplomat* (New York: Macmillan Co., 1957).

Warsh, David. *Knowledge and the Wealth of Nations: A Story of Economic Discovery* (New York: W. W. Norton and Co., 2006).

Webber, Carolyn and Aaron Wildavsky. *A History of Taxation and Expenditure in the Western World* (New York: Simon and Schuster, 1986).

Webster, Pelatiah. *A Seventh Essay on Free Trade and Finance* (Philadelphia: Eleazar Oswald, 1785).

——. *A Plea for the Poor Soldiers* (Philadelphia: Francis Bailey, 1790).

Weise, Arthur James. *The History of the City of Albany, New York: From the Discovery of the Great River in 1524, by Verrazzano, to the Present Time* (Albany: E. H. Bender, 1884).

Wermiel, Sara. *The Fireproof Building: Technology and Public Safety in the Nineteenth-Century American City* (Baltimore: Johns Hopkins University Press, 2000).

Werner, Walter and Steven Smith, *Wall Street* (New York: Columbia University Press, 1991).

Whisker, James B. *Virginia Clockmakers and Watchmakers, c. 1660–1860* (Lewiston, N.Y.: Edwin Mellen Press, 1999).

White, Leonard. *The Federalists: A Study in Administrative History* (New York: Macmillan Company, 1948).

White, Patrick, ed. *Lord Selkirk's Diary, 1803–1804: A Journal of His Travels in British North America and the Northeastern United States* (Toronto: The Champlain Society, 1958).

Whiteside, John F. "The Toronto Stock Exchange and the Development of the Share Market to 1885," *Journal of Canadian Studies* 20 (1985), 64–81.

Winterbotham, William. *An Historical, Geographical, Commercial and Philosophical View of the American United States, and of the European Settlements in America and the West-Indies* (London, Printed for the editor, 1795).

Worth, Gorham A. *Random Recollections of Albany from 1800 to 1808* 3rd ed. (Albany: J. Munsell, 1866).

Wright, Donald R. *African Americans in the Early Republic, 1789–1831* (Arlington Heights, Ill.: Harlan Davidson, Inc., 1993).

Wright, Gavin. *The Political Economy of the Cotton South: Households, Markets, and Wealth in the Nineteenth Century* (New York: W. W. Norton and Co., 1978).

——. *Old South, New South: Revolutions in the Southern Economy Since the Civil War* (Baton Rouge: Louisiana State University Press, 1986).

Wright, Robert E. "Banking and Politics in New York, 1784–1829," (Ph.D. diss., State University of New York at Buffalo, 1997).

——. "Women and Finance in the Early National U.S.," *Essays in History,* 42 (2000): http://etext.lib.virginia.edu/journals/EH/EH42/Wright42.html.

——. *Origins of Commercial Banking in America* (New York: Rowman and Littlefield, 2001).

——. *Hamilton Unbound: Finance and the Creation of the American Republic* (New York: Praeger, 2002).

——. *The Wealth of Nations Rediscovered: Integration and Expansion in American Financial Markets, 1780–1850* (New York: Cambridge University Press, 2002).

——. *The First Wall Street: Chestnut Street, Philadelphia, and the Birth of American Finance* (Chicago: University of Chicago Press, 2005).

———, ed. *The U.S. National Debt, 1787–1900* (London: Pickering & Chatto, 2005).

———. "On the Economic Efficiency of Organizations: Toward a Solution of the Efficient Government Enterprise Paradox," *Essays in Economic and Business History* 25 (April 2007), 143–54.

Wright, Robert E., Wray Barber, Matthew Crafton, and Anand Jain, eds. *History of Corporate Governance: The Importance of Stakeholder Activism* 6 vols. (London: Pickering and Chatto, 2004).

Wright, Robert E. and David J. Cowen, *Financial Founding Fathers: The Men Who Made America Rich* (Chicago: University of Chicago Press, 2006).

Wright, Robert E., Timothy Jacobson, and George D. Smith. *Knowledge for Generations: Wiley and the Global Publishing Industry, 1807–2007* (Hoboken, N.J.: John Wiley & Sons, 2007).

Wright, Robert E. and Laurie M. Wolfe, "Michael Hillegas," in Craig Horle et al., eds., *Lawmaking and Legislators in Pennsylvania: A Biographical Dictionary* Vol. 3 (Harrisburg: Pennsylvania House of Representatives, 2005).

Young, John H. "Comparative Economic Development: Canada and the United States," *American Economic Review* 45 (1955), 80–93.

INDEX

ABOUT THE AUTHOR

Robert E. Wright, Ph.D. is Clinical Associate Professor of Economics at New York University's Stern School of Business. A prolific author and engaging speaker, Professor Wright (Ph.D., History, SUNY Buffalo, 1997) is a curator for the Museum of American Finance and editor of Pickering & Chatto's financial history monograph series.